W9-BEF-868

The
HISPANIC
10 0

The
HISPANIC
100

*A Ranking of the
Latino Men and Women
Who Have Most Influenced
American Thought and Culture*

Himilce Novas

A Citadel Press Book
Published by Carol Publishing Group

In memory of Jeanne Silva,
who graced us and left much too early.

A Citadel Press Book
Published by Carol Publishing Group
Citadel Press is a registered trademark of Carol Communications, Inc.

Editorial Offices: 600 Madison Avenue, New York, NY 10022
Sales and Distribution Offices: 120 Enterprise Avenue, Secaucus, NJ
    07094
In Canada: Canadian Manda Group, One Atlantic Avenue, Suite 105,
    Toronto, Ontario M6K 3E7

Queries regarding rights and permissions should be addressed to:
Carol Publishing Group, 600 Madison Avenue, New York, NY 10022

Carol Publishing Group books are available at special discounts
for bulk purchases, sales promotions, fund-raising, or
educational purposes. Special editions can be created to specifications.
For details, contact: Special Sales Department, Carol Publishing Group,
120 Enterprise Avenue, Secaucus, NJ 07094.

Manufactured in the United States of America
10 9 8 7 6 5 4 3 2 1

Design by Ardashes Hampartzoomian

Library of Congress Cataloging-in-Publication Data

Novas, Himilce.
    The Hispanic 100 : a ranking of the Latino men and women who have
most influenced American thought and culture / by Himilce Novas.
        p.   cm.
    "A Citadel Press Book."
    Includes index.
    ISBN 0–8065–1651–8
    1. United States—Civilization—Hispanic influences. 2. Hispanic
Americans. I. Title. II. Title: Hispanic one hundred.
E169.1.N77 1995
920′.009268—dc20
[B]   94–44289
                                                        CIP

CONTENTS

ACKNOWLEDGMENTS

My thanks go first and foremost to my partner, Rosemary Silva, a gifted writer and indefatigable editor and researcher, whose work in the compilation and execution of this book made this volume possible.

To New York City, California, Texas, New Mexico, and Miami, a debt of gratitude for all the people, public libraries, universities, and cultural institutions that enabled us to unearth a glorious history.

Thanks also to Dorothy Tate, the American Program Bureau, KQSB AM, my agent Susan Herner, Ruth Elizabeth Jenks, Theresa Mantenfel, Carolyn Howe, Teri and Jack Lindsey, Harriet Harkavy, Penny Davies and her Earthling Book Store, Judy Babcock, Elaine St. James, Gail Humphreys, Fran Halpern, Carol Storke, Miguel A. Bretos, and the Smithsonian Institution, UCSB professors Mario Garcia and Jill Levine, and to Bunny and Jellybean for love and friendship.

And to the millions of Latinos, sung and unsung, across our blessed homeland: arriba y arriba!

INTRODUCTION

"That was how I became part of Los Indios, which was what we called ourselves. It was all pretty innocent, not at all what people think of when they see brown faces, hear Spanish words, and are told about gangs.... What we mostly did was walk home together through enemy territory. Since we were Los Indios, it was the cowboys and the settlers we had to watch out for. The Anglo ones.... Also, it was a relief to slip into Spanish again after guarding my tongue all day so it wouldn't incite Sister Mary Margaret."

From *The Day the Cisco Kid Shot John Wayne*, by Nash Candelaria*

Ｂy the year 2000, Latinos will be the largest single minority in the United States, and by the year 2040 one out of three U.S. citizens will be of Latino ancestry.

For a group that looms so large in numbers and cultural contributions, there is still very little known in mainstream America—including our schools—about whom we choose as heroes and heroines and about the enormous impact these sung and unsung Americans have had upon our country.

As a youngster in the New York City public school system in the 1960s, most of the literature about Latinos I read consisted of books by Anglos. But where were the works by writers like some of the ones presented in this book? And when it came to texts,

---

*Nash Candelaria was born in Los Angeles in 1928. His American roots go deeper than those of most Anglos: His family helped found Albuquerque, New Mexico, in 1706. *The Day the Cisco Kid Shot John Wayne* was published in 1988 (Tempe, Arizona: Bilingual Press/Editorial Bilingüe).

xi

schoolbooks made us think all Latinos were recent immigrants—
"the children of Sanchez"—and that Texas, California, and most
of the Southwest was deserted before Davy Crockett went hunting
for beaver and lost it all at the Alamo.

True, we have come a long way since then, thanks, in part, to
Latino activism, media attention, and a handful of schools that
have made multicultural studies part of their curriculum. But
even now, in spite of the progress, Latino life in the United States
is like a partial eclipse: Now you see us, now you don't.

There's an ethnic "joke" I once heard in Los Angeles that
goes like this: "Why aren't there any Chicano writers? Because
spray paint was only invented two years ago!" In fact, can most
people name any Mexican-American writers? Any Puerto Rican
educators? Any Cuban-American fashion designers? Any
Panamanian-American theater directors? Any Spanish-
American scientists? How many people can name even just one
outstanding Latino?

Often the only names that come up when I ask this question
to audiences across the country are Geraldo, Rita Moreno, and
Desi Arnaz....

*   *   *

Perhaps no other ethnic group in America is as diverse in its
culture, appearance, and traditions as Latinos. Mexican
Americans, Puerto Ricans, Cuban Americans, Dominicans,
Spanish Americans, and Central and South Americans are all
part of the rich mosaic we've come to know as Latino, or
Hispanic.

Today, some prefer the term Latino (*Latina* when referring
to a woman), meaning people of mixed Native American and
Spanish ancestry, rather than Hispanic, meaning people of
Spanish ancestry. The U.S. Bureau of the Census still classifies
Latinos as Hispanics, and, indeed, so do many Latinos
themselves, particularly on the East Coast. After much
consideration, my publisher has elected, therefore, to title this
book *The Hispanic 100*.

Latino writers and thinkers who take issue with what critics
claim to be a non-issue (namely, what's in a name?) are quick to
explain that to label them "Hispanic" means to think of them as
merely a language, the language that the Spanish conquistadors
imposed on peoples such as the Mayas, Aztecs, Incas, Toltecs,
Africans, mulattoes, mestizos, and even Caucasian Iberics—all of

whom were speaking colorful, sophisticated tongues long before there was such a thing as a country called Spain.

According to the latest U.S. census, Americans of Latino origin number 22,354,059, representing roughly 9 percent of the population. This figure is up from 16,940,000 in 1985, and fails to take into account hundreds of thousands of undocumented aliens. With this sharp population increase and a median age just below thirty as recently as 1988, Latinos have emerged as the fastest growing ethnic minority in the United States.

Mexican Americans, or Chicanos, who comprise the largest group (upward of 13 million) are mainly mestizo, or of mixed Native American (Mayan, Aztec, Hopi Pueblo) and Spanish-Caucasian descent. They live mostly in the Southwest, particularly Texas, New Mexico, Arizona, Colorado, and California. Officially, over 8 million Chicanos live in California and almost 5 million in Texas.

Chicano history begins before 1325, with the founding of a homeland called Aztlan, which encompassed part of the present-day United States and Mexico. The Chicano national culture predates Columbus and even European culture for, as we know, the "new" world is indeed much older than the "old" one.

Another Mexican-American group, known as *Hispanos,* are the direct descendants of Mexicans from the vast domain the U.S. government annexed as part of the Treaty of Guadalupe Hidalgo after the Mexican War. These *Hispanos* have actually been in America longer then the Anglo descendants of the Mayflower. Santa Fe, one of America's oldest cities, was founded in 1609, the same decade the English settled Jamestown. For the most part, *Hispanos* have assimilated into the non-Latino population of the United States. A majority are Caucasian, direct descendants of the Spanish conquistadors, but many are also mestizo.

Puerto Ricans make up the second largest Latino group. Thanks to the Spanish-American War, the annexation of Puerto Rico by the United States, and its present U.S. commonwealth status ("Estado Libre Asociado"), which makes Puerto Ricans U.S. citizens, the movement of Puerto Ricans between Puerto Rico and the U.S. mainland is considered internal migration within the country, not "immigration."

According to the latest census, Puerto Ricans number almost 2.5 million on the U.S. mainland alone. They are concentrated in the Northeast, especially New York City—although barrios, or "little borinquens" (the native peoples' word for the island) thrive in far-flung places like Chicago, Providence, and Miami. Puerto Ricans are also the youngest group of Latinos, with almost half under the age of twenty-one.

Cuban Americans comprise the third largest group of Latinos, numbering over 1 million. They are mainly concentrated in south Florida, particularly Miami. Cuban Americans have long identified themselves with other Europeans who came to our shores escaping totalitarian governments. Most Cuban-born U.S. citizens came to America in the early 1960s, fleeing Fidel Castro's revolution. Later, in the mid-1970s, another group of Cubans known as *marielitos*, reached the Unites States as part of a massive seven-week-long air- and seaborne evacuation known as the Mariel Boat Lift, orchestrated by President Jimmy Carter. The first wave of Cuban Americans was largely made up of white-middle-class people who strongly identify with their Spanish roots—although, to be sure, Afro-Cuban rhythms and Yoruba religious practices, known as *Santería,* have greatly influenced their culture and ethnic makeup. Just listen to Celia Cruz and Gloria Estefan.

There are over 2.5 million Dominicans and Central and South Americans. Most are here as a result of revolutions and political upheavals in their native countries. They comprise the most recent community of immigrants and are generally scattered among dominant Latino populations in the Northeast, such as New York, Boston, and Washington, D.C.

Iberians, or people of direct Spanish descent, represent the smallest segment of Hispanics. Some came to America fleeing the Spanish Civil War in the 1930s, while others immigrated to the United States after first immigrating to Latin America.

Ranking people and their contributions is always difficult— particularly when they represent entirely different disciplines and span the centuries. We used three criteria in compiling this book and in ranking the Latinos within in order of importance from 1 to 100: Our heroes and heroines had to be trailblazers, "legends" either in their own time or later, and their influence had to be of a far-reaching and international scope. We ranked them through an often difficult and, no doubt, somewhat subjective assessment of how much impact each particular "legend" had or is having upon Latinos and Americans as a whole.

Because Latinos, for the most part, began attaining significant positions outside their communities, in mainstream "Anglo"** society, only toward the last half of the twentieth century, most of the biographies presented here are of nineteenth- and twentieth-century legends.

By narrowing our selection to 100 names, I feel we have set the stage for another yet-unwritten volume of hundreds of others who, in large and small ways, have contributed to the new face and voice of America.

In telling about the remarkable lives of the men and women in this book—Latinos who have excelled in the arts, sciences, sports, government, and so on—we also pay homage to countless unnamed others and to new generations who will follow in their footsteps.

The Hispanic 100 is only a beginning—what we call in Spanish *un abrir la puerta*—but it *is* a *puerta* (door), and a sunny and splendid one at that! Bienvenidos!

**Originally, Anglo meant an American of English descent. However, today the term refers to any American of European descent.

The
HISPANIC
100

Cesar Chávez

1927–1993

One of five children, Cesar Estrada Chávez was born on a small farm near Yuma, Arizona, on March 31, 1927. His parents, Juana Estrada and Librado Chávez, were Mexican-American migrant workers. The Chávez clan, headed by Cesar's grandparents, had come to America to escape the Mexican Revolution of 1910. They made their way to Arizona and saved enough money for a down payment on the farm where Cesar Chávez was born. During the Great Depression, the Chávez family lost the farm, and for the next several years they moved with the harvests in their old Studebaker and lived alongside other downtrodden migrants in a string of farm labor camps in California and Arizona.

This difficult way of life provided Cesar with little formal education. He attended over thirty elementary schools and finally dropped out when he was in seventh grade to harvest crops in the fields full-time. Even as a child Cesar fought for equality. In 1943, when he was only fifteen, he refused to conform to the rules of segregated seating at a Delano, California, movie theater and was forced off the premises. During World War II, Chávez served in the U.S. Navy and saw action in the Pacific. Upon receiving an honorable discharge, he returned to migrant farmwork in California and Arizona. When the National Farm Labor Union began organizing in the San Joaquin Valley in the late 1940s, young Cesar became a member and marched in picket lines.

While working in Delano, Cesar met Helen Fabela, the daughter of a Zapatista hero of the Mexican Revolution, and the two married in 1948. They settled in San Jose, California, where they shared a house with Cesar's parents and other family members. The entire family devoted itself to sharecropping strawberries seven days a week. In 1949, Fernando, the first of Cesar Chávez's eight children, was born. The family was barely getting by, so Cesar and his brother Richard found work as lumberjacks in northern California. Upon their return to San Jose, the family left the strawberry farm and moved to the edge of town. Cesar worked in a lumberyard and in fruit orchards and was plagued by worries about meeting the needs of his growing family. He identified with the thousands of migrant workers who faced starvation as they toiled in the fields.

One of Chávez's early mentors in San Jose was Father Donald McDonnell, who built a mission in the poor section of town. The priest taught Chávez about labor history, thus preparing him for a role in organizing agricultural workers. Another influential figure in Chávez's life was Fred Ross, an agent of Saul Alinsky, the community organizer. Alinsky sent Ross to Southern California to recruit local talent to staff the Community Service Organization (CSO), an agency geared toward aiding poor communities across the nation. At Father McDonnell's insistence, Chávez attended one of Ross's house meetings in 1952. Chávez was impressed by Ross and by the CSO's tactics of recruiting members at small meetings and gradually building an organization that in time could confront injustice through nonviolent, direct-action tactics, such as boycotts and sit-ins.

Chávez was soon employed at the CSO office in San Jose, first as an unpaid volunteer, then as a paid staff member. He organized voter-registration drives in San Jose and helped farm-workers cope with police, immigration authorities, and welfare boards. While at the CSO, he learned how to recruit and train volunteers. Soon he became a statewide organizer for the CSO and traveled around California organizing CSO chapters in towns in the San Joaquin Valley. In 1958 he was appointed general director of the national CSO. With the help of Dolores Huerta, his principal assistant, and others, the CSO was expanded to twenty-two chapters in California and Arizona.

As it grew, the CSO attracted more middle-class liberals and fewer poor farmworkers. Chávez grew disenchanted, believing that the CSO had lost sight of its original purpose of mobilizing the poor. Furthermore, he felt the solution to the economic and social woes of farmworkers lay in agricultural reform, while CSO leaders wanted Latinos to abandon agricultural work altogether. As Chávez recalled in Jacques E. Levy's 1975 book *Cesar Chávez: Autobiography of La Causa:* "While the CSO was doing some good for the poor in the communities, after a few years I began to realize that a farm workers' union was needed to end the exploitation of the workers in the fields, if we were to strike at the roots of their suffering and poverty."

When, in 1962, the CSO refused to support his proposal to form a farmworkers union, Chávez resigned his post, turned down other job offers, moved his family to Delano, and without any financial support began organizing farmworkers. On September 30, 1962, he founded the Farm Workers Association (FWA), which later became known as the National Farm Workers Association (NFWA). By 1965, the NFWA had enrolled seventeen hundred families, enabling it to negotiate pay raises from two local growers. While Cesar Chávez feared that the NFWA was still too small to confront large growers, he was forced to act when migrant Filipino grape pickers, represented by the AFL-CIO–sponsored Agricultural Workers Organizing Committee (AWOC), went on strike on September 8, 1965, in protest of the low wages Delano growers offered. Chávez and the NFWA joined with the strikers. The long *huelga* (strike) against grape growers in the San Joaquin, Imperial, and Coachella valleys began.

In July 1966, Chávez's grape workers voted to merge with the AWOC under the AFL-CIO banner to form the United Farm

Workers Organizing Committee (UFWOC) of the AFL-CIO. Even with such strength in numbers, Chávez knew that victory was uncertain. Previous strikes had failed because workers ran out of money or growers simply replaced strikers with imported Mexican farmworkers. As an offensive move, Chávez sought the assistance of labor unions, the liberal clergy, publications such as the *New Republic,* and political figures like Hubert H. Humphrey and Robert F. Kennedy. With publicity provided by such allies and through such nonviolent actions as sing-ins and marches, Chávez succeeded in forcing wine-grape growers to capitulate within one year.

Table-grape growers did not bow to the pressure so easily. They had won a court battle allowing them to import Mexican workers, and they replaced the striking workers with "scab" labor. Unable to prevent table-grape growers from harvesting grapes and shipping them out of state for sale, Chávez had no alternative but to take on the entire grape industry and publicize his cause across the nation. In the spring of 1968 he organized a national boycott of all California table grapes, mobilizing concerned consumers, peace groups, religious supporters, Hispanic associations, unions, and activists. Representatives of the United Farm Workers (UFW) traveled across America gathering support in such forums as church meetings, rallies, marches, and sing-ins. Their drive was so successful that the national consumption of grapes nosedived by approximately 20 percent by August 1968.

The grape strike lasted for five years. The hardship the strike wrought on the table-grape growers finally forced them to the bargaining table, and in 1970 the UFW, a member union of the AFL-CIO, signed a table-grape labor contract with David Freedman & Co. and the Wonder Palms Ranch, the first contract of its kind in the nation. It provided for a wage increase, health insurance, and regulations restricting the use of certain pesticides. The stress of the grueling battle with the table-grape industry took a physical toll on Chávez, who suffered pain from an old back ailment and was bedridden for months. Sen. Edward Kennedy showed concern for his condition and arranged to have Dr. Janet Travell, who had successfully treated a similar condition in President John F. Kennedy, visit Chávez. She restored the labor leader to health.

Cesar Chávez's victories in California were sharply diminished, however, due to a jurisdictional dispute with the International Brotherhood of Teamsters over the organization of field workers. In 1973 the Teamsters cut heavily into the UFW membership by signing contracts with former UFW grape growers. In March 1977, the dispute with the Teamsters Union was settled, and the UFW concluded agreements with the other large table-grape growers. Chávez then expanded his efforts to include all California vegetable pickers and launched a lettuce boycott.

To the very end of his life Chávez fought for the rights of farm laborers. On April 23, 1993, at age sixty-six, he died in his sleep of natural causes at the home of family friends in San Luis, Arizona. He had been staying there during a trial in which he testified on behalf of farmworkers who were being sued by a lettuce grower. On April 29, 1993, over twenty thousand people, among them former governor of California Edmund G. Brown Jr., the Reverend Jesse Jackson, and Ethel Kennedy, gathered on a dusty field in Delano to pay homage to Cesar Chávez.

2

Henry Barbosa González

1916–

One of six children, Henry Barbosa González was born on May 3, 1916, in San Antonio, Texas, to Leonides and Genoveva (Barbosa) González. On the paternal side, Henry was descended from early Spanish settlers who ventured to Mexico in 1561 and grew powerful and wealthy from investments in ranch land and silver mines. In 1911, Henry's father, once the mayor of Mapimi in the Mexican state of Durango, came under attack from revolutionaries led by Pancho Villa during the Mexican Revolution.

Leonides González fled across the Rio Grande and settled in San Antonio. On the maternal side, Henry was descended from Cosmo Prince, a Scotch-Irish Pennsylvania Presbyterian who went to Mexico in 1855. González's family was part of what historians call "the Mexican-American generation." Later generations came to be called Chicanos and post-Chicanos.

In his boyhood Henry knew the face of poverty and discrimination. When he went to work at age ten, he had to battle racial injustice unceasingly. He was labeled a "greaser" and was barred from restaurants and swimming pools reserved "for whites only." Henry found solace from the perils of a racist society in books, and by age eight he was frequenting the public library. He attended the Mark Twain Junior High School and Thomas Jefferson High School in San Antonio. He then enrolled at San Antonio Junior College, graduated in 1937, and went on to the University of Texas at Austin to study engineering and law. The Great Depression was ravaging the country, and González was forced to return to San Antonio, where he earned a B.A. degree and an LL.B. degree at St. Mary's University School of Law in 1943.

Instead of practicing law, González joined his father as co-owner of a Spanish-English translation service geared toward radio and television clientele and worked in public relations at a local insurance company. In 1940, González married Bertha Cuellar of Floresville, Texas, and the couple had eight children. From 1943 to 1946 he worked as a juvenile probation officer for the Bexar County Juvenile Court. González was appointed chief probation officer in 1946 but resigned when he was not permitted to hire an African-American staff member. During World War II he served as a civilian cable and radio censor for the U.S. Army and Navy.

In 1950, González entered the political arena without any outside support and with campaign funds of less than $300. He ran for the San Antonio City Council but was defeated by a narrow margin. That year, González was named deputy family-relocation director for the San Antonio Housing Authority to aid with the city's slum-clearance program. In 1953, González was elected to the San Antonio City Council. During the first of his two terms in office, he sponsored an ordinance that put an end to segregation in San Antonio's recreational facilities. During this time period, he also served briefly as mayor pro tem.

In 1956, González was elected to a four-year term in the Texas Senate, becoming the first citizen of Mexican descent to be seated in that body in 110 years. He continued to be an outspoken advocate of equal rights for all minorities and immediately set to work combating racist legislation. In 1957, González attracted national attention in a regular session of the legislature by conducting, with state senator Abraham Kazen Jr. of Laredo, the longest filibuster in the history of Texas. González opposed ten "race" bills, designed to intensify racial segregation, previously passed by the House of Representatives. The two senators held the floor for just over thirty-six hours, a state record. Eight of the bills were defeated, and two were passed, one of which was subsequently declared unconstitutional. Later in 1957, Henry González filibustered alone, for twenty consecutive hours against three more "race" bills which were passed and signed by Governor Price Daniel. In 1958, Henry González unsuccessfully challenged the reelection of Price Daniel for a second term as governor in the democratic primary; he was defeated by a margin of more than three to one.

During the five years he served in the Texas Senate, González handled forty-two bills, including those addressing slum-clearance programs and the control of lobbying. In November 1961, he won a special election to fill a vacancy in the U.S. House of Representatives caused by the resignation of Paul J. Kilday, the representative of the Twentieth District. As the first Texan of Mexican ancestry, González was seated in the Eighty-seventh Congress in January 1962 and assigned to the House Banking and Currency Committee. In those early years in the House, Henry González introduced or sponsored legislation providing for a Youth Conservation Corps, adult basic education, civil service salary increases, Puerto Rican rights, and an increase in income-tax exemptions, among many other measures.

Over the years Henry González has been regularly reelected to his post in the House. In the more than three decades he has served in that body, González has been scoffed at for being a hot-tempered, obstinate populist beholden to no one, not even fellow Democrats. He earned this reputation from events that have taken place in the House. When he was a freshman, Cong. Ed Foreman, a fellow Texas lawmaker, called him a Communist. González invited Foreman into the Speaker's lobby and retaliated, some say with his fist. Members of the House Banking Committee say González runs the panel unlike any other in the House. He is frequently on the losing side of votes on legislation, in part, they say, because he seldom strategizes in private with Democratic committee members.

González's sympathizers hold a different view of the representative. They consider him an individual endowed with a high moral sense and intellectual honesty, a fearless maverick who will oppose the powers that be in the executive branch and in regulatory agencies without bowing under pressure. Some of his fellow Texans place him in the exalted ranks of Thomas Jefferson and Franklin Delano Roosevelt, and even Gandhi, for his passionate and at times mystic devotion to the pursuit of justice and freedom for all. They believe his actions in the House of Representatives support this view. For instance, in 1977, González resigned as head of the House Select Committee on Assassinations because he realized that the riddle of John F. Kennedy's murder would never be solved because "vast and powerful forces, including the country's most sophisticated crime element, won't stand for it."

In 1981, González became chairman of the powerful House Banking Committee. Over the next eight years he fought the Reagan adminstration's opposition to federal housing programs that would help lower-income citizens but made little headway. Only in 1990, under a new administration, did González succeed in passing the Affordable Housing Act. He tried to have Ronald Reagan impeached for the United States' invasion of Grenada in 1983 and again in 1987 for allegedly trading arms for hostages with Iran and diverting profits from those sales to the Contra rebels in Nicaragua. In 1988, González was chosen to chair the Banking, Finance, and Urban Affairs Committee. As chairman, he was instrumental in uncovering wrongdoing in the savings-and-loan crisis in the late 1980s. He oversaw the drafting of the comprehensive savings-and-loan bailout bill signed by President Bush in 1989, which provided funds to prosecute fraud and placed restrictions on accounting and lending procedures.

His commitment to justice showed clearly in the early 1990s. He was among the first in Congress to object to America's involvement in Iraq and called for the impeachment of President Bush and the removal of other federal officials as the United States braced for war in the Persian Gulf. In 1992 the House Banking Committee, with González as chairman, held hearings that charged the Bush administration with conspiring to sell advanced weapons to President Saddam Hussein of Iraq, thus helping him build up an arsenal that would be used against American and allied forces. The House Banking Committee also exposed the link between President Bush's son Neil and a bankrupt savings and loan. In 1993, González shifted his focus to domestic affairs. He has aided American consumers by cosponsoring a bill enabling individuals to correct erroneous credit reports more easily.

Since his early days as a congressman, González has fought for the civil rights of those groups that have been historically disadvantaged. In the decades he has spent in the House, he has pushed bills for better housing, benefits for farmworkers, a Youth Conservation Corps, and adult basic education. He proposed to raise the amount of punitive damages women and religious groups can seek under Title VII of the Civil Rights Act and the Violence Against Women Act. He is a strong advocate of national lesbian and gay rights. For his efforts to better the lives of Americans, González received an honorary Doctor of Laws degree from his alma mater St. Mary's University School of Law in 1965, the Shallcross Award in 1985, and the M. Justin Herman Memorial Award in 1988. In 1991 he was honored with the National Alliance to End Homelessness Award and the Texas Civic Leadership Award. In 1992, Henry González was chosen the National Rural Housing Legislator of the Year.

3

Luis Alvarez

1911–1988

One of four children, Luis Walter Alvarez was born on June 13, 1911, in San Francisco, California, to Harriet Skidmore Smyth Alvarez and Walter Clement Alvarez, a physician, a professor at the University of California, and a medical journalist. Luis grew up in San Francisco and later in Rochester, Minnesota, where his father joined the Mayo Clinic. Luis graduated from Rochester High School in 1928 and then entered the University of Chicago, where, encouraged by a professor, he switched his major from chemistry to physics. Luis achieved academic excellence at the University of Chicago and was initiated into Phi Beta Kappa and Sigma Xi, the science-research honor society. After receiving his B.S. degree in 1932, he pursued graduate study at the University of Chicago and was awarded an M.Sc. in 1934 and a Ph.D. in 1936.

In 1936, Alvarez wed Geraldine Smithwick, and the couple had a son and a daughter. The marriage ended in divorce, and in 1958, Alvarez married Janet L. Landis, with whom he had two children.

After receiving his doctorate, Alvarez joined the faculty of the University of California at Berkeley as a research assistant. From 1938 to 1945 he climbed the academic ladder from instructor to professor of physics. In the late 1930s, Alvarez and Berkeley colleague Jacob H. Wiens created the artificial isotope mercury-198 with the cyclotron. A mercury-vapor lamp filled with this isotope emitted a wavelength of light that was later adopted by the U.S. Bureau of Standards as a standard of length. In further research in 1937, Alvarez demonstrated that nuclei can capture some of the innermost electrons that orbit an atom through magnetic movement. The method he developed for producing beams of very slow neutrons laid the groundwork for fundamental studies of neutron scattering. On the eve of World War II, Alvarez and a colleague discovered tritium, a radioactive isotope of hydrogen, and helium-3, a radioactive isotope of helium.

From 1940 to 1943, Alvarez took a leave of absence from Berkeley to work on the development of radar at the Radiation Laboratory of the Massachusetts Institute of Technology (MIT). Because of his extraordinary powers of invention, Alvarez was invited to head a group, dubbed "Luie's Gadgets," whose sole objective was to turn ideas into technological advances. It was not long before he perfected a microwave radar system, called the ground-controlled approach (GCA) system, for landing aircraft. In 1946 his work on the GCA system earned Alvarez the Collier Trophy from the National Aeronautical Association, the most prestigious award in aviation in the United States. On December 17, 1946, the forty-third anniversary of the Wright brothers' first flight, President Truman presented the Collier Trophy to the physicist. While at MIT, Alvarez also both orchestrated both the development of the Eagle, a high-altitude radar device that facilitated pinpoint bombing, and the microwave early-warning (MEW) set, which transmitted images of aerial combat and was employed to control aircraft from the ground.

In 1943, Alvarez left MIT for Los Alamos, where he worked with Enrico Fermi, J. Robert Oppenheimer, Edward Teller, and other scientists on the Manhattan Project. After witnessing the first nuclear explosion at Alamogordo, New Mexico, in 1945,

Alvarez flew as an observer in a B-29 accompanying the *Enola Gay*, which dropped the atomic bomb on Hiroshima. After World War II, Alvarez returned to academia as a professor of physics at the University of California at Berkeley, where he turned his attention to the field of elementary particle physics. In 1947 he supervised the construction of a radiation laboratory at Berkeley to be used for research on atomic energy. The plans included a forty-foot-long linear accelerator for protons. As a way to study the many subatomic particles produced by the new accelerator, Donald A. Glaser had constructed a bubble chamber in 1952, in which particles, passing through a superheated fluid, left a trail of gas bubbles.

After examining of Glaser's work, Alvarez developed a much larger device, enabling scientists to observe many more subnuclear particles by 1960. Alvarez was honored with the 1968 Nobel Prize in physics "for his decisive contribution to elementary particle physics, in particular the discovery of a large number of resonance states, made possible through his development of the technique of using hydrogen bubble chamber and data analysis." While in Stockholm to attend the Nobel Prize ceremony, he revealed to the press his quest to learn if a chamber laden with treasure was hidden deep within the Chephren pyramid at Giza in Egypt. Chambers had been uncovered in other pyramids, but not in the Chephren; therefore, in 1965, Alvarez mounted a joint American-Egyptian expedition to the site. Since the Chephren pyramid is constructed from rock which absorbs cosmic rays, Alvarez placed detectors under the pyramid that would show a "bright spot" where there was less stone, indicating the existence of a chamber. No bright spots were detected, and Alvarez abandoned the project.

In the 1970s, Alvarez's career shifted in another direction. He developed the impact theory of dinosaur extinction, which arose from the work done in Gubbio, Italy, by his son, Walter Alvarez, a geology professor at Berkeley. In Gubbio the younger Alvarez discovered a curious iridium-rich layer of sediment about an inch thick and determined that it was laid down between the Cretaceous and the Tertiary periods, found frequently 65 million years ago. Since iridium is in meteorites but rarely on earth, Luis Alvarez and his son theorized that an asteroid or a comet had collided with the earth, causing the extinction of dinosaurs. Critics of the theory argued that iridium also occurs in volcanic debris and that the extinctions took place over time and some species were around during survived the Tertiary period. Those scientist in support of the impact theory countered that one or a succession of collisions created a cloud that chilled the planet and led to the widespread extinction of dinosaurs. The impact theory of Luis Alvarez and Walter Alvarez has inspired much debate on the theory of evolution and more research in the fields of paleontology, geology, geophysics, and astrophysics.

Alvarez's long list of other accomplishments includes the invention of a color-television system and the nightscope used in Vietnam. He even devised an electric indoor golf training system that President Dwight D. Eisenhower used. In his last two years Alvarez was at work on developing methods to prevent airplane collisions and devices to detect explosives. Luis Alvarez was also quite an entrepreneur, and he launched several successful companies, including Humphrey Instruments and Schwem Technologies. He also served as a consultant for several high-tech corporations, such as Polaroid and Hewlett-Packard. As a government adviser, Alvarez was twice a member of the President's Scientific Advisory Committee, and served on the Land Committee that worked toward developing reconnaissance from space, and in other high-level technical groups.

In the course of his long career of scientific inquiry, Alvarez was recognized on numerous occasions for his contributions. In 1953 the city of Philadelphia bestowed upon him the John Scott Award, and in 1960 he was named California Scientist of the Year. In 1961, Alvarez won the Albert Einstein Award of the Lewis and Rosa Strauss Memorial Fund, and in 1963 the scientist received the Pioneer Award of the Institute of Electrical and Electronic Engineers. In 1964 he was honored with the National Medal of Science of the National Science Foundation. Luis Alvarez was inducted into the National Inventors Hall of Fame in 1978. In 1986 he was honored with a Rockwell Medal, and a year later, Alvarez won the Enrico Fermi Award. In 1988, Luis Alvarez and Walter Alvarez received a great honor rarely bestowed on living scientists. The International Astronomical Union named a new asteroid Asteroid Alvarez after the father-and-son team, upon the recommendation of its discoverer, Eugene Shoemaker. On August 31, 1988, Luis Alvarez died at his Berkeley home, having developed innovative ideas until his last days.

4

Junípero Serra

1713–1784

Junípero Serra was born Miguel José Serra in the village of
Petra on the island of Majorca off the coast of Spain, on
November 24, 1713, to farmers Antonio Nadal Serra and Margarita Rosa Ferrer Serra. Upon his son's birth, Antonio Serra
nailed a laurel branch to the front door of the house, announcing
to the world that God had given the family a baby boy. A few
hours later, the newborn was carried by a midwife at the front of a

procession of relatives and friars to the parish church, where he was christened Miguel José. Amid a life of simplicity and religious piety, Miguel grew up memorizing the catechism, reciting prayers, and helping with chores. By age seven he accompanied his parents to the distant fields they farmed. On his own, the young Miguel would often visit the friary of San Bernadino, one of the island's intellectual and spiritual havens, where he was always welcomed by the friars, who admired his intelligence and devout nature. Those same friars were Miguel's early teachers and instructed him in reading and writing. The young boy was eager to learn religion and asked permission to study music, particularly Gregorian chant. When he was eight years old, one of the friars would take him to chant with the other Franciscans on feast days.

Delighted by their son's devout nature and thirst for knowledge, Antonio and Margarita Serra took the fifteen-year-old Miguel to the capital city of Palma, where they selected a priest at the Cathedral of Palma to oversee his religious training. The canon taught Miguel to pray and supervised his daily studies and responsibilities. After a year passed, the youth was enrolled as a student of philosophy in the classes conducted by the Franciscans at the Convent of San Francisco. Miguel Serra studied there for one year, and then, in 1730, he was admitted to the Franciscan order and entered the Convent of Jesus outside Palma's walls. Soon he took the name Junípero, after Brother Juníper, the constant companion of Saint Francis of Assisi. On September 1731, Junípero Serra knelt before the Very Reverend Antonio Perello Moragues in the sanctuary of the Convent of Jesus and took the vow of the Franciscans.

Serra spent the next six years studying philosophy and theology at the Convent of San Francisco. His fine intellect was recognized at once, and he was singled out to be a professor within the order. After passing a battery of difficult exams, Serra was unanimously declared lector of philosophy on November 29, 1737. By Christmas 1737 he was ordained a priest, although the date of his ordination remains a mystery. He was commissioned to teach for three years. One of the students in his first class was Francisco Palóu, who would later accompany Serra on his travels in the New World and become his devoted disciple and biographer. While he taught, Serra also pursued graduate studies in sacred theology at Lullian University and was awarded his doctorate in the field in 1742. From 1743 to 1749, Serra remained at the Lullian University at Palma as a professor of theology. During his time as a student and then a professor at Lullian University, Serra also toured the island, preaching to the learned and the unlettered, the wealthy and the poor, an activity that gave him great joy.

In the fall of 1748, Fray Junípero Serra heard talk of King Carlos III's royal edict to banish the Jesuit order from Spain and its colonies, and he began to secretly consider going to the New World, leaving developments in the hands of God. Soon Father Mezquia, a representative of the Apostolic College of San Fernando in Mexico City, which was ordered by the same royal edict to replace the Jesuits, arrived in Spain to recruit new missionaries for the perilous work, which entailed converting the Native Americans of northeastern Mexico to Christianity. Fray Junípero Serra volunteered for missionary service in Mexico, and the authorities of the Apostolic College of San Fernando unanimously selected him based on his work in Palma. In 1749 he bid farewell to his family in a letter, fearing that if he confronted them face to face with his plans they would plead for him to stay and weaken his resolve. Accompanied by his lifelong friend Palóu, Serra went to Mexico City, where he taught briefly at the Apostolic College of San Fernando. Soon he began nine years of missionary work in the Sierra Gorda region of Mexico, working among the Pame Indians.

Within a few months among the Pame, Junípero Serra had mastered enough of their language to translate the Christian doctrine and prayers and to preach to the Native Americans. He used persuasion, passionate preaching, and example to get them to come to church. During the years he spent in the region, Serra labored unceasingly to improve living conditions. Through the college he obtained oxen, cows, asses, sheep, goats, and farm implements and taught the Pame how to plant and harvest crops and sell their products to buy more animals, tools, and clothing. Soon the Native Americans were given their own plots of land and seeds and oxen for planting. The women were taught spinning wool, knitting, and sewing. As one of his last acts among the Pame, Fray Junípero Serra finished supervising the construction of the Mission of Santiago de Jalpán in the village of Jalpán, still in use today. With his bare hands, Serra helped build the entire building.

For nine years after he left the Pame Indians, from 1758 to 1767, Junípero Serra devoted himself to administrative work at the Apostolic College of San Fernando, supervising missionary efforts and gaining a large and devoted following due to his intellectual attainments, passionate preaching, and stern asceticism. In those ten years, he traveled over fifty-five hundred miles to preach to Spaniards, Creoles, and Native Americans. After the Jesuit order was forced to leave Mexico in 1767, Fray Junípero Serra was chosen to serve as president of the missions of Baja California, which were originally planted by the Society of Jesus. Junípero Serra was sent to the mission in Loreto, where he remained for over a year while his men conducted their conversion efforts in the surrounding mountains and deserts. The period of his greatest effort began in 1769, when he accompanied a military expedition commanded by Gaspar de Portolá into Alta California, where the government of New Spain was establishing colonial settlements to prevent the Russians or the English from moving down the Pacific coast.

When they reached San Diego, Junípero Serra left the party to found the first mission in the area, while the others went on in search of the harbor of Monterey. When they returned with no success, Serra was one of those responsible for sending another expedition, which he accompanied. They reached Monterey on Ascension Day, May 24, 1770, and on June 3, 1770, Mission San Carlos Borromeo was founded. Serra stayed at San Carlos Borromeo as president of Alta California missions until 1771, when he transferred the mission to Carmel-by-the-Sea, which became his headquarters for the rest of his days. He felt a particular affinity to the Native Americans of the region and defended them against the abuses of colonists; he personally baptized over six hundred of them and confirmed almost as many. Under Serra's presidency a chain of nine prosperous missions was founded from San Diego to San Francisco, including Mission San Antonio de Padua and Mission San Gabriel Arcángel in 1771, Mission San Luis Obispo in 1772, Mission San Juan Capistrano in 1776, Mission San Francisco de Asís in 1776, Mission Santa Clara de Asís in 1777, and Mission San Buenaventura in 1782.

By August 1784, having devoted fifteen years to the mission effort, Junípero Serra had a strong premonition of approaching death. On August 28 he lay down on his cot and passed away, with his friend Francisco Palóu at his side to read the Commendation for a Departing Soul. Until nightfall on August 28, Native Americans, colonists, soldiers, and sailors entered Serra's chamber to pay their last respects. That evening, a long procession accompanied the priest's remains into the church, and on Sunday morning a service was held for Fray Junípero Serra. In attendance were all six hundred Native American converts living at Mission San Carlos Borromeo in Carmel. Throughout the day, at half-hour intervals, a cannon shot was fired from the ship *San Carlos,* anchored in Monterey Bay, answered by a volley from the cannons at the presidio. That evening, Fray Junípero Serra was buried in the sanctuary of a church at Mission San Carlos Borromeo. Fray Francisco Palóu temporarily aassumed the presidency of the California missions. Over the years Franciscan zeal waned as the first generation of missionaries that settled California completed their work for God and King Carlos III of Spain.

In 1988, Junípero Serra was beatified by Pope John Paul II in spite of protests from groups of Native Americans and their supporters, who associated Serra with the colonial effort that had led to the destruction of their way of life. The church's position remains that Fray Junípero Serra protected the Native Americans from imminent harm.

5

George Santayana
1863–1952

George Santayana was born in Madrid, Spain, on December 16, 1863, the son of Augustín Ruiz de Santayana and Josefina Borrás. On New Year's Day, 1864, he was christened Jorge Augustín Nicolás de Santayana. George's mother was previously married to a Boston merchant named George Sturgis with whom she had had five children. Before his death, she promised Sturgis she would educate their children in America. On a visit to Madrid, Josefina Borrás married Augustín Ruiz de Santayana, a retired civil servant, who had translated works by Lucius Annaeus Seneca into Spanish and had assisted a painter in the school of Goya. The young George thus found himself in a home where art and literature were revered. When he was three years old, the family moved from Madrid to Avila, a small town in Castile. In keeping her promise to her first husband, Josefina Borrás soon left for Boston with the three surviving Sturgis children, leaving George and his father behind in Avila. Until age eight, George received a basic Spanish education, mainly studying the *cartilla,* an alphabet book, and the catechism.

When George was nine years old, he and his father set sail for Boston so that the boy could receive a quality education. George arrived in Puritan America speaking only Spanish, and despite his years, he was enrolled in Miss Welchman's Kindergarten in 1872 to learn English. Under the tutelage of his half sister Susana, who showered him with the affection that his emotionally ill mother could not, George swiftly grasped the new language. In 1873 and 1874 he was enrolled at the Brimmer public grammar school. In 1874 ten-year-old George entered the Boston Latin School for eight years of a centuries-old regime of intellectual discipline, studying languages, math, English, and rhetoric. As a youth, George delighted in poetry; his greatest ambition was to be a poet. His first literary accomplishment, the witty *Lines on Leaving the Bedford Street Schoolhouse,* showed promise and was printed at the Boston Latin School. George won numerous scholastic prizes for his verses, and in 1881 he became an editor of the school periodical the *Latin School Register.*

George's father was so appalled by the New England weather and his wife's allegiances to the Sturgises that a year after his arrival he sailed back to Spain to live out the rest of his days in Avila. As George neared his nineteenth birthday in 1882, he enrolled in Harvard College, where he distinguished himself in philosophy and English composition. During his Harvard days he contributed drawings regularly to the *Harvard Lampoon,* played the lead in theatrical productions, helped found the *Harvard Monthly,* and became a member of eleven clubs, including the Chess Club, the Art Club, the Everett Athenaeum, Hasty Pudding, the Institute of 1770, the O.K. Society, the Shakespeare Club, and the Philosophical Club, of which he was president. At the end of his freshman year, George took the first of many summer trips to Europe and visited his father in Spain. He contracted smallpox on the trip but returned to Harvard Yard fit to start his sophomore year.

Santayana received his B.A. degree summa cum laude in 1886 and spent the next two years on a Walker fellowship, enjoying the academic freedom of the University of Berlin. He then returned to Harvard to pursue a doctorate, studying philosophy and psychology under William James and writing his dissertation on the philosophy of Rudolf Hermann Lotze under Josiah Royce. In 1889, Santayana was awarded the combined degrees of master of arts and doctor of philosophy. That fall, at the age of twenty-six, he joined the distinguished faculty at Harvard as an instructor in the Department of Philosophy and soon won a reputation as a superb lecturer. Among his most notable students were T. S. Eliot, Conrad Aiken, Walter Lippmann, and Robert Benchley. Santayana lived on campus and paid regular visits to his mother and sister at their home in Brookline. In 1898, Santayana was made an assistant professor of philosophy, and in 1907 he was appointed professor of philosophy.

Santayana's first poems, *Sonnets and Other Verses*, were published in 1894, but they were ignored by literary critics until the turn of the century. The poems express Santayana's rejection of Catholicism and his allegiance to naturalism. His other poetic works around this time were *Lucifer: A Theological Tragedy* (1899) and *The Hermit of Carmel and Other Poems* (1901). Opinion was divided in literary circles as to the merit of his verse, and Santayana himself declared that he was "no poet."

His philosophical works, on the other hand, were well received. He caught the attention of the reading public with his first philosophical publication, *The Sense of Beauty* (1896), which offers the first treatment on aesthetics from the vantage point of psychological research as well as a philosophy of art. Santayana stunned readers with *Interpretations of Poetry and Religion* (1900), in which he attacks the poetry of Whitman, Browning, Keats, and Shakespeare on moral grounds and explores the intersection of poetry and religion. The publication of *The Life of Reason* (1905–1906, 5 vols.), an inquiry into the facts of existence and the values of humanity, and *Three Philosophical Poets: Lucretius, Dante, and Goethe* (1910), Santayana's most scholarly contribution to literary criticism, established Santayana's merit as a moral philosopher.

In 1911, Santayana received an honorary doctorate from the University of Wisconsin at Madison. The next year, at the height of his brilliant teaching career at Harvard, he resigned his faculty post to devote all of his time to literary pursuits. He yearned to return to Europe to travel, read, write, and contemplate, and an inheritance from his mother's estate made such a life financially possible. Santayana spent time in Seville and Paris before settling in England, where he set to work on *Egotism in German Philosophy* (1916), an attack on German idealism that made even international war morally acceptable. He next published *Character and Opinion in the United States* (1920), which contains his renowned essays "Materialism and Idealism in American Life" and "The Genteel Tradition in American Philosophy."

During the first half of the twentieth century Santayana wielded a great deal of influence on the philosophical movement called naturalism. *Soliloquies in England and Later Soliloquies* (1922) established him as an essayist of considerable distinction. Some critics have perceived the quintessence of Santayana's philosophy of life in an essay belonging to the collection entitled "Carnival" in which the philosopher asserts that "everything in nature is lyrical in its ideal essence, tragic in its fate, and comic in its existence." Throughout his life Santayana remained a naturalist and held firm to the philosophical tenet that the ideal has a natural basis.

After World War I, Santayana lived in Paris for a short while before finally settling in Rome. In 1927 he met David Cory, who became his secretary and later his literary executor. In his earlier works, Santayana had adopted a more psychological approach to the life of the mind; in his later works he took a more classical philosophical approach. In *Scepticism and Animal Faith* (1923) and the four volumes of *The Realms of Being*—*The Realm of Essence* (1927), *The Realm of Matter* (1930), *The Realm of Truth* (1938), and *The Realm of Spirit* (1940)—Santayana essentially organizes his philosophical naturalism into four major "realms" of being: essence, matter, truth, and spirit, what some critics hold to be one of the great philosophical systems of modern times. While at work on *The Realms of Being*, Santayana rarely made public appearances, an exception being the lectures he delivered at The Hague as part of the tercentenary celebration of the births of Locke and Spinoza in 1932. In 1935, the philosopher published his first and only novel, entitled *The Last Puritan*, which immediately made bestseller lists. The novel, which has no plot, characters, or dialogue, is essentially a vehicle by which Santayana could apply his philosophy of materialism to his experiences in America.

At the outbreak of World War II, George Santayana moved to a convent of an order of English nuns in Rome, where he would remain for the rest of his days. In 1944 he said, "I shall never leave here [the convent]. There has been so much killing and so much suffering in the world's history." He took many solitary walks, carried on a wide correspondence, but generally remained detached from people and events. Santayana once explained that his detachment was "affectionate and simply what the ancients called philosophy." In 1940 the philosopher set to work on his autobiography, *Persons and Places* (3 vols., 1944–1953), the last volume of which was published posthumously. In the first volume, *The Background of My Life* (1944), Santayana offers an account of his first thirty years and of the Spanish and American influences in his life and work. In 1946, Santayana published *The Idea of Christ in the Gospels*, a reiteration of the ideas he had put forth forty years earlier in *Interpretations of Poetry and Religion*, in which he translates theological dogma into dramatic symbols and poetic myths.

When Rome was liberated in 1944, the philosopher was swamped with American visitors, among them servicemen and intellectuals familiar with his work. By this time he was writing *Dominations and Powers* (1951), an analysis of the individual and society. Upon its completion, Santayana devoted himself to translating Lorenzo de' Medici's love poem "Ambra," even though he was partly deaf and half blind. His last illness put an end to his writing, and on September 26, 1952, at age eighty-eight, George Santayana succumbed to stomach cancer. According to his wishes, the philosopher was buried in the Catholic cemetery of Rome in a plot reserved for Spanish nationals.

6

Pablo Casals

1876–1973

Pablo Casals was born Pau Carlos Salvador Defilló de Casals on December 29, 1876, in Vendrell, a seaside village approximately forty miles from Barcelona, the capital of Catalonia in Spain. He was the second of eleven children of Carlos Casals, an organist at a local church, and Pilar Defilló de Casals, who had been born in Puerto Rico. Pablo absorbed his parents' interest in music and sang in tune before he could speak clearly. At the age of five he became a second soprano in the local church choir. His father taught him piano and organ—as soon as his feet could touch the pedals—and the violin. By age seven, Pablo could compose and transpose music, and at eight he began filling in at the organ for his father when the latter could not be in church. Pablo Casals told his lifelong friend José María Corredor: "From my earliest days music was for me a natural element, an activity as natural as breathing."

Pablo first laid eyes on a makeshift cello when a group of traveling minstrels stopped in Vendrell. The young boy asked his father to build him a cello, with a gourd as the sounding board. He saw and heard a real cello for the first time when José García played at the Catholic Center in Vendrell. At age eleven, Pablo decided to study the cello under García at the Municipal School of Music in Barcelona. Ironically, Pablo's commitment to a musical education set off a bitter family quarrel. Despite the lengths he had gone to introduce his son to music, Carlos Casals, a man of limited vision, thought Pablo should become a carpenter's apprentice. His mother, on the other hand, was devoted to fostering Pablo's musical talent and placed the boy with relatives in Barcelona, where she stayed with him during his second year of study.

At the Municipal School of Music, Pablo rebelled against the technical restraints of the cello that required stiffness of the right arm and restricted the fingering of the left hand. With his technique of bowing and fingering the cello, the young Pablo purified phrasing and enriched intonation in ways that had not been thought possible. With his innovative technique, Pablo gave the cello, which had traditionally been played within an ensemble, solo status. At the Municipal School of Music, Casals also took instruction in harmony and counterpoint from José Rodereda. His parents' quarrels did not abate while he was studying at the Municipal School of Music, and during his last year in Barcelona their disagreements threw Pablo into a prolonged spiritual crisis, what he described as "mental revulsion in the face of a horrible world." Meanwhile, he earned a living by performing in a local bistro, the Cafe Tost, where he impressed pianist and composer Isaac Albéniz. Albéniz gave the young musician a letter of introduction to the Count Guillermo de Morphy, a renowned devotee of music and the private secretary of the Queen Regent of Spain, Maria Cristina, in Madrid.

In 1894, Casals went with his mother to Madrid. With a 250-peseta scholarship from Queen Cristina, Casals studied chamber music under Jesús de Monasterio and composition under Tomás Breton at the Royal Conservatory of Music in Madrid. A disagreement between Count Guillermo de Morphy, who wanted

Pablo to compose Spanish operas, and Casal's mother, who insisted that he devote himself to the cello, brought an end to their stay in Madrid in 1897. The family traveled to Brussels and then to Paris, where the four francs Casals earned each day as a cellist at the Folies Marigny, a music hall, kept them barely afloat. The family then returned to Catalonia, where Pablo Casals taught at the Municipal School of Music in Barcelona, played principal cello at the Barcelona Opera, and gave concerts in posh resorts until he saved enough money to return to Paris and leave his family behind with some financial security.

With a letter of introduction from Count Guillermo de Morphy, Casals made the acquaintance of French conductor Charles Lamoureux, who proclaimed the cellist "one of the elect." On November 12, 1899, Casals made his Paris debut as a virtuoso in a concert conducted by Lamoureux. Around this time, Casals began playing Bach's unaccompanied suites for cello in their entirety, even though they were considered mere finger exercises. Casals felt the suites had a richness and poetry, and by his subtle interpretations, he gradually unmasked their beauty and transformed them into the benchmark by which all cellists are judged. Casals practiced the suites every day for over a decade before he played them in public, and then played one suite every day for the rest of his life.

After his Paris debut, the young cellist was flooded with invitations to perform, and for twenty years he took his cello across Europe and the Americas, touring the United States over a dozen times. Around the turn of the century, Casals performed for England's Queen Victoria, Belgium's Queen Elizabeth, and President Theodore Roosevelt. He appeared in concert on numerous occasions with violinist Jacques Thibaud and pianist Alfred Cortot, with whom he helped Auguste Mangeot found the Paris Normal School of Music in 1914. After World War I, Casals devoted himself to promoting musical excellence in Spain. In 1920 he founded the Pau Casals Orchestra in Barcelona, which he subsidized for seven years before the orchestra became self-supporting. In the mid-1920s, Casals founded the Workingmen's Concert Association to make music available to all the classes of Catalán society. In the years after he founded the Pao Casals Orchestra, Casals stepped up his international tours and guest-conducted such orchestras as the London Symphony, the New York Symphony, and the Vienna Philharmonic.

Throughout his career, Casals came to the defense of oppressed peoples by refusing to perform in countries practicing tyranny and repression, and by writing protest letters and holding benefit concerts. In 1936, when Franco and conservative forces rose against a popularly elected Second Spanish Republic government that recognized the regional autonomy of Catalonia, Casals took the Republican side, and during the Spanish Civil War he performed benefit concerts for the victims of Franco's major offenses against Catalina. Once Franco came to power, in 1939, Casals chose exile, moving to Prades, a French village just across the Spanish border with a strong Catalán presence. He vowed to return to Spain only when the country had a freely elected government. Despite numerous invitations from the United States, Casals remained in France during World War II, by the side of his fellow exiles and in an active stance against totalitarianism. After the German occupation, Casals ceased to make public appearances.

When the war ended, Casals resumed his public performances until he realized in the fall of 1945, while touring England, that democratic nations would allow Franco to remain in power. Casals protested by turning down all invitations to play or conduct after 1947. His only audiences were his pupils and the friends he invited to his home. In 1950 prominent musicians from around the globe, led by American violinist Alexander Schneider, descended on Prades, with Casals's permission, for Bach bicentenary concerts. Urged on by friends, Casals resumed conducting and playing for the event, which gave birth to the annual Prades Festivals. At the close of the festival, as he would after every concert, Casals played the Catalonian folk ballad "The Song of the Birds" as a gesture of protest against the continued oppression of the Spanish people. Casals appeared in subsequent Prades Festivals and eventually resumed his busy career.

On January 28, 1956, at Veracruz, Mexico, Casals performed in concert outside Prades for the first time after nine years in exile. For three months Casals visited Puerto Rico, his mother's birthplace, and returned to settle on the island a year later. In August 1957, Casals wed Marta Montañez, a Puerto Rican cello student, after failed marriages to Portuguese cellist Guilhermina Suggia and American singer Susan Metcalfe. Casals would call Puerto Rico home for the rest of his days and would never return to live in Spain. Casals mapped out an ambitious cultural plan for

Puerto Rico, which included the inauguration in 1957 of the world-famous Festival Casals and the incorporation of a symphony orchestra and a conservatory of music.

When he resumed concert appearances in 1956, Casals refused to play in any country that officially recognized Franco's Fascist regime. In 1958, Casals performed at the United Nations and joined Albert Schweitzer, the Nobel Prize–winning French philosopher and musicologist, in a speech advocating nuclear disarmament before the UN General Assembly. In 1961 he performed at the White House at the request of President John F. Kennedy, whom he greatly admired. On that occasion he spoke privately for one hour with President Kennedy about the threat to world peace that nuclear proliferation posed.

Beginning in 1962, Casals performed the chief choral work of the Festival Casals each year at Carnegie Hall in New York. At the conclusion of the Carnegie Hall performances, Casals traveled almost every summer until 1973 to the Marlboro School in Vermont to teach classes and conduct the school's chamber orchestra during the annual Marlboro Festival. In his later years, Casals also became increasingly active as a composer, writing symphonies, string quartets, songs, motets, sonatas for piano and violin and piano and cello, and pieces for violin solo and cello solo.

In 1971 the great musician and humanitarian appeared before the UN General Assembly once again, at the age of ninety-five, to conduct the first performance of his "Hymn of the United Nations." Two years later, on October 22, 1973, Pablo Casals died in San Juan, Puerto Rico. At his funeral, a recording of "The Song of the Birds" was played.

Desi Arnaz

1917–1986

An only child, Desi Arnaz was born Desiderio Alberto Arnaz y de Acha III in Santiago de Cuba, Cuba, on March 2, 1917, to Desiderio Arnaz and Dolores de Acha. Desi's paternal great-grandfather had been appointed mayor of Santiago de Cuba by the queen of Spain, and his paternal grandfather, Don Desiderio, was a Cuban doctor who tended to Teddy Roosevelt's Rough Riders when they charged up San Juan Hill during the Spanish-American War. Desi's maternal grandfather was Alberto de Acha, one of the founders of the Bacardi rum company. In 1916, Desi's parents married, and in 1923 Desiderio Arnaz was elected mayor of Santiago de Cuba.

Desi was raised in an atmosphere of privilege, wealth, and power. His childhood was spent at the family's house in Santiago de Cuba, on three farms his father ran, and at a beach house at Cayo Smith. He attended a Jesuit school, Colegio de Dolores, in Santiago de Cuba, and during school vacations he often worked on one of the farms and learned to ride horses and to fish. In 1932, Desiderio Arnaz was elected to Congress and went to Havana to serve his term, with plans of moving the family there at a later date. In 1933, Fulgencio Batista led a "sergeant's revolt" against the despotic rule of General Gerardo Machado. Machado fled Cuba. Since Desiderio Arnaz was among General Machado's followers, the Arnaz family was targeted during the revolt. The family lost its entire fortune, and Desiderio Arnaz was imprisoned at La Cabana in Havana for six months.

Upon his release, father and son fled Cuba on a ferryboat to begin a new life from scratch in Miami; Desi's mother stayed behind until they were set up. Desi was enrolled at Saint Patrick's High School in Miami, even though he already had enough credits to graduate, and he took two courses, played basketball, and swam on the school team. Desi's best friend then was Al Capone Jr., whose infamous father was imprisoned at Alcatraz. Desiderio Arnaz started several businesses in Miami that did poorly, so Desi had to earn money after school in various jobs, such as cleaning canary cages. His next job would lead to show business. Desi was invited to sing and play the guitar with a rumba band in Miami called the Siboney Septet for thirty-nine dollars per week, starting in December 1936. His mother joined the family in Miami at around that time.

In 1936, Arnaz's performance in the rumba band at the posh Roney Plaza Hotel caught the eye of Xavier Cugat, the king of rumba. Cugat auditioned Desi for his orchestra, and the young singer belted "Para Vigo me voy" ("In Spain They Say Si Si") and was hired on the spot. After graduating from Saint Patrick's, Arnaz traveled from city to city with the orchestra as its featured vocalist. In Cleveland, Bing Crosby heard Desi sing, and he was so impressed that he told Xavier Cugat to give the young performer a raise. After six grueling months on the road, Desi decided to go back to Miami and start his own Latin dance band. For twenty-five dollars a month Cugat allowed Desi to bill his band as "Desi Arnaz and his Xavier Cugat Orchestra," direct from the Waldorf-Astoria Hotel in New York City. Desi made his first appearance in 1938 at the Park Central bistro in Miami, where he introduced the conga to American audiences. The dance was so successful that the club was renamed La Conga Cafe.

Desi Arnaz was a sensation and soon attracted the attention of Broadway director George Abbott. Abbott gave the young singer a major break, casting him as a Cuban football star in Rogers and Hart's 1939 Broadway musical *Too Many Girls*. That same year, Desi's parents divorced, and his mother came to live in his penthouse on Central Park West. Soon after, RKO purchased the motion-picture rights to *Too Many Girls*, and Desi was signed for the film. On the set at the RKO studios in Hollywood, Desi Arnaz met Lucille Ball, a contract player for RKO. They began dating during shooting and married on November 30, 1940, in Greenwich, Connecticut, while Desi was doing a four-week solo engagement at the Roxy Theatre in New York. Soon RKO offered Desi a contract to make three more films, so the couple returned to California, where they bought a five-acre ranch in the San Fernando Valley, christened Desilu.

In 1941, Arnaz acted in the mediocre motion picture *Father Takes a Wife*. That year, he joined movie stars like Clark Gable and Bing Crosby to kick off President Roosevelt's Good Neighbor Policy in Mexico. After the bombing of Pearl Harbor, Arnaz received a commission as a lieutenant in the Cuban army; he resigned the commission and joined the U.S. Navy and toured with Hollywood stars in 1942 as part of the Army and Navy Relief. Before the tour, Arnaz acted in the box-office dud *Four Jacks and a Jill* and his last RKO picture *The Navy Comes Through* (1942), which the critics applauded. Louis B. Mayer spotted him that year in the show *Ken Murray's Blackouts*, and Arnaz was put under contract at Metro-Goldwyn-Mayer (M-G-M). After performing for the troops in the Caribbean with the USO, Desi Arnaz made a brief appearance in M-G-M's 1943 war film *Bataan*, which won him recognition and a Photoplay Award for Best Performance of the Month.

In 1943, Arnaz was assigned to the U.S. Army Medical Corps, and he entertained hospitalized servicemen until his discharge in November 1945. He then assembled a rumba band and opened at Ciro's in Hollywood in January 1946, introducing the conga song "Babalu," which became his trademark later. In 1946, Arnaz appeared in Universal's *Cuban Pete*, a film showcasing the rumba band which was good publicity. He played at the Copacabana in New York and then cut his first album for RCA Victor. In 1946 and 1947, Arnaz served as musical director of Bob Hope's radio show. A film for Columbia, *Holiday in Havana* (1949), another tour with his band, and a stint on the musical quiz show *Tropical Trip* in early 1951 for CBS radio followed.

Beginning in 1948, Lucille Ball starred in *My Favorite Husband,* a radio series for CBS about a scatterbrained housewife and her banker-husband. The network approached Ball about converting the radio show into a TV series. Lucille Ball insisted that Arnaz play her husband on the show, but the network doubted the pair would succeed. The two went on a nationwide vaudeville tour to test their act, and audiences reacted enthusiastically. CBS bigwig William Paley then agreed to do a pilot for their show; within two days Philip Morris bought the series. At first the story line concerned the real life of Lucille and Desi, but later the characters were made more recognizable to a 1950s audience. Desi became Ricky Ricardo, the struggling bandleader, and Lucy became a talentless housewife. Arnaz suggested that the series be filmed before a live audience, a hitherto untried approach. CBS agreed to do so if the couple took a salary cut. Arnaz and Ball consented under the stipulation that they would own all the episodes outright after one network airing. It proved a brilliant business decision on their part.

In 1950, Ball and Arnaz formed Desilu Productions to produce the show. The series became *I Love Lucy* and debuted on October 15, 1951, setting the standard for sitcom productions. Desi Arnaz did not yet realize that since the show was filmed, it would lend itself easily to reruns and network syndication that would make them a fortune in future decades. *I Love Lucy* ran on CBS with rave reviews through the 1956–1957 season, and Desilu Productions blossomed into a high-profile Hollywood television studio, producing or providing aid to such shows as *Our Miss Brooks* and *Make Room for Daddy*. Arnaz then sold the 180 episodes of *I Love Lucy* back to the studio for $4,500,000 in order to finance the expansion of Desilu. *I Love Lucy* received top ratings, so Arnaz and Ball made it a series of hour-long shows renamed the *Lucille Ball–Desi Arnaz Show*. In 1957, Arnaz purchased the RKO Gower and RKO Culver studios from General Tire, enormously increasing Desilu holdings to thirty-five soundstages.

During the *I Love Lucy* years, Desi and Lucy starred in two feature films, the well-received *Long, Long Trailer* (1954) and *Forever Darling* (1956). They also had two children, the actors Lucy Arnaz and Desi Arnaz Jr. The couple shocked the nation when they divorced in 1960, marking the end of the *Lucille Ball–Desi Arnaz Show*. They split their financial empire evenly. Arnaz continued to head Desilu and even served as executive producer until he sold his portion of the company to Ball soon after she launched the series *The Lucy Show* in 1962. Ball eventually sold the studio to Gulf & Western, now Paramount Communications.

In 1963, Arnaz married Edith Mack Hirsch. The couple remained married until her death in 1985. In 1967, Arnaz returned to television production with *The Mother-In-Law*, a series produced by Desi Arnaz Productions at Desilu. The show ran for two seasons. Desi Arnaz's later activities were limited to guest appearances on such TV shows such as the *Kraft Music Hall*, *Saturday Night Live*, and *Ironside*. In 1982 he acted in his last film, *The Escape Artist*, using the name Desiderio Arnaz in order to make room in the limelight for his son Desi Arnaz Jr. In 1976, Arnaz published his autobiography, entitled *The Book*, which chronicles his life up until his divorce from Lucille Ball. In the epilogue of *The Book*, Arnaz writes in praise of America: "I want to thank the United States of America and her people. I cannot think of another country in the world in which a young man of sixteen, broke and unable to speak the language, could have been given the chances to accomplish what I did, or the welcome, *cariño*, praise and honor which were given to me." Desi Arnaz died of cancer on December 2, 1986, in Del Mar, California.

Joan Baez

1941–

One of three sisters, Joan Baez was born Joan Chandos Baez in Staten Island, New York, on January 9, 1941, to Albert Baez, a physicist who came to America at age two from Puebla, Mexico, and Joan (Bridge) Baez, born in Edinburgh, Scotland, and raised in the United States. Her parents' Quaker beliefs of nonviolence engendered in Joan a devotion to issues of justice and peace, which was fueled by the discrimination she endured in childhood. Joan's classmates ostracized her because of her Latino roots and dark complexion, and this treatment left an indelible mark on her psyche. As an escape from prejudice, Joan immersed herself in music, spending a summer developing her voice and learning to play the ukulele. She soon envisioned music as a path that would lead to her popularity. This was a self-fulfilling prophecy, for not long after, Joan made her first stage appearance in a school talent show, and the warm reception bolstered her self-confidence.

Throughout Joan's childhood, her father assumed teaching and research posts that kept the family moving to various college communities in New York State, Iraq, Redlands, Palo Alto, Boston, and finally Paris. After Joan completed high school in Palo Alto, where she excelled in music and sang in the school choir, the family relocated to Belmont, Massachusetts, so that Albert Baez could teach at Harvard University and the Massachusetts Institute of Technology. In 1958, Baez entered Boston University's Fine Arts School of Drama, but she became distracted by the folk scene on Harvard Square and abandoned her studies after one month. In those days folk music was enjoying a revival, and musicians such as the Kingston Trio and Pete Seeger enjoyed the spotlight. Coffeehouses on the East Coast featured local singers and became favorite gathering places for college students. Before long Baez made a modest start in the coffeehouses singing American ballads, blues, and spirituals with a roommate, but soon went solo.

In 1959, Baez sang for several weeks at the Gate of Horn, a nightclub in Chicago, where she met pop folk singer Bob Gibson. Gibson invited the teenage singer to appear with him that August at the first Newport Folk Festival. Singing as an unlisted entertainer, Baez stole the show and became an overnight celebrity. Her success led to friendships with folk singer Odetta and the Weavers and spawned offers to make recordings and go on concert tours. Baez chose instead to return to the coffeehouse circuit in Boston. Soon after, however, she signed her first contract with Vanguard, a small label known for the quality of its recordings, turning down more lucrative deals with larger recording companies. In 1960, Baez appeared again at the Newport Folk Festival, and on November 5 of that year she gave her first solo concert at the 92nd Street Y in New York City. That fall, Baez also held solo concerts in New York City's Town Hall and at the prestigious Carnegie Hall.

Before Christmas in 1960, the singer's first solo album *Joan Baez* was released. On November 23, 1962, *Time* magazine caught the Baez fever by featuring the singer on its cover holding a guitar. In 1963, Baez's third album, *Joan Baez in Concert*, was released, and she performed at the Forest Hills Music Festival and the Hollywood Bowl. That year, she began touring with Bob Dylan, and in her Forest Hills Music Festival concert in New York, she performed numerous Dylan songs, some sung alone and others with Dylan. From 1963 to 1965, Baez and Dylan were involved romantically. Later, she would record *Any Day Now,* a double album of Dylan tunes.

In the 1960s, Baez took an active role in the civil rights movement and the Vietnam War protest. In 1962 she joined Martin Luther King Jr. at a banned march in Birmingham, Alabama, risking both her life and career. She marched with King again in 1963 in Montgomery, Alabama, and on August 28, 1963, led 350,000 people in "We Shall Overcome" at the Lincoln Memorial when King gave his "I Have a Dream" speech. In 1963, Baez sang at the White House for President Lyndon Johnson; in between songs the singer told the president that the American people wanted to stay out of the war in Vietnam. In 1964, Joan Baez protested U.S. involvement in the conflict by keeping 60 percent of her federal income taxes, the portion she figured went into the U.S. Defense Department. In a show of her commitment to nonviolent protest and to world peace, the singer founded the Institute for the Study of Nonviolence (now called the Resource Center for Nonviolence) in 1965.

In 1967, the Daughters of the American Revolution refused Joan Baez permission to play at their Constitution Hall in Washington, D.C., because of her stance against the war. Mo Udall, secretary of the interior, granted the singer permission to give an outdoor concert at the base of the Washington Monument, where an estimated 300,000 people gathered to hear her sing. Several months later, Baez was arrested and jailed for her civil disobedience in opposition to the draft. The next year, she married David Harris, a draft-resistance leader who spent time in jail for refusing induction. They had a son, Gabe, but their tempestuous marriage ended in divorce a few years later. In 1969, Baez performed at Woodstock, a five-day concert bringing together some of the most influential singers of the decade.

Baez wrote the songs on her next album *Blessed Are...*; "The Night They Drove Old Dixie Down," a cut from the album, became a popular hit of the 1970s. In 1971, Baez and Harris divorced, and she left Vanguard. In 1972, she toured North Vietnam to witness the devastation of the war, spending eleven days in Hanoi. Upon her return to the United States, Baez edited the tapes she had recorded on the trip to make her most political album—entitled *Where Are You Now, My Son?*—released in 1973. In that same year, she was also involved in an antiwar protest at the Congress building in Washington, D.C. In 1975, Joan Baez recorded *Diamonds and Rust,* which she believes is in many ways the best album she ever made. It eventually went gold, giving a boost to her career. The title song, about her affair with Bob Dylan, received strong airplay. She joined Dylan on the fabled Rolling Thunder tour and released a live album entitled *Gulf Winds.*

Since 1973, Joan Baez has served on the national advisory board of Amnesty International. She was instrumental in forming Amnesty West Coast, a California branch of the organization. In 1979 she founded the Humanitas International Human Rights Committee, whose purpose was to address global human rights violations. On July 19, 1979, Baez gave a concert at the Lincoln Memorial with ten thousand people in attendance to gather support for the Vietnamese boat people. In seeking to end the suffering of the boat people, she urged President Carter to send the Sixth Fleet into the South China Sea on a rescue mission, which he did. In 1979, Baez received the American Civil Liberties Union's Earl Warren Award for her long commitment to civil liberties and human rights.

By the 1980s, Baez's singing career was floundering as her fans of the protest era gradually drifted away. In an effort to widen her repertoire, Baez mixed genres, adding reggae songs, like her 1983 "Warriors of the Sun," Latin American nonsalsa songs, and new African styles to her list of protest songs, Scottish hymns, and American spirituals. Nevertheless, eight years would pass before Baez released her next album, the 1987 LP *Recently.* That same year, she published her memoir *And a Voice to Sing With,* in which she condemns the materialism rampant in American society. In 1989, the singer released *Speaking of Dreams* in celebration of the thirtieth anniversary of her album *Joan Baez.*

Speaking of Dreams was not enough to revive the singer's career, and she had serious thoughts of retiring. Instead, she opted for change, hiring her first singing teacher and an enterprising manager, Mark Spector. By 1990, she signed with Virgin Records, and for a year Baez collaborated with songwriters she admired, who provided her with material for a new album and helped her write her own songs. In 1993 she released the results:

Play Me Backwards, her first album on a major label since the late 1970s and one of the finest recordings of her career. The high points of the album include a folk-rock ballad, "Stones in the Road," Mary Chapin Carpenter's lament for a lost generation, and a haunting love song by Janis Ian called "Amsterdam." For her renewed persistence and effort, Baez was rewarded with both a nomination for a Grammy in the category of Best Contemporary Folk Album and a revival of her popularity as old and new fans "discovered" the singer.

Throughout the 1980s and early 1990s, Baez continued to actively protest the injustices of the world. In 1982 she appeared with Paul Simon in a benefit concert for the National Nuclear Weapons Freeze Campaign. Three years later, in 1985, Baez opened the U.S. portion of the Live Aid concert to raise money for relief to victims of famine in Africa, and in 1986 she took part in the "Conspiracy of Hope" concert, which celebrated the twenty-fifth anniversary of Amnesty International. In the late 1980s, Baez toured Israel and the occupied territories, seeking a peaceful resolution to the conflict. In April 1993, at the invitation of refugee-aid organizations, the singer offered a musical message of hope to the peoples in the war-ravaged cities of Sarajevo and Zagreb. In the last two decades, Baez has been honored with numerous awards for her peace efforts, most notably the 1982 Lennon Peace Tribute Award, the 1982 Americans for Democratic Action Award, the 1983 SANE Education Fund Peace Award, and the 1988 Gandhi Memorial International Foundation Award. To this day, Joan Baez continues to advocate an end to violence and war in the world and to help those less fortunate at home and abroad.

Antonia Novello

1944–

The oldest of three children, Antonia Novello was born in Fajardo, Puerto Rico, on August 23, 1944, to Antonio Coello and Ana Delia (Flores) Coello. After her parents divorced, Antonia and her brother were raised by their mother. During her childhood, Antonia suffered from congenital megacolon, a debilitating condition which required that she be hospitalized for a minimum of two weeks each summer. She was supposed to undergo corrective surgery on her colon at age eight, but her busy mother kept postponing it. The surgery was not performed until Antonia was eighteen, and during the next several years she had to endure additional operations to correct the condition. Novello has cited this illness as a motivating factor in her decision to pursue a career in medicine and administer to those who have fallen by the wayside. In May 1991 she told the *Saturday Evening*

Post: "I thought, when I grow up, no other person is going to wait 18 years for surgery."

Ana Delia Coello, the principal of a local junior high school for thirty years, inspired her daughter to excel in all her endeavors. Beginning at an early age, Antonia devoted herself to her studies and dreamed of someday becoming a pediatrician. Upon graduating from high school, Antonia became a premedical student at the University of Puerto Rico at Rio Piedras, where she received her B.S. degree in 1965. Antonia went on to study medicine at the University of Puerto Rico at San Juan and received her M.D. degree in 1970, the same year she married Joseph Novello, then a navy flight surgeon. The couple moved to Ann Arbor, Michigan, where Antonia continued her medical training as an intern at the University of Michigan Medical Center. In 1971, Antonia Novello became the first woman to receive the Intern of the Year Award, in recognition of her outstanding performance, from the Department of Pediatrics, the University of Michigan Medical Center.

Novello spent the next two years as a pediatrics resident at the University of Michigan Medical Center. During her residency, her favorite aunt died of kidney failure, and she herself suffered from a severe kidney ailment that required hospitalization. These experiences led her to pursue subspeciality training in pediatric nephrology as a fellow at the University of Michigan in 1973 and 1974. As she monitored the progress of patients awaiting kidney transplants and saw that many could not be helped, her resolve to improve the lot of kidney patients was strengthened. In 1974 and 1975, she continued her study of pediatric nephrology as a fellow at the Georgetown University Hospital in Washington, D.C. She then opened her own private pediatrics practice in 1976 in Springfield, Virginia.

Two years later, Novello gave up private practice and applied for a position with the U.S. Public Health Services. In 1978 she was hired as a project officer in the artificial-kidney and chronic-uremia program of the National Institute of Arthritis, Metabolism, and Digestive Diseases, at the National Institutes of Health (NIH) in Bethesda, Maryland. Novello remained at that post until 1979 and then rose swiftly through the ranks of the NIH. In 1979 and 1980 she was a staff physician at the NIH, and from 1981 to 1986 she was the executive secretary in the Division of Research Grants at the NIH.

In 1982, Novello earned a master's degree in public health from Johns Hopkins University. That year, she was selected as a congressional fellow on the staff of the Labor and Human Resources Committee, chaired by Sen. Orrin Hatch, the Republican from Utah. As a congressional fellow until 1983, Novello contributed to the drafting and enactment of the National Organ Transplant Act of 1984, which provided for the creation of a national network for acquiring, allocating, and transporting human organs for transplantation. From 1986 until her appointment as U.S. surgeon general in 1989, Antonia Novello was deputy director of the National Institute of Child Health and Human Development, one of the twenty-six highest positions at the NIH. In that capacity, she came face-to-face with the devastation wrought by AIDS and developed a special interest in pediatric AIDS research.

When she was appointed deputy director of the National Institute of Child Health and Human Development, Novello felt she had reached the pinnacle of her career, and she envisioned remaining in that position until retirement. Then, on October 17, 1989, President George Bush nominated Novello for the post of U.S. surgeon general. The nomination was heartily endorsed by Congress, and on March 9, 1990, Antonia Novello was sworn in as the fourteenth surgeon general of the United States. In the speech she delivered at the swearing-in ceremonies in the Roosevelt Room of the White House, Surgeon General Antonia Novello told the audience, which included George Bush and Supreme Court Justice Sandra Day O'Connor, that "the American dream is alive and well...today the West Side Story comes to the West Wing."

As surgeon general, Novello's myriad responsibilities included commissioning research focusing on major health concerns, issuing warnings to the American people about threats to their health, serving as a spokesperson for the Bush administration on matters of public health, and overseeing the fifty-seven hundred commissioned officers of the Public Health Service. Antonia Novello would prove herself uniquely qualified to meet the challenges of her post. In her first year as surgeon general, Novello consulted with experts in many fields in preparation for several major campaigns she would launch to combat serious threats to the health of Americans. She targeted such major threats to the general population as AIDS, substance abuse, smoking, and drinking and driving.

Novello launched an aggressive campaign against smoking, rallying against what she called "the self-serving, death-dealing tobacco industry and their soldiers of fortune, advertising agencies." In September 1990, Surgeon General Novello released a comprehensive report on the hazards of cigarettes and the health benefits to those individuals who quit smoking. She voiced grave concern about the slow decline in smoking among women, which resulted in lung cancer surpassing breast cancer as the number-one cause of cancer fatalities in women. In March 1992 the surgeon general made headlines across the nation when she and James S. Todd, the executive vice president of the American Medical Association, held a news conference to urge R. J. Reynolds to stop featuring Joe Camel in its ads, since the cartoon character has a special appeal to children.

As U.S. surgeon general, Novello targeted the health concerns of the nation's constituencies that have historically been neglected: children and youth, women, and minorities. She sought not only to provide better health care for these groups but to address their pressing health problems. With regard to children, Novello warned the nation about the crisis in the system of immunization in America and the critical absence of quality prenatal care. She also stressed the growing threat of AIDS among children and the pressing need to make AIDS education widely available. Novello also emphasized injury prevention for children, who fall victim in high numbers to machinery-related accidents and the effects of harmful chemical or biological agents. In addressing the special problems facing youth, the surgeon general concentrated on smoking, teenage violence, and rampant drug abuse and drinking. In 1991, Novello met with some of the largest beer and wine companies in the United States and requested that they stop targeting children and teenagers with their advertising.

With regard to women and health care in the United States, Novello grappled with health problems of enormous proportions, particularly domestic violence, breast cancer, and heterosexual AIDS. She expressed great concern about the prevalence of domestic violence in households across the United States and the fact that this ubiquitous problem has been swept under the rug.

At an American Medical Association Conference held in January 1992 the surgeon general reported that domestic violence is "the most common cause of injury among women overall and the leading cause of injuries to women ages fifteen to forty-four." She called for more research into ways of halting violence against women in the United States.

With regard to minorities, Novello shed light on the serious faults in the health-care system, of consequence to Latinos in particular. In an editorial published in the January 9, 1991, issue of the *Journal of the American Medical Association,* the surgeon general cited the critical lack of health-care coverage among Latinos, who are uninsured at a higher rate than any other group in America. She expressed concern about the fact that Latinos suffer from diseases such as AIDS, high blood pressure, diabetes, kidney disease, and cancer in disproportion to their percentage of the general population.

Since 1986, Novello has held the position of clinical professor of pediatrics at the Georgetown University School of Medicine in Washington, D.C., concurrently with her other posts. For her service in the medical profession, Novello has received numerous awards. In 1983, she was awarded the Public Health Service Commendation Medal; in 1985, she was honored with the NIH Certificate of Recognition; and in 1989 she was given the Surgeon General's Exemplary Service Medal. In the course of her illustrious career, Antonia Novello has authored over seventy-five articles and chapters of books related to nephrology, pediatrics, and public health policy.

10

Plácido Domingo

1941–

Plácido Domingo was born on January 21, 1941, in Madrid, Spain, to famous singers Plácido Domingo, an Aragonese, and Pepita Embil Domingo. His parents performed in Spain and Latin America as a duo in the *zarzuela,* a uniquely Spanish comic opera. Known as the "Queen of the Zarzuela" during the genre's golden years from 1940 to 1946, Pepita Embil Domingo commissioned many operettas for the duo. From early childhood Plácido loved music; he studied the piano, and for a time he dreamed of becoming a conductor. His mother was the first to realize that Plácido had the makings of a great tenor, and she encouraged him in his musical pursuits. When he was eight years old, the family moved to Mexico, where Plácido's parents eventually formed their own operetta company, based in Mexico City. Plácido sometimes accompanied his family's singing troupe on the piano.

Plácido studied piano and voice at the National Conservatory of Music in Mexico City from 1955 to 1957, where Carlo Morelli, a former Metropolitan Opera singer, coached him and helped him switch from baritone to tenor. He attended the Instituto Mexico, a high school, where he played soccer, his favorite sport. Domingo is such a fan of soccer that when the World Cup came to the United States in June 1994, he postponed all professional obligations to concentrate on the soccer competition. In his youth, he also enjoyed bullfighting and performed as an amateur matador at private fiestas.

At age nineteen, he sang the minor role of Borsa in *Rigoletto,* but he made his official operatic debut as a tenor in 1961 in Monterrey, Mexico, as Alfredo in *La Traviata.* Later that year, the Dallas Civic Opera signed him, and soon the tenor had the opportunity to perform with two great divas of the opera world. In 1961, he sang Arturo in *Lucia di Lammermoor* with Joan Sutherland as the heroine. In 1962 the tenor sang the important role of Edgardo in the Fort Worth production of the same opera, in which the French American coloratura soprano Lily Pons sang the title role in her farewell to the stage. During these early years Plácido also performed in *Tosca* and *Adrienne Lecouvreur.*

Domingo then went to Tel Aviv to join the Israel National Opera Company, which was searching for a tenor. Shortly before he left, he married Marta Ornelas, a lyric soprano, who later gave up her musical career to raise their three sons. Ornelas has been a great source of encouragement and inspiration to Domingo and always insists that he strive for the high tenor notes. Domingo intended to stay in Israel for six months to enlarge his repertory but ended up remaining for two and a half years, singing 280 performances of eleven roles, all in their original language except for two. In 1965, Domingo returned to the United States to perform with the New York City Opera, singing the role of Don José in *Carmen* and Pinkerton in *Madame Butterfly.* Few critics took note of the tenor, since the operas were scheduled late in the season. However, Domingo's spectacular singing and acting in *Don Rodrigo* in the opening of the 1966 season of the New York

City Opera captured the attention of major New York critics.

In the summer of 1966, Domingo sang with the Metropolitan Opera in concert performances of *Cavalleria Rusticana* and *I, Pagliacci*. During the 1966 fall season of the New York City Opera, he continued to win plaudits for his lyrical attainments as Don José in *Carmen* and Alfredo in *La Traviata*. In the next few years Domingo became known to opera audiences in the rest of the United States and in Europe, performing in, among others, *Manon Lescaut*, and *Don Carlos, Un Ballo in Maschera*, and *Faust* with the Berlin, Hamburg, and Vienna opera companies during the summer of 1968. Domingo was scheduled to make his official debut with the Metropolitan Opera Company on October 2, 1968, as Maurizio in *Adrienne Lecouvreur*, a role he had sung just once six years earlier. But on September 28, with thirty-five minutes remaining before curtain time, Franco Corelli, who was to perform Maurizio that evening, canceled, and Domingo was summoned to replace him. Despite having to appear four days earlier than planned, Domingo gave a stellar performance.

In 1969, Domingo obtained a release from the New York City Opera and again came to the rescue of Corelli, this time as Manrico in the Metropolitan's production of *Il Trovatore*. He performed his first Edgardo for the Met in June 1970, with Joan Sutherland again as the heroine of *Lucia di Lammermoor*. Meanwhile, he was building an international reputation, debuting at La Scala in December 1969 in the title role of *Ernani* and singing Cavaradossi in a Covent Garden revival of *Tosca* in London in December 1971. Later that month, he performed Chevalier des Grieux in *Manon Lescaut* in Barcelona.

By 1979, when he opened the Metropolitan Opera with *Otello*, Domingo had sung in an estimated eighty operas, had recorded fifty, and had performed fourteen hundred times. As the 1980s dawned, televised and filmed opera became increasingly popular in the United States, providing another niche for Plácido Domingo. In the decade of the 1980s the tenor appeared in fully staged operas and recitals on the Public Broadcasting Service's *Live from Lincoln Center* and *Live from the Met*, for which he was highly praised. Domingo's opera films were just as well received. In 1983, he won praise for his Alfredo in Franco Zeffirelli's highly acclaimed film version of *La Traviata*, and in 1984 he was applauded for his passionate Don Juan in Francesco Rosi's spectacular screen version of *Carmen*.

Nonoperatic music has also appealed to Plácido Domingo despite grumbling from archconservatives of the opera world. In 1981 his pop recording of "Perhaps Love" with John Denver was a hit and made him popular with listeners unfamiliar with opera. Domingo has also recorded tangos and songs from Viennese operettas. In addition to releasing pop recordings, Domingo has also performed nonoperatic music in televised performances. In 1984 he costarred with Carol Burnett in a variety special in which he sang "Be a Clown" and "Vesti la giubba" from *I, Pagliacci* and accompanied Burnett in Cole Porter's "Night and Day." In his own special, *Steppin' Out with the Ladies*, which aired in 1985, he sang pop standards and duets from Broadway musicals with Maureen McGovern, Marilyn McCoo, Leslie Uggams, and Patti LaBelle. Plácido Domingo has also collected his family's native zarzuela on recordings entitled *Zarzuela Arias* and *Zarzuela Arias and Duets*. He has given zarzuela performances all over the world.

During the 1984–1985 Met season the charismatic tenor made his U.S. Wagnerian debut in the title role in *Lohengrin* and his conducting debut in *La Bohème*. In September 1985, Mexico City was hit by earthquakes, and Domingo lost several family members in the disaster. He took time off from his opera schedule to hold benefit concerts on behalf of earthquake victims. In 1986, Domingo played the part of Verdi's tragic Moor in Franco Zeffirelli's film version of *Otello*. On November 15, 1986, Domingo sang the title role in Menotti's *Goya*, an opera the tenor had commissioned, at its premiere in Washington, D.C. In 1987 he had the honor of singing *Otello* at the 100th anniversary performance at La Scala.

On New Year's Eve, 1988, Domingo appeared as a soloist with Zubin Mehta and the New York Philharmonic in a gala concert televised live to millions of viewers, during which he also conducted the orchestra in the overture to *Die Fledermaus*. The year 1993 heralded Plácido Domingo's twenty-fifth anniversary at the Met, which he shared with Luciano Pavarotti, whose debut took place the same year. Plácido Domingo sang the first act of *Die Walküre* and then performed in the finale with Pavarotti for the third act of *Il Trovatore*, with its famous two-tenor aria. By 1992, Domingo had made over seventy-one recordings of fifty-five different operas and had received two Emmy Awards, six Grammy Awards, and countless other international awards.

Throughout his career, Domingo has shown considerable

talent as a conductor. He made his formal debut as an opera conductor with *La Traviata* at the New York City Opera on October 7, 1973. On October 25, 1984, the tenor appeared at the Metropolitan Opera, conducting *La Bohème*. While he enjoys conducting, Domingo expects singing to be his major focus until the mid-1990s. He will not be satisfied until he has sung *Tristan* in Vienna in 1996, the most demanding role for a tenor in all of opera.

11

Henry Cisneros

1947–

Henry Gabriel Cisneros was born in the Prospect Hill section of San Antonio, a Latino middle-class neighborhood, on June 11, 1947. His maternal grandfather, Mexican emigrant José Rómulo Munguia, was an intellectual and reformer who in 1926 fled across the border and eventually started a printing company in San Antonio. Henry was the oldest of five children born to George Cisneros and Elvira (Munguia) Cisneros, who were active in local politics and numerous civil organizations in San Antonio. George Cisneros was a civilian administrator for the U.S. Army and later became a colonel in the army reserve.

Henry's mother cultivated a strict and supportive atmosphere in the Cisneros home. Each summer she engaged the children in reading, creative projects, family debates, and daily chores. She insisted that the children speak English, and she forbade them to watch television. Henry was enrolled at the Roman Catholic parochial school of San Antonio's Church of the Little Flower. A bright child, he skipped third grade and graduated at age sixteen from Catholic Central High School. After his high school graduation, Henry wanted to enter the U.S. Air Force Academy to pursue his dream of becoming a pilot, but he was rejected due to his young age and small stature. Instead, he entered Texas A&M University in the fall of 1964. A turning point in Henry Cisneros's life came in 1967, while he was an undergraduate at Texas A&M. He participated in a conference of student leaders held at West Point and became painfully aware of his shortcomings when the students from Ivy League schools outshined him with their polish and knowledge. From that day on, Cisneros devoured information and set high standards of achievement for himself.

After graduating in 1968 from Texas A&M with a B.A. degree in city management, Cisneros returned to San Antonio. He soon landed a job as an analyst with President Johnson's Model Cities effort, a Great Society program committed to urban renewal. Roy Montez, the program's director, admired Cisneros's knack of wading through bureaucracy and promoted him to assistant director in January 1969. On June 1, 1969, Cisneros married Mary Alice Perez, his high school sweetheart. The couple had two daughters and one son, John Paul, who was born with a serious congenital heart defect.

Henry Cisneros's growing interest in urban-management led him to pursue an M.A. degree in urban and regional planning from Texas A&M. He received the degree in 1970 and then applied to the doctoral program in public administration at George Washington University. He would earn a Ph.D. in 1975. In January 1970, Cisneros went to Washington, D.C., where he secured a position as an administrative assistant to the executive vice president of the National League of Cities. The following year, he submitted an application to the White House Fellows program and was selected for the year 1971 as the youngest House Fellow in U.S. history. He was assigned to work under Elliot L. Richardson, secretary of health, education, and welfare, who was influential in furthering Cisneros's political career.

In 1972 and 1973 Cisneros worked toward a second master's degree in public administration from the John F. Kennedy School of Government at Harvard University. He financed his studies at Harvard with a Ford Foundation Grant and served as a teaching assistant at the Massachusetts Institute of Technology (MIT); in 1974 he turned down a full-time teaching job at MIT. Instead, he took the advice of Elliot Richardson and returned to San Antonio that year. The atmosphere in the city was charged by social unrest and minority activism. Cisneros took a teaching position as a professor of urban affairs at the University of Texas at San Antonio, but against the backdrop of San Antonio politics, academia seemed dull to Cisneros. His goal was a political post and the mayor's seat.

Henry Cisneros found an ally in the Good Government League (GGL), a community organization that since the mid-1950s had effectively controlled city hall but in the late 1960s had begun to lose Latino support. The league had lost the last mayor's election and needed to attract Latino votes in the campaign for city council to reestablish its dominance. Cisneros's uncle, Ruben Munguia, supported his nephew's political aspirations and lobbied to get him on the GGL ticket. In 1975, at the age of twenty-seven, Cisneros was easily elected to the city council as its youngest member in San Antonio's history. As one of the city's brightest young politicians, he was reelected in a landslide in 1977, and again in 1978, and served a total of six years. He allied himself with Communities Organized for Public Service (COPS), a grassroots Latino advocacy group, but spent most of his term in the San Antonio City Council mending fences with COPS because he did not always agree with the organization's strategies.

In December 1980, the popular mayor of San Antonio, Lila Cockrell, withdrew from the mayoral race for personal reasons, and the door was wide open for Henry Cisneros to assume the post he had been dreaming of for a decade. Among his opponents in the race was councilman John Steen, who had been chair of the GGL when Cisneros was asked to run on its ticket. Steen was no match for Cisneros, who easily won the election on April 4, 1981, capturing 62 percent of the votes cast. With this victory, Cisneros became the first Mexican American elected mayor of San Antonio since 1842.

Cisneros had a vision of San Antonio as a high-profile city on the cutting edge of change. He implemented a plan of intensive urban renewal and economic development to realize his vision. Cisneros's strategy was to boost the city's image as a center of tourism, accomplish public works, and recruit business. In an effort to increase tourism, he built the Alamodome stadium, a resplendent mall named Rivercenter, and numerous theme parks. Mayor Cisneros concentrated heavily on improving San Antonio's business climate. Early in his first term, in hopes of luring high-tech companies to the region, he convinced the Texas College and University System to introduce an engineering program at the University of Texas at San Antonio that would serve as a center for high-tech development. He also pushed for the creation of a high-technology high school and a health-careers high school in Bexar County, of which San Antonio is county seat. For his accomplishments, Cisneros received the Jefferson Award from the American Institute of Public Service in 1982.

In his 1983 reelection campaign, Cisneros touted his "Target 90—Goals for San Antonio" program, which assigned five hundred individuals from various fields of expertise to study the major issues affecting San Antonio. The positive response to "Target 90" and to the mayor's general performance showed in the polls; Cisneros won reelection that April with more than 93 percent of the vote. In the fall of 1983 President Reagan selected Cisneros as a member of the National Bipartisan Commission on Central America, presided over by former secretary of state Henry A. Kissinger. The mayor spoke out against the administration's policies regarding Central America, and with the spotlight of the national media focused on him, Cisneros became a major voice for Latinos across America.

Reports in 1984 that Democratic candidate Walter F. Mondale was considering the mayor as his second choice for a running mate in the presidential race intensified the media's attention on Cisneros. But he renounced any desire to seek a national post and focused on his job as mayor. For his contributions as leader of San Antonio, Cisneros was elected president of the Texas Municipal League in the fall of 1984. Several months later he was chosen vice president of the National League of Cities. In 1985, Cisneros was elected for a third term as mayor of San Antonio, with 72 percent of the vote. Two years later, Cisneros was reelected for a fourth term as mayor with 67 percent of the vote, and he publicized his wish to remain mayor through 1990, the year his "Target 90" program would reach fruition. Yet he approached the end of four terms as mayor in 1988, Cisneros was poised to run for governor. However, he had been having an affair with another woman, and news of it came out during an agonizing press conference, jeopardizing his bid for office. Cisneros ended the affair and decided not to run for governor. His wife filed for divorce, then had a change of heart and withdrew the petition.

Rather than pursuing another term as mayor of San Antonio, Cisneros left office in 1988 to work on a new business venture. With a boost from the Houston-based financial-services company Transamerica Criterion, he founded Cisneros Asset Management, a business managing pension funds. In 1993, Cisneros Asset Management held over $500 million in various investment equities. In 1992, Henry Cisneros campaigned for Bill Clinton as he sought the office of the president of the United States. After the election, Clinton had his eye on Cisneros for his cabinet, while Ann Richards, who had been elected governor of Texas, tried to convince the ex-mayor to fill the Senate seat left vacant by Lloyd Bentsen's appointment to the Treasury.

Henry Cisneros chose the cabinet position and his appointment as secretary of Housing and Urban Development (HUD) was announced on December 18, 1992. The HUD post was more in line with Cisneros's ideal of being a public servant pursuing policies to help the poor and oppressed of America's cities. In taking over at HUD, Cisneros assumed the worst job in the cabinet. For years, the agency had been riddled with corruption; several HUD officials had even been indicted on conspiracy, bribery, and mail-fraud charges. Cisneros and the Clinton administration targeted homelessness as HUD's number-one priority. Henry Cisneros told *Time* magazine in a December 6, 1993, article: "I came to this job because I believe that time is running out on the American way of life as we know it. I don't want to be overly pessimistic, but how long can we go on with random killings and a permanent underclass and the homeless?"

Rita Hayworth

1918–1987

Rita Hayworth was born in New York City on October 17, 1918. Christened Margarita Carmen Cansino, she was the first child of Eduardo Cansino and Volga (Haworth) Cansino, both of whom had made careers in show business. Volga Cansino, a Ziegfeld Follies showgirl, came from an English family whose theatrical heritage dated back many centuries. Eduardo Cansino was descended from a long line of famous professional dancers in Spain. In 1913 he emigrated to the United States to work as a vaudeville headliner with his sister. After Margarita's birth the family moved from a high-class theatrical hotel to Jackson Heights, Queens.

Before Margarita could walk, her parents envisioned a career for her on the stage.

Margarita and her two younger brothers went to PS 79 in Jackson Heights. When she was nine, the family moved from Queens to Los Angeles so that her parents could join the rapidly expanding motion-picture industry. In Los Angeles, Eduardo Cansino directed dance scenes for various studios and taught dancing. Rita attended the Carthay School and later spent her first and only year of middle education at Hamilton High School. As a child she took acting and dancing lessons, and at age eleven, she made her stage debut in a school play.

In 1932, Margarita made her professional debut at Carthay Circle Theater in a stage prologue for the motion picture *Back Street*. At that moment, Eduardo Cansino, realizing his twelve-year-old daughter's immense potential, made Margarita his dance partner, passing her off as his wife. "The Dancing Cansinos," as they called themselves, performed for a year and a half in Tijuana, Mexico, at the Foreign Club Cafe de Luxe, a favorite watering hole of the film industry. After that they moved their act to one of California's floating casinos, a gambling boat moored three miles off Long Beach shore. They were a smash hit, but according to biographer Barbara Leaming in her book *If This Was Happiness*, Rita suffered both brutal beatings and sexual abuse at the hands of her father. As Orson Welles confessed to Leaming in 1983, the abuse continued until Rita left home, although her alcoholic mother attempted to intervene.

Margarita Cansino soon got her big break in film when Hollywood producers and casting directors saw her dancing with her father at the Caliente Club in Agua Caliente, Mexico. Winfield R. Sheehan, then at Fox, hired the sixteen-year-old dancer for a role in the 1935 film *Dante's Inferno*, starring Spencer Tracy. For *Dante's Inferno*, Margarita's name was shortened to Rita, and her Latin looks were enhanced. Although the film failed, Rita obtained a one-year contract with Fox. During this year, she played a string of minor roles, which capitalized on her Latin looks, in the films *Charlie Chan in Egypt* (1935), *Under the Pampas Moon* (1935), *Paddy O'Day* (1935), and *Human Cargo* (1936).

Her contract with Fox was not renewed, and Hayworth spent the next year portraying Native Americans and Mexicans in several motion pictures. In 1937, at age eighteen, Rita Cansino married Edward C. Judson, a businessman who became her manager. Much later, Hayworth learned that she was Judson's third wife. In an effort to enhance the actress's appeal, Judson altered her hairline and her eyebrows by electrolysis and changed her professional name to "Hayworth," her mother's maiden name with a minor alteration. Judson also encouraged the young actress to sleep with studio executives to promote her career. Hayworth captured the attention of Harry Cohn and secured a seven-year contract with his Columbia Pictures. She made fourteen low-budget movies before landing a starring role opposite Cary Grant in the 1939 box-office success *Only Angels Have Wings*. In 1941 she teamed up with James Cagney in *The Strawberry Blonde* for Warner Brothers, and then joined Fox to film *Blood and Sand*.

When Hayworth costarred with Fred Astaire in *You'll Never Get Rich* (1941) for Columbia, she struck it rich and achieved celebrity status. She appeared on the cover of *Time* magazine and was named "the Great American Love Goddess" by Winthrop Sargent of *Life*. In 1942, Hayworth starred in three hit movies, dancing opposite Fred Astaire in *You Were Never Lovelier*. As her career blossomed, Hayworth tried to end her marriage to Edward Judson, but he threatened to throw lye in her face if she did. Finally, in 1942, he consented to a divorce when Hayworth handed over all her assets to him. The next year, Hayworth married Orson Welles. In 1944, she costarred with Gene Kelly in the Technicolor musical *Cover Girl*. She was cast as Rusty Baker, a Brooklyn singer who achieves fame and decides it isn't everything. *Cover Girl* was a smash hit. Soon after its release, *Life* magazine featured Hayworth on the cover wearing black lace in a photograph, which, according to the *New York Times*, "became famous around the world as an American serviceman's pinup."

In 1945, Hayworth played a bit part in *Tonight and Every Night*, staring Les Bowman, Janet Blair, and Shelley Winters. While the film was in production, Hayworth discovered that she was pregnant, and on December 14, 1944, she gave birth to a daughter, Rebecca. Her elation over the birth turned to grief a month later when her mother died tragically at age forty-five from a ruptured appendix. In 1946, Hayworth played what is perhaps her most unforgettable role in *Gilda*, a classic example of the film noir of the period. The "scandalous" scene in which Hayworth sings "Put the Blame on Mame" and strips off her long black gloves sent scores of moviegoers rushing to the box office, and *Gilda* set all-time Columbia box-office records.

In 1947, Hayworth shed her love-goddess image, cut her hair, and played a sophisticated blonde in *The Lady from Shanghai,* a film Orson Welles starred in and directed. The film was released in 1948 to harsh reviews and turned out to be a major failure. Hayworth's marriage to Orson Welles was also doomed to failure that year. After a brief interlude with Howard Hughes that led to an unwanted pregnancy and abortion, Hayworth went to Europe, where she spent time in the company of Prince Aly Khan, reputedly one of the richest men in the world. Harry Cohn ordered the actress back to Hollywood to play in *The Loves of Carmen* (1948), for which her love-goddess image was resurrected. Rumors about an affair with Aly Khan proved true, and in 1949 she married the prince. An offscreen scandal erupted when it was revealed that Rita Hayworth was already pregnant with their daughter, the Princess Yasmin Aga Khan. This marriage was also destined to end, and the couple divorced in 1953.

In 1952 she acted in *Affair in Trinidad,* a box-office hit which outgrossed *Gilda.* At around this time, Hayworth became embroiled in another romance fraught not only with failure but with danger. Her fourth husband, the actor-singer Dick Haymes, whom she married in 1953 and divorced in 1955, physically abused the actress as he tried to capitalize on her fame as a way to get ahead in his career. This disastrous marriage took its toll on her, and she went into temporary retirement until 1957. She reemerged on the Hollywood scene in the 1957 motion pictures *Fire Down Below,* which received favorable reviews, and *Pal Joey,* her final role as a contracted actress.

Soon after completing *Pal Joey,* Hayworth began to date the producer James Hill, and in 1958 they were married. Hill gave Rita Hayworth, by then a freelance actress, the role of a sexually tormented wife who brings about the downfall of her husband in *Separate Tables* (1958). Hayworth got top billing in the film, and she performed the role to critical acclaim. *Separate Tables* turned out to be a memorable film. In 1959, Hayworth played in *They Came to Cordura,* and she portrayed a housewife who, with her lover, is charged with murdering her husband in the courtroom drama *The Story on Page One.*

At this time, Hayworth was having as little success in her marriage as the female characters she portrayed. In 1961 she and Hill divorced. Hayworth stayed away from Hollywood until 1964. She struggled to make a handful of films in the mid-1960s and early 1970s, such as *The Poppy Is Also a Flower* (1966), *The Naked Zoo* (1971), and *The Wrath of God* (1972), but by then she was suffering from Alzheimer's disease and had difficulty remembering her lines. In 1981, her daughter Yasmin became Hayworth's conservator. Yasmin remained her mother's nurse and constant companion, providing the love Rita Hayworth had always longed for, until the actress succumbed to Alzheimer's on May 14, 1987, at age sixty-eight. Her death saddened the nation and alerted Americans to the plight of those suffering from Alzheimer's.

13

Oscar de la Renta

1932–

The youngest of seven children and the only boy, Oscar de la Renta was born Oscar Ortiz de la Renta on July 22, 1932, in Santo Domingo, the Dominican Republic, to Oscar de la Renta and Mariá Fiallo. Oscar's mother had a strong influence on him and was the first to introduce him to the world of European fashion. Since it was impossible at the time to buy fine clothes in the Dominican Republic, she would make frequent trips to Havana to shop at El Encanto, a famous European clothing store. Oscar attended high school and art school at the same time in Santo Domingo and held a one-man show of paintings when he was only seventeen years old. After graduating from high school, he convinced his mother to send him to Madrid to study art at the Academia de San Fernando, where he had private lessons with Vasquez Díaz. Oscar's ambition was to become an abstract painter, despite his father's wishes that he follow in his footsteps and become an insurance salesman.

When Oscar was nineteen, his mother passed away, and his father ordered him to return home from Madrid. The future designer refused to leave Spain, and his sisters continued to send him money so that he could remain abroad. Oscar took part in many gallery shows in Madrid, but he did not sell a single painting. He realized that he could not rely solely on his sisters for his livelihood, so he decided to market his artistic skills by doing fashion illustrations for newspapers and magazines in Spain. He was soon drawing his own designs; Mrs. John Lodge, wife of the American ambassador to Spain, saw a few of his sketches and asked him to design the debut gown for her daughter. *Life* magazine featured the debutante in her white tulle gown on the cover, and de la Renta's career in fashion was launched. Soon after, the designer Cristobal Balenciaga offered Oscar work at Aisa, the Balenciaga couture house in Madrid. Balenciaga's main house was in Paris, where he and Christian Dior were the pillars of couture in those days.

After spending six months at Aisa, Oscar de la Renta decided it was time to go to Paris, even though Balenciaga thought the young designer would make a greater contribution if he stayed in Madrid. With letters of introduction in hand, de la Renta left for Paris in 1961, where, on his first day searching for a job, he was offered a position at Dior. On the second day he visited Antonio del Castillo, the Spanish designer for Lanvin-Castillo, who was searching for an assistant. Castillo took an instant liking to Oscar because he spoke Spanish, and with assurances from the young designer that he could drape, Castillo offered him a job starting in two weeks. That evening, Oscar de la Renta flipped through the Yellow Pages in search of a fashion school. He chose the one with the biggest ad and petitioned the head teacher at the school to teach him a year-long course in two weeks.

In November 1962, de la Renta decided to try his luck in New York. He knew he could not practice his profession back in the Dominican Republic, and New York seemed like a good compromise. Armed with letters to Christian Dior, whose manufacturing business was on Seventh Avenue, and to Elizabeth Arden, who had a custom salon in Manhattan, Oscar left Paris. Two months later, he joined Antonio del Castillo at Elizabeth Arden to work on the ready-to-wear collection, where his designs were labeled "by Oscar de la Renta for Elizabeth Arden." De la Renta's collections for Elizabeth Arden were met with accolades for their elegant exuberance, and he quickly gained a devout following. In 1965, after two years at Elizabeth Arden, de la Renta began designing for the American Jane Derby, and many of the clients he cultivated at Arden followed him. After Derby's death the company became known as Oscar de la Renta.

Oscar de la Renta came of age as part of a new breed of designers, who ceased creating costly, labor-intensive, made-to-order clothes but considered their designs "couture" because of their superior quality. Along with contemporaries like Bill Blass and Galanos, de la Renta built his career on clothes that, while ready-to-wear, felt luxurious and opulent. In the 1960s, his day clothes were somewhat austere; he designed dresses that buttoned down the side and suits trimmed with cheetah or lynx. His evening dresses were ornate, with close-fitting, bejeweled bodices and full skirts. In 1967, de la Renta's Gypsy and Russian ensembles were cited as trendsetters for the era of ethnic fashion that swept the globe. That year, de la Renta started other trends, among them Belle Epoque designs inspired by Toulouse-Lautrec and Gustav Klimt and clothes made of transparent fabrics.

In 1967, Oscar de la Renta married Françoise de Langlade, who was then editor in chief of French *Vogue*. The two met in 1966 at a dinner given by the duke and duchess of Windsor at Maxim's in Paris and fell in love. After their marriage, the couple took New York by storm. Françoise de Langlade dictated style in Manhattan high society, running a Parisian salon where the rich, the powerful, and the cultured rubbed elbows. Her connections provided de la Renta with a window into the lifestyles of luxury, which served him well as he began to build a fashion empire that in 1991 was reported to gross $450 million a year.

In 1967, Oscar de la Renta received the "Winnie" of the Coty American Fashion Critics' Award, and in 1968 he captured a "Winnie" Return Award. As the decade of the 1970s dawned, de la Renta emerged as one of the leading American men's wear designers of both leisure and formal clothes. Among de la Renta's many noteworthy creations for women in the 1970s were suits with safari jackets; dresses in caftan, butterfly-wing, or sarong shapes; and "portrait" dresses of rustling paper taffeta with a fitted bodice and full, ruffled sleeves, a design he has never abandoned. In the 1970s, as a fashion designer of international reputation, de la Renta began to dress some of the most socially prominent women in America for ubiquitous charity benefits, lunches, dinners, and gala evenings.

In 1971, Oscar de la Renta became a naturalized American citizen. In 1972, he and Françoise sought a retreat from the hustle and bustle of Manhattan and they purchased a house in Kent, Connecticut, where the designer, with the advice of the great landscape architect Russell Page, created breathtaking vistas on the property. He also became involved in several charitable projects in Santo Domingo. In the 1970s, in a rural area of his homeland, he discovered an Episcopal priest trying desperately to care for forty orphaned children in the stable of an abandoned estate. The designer decided to found an orphanage and day school for the children on the scale of Boys Town. The Dominican government contributed land and his friends in the construction business built the dormitories and classrooms. Each year de la Renta puts on a fashion show to benefit the orphanage, which shelters and educates approximately 375 children.

By the 1980s the industrious fashion designer had reached the apex of his career. De la Renta built part of his empire by designer licensing, lending his label to more than eighty different products. During his stint in the early 1980s as president of the Council of Fashion Designers of America (CFDA), de la Renta endeavored to enlarge the profile of the fashion industry. He wanted to set up regularly scheduled fashion shows at the Jacob K. Javits Convention Center, as the French had at the Louvre and the Italians at the fashion fair in Milan, but his plan generated no interest among New York City officials. He did succeed, however, in shining the spotlight on American fashion with gala events like those held at New York's Metropolitan Museum of Art to celebrate the CFDA's Lifetime Achievement Awards.

In 1983, Françoise de Langlade, a legend in high society, succumbed to cancer. In 1984, de la Renta took in one of the foundlings from the orphanage in the Dominican Republic. The baby, named Moises, weighed only two pounds when he was found, and doctors feared the worst. Although the designer had fourteen servants at the time, he fed, washed, and diapered

Moises himself and decided that the child would remain in his household. Five years later, in 1989, de la Renta married Annette Reed, daughter of the late metals industrialist Charles Engelhard and his wife, Jane. De la Renta met Annette Reed at a weekend party given by her mother. Reed is popularly considered heir to the title of doyenne of New York society currently held by Brooke Astor. The couple places high priority on the cultivation of culture in New York. Reed is vice chairperson of the board of trustees of the Metropolitan Museum of Art, while Oscar de la Renta is on the boards of the Metropolitan Opera and Carnegie Hall.

In 1991, Oscar de la Renta earned the distinction of being the first American designer to show at the Paris ready-to-wear collections, staged twice each year in the courtyard of the Louvre. The designer received a standing ovation at this bastion of French fashion; even the trendsetters of fashionable Paris society, including Paloma Picasso, São Schlomberger, and Inès de la Fressange, rose to their feet. Then, in 1993, de la Renta became the first American designer to take over a French couture business when the classic house of Pierre Balmain took him on. The house of Balmain had been on a financial losing streak, since couturiers could no longer reap profits from haute couture. Balmain knew that the prestige the American designer brought to couture would help sell its more profitable ready-to-wear clothing, accessories, and perfume. The show of de la Renta's debut haute couture collection for Balmain, held two months later, was a resounding success.

In addition to the many commendations the fashion world has bestowed on one of its greatest designers, Oscar de la Renta was honored with the order of Jean Pablo Duarte, grado Caballero, and the order of Cristobal Colón, grado de Gran Comandante, from the Dominican Republic, as one of the nation's most distinguished citizens. On several occasions he was offered the post of Dominican ambassador to the United States, but he refuses to part with his American citizenship.

14

José Vicente Ferrer

1912–1992

José Ferrer was born José Vicente Ferrer de Otero y Cintrón in Santurce, Puerto Rico, on January 8, 1912. His well-to-do parents, Rafael Ferrer and María Providencia Cintrón, were both from Spain. Rafael Ferrer brought José to the mainland when the boy was six years old. As soon as José finished high school, Rafael Ferrer, a prominent attorney, enrolled the fourteen-year-old boy at Princeton University in the hope that his son would someday join his law firm. Once at Princeton, however, the young José decided to study drama, which, much to his father's distress, was the only reason José stayed at Princeton rather than dropping out to join one of the many popular traveling theater companies of the day. José acted with such budding actors as James Stewart and Joshua Logan in the Princeton Triangle Club, the undergraduate acting society. He also organized a dance band at Princeton called "José Ferrer and His Pied Pipers." In 1933 he received his B.A. from Princeton, and in 1934 and 1935 he completed graduate work in romance languages at Columbia University.

During the summer of 1934, Ferrer made his professional appearance in *The Periwinkle*, a showboat melodrama that made one-night stands in towns on Long Island Sound. In the summer of 1935, Ferrer was cast in walk-on parts and acted as assistant stage manager for Joshua Logan's stock company, the Suffern Country Playhouse, in New York. In September 1935 he made his Broadway debut in a walk-on part as the Second Policeman in *A Slight Case of Murder*, and from 1936 to 1940 he won roles in many more theater productions, including *Spring Dance* (1936), *Brother Rat* (1936), *In Clover* (1937), and *Key Largo* (1939). In 1937, Ferrer made his directorial debut in Princeton University's annual production at the Triangle Club, *Fol-de-Roi*, which then went on tour. On December 8, 1938, Ferrer married the actress Uta Hagen; the couple had one daughter and divorced in 1948.

In the 1940s, Ferrer's productivity increased. In 1940 he directed summer stock at the Westchester Playhouse in New York. That year he landed his first major stage role, the lead in the successful Broadway revival of *Charley's Aunt*. In 1941, Ferrer produced and directed the pre-Broadway tryout of *The Admiral Had a Wife*, in which he played the admiral. This comedy was scheduled to open in New York City on December 7, 1941, but was canceled because of Pearl Harbor. Ferrer then directed and starred in *Vickie*, which opened in September 1942. A year later, he played Iago opposite Uta Hagen, as Desdemona, in the Paul Robeson production of *Othello*. Ferrer toured with the production in 1943 and 1944 and won a Donaldson Award for his perform-ance. *Othello* enjoyed a long-running engagement and was one of the most memorable moments in his stage career. Ferrer then produced and directed *Strange Fruit*, which opened on November 29, 1945. In 1946 he played the title role of *Cyrano de Bergerac;* for his performance in *Cyrano*, he was awarded a Tony. Ferrer then toured as Kenneth Bixby in *Goodbye Again* and as Leo in *Design for Living* in 1947. That year, Princeton University awarded him an honorary master's degree.

Ferrer later became general director of the New York City Theater Company at the New York City Center, where he played the lead in *Volpone* in 1948. Ferrer married the actress Phyllis Hill on June 9, 1948, but they divorced in 1953. In 1948 he made his professional film debut as the Dauphin with Ingrid Bergman in *Joan of Arc* and was nominated for an Academy Award for Best Supporting Actor for his performance. In 1949 the University of Puerto Rico presented Ferrer with an honorary degree of doctor of humanities, and he was also awarded an honorary degree from Bradley University. In 1950 he played a lovelorn poet in Richard Brooks's film version of *Cyrano de Bergerac*. With his witty performance, Ferrer captured the film's only Oscar nomination and won the award for Best Actor of 1950. That same year, he won the Lingaphone Institute's Annual Award for diction in films and played opposite Gloria Swanson in the stage production of *Twentieth Century*, in accordance with Swanson's contract, which stipulated that she appear only with Ferrer.

The 1951–1952 season proved to be Ferrer's year. He directed, produced, and starred on Broadway in *The Shrike*. His efforts in *The Shrike* won him a Tony for Best Director and Best Dramatic Performance in 1952 as well as the Donaldson Award for acting and directing. On Broadway, Ferrer directed and produced *Stalag 17* and *The Fourposter* and won Tony Awards for Best Director of these productions. He also appeared in the 1952 Hollywood films *Anything Can Happen,* a chronicle of the adventures of a Russian immigrant family in New York, and *Moulin Rouge*. His portrayal of Toulouse-Lautrec in the latter film, which many critics considered even stronger than his performance as Cyrano, won him an Academy Award nomination for Best Actor. In 1952 he won many other awards, including *Variety*'s New York Critics Poll for directing and acting, the New York Newspaper Guild's Page One Award for dramatic art, and the Federation of Motion Picture and Stage Actors of Cuba Annual Award for acting.

On July 13, 1953, José Ferrer married the popular singer Rosemary Clooney, and the couple had five children. They divorced twice, the last time in 1967, but remained friends throughout. In 1953, Ferrer played opposite Rita Hayworth in the 1953 motion picture *Miss Sadie Thompson,* a semimusical remake of the early talkie *Rain*. Today Ferrer is probably best remembered by American audiences for his Lt. Barney Greenwald, the sharp navy lawyer who outsmarts Captain Queeg, played by Humphrey Bogart, on the witness stand in the 1954 film *The Caine Mutiny*, about World War II. In 1955 he starred in and directed the screen version of *The Shrike* with June Allyson. Five years later, in 1960, Ferrer made his operatic debut in the title role in *Gianni Schicchi*, which ran at the Santa Fe Opera Company and then at the Brooklyn Academy of Music. The next year, he sang Amonasro in *Aida* in Beverly Hills. He appeared as Pseudolus in *A Funny Thing Happened on the Way to the Forum* in 1965 in Florida and New York. In 1966 he replaced Richard Kiley in the role of Don Quixote in *Man of La Mancha* and subsequently toured with the national company in 1966 and 1967.

In the course of his long career José Ferrer also made countless television appearances in series, miniseries, episodes, TV movies, and specials. Ferrer enjoyed playing in dramatic television series and once confessed that one of his favorite parts had been that of a villain in a 1974 television episode of *Columbo*, starring Peter Falk. He was also a guest on most major talk shows and variety hours.

In 1990, Ferrer appeared onstage for the last time in a musical version of Ionesco's *Rhinoceros*, which ran in England. He continued to direct and was involved in such productions as *The Best Man* at the Mark Taper Forum in Los Angeles. In March 1992, Ferrer was scheduled to appear with Judd Hirsch in the Broadway production of Herb Gardner's play *Conversations With My Father*, but withdrew from the production because of illness. On January 26, 1992, at the age of eighty, José Ferrer died in Coral Gables, Florida, a cancer victim. His fourth wife, the former Stella Daphne Magee, survived him. Ferrer loved the stage and screen. This was apparent to follow actor Ronald Reagan who bestowed upon Ferrer the National Medal of Arts in 1985. Jose Ferrer once described his devotion to acting in this way: "You know you're in the right racket if you love the drudgery that goes with it."

15

Fabiola Cabeza de Baca Gilbert

1898–?

Fabiola Cabeza de Baca Gilbert was born on May 16, 1898, to distinguished parents at La Liendre, headquarters of the family's large ranch in northeastern New Mexico. The Cabeza de Baca and Delgado families, from whom Fabiola is descended, first entered New Mexico in the seventeenth century. In 1823 her ancestor Don Luis María Cabeza de Baca received a land grant of a half million acres in the llano region near Las Vegas, New Mexico. Her mother passed away when she was four years old, so Fabiola was raised by her paternal grandmother, a traditional Latina of the patrón class. In childhood, Fabiola was fascinated by the culinary and folkloric traditions of the American Southwest handed down to her by her Spanish ancestors, and these traditions became a major focus of her later writing.

Fabiola was enrolled at the Loretto school in nearby Las Vegas, and upon graduating in 1916, she received her first teaching assignment. Later, she continued her education at New Mexico Normal (later Highlands) University in Las Vegas, New Mexico, spending one year of undergraduate study at the Centro de Estudios Históricos in Madrid, where she immersed herself in languages, history, and art. Upon graduating from New Mexico Normal University with a degree in pedagogy in 1921, she taught for several years in rural schools across New Mexico, from Santa

Rosa to El Rito. Early in her teaching career, she received an assignment to teach "domestic science," which sparked a lifelong interest in the field and inspired her to pursue a second bachelor's degree, this time in home economics, at New Mexico State University in Las Cruces.

Immediately after being awarded a B.S. degree in 1929, Cabeza de Baca Gilbert took a job with the New Mexico Extension Service as a home-demonstration agent. With a pressure cooker in her car, she spent the next thirty years roaming New Mexico. In Native American pueblos and Hispanic villages all over the state, she taught the basic principles of food preparation and also resurrected more traditional methods, such as food drying. Cabeza de Baca Gilbert is probably the first American-trained nutritionist to recognize the merits of combining culinary innovations and age-old culinary traditions which have withstood the test of time. From her work in the Taos and Española valleys, she gained an intimate knowledge of the indigenous Pueblo Indians, the Tiwa and Tewa, of northern New Mexico. She learned the Tiwa and Tewa dialects and became the only agent to succeed in working with the women of the Native American pueblos.

During the years she spent with the New Mexico Extension Service, Cabeza de Baca Gilbert also worked tirelessly to organize markets where the native women of New Mexico could sell their handicrafts. As the first outlet in New Mexico for native rugs, baskets, pottery, canned delicacies, and other handicrafts, these markets served to popularize the creative work of local women artists and artisans. By supplying women artists with a forum in which to present and sell their work, Cabeza de Baca Gilbert made enormous strides in empowering and liberating women in New Mexican society. Her concept of popularizing native work served as a model for communities around the world.

In 1951, Cabeza de Baca Gilbert's pioneering efforts attracted the attention of the United Nations Educational, Scientific, and Cultural Organization (UNESCO). UNESCO requested that she establish a home economics program among the Tarascán Indians in the state of Michoacán in Mexico and teach agents from other Latin American countries about her food-preparation techniques. Since glass jars and pressure cookers were unavailable in Mexico, she introduced other food-processing and fish-drying techniques in the Lake Pátzcuaro region still in use today. While in Mexico, Cabeza de Baca Gilbert established eighteen demonstration centers for food preparation and preservation.

Cabeza de Baca Gilbert devoted much of her time to describing her work in home economics. For twenty years she contributed a column in Spanish to *El Nuevo Mexicano,* a newspaper in Santa Fe, and made weekly broadcasts in English and Spanish on a Santa Fe radio station. In the mid-1930s she began to write pamphlets in Spanish on food preparation, including *Los Alimentos y su Preparación,* which was published in 1934 and reprinted in 1937 and 1942, and *Boletín de Conservar,* which appeared in 1935 and was republished in 1937 and 1941. The pamphlets soon evolved into a groundbreaking two-volume cookbook entitled *Historic Cookery,* which was published in 1939 and reissued in 1956 and which sold over 100,000 copies in its initial years in print. *Historic Cookery* was the first definitive collection of authentic New Mexican recipes, passed from generation to generation by word of mouth. Working from her copious field notes and observations in Latino, Anglo, and Native American kitchens across the state, Cabeza de Baca Gilbert recorded the recipes on paper. In 1983 the Museum of New Mexico Press republished *Historic Cookery*, and it became a bestseller.

As Cabeza de Baca Gilbert traveled throughout the state of New Mexico spreading information on food preparation and preservation and establishing markets, she also collected folklore, a big passion in her life. In 1952 she published a novel entitled *The Good Life,* which traces a family's annual cycle of work and leisure in a northern New Mexico village.

Cabeza de Baca Gilbert is invariably best known for *We Fed Them Cactus* (1954), her chronicle of life on the Llano Estacado (Spiked Plain), the grasslands of eastern New Mexico, at the turn of the nineteenth century. The title of the book refers to the method of keeping cattle alive during a drought. She relied on archival material, interviews, and her own memories of her family's past to explore the history of settlers on the plains. In *We Fed Them Cactus* the author underscores the critical role of women in the Hispanic frontier and pays tribute to their bravery and ingenuity. In addition, the book contains fascinating accounts of the range wars, the infamous Vicente Silva bandit gang, and the arrival of the homesteaders. At the time of its publication *We Fed Them Cactus* played a significant role in promoting cultural and historical awareness about a little-documented region of the United States.

Throughout her life, Cabeza de Baca Gilbert worked on behalf of numerous community organizations, including the New Mexico Museum Board, the Red Cross, the Girl Scouts, the New Mexico Laboratory of Anthropology, the Santa Fe Opera Guild, the International Relations Women's Board, the School of American Research, and La Sociedad Folklórica de Santa Fe. In 1957, she received the Superior Service Award of the U.S. Department of Agriculture in recognition of her many outstanding contributions to the quality of life in New Mexico. She was also the recipient of a National Home Demonstration Agents Association Distinguished Award for Meritorious Service. In 1976 the American Association of University Women honored Cabeza de Baca Gilbert by including her works in the Museum of New Mexico Bicentennial Exhibit, which portrayed influential women in New Mexico history. Her inclusion in the exhibit sparked a new wave of interest in her writing.

Cabeza de Baca Gilbert's contributions in home economics spanned many decades, and her work continued without interruption even after an automobile accident claimed her right leg. For years she was married to Carlos Gilbert, an insurance agent, but the couple separated. After her retirement in 1959 she was active on the lecture circuit, wrote articles on cookery and folklore, and worked as a consultant for the Peace Corps. She spent her last years at a retirement home in Albuquerque, having contributed a wealth of research on the history, culinary traditions, and folklore of New Mexico.

16

Roberto Goizueta

1931–

The son of a wealthy sugar grower and refiner, Roberto Crispulo Goizueta was born on November 18, 1931 in Havana, Cuba, to Crispulo D. Goizueta and Aida (Cantera) Goizueta. Roberto enjoyed the many privileges of an aristocratic upbringing and was educated in the finest schools in the United States. He attended the Connecticut prep school Cheshire Academy, where he spent evenings flipping through the dictionary, since he did not speak English upon his arrival in America. After completing his studies there, Goizueta went on to Yale University. In 1953 he graduated from Yale with a B.S. degree in chemical engineering as one of the top-ten students in his class. That year he married Olga T. Casteleiro; the couple has three children. In 1954, Goizueta returned to Havana, where he decided to take a technical job as a quality-control chemist at Coca-Cola's Havana subsidiary rather than help run the family's sugar plantation.

After Fidel Castro rose to power in Cuba, it became extremely difficult for the Goizueta family to maneuver in business, so they fled the country in 1961, on the eve of Castro's announcement that Coca-Cola's operations on the island would be nationalized. According to Roberto Goizueta, if Castro had not taken power, his father would have purchased the Havana Coca-Cola bottling franchise. Today that business would be in the hands of Roberto Goizueta. Instead, he was transferred to Coke's operations in Nassau, in the Bahamas, where he was named staff assistant to the senior vice president in charge of Latin America. In 1965, Goizueta was moved to Coca-Cola headquarters in Atlanta, and a year later, at age thirty-five, he was named Coke's youngest vice president in charge of quality and research. In 1969, Goizueta became a naturalized American citizen. In 1975 he moved up the corporate ladder to become senior vice president of the technical division at Coca-Cola, and in 1978 he was also put in charge of legal affairs, administration, and external relations.

After 1978 a struggle for power began as corporate executives at Coca-Cola jockeyed for position when the company began to search for a successor to its president J. Paul Austin. Austin had become Coca-Cola's president in 1962, although Robert Woodruff, who had been chairman of the firm until 1955, directed the company's fortunes until the 1970s. Everyone was aware that Woodruff had forged a close bond with Goizueta, who, by the late 1970s, had earned a reputation at Coca-Cola as an able corporate executive who knew how to listen and organize, though he lacked experience in operations and marketing. Nevertheless, when Goizueta was selected as president in 1980 and then assumed full command as chairman and CEO of the Coca-Cola Company in March 1981, many in the ranks were astonished that an individual who was not born in America and spoke English with an accent could head a company as American as apple pie. Furthermore, they were shocked that a technocrat was chosen to lead a firm that had achieved success through marketing. Many believed Woodruff had chosen Goizueta as an interim leader who would step to the wings as soon as the right person for the job was found. They entirely underestimated the ability of Goizueta.

Goizueta had inherited a wealthy and influential company,

but one that also had many hidden problems. His predecessor, J. Paul Austin, had been suffering from both Alzheimer's and Parkinson's diseases, unbeknownst to the company, and had allowed management to drift. Soon after he took the helm Goizueta made the disturbing discovery that most of the capital the company was investing was equity capital, which cost about 16 percent. All of Coca-Cola's business, except soft drinks and juices, returned only 8–10 percent a year, and therefore, by borrowing money at 16 percent and investing it at 8, Coca-Cola was gradually liquidating its business. Goizueta swiftly sold all the unproductive parts of the business and pulled Coke out of markets where it had little expertise. He then forced the company make decisions based on what he called economic profit: after-tax operating profit in excess of charge for capital.

In March 1981, Goizueta summoned all senior executives to a five-day meeting in Palm Springs, California, where he informed them that Coca-Cola was about to increase profits dramatically. He laid out his strategy to accomplish this goal and told them that the company from now on would reward performance, not attendance. Goizueta promised that executives who produced good results would reap bonuses, stock options, and stock grants that mature upon retirement. As part of the strategy to get Coca-Cola back on track, early on Goizueta picked Coke executive Donald Keogh as his right-hand man and named him president. Together they made a dynamic team: While Goizueta was an introverted intellectual from Yale, Keogh was a charismatic and energetic salesman. Goizueta also chose Bryan Dyson to head Coca-Cola USA and to come up with innovative marketing and advertising campaigns to enable Coke to establish a competitive edge over Pepsi. After 1977, Pepsi-Cola had pulled ahead of Coke in supermarket sales, which account for 40 percent of all soft-drink sales. As part of the advertising campaign, Goizueta adopted a new corporate slogan—Coke Is It!—to compete with Pepsi's highly effective Pepsi Challenge.

In another move to get Coke shipshape, Goizueta also implemented a controversial program to restructure its network of bottlers. In the 1970s, Coca-Cola had run into problems with bottlers over syrup prices, so Roberto Goizueta began buying out bottlers in key markets who he thought were not "sufficiently aggressive." This costly operation was financed at least in part by the reduction of dividend payments. The move that caused the most reaction was Goizueta's purchase of Columbia Pictures in 1982 for $750 million. Several analysts were critical of the purchase because they believed that the motion-picture industry was risky business that could impact negatively on Coke's profitability. Furthermore, analysts felt that Goizueta had been cheated by Hollywood and had paid too much for Columbia. Six months later, most of Goizueta's critics had changed their tune, and they agreed that Coca-Cola's CEO had made a remarkably clever deal. By 1985, Columbia Pictures was contributing 14 percent of Coca-Cola's operating costs, and in terms of profits, it was larger than any other entertainment division in America. In 1989, Goizueta sold the company's stake in Columbia Pictures to Sony for $1.55 billion, reaping a healthy profit.

By 1984, Coca-Cola was enjoying extraordinary success. In 1979 it had reaped $5 billion in sales, as well as profits of $420 million; by 1984 both of these figures had doubled. Furthermore, Coke's return on equity by 1984 had skyrocketed to 22 percent, its highest in eleven years. To top it all off, the firm's share of the American soft-drink market that year was an all-time high of 36 percent. However, Goizueta had managed to increase the Coca-Cola Company's market share not by bolstering sales of Coke but by introducing Diet Coke in 1982, the first extension of the company's trademark. Goizueta's predecessors forbade putting the Coke name on a new product, and the company's lawyers had opposed the idea on the grounds that it was a risk to the copyright. Diet Coke was a smash hit, soon becoming the third most popular soft drink in the world, after Coke Classic and Pepsi. Many viewed Diet Coke as the most successful consumer launch of the 1980s.

Meanwhile, sales of the company's flagship product, Coke, were still sinking. In fact, in 1984 old Coke lost another 1 percent of the market to Pepsi. In 1985, Goizueta made a decision that sent shock waves across America. He changed the century-old formula for Coca-Cola and launched a new smoother and sweeter Coke, which tasted more like Pepsi than like the old Coke. Goizueta realized that not all Americans would react positively to the change, so the company hired Bill Cosby to appear in a series of commercials praising "new" Coke. After Goizueta made the announcement about "new" Coke on April 23, 1985, Pepsi exploited Coke's change by running as a full-page ad a letter to Pepsi bottlers essentially declaring that the Coca-Cola Company had finally withdrawn its product and reformulated Coke to taste like Pepsi, the superior soft drink. Just as unnerving for Coca-Cola executives was the barrage of phone calls at the company's headquarters. The switchboard was hit with more than a thousand calls a day from consumers across America, who were upset, shocked, or irate that Coke had been changed. The media joined the anti–new Coke campaign; newspapers ran stories on what may have prompted Coca-Cola to take such a drastic measure.

By June 1985 the public's resentment was actually having an adverse effect on the quality of life of Coke executives, who were even accosted on the street by angry strangers. Sales volume for Coke declined, and by early July, Goizueta and Coke executives decided they had to bring back the old Coke, but in such a way that they would not lose face. Rather than admitting that "new" Coke was a fiasco, they created two Cokes: "new" Coke and old Coke, named "Coca-Cola Classic." When American consumers learned that old Coke was making a comeback, they responded with a deluge of phone calls to thank the company, and in one day Coca-Cola headquarters received eighteen thousand calls. By 1986, Coke Classic was the number one soft drink in virtually every major market in America.

While the introduction of "new" Coke had at first been interpreted as one of the biggest fiascos in business history, ironically, in the end, it was an incredible marketing coup. With two products to suit diverse tastes, Coca-Cola's market position was bolstered. Furthermore, "new" Coke and Coke Classic grabbed more shelf space in supermarkets away from Pepsi and other competitors. All the Coke products combined gave the company 39.9 percent of the $38 billion American soft-drink market in 1986, an increase of nearly 4 percent from 1984 and the first major challenge Coca-Cola had posed to Pepsi in decades. As a result of these achievements, Goizueta was voted one of the "most admired CEOs" in America by *Industry Week* in January 1986.

Goizueta realized that Coke's dominance on the international front would account for most of its earnings growth, and early on in his tenure he sought to capitalize on overseas markets. Goizueta hired a number of internationalists to replace several tenured southerners in the company and soon saw results. While consumption per capita in foreign markets in 1988 was only 15 percent of that in the United States, by 1989 fully half of Coca-Cola sales were made abroad, where the company garnered 75 percent of its profits. By 1993, Coke earned more than 80 percent of its profits internationally and posted 6 percent volume growth overseas. The company has pinned its future on rapid volume growth overseas, in such emerging markets as India, China, the Middle East, and Latin America, and catchy marketing initiatives, such as new alternative drink lines and alterations in packaging.

In 1980, before Goizueta took the helm, Coca-Cola's market value was only slightly higher than $4 billion, making it a prime target for a takeover. By the end of 1992 its market value had risen to approximately $56 billion, making Coca-Cola the sixth most valuable public company in the United States. Under Goizueta, Coke's total return to investors averages almost 30 percent; before Goizueta became CEO, Coke's ten-year total return averaged less than 1 percent. In 1994, Coca-Cola, pleased with its decade-long winning streak, invited Goizueta to stay on after his tenure ends in November 1996, when he turns sixty-five. Goizueta, who loves his job, was delighted by the prospect of remaining with the company.

As the highest-paid CEO in the United States, Goizueta earned $2,962,000 in 1990. He owns Coca-Cola stock worth over $140 million, which constitutes almost his entire net worth. He has never sold a share of Coke stock, and to this day he owns the first one hundred shares he bought when he started with the company. Goizueta is a trustee of the Robert W. Woodruff Arts Center and is a member of the board of Atlanta's Symphony Hall, the Trust Company Bank of Georgia, Sun Trust Banks, Inc., SONAT Inc., the Ford Motor Company, and Eastman Kodak. He once told *Time* magazine: "I am not of the Cuban culture. I am not of the American culture. I suppose I am of the Coca-Cola culture."

17

Edward R. Roybal

1916–

Edward Ross Roybal was born on February 10, 1916, in Albuquerque, New Mexico, into one of the original families that had founded Santa Fe, and had received a New Mexico land grant from the king of Spain around 1610. In 1922, the family moved to the Boyle Heights area of Los Angeles, following a strike against the railroad that left Edward's father unemployed. Edward attended L.A. public schools and graduated from Roosevelt High School in 1934, when America was in the throes of the Great Depression.

Upon graduating from high school, Roybal joined the Civilian Conservation Corps (CCC), which Congress had established as a measure of the New Deal program in 1933 to provide work and vocational training for young men through conserving and developing the country's natural resources. Edward Roybal remained with the CCC until April 1, 1935, when he decided to continue his education. He went on to the University of California at Los Angeles and Southwestern University, where he studied business administration. From 1942 to 1944 he worked as a public-health educator with the California Tuberculosis Association. His work came to a halt during World War II, when from April 1944 to December 1945, Roybal served in the U.S. Army. After receiving his discharge, he again devoted himself to health work. From 1945 to 1949, Roybal was employed as health-education director for the Los Angeles County Tuberculosis and Health Association.

As the postwar decade dawned, many Mexican Americans in Los Angeles began to organize in order to address the rampant discrimination they faced in American society. They formed an activist group and sought the political representation they had been deprived of for a century. These Mexican Americans targeted the Los Angeles City Council and chose as their candidate Edward Roybal, who himself was concerned about the abuse and discrimination against Latinos he had witnessed in his East Los Angeles neighborhood. Roybal's 1947 campaign for a seat on the Los Angeles City Council met with defeat, but the political group behind him only intensified their effort. With the help of community organizer Fred Ross, the group reorganized Roybal supporters into a local chapter of the Community Service Organization (CSO), a grassroots organization launched in Chicago. Before the next election, in 1949, the CSO chapter organized enormous voter-registration and get-out-the-vote drives in East Los Angeles to strengthen Roybal's campaign.

Their hard work paid off when Roybal defeated the incumbent in the race by a two-thirds margin to become the first Mexican American to serve on the Los Angeles City Council since 1881. Once elected he immediately set about to address specific social problems plaguing his community, such as substandard housing and a lack of recreational and health facilities, and stirred open debate about discrimination against Latinos that had gone unaddressed for so long. In 1950, Roybal became embroiled in another battle, this one waged by Sen. Joseph McCarthy. While other public officials joined McCarthy's extremist camp or were silenced by the "Red Scare," Roybal attacked censorship and espoused the protection of civil liberties for all Americans, regardless of their political affiliation.

In 1954, the Democrats nominated Roybal for lieutenant governor. He campaigned hard for social change as he had in Los Angeles but was defeated in statewide elections. In 1958, he again sought election to higher office and ran for a seat on the Los Angeles County Board of Supervisors. His efforts were again met by defeat, although the race had been neck and neck and many felt that Latino voters had been harassed at the polls. In 1958, Roybal became president of Eastland Savings & Loan Association and remained at that post until 1968, when he was elected chairman of the board. At the same time Roybal continued to serve on the Los Angeles City Council and was reelected on two occasions with no opposition. For thirteen years, as a council member, he was active on many important committees, and in 1961 he served as president pro tempore. Roybal devoted his efforts in the Los Angeles City Council toward developing child care and community-health programs.

While serving his thirteenth year on the council in 1962, Roybal ran for a seat in Congress representing the Twenty-fifth District of California, a heavily Latino area including downtown Los Angeles and East Los Angeles. With the solid support he garnered from Latinos, he was elected as a Democrat to the Eighty-eighth U.S. Congress. He took his place in the House of Representatives when the session was officially opened on January 3, 1963, and would remain for the twelve succeeding Congresses. Edward Roybal was usually reelected by a huge margin, never receiving less than 66 percent of the popular vote from his constituents in California's Twenty-fifth district.

Roybal arrived in Washington at a time when there were few Latino congressmen. During his tenure, Roybal consistently championed the rights of Latinos and continued to espouse social and economic reforms to benefit all Americans. In 1963, Congressman Roybal introduced a bill that would add an Equal Rights for Women amendment to the Constitution. In 1967, Roybal introduced and won approval for the first federal bilingual education act, and in 1969 his bill establishing a cabinet-level Committee on Opportunities for Spanish-Speaking People was enacted. Later, Congressman Roybal led the opposition to the Immigration Reform and Control Act of 1986. He argued that the measure's sanctions against U.S. employers who hired undocumented workers would lead to a rash of false accusations against Latinos and, therefore, greater discrimination. On behalf of Latinos, Roybal founded and served as president of both the National Association of Latino Elected and Appointed Officials and the Congressional Hispanic Caucus.

Congressman Roybal also fought for the rights of the elderly in America. He served for numerous years on the Select Committee on Aging, which he chaired from 1983 until his retirement in 1992. In 1980 he convinced the House to restore $15 million in cuts from senior citizens' programs. In 1991, as chairman of the Select Committee on Aging's Subcommittee on Health and Long-term Care, Roybal authored the National Guardianship Rights Act, which guaranteed safeguards, such as the right to a jury trial, for those living under or threatened with guardianship. In 1992, just before retiring, Congressman Roybal established the Edward R. Roybal Foundation, committed to generating funds to establish a community-based gerontology center in East Los Angeles that would provide care, conduct research, and award scholarships in gerontology.

During nearly thirty years of service in the House of Representatives, Roybal served on a number of important committees, including the Interior and Insular Affairs Committee, the Post Office and Civil Service Committee, the Committee on Foreign Affairs, the Veterans Affairs Committee, and the House Appropriations Committee. Among the many honors bestowed upon him are honorary doctor of law degrees from Pacific States University and Claremont Graduate School. In 1973, Roybal was appointed a Visiting Chubb Fellow by Yale University. In 1976 he received the Excellence in Public Service Award from the American Academy of Pediatrics, and in the early 1980s he was the recipient of the Joshua Award for his support of improved Jewish-Latino relations.

After three decades as the representative of the Twenty-fifth Congressional District of California, Roybal stunned his East Los Angeles constituency in February 1992 by announcing that he would not seek reelection to the House of Representatives. He made the decision to end his career in public service when doctors warned him of his wife, Lucille's declining health. Roybal was quoted in the November 1992 issue of *Hispanic Business* as saying: "I don't want to be away from my wife." The Roybal legacy in politics lives on in Lucille Roybal-Allard, Edward Roybal's daughter, who became the first woman of Mexican-American ancestry in the U.S. Congress when she was elected representative of the Thirty-third Congressional District in November 1992.

18

Herman Badillo

1929–

An only child, Herman Badillo was born in Caguas, Puerto Rico, on August 21, 1929, to Francisco Badillo and Carmen (Rivera) Badillo. The paternal side of his family dates back to the island's earliest Protestant settlers, and his ancestors brought the first Protestant Bible to Puerto Rico. Badillo's mother was a Catholic of Spanish-Italian stock. Herman was born at the time of the Great Depression, which brought rampant hunger and disease to Puerto Rico. When Herman was only a year old, an epidemic of tuberculosis swept the island, taking the life of Francisco Badillo, an English teacher, who was in the midst of compiling a Spanish-English dictionary. Four years later, Carmen Badillo succumbed to the disease, and Herman was left an orphan. Herman had grown accustomed to going hungry and barefoot when an aunt took the boy in. Living conditions did not improve in his aunt's household, and Herman went hungry most of the time.

At age eleven he took a job cleaning seats at a cinema to contribute to the family. Herman's teachers and relatives knew he was extremely bright and felt he deserved a better education than the one he could receive in Puerto Rico. The only way they could secure a more promising future for him was to take him to the U.S. mainland. In 1941, Herman accompanied his aunt and a cousin to New York. He was sent to live with three or four different families in various tenements in the barrio, where he was fed three meals a day and given a pair of shoes. His aunt had difficulty earning enough to support the children, so Herman was shunted among relatives and ended up at an uncle's house in Burbank, California. He liked the mountains and climate of Burbank, and before long he found a job mowing lawns and delivering newspapers.

After two years, Herman's aunt in New York had found steady work and invited him to return and be a part of the family. Though he had grown attached to life in California, Herman went back to the barrio and was enrolled at Haaren High School, an academic and trade school. At the end of the fourth term, he had the highest average in his class. He earned money at a series of odd jobs as a pin boy in a bowling alley, an elevator operator, a busboy, and a short-order cook at Horn & Hardart. Upon graduating from high school, Badillo enrolled at the College of the City of New York as an engineering student and worked after class to support himself. He soon switched his major to business administration and received the highest marks in all of his classes. Herman enjoyed the intellectual atmosphere at City College, where, in his last years of study, he trained to become a certified public accountant (C.P.A.) and worked under accountants during summer vacations to gain experience.

In 1949, Herman Badillo married Norma Lit. The couple had a son, and in 1960 they divorced. In 1951, Badillo graduated magna cum laude from City College and landed a position as an accountant in the firm Ferro, Berdon and Company, Certified Public Accountants. He was employed full-time at the firm and studied law at Brooklyn Law School in the evenings. Badillo received the Dean's Scholarship for his second and third years of study and earned the highest distinction at the law school with his appointment as editor of the *Law Review*. In 1954 he was awarded an LL.B. degree cum laude and was valedictorian of his class at Brooklyn Law School. In 1967 he would receive a J.D. degree cum laude. Badillo was admitted to the bar in 1955 and earned his accreditation as a C.P.A. Between 1955 and 1962 he built a law practice, Permut and Badillo, and divided his time between tax and real-estate law and criminal-defense cases.

In 1960, Badillo entered the political arena for the first time as chairman of the John F. Kennedy for President Committee, which conducted an intensive registration drive aimed at Puerto Rican and black voters in East Harlem. His organization then supported Robert Wagner in his successful bid for reelection as mayor of New York City in 1961. On May 18, 1961, Herman Badillo married the former Irma (Deutsch) Leibling. That year, he launched his first campaign for political office by running for district leader of the Sixteenth Assembly District. Badillo was seventy-two votes shy of winning the election and demanded a recount, but before the courts handed down a decision, Mayor Wagner named Badillo deputy commissioner of real estate. Eleven months later, Wagner appointed Badillo commissioner for housing and relocation. As commissioner, Badillo's most important task was to relocate minorities who were to lose their home through slum clearance. He moved Puerto Ricans into low-cost housing in white ethnic areas in the Bronx, precipitating a massive white flight.

Voters did not blame Badillo for the fiasco in the Bronx, and by 1965 he had enough backing to run for borough president of the Bronx on a Democratic Reform ticket. He won more votes in the election than the incumbent Joseph F. Periconi. However, Periconi demanded a recount when a federal court in Washington invalidated the sixth-grade provision of the Voting Rights Act, which did away with a literacy test for voters and granted persons who could prove they had completed the sixth grade the right to vote. A New York court upheld the victory. As borough president, Herman Badillo initiated public budget hearings in the Bronx so that members of his constituency could voice their requests. On the basis of these requests, City Hall allocated Badillo approximately $1 billion for improvements and new construction. During his tenure as borough president of the Bronx, Badillo also chaired the Health, Housing and Social

Service Committee at the 1967 New York State Constitutional Convention. He opposed U.S. military involvement in Vietnam and supported Sen. Robert F. Kennedy's bid for the presidency and that of Sen. Eugene J. McCarthy. Badillo was also a delegate and a member of the Credentials Committee at the 1968 Democratic National Convention.

Rather than seek reelection as borough president, Badillo ran for mayor of New York City in 1969, billing himself as "the only liberal candidate." When the primary election was held on June 17, 1969, five Democratic candidates were on the ballot, including Badillo's former supporter Robert Wagner. Norman Mailer entered the race, further splitting the ticket and capturing Badillo's liberal constituency. Badillo placed third and after his defeat became a partner in the distinguished Wall Street law firm of Stroock, Stroock and Lavan, with which he remained affiliated until 1982. Before long he announced his candidacy for the Democratic nomination for congressman from the Twenty-first Congressional District. The *New York Times,* the *New York Post,* Mayor Lindsay, Governor Rockefeller, many union groups and educators, and the underprivileged of the city supported Badillo in his campaign. With a solid victory, Herman Badillo joined the Ninety-second Congress in January 1971. He vowed to represent his New York district and all Puerto Ricans.

Once in Washington, Herman Badillo was assigned to the House Agricultural Committee, a waste of his talent. He challenged the appointment and was reassigned to the Education and Labor Committee in charge of most of the antipoverty legislation. When riots broke out in Attica state prison in upstate New York in late 1971, Governor Rockefeller appointed Badillo as an "observer" to analyze the situation. This appointment gave rise to the book *A Bill of No Rights: Attica and the American Prison System,* which Badillo coauthored with Milton Haynes. In *A Bill of No Rights,* Badillo condemns the traditional practice of incarcerating criminals rather than rehabilitating them as "a destructive and monumental failure." He advocates revamping the prison system to ensure that prisoners' rights, guaranteed under the Constitution of the United States and federal and state statutes, are protected.

Badillo served in the House of Representatives until 1978, his last elected office. In 1981 he became a staff member at the corporate law firm of Fischbein, Olivieri, Rozenholc & Badillo, and he chaired the New York State Mortgage Agency from 1983 to 1986. In 1985 he almost ran for the mayor's office and would have posed a serious threat to then mayor of New York City Ed Koch. In 1986, Badillo carried New York City in the election for state comptroller, but he came up short when the votes were counted. These setbacks did not sap Badillo's desire to run for political office again. In 1993, Badillo decided to campaign for mayor of New York, but he dropped out of the race when he only managed to raise $200,000 among his poor supporters. That same year, he ran for New York City comptroller on a fusion ticket with Rudolf W. Giuliani, the Republican-Liberal candidate for mayor. Badillo expected to woo Hispanic voters to the Republican-Liberal ticket based on name recognition. Ultimately, Badillo could not persuade the Hispanic community to abandon the Democratic ticket, and he was defeated at the polls by Democrat Alan G. Hevesi in the November 2, 1993, election.

Badillo has remained a partner at same law firm, which was renamed in 1987 Fischbein, Badillo, Wagner & Itzer, and has served as an adviser on many occasions to elected officials in New York. In 1994, Mayor of New York City Rudolph Giuliani appointed Herman Badillo special counsel.

19

Rita Moreno

1931–

Rita Moreno was born Rosa Dolores Alverio on December 11, 1931, in the small town of Humacao in Puerto Rico. Her parents, Paco Alverio and Rosa María Marcano Alverio, divorced when Rosa was still a baby. She was left in the care of relatives while her mother went to New York to work as a seamstress. When Rosa was five years old, her mother brought her to New York, where they set up a household with other family members in a tenement in the Washington Heights section of Manhattan. A year later, Rosa began to study dance with the gifted teacher Paco Cansino, an uncle of Hollywood legend Rita Hayworth. Before she was a teenager she was performing in the children's theater at Macy's and at weddings and bar mitzvahs.

Rosa attended Public School 132, soon traded schoolwork for the stage. Billed as "Rosita Cosio," she landed her first part on Broadway at age thirteen in Harry Kleiner's 1945 war drama *Skydrift*, starring Eli Wallach. As a teenager, she also performed in nightclubs in Boston, Las Vegas, Montreal, and New York. In the mid-1940s, she did the Spanish dubbing of such child stars as Elizabeth Taylor, Margaret O'Brien, and Peggy Ann Garner for films sent abroad. In 1950, Rita appeared in her first major role in the film *So Young, So Bad,* under the name Rosita Moreno, the surname of her stepfather, Edward Moreno. At the request of Metro-Goldwyn-Mayer (M-G-M), she changed her first name to Rita. After her film debut a talent scout arranged to have Rita meet Hollywood mogul Louis B. Mayer, who signed the seventeen-year-old actress to a contract with M-G-M.

Moreno was then cast in two minor parts in the 1950 films *The Toast of New Orleans* and *Pagan Love Song*; after shooting, she was dropped by M-G-M. She freelanced and was invariably cast as a Latin temptress in movies like *The Fabulous Señorita* (1952), *The Ring* (1952), *Cattle Town* (1952), *Latin Lovers* (1953), and *Jivaro* (1954). Since the modus operandi in Hollywood regarding Latinos at the time was that they were ethnically versatile, Moreno was also cast as an Arab in *El Alamein* (1953) and as a Native American in both *Fort Vengeance* (1953) and *The Yellow Tomahawk* (1954). Although these roles won Rita Moreno recognition in the 1950s, they further pigeonholed her as a "Latin." She was labeled "Rita the Cheetah," and her highly publicized relationships with Marlon Brando and Geordie Hormel of the meatpacking empire reinforced this image. Unchallenged by these unchallenging, demeaning roles, Moreno sought refuge in theater. However, she was dropped from the cast of *Camino Real* because its author, Tennessee Williams, thought her voice was unsuitable for the part.

Moreno's career seemed to be on the upswing when she was featured on the cover of *Life* magazine in 1954. The publicity helped her obtain a contract with Twentieth Century-Fox, and after a minor role in the 1954 motion picture *Garden of Evil*, she landed parts with more substance. Still, Moreno was not treated as a serious actress and was again assigned ethnic roles, as in the 1955 film *Seven Cities of Gold*, in which she played an Indian savage who asks a U.S. soldier, "Why joo no luv Oola no more?" and then leaps off a cliff to her death. Years of discrimination took an emotional and professional toll on the actress, who began six and a half years of therapy to recover from distress and depression.

After imitating Marilyn Monroe in the Tom Ewell comedy *The Lieutenant Wore Skirts* (1956), Rita Moreno was finally cast in what she considered a satisfying role as a Burmese slave girl in the 1956 film adaptation of the hit musical *The King and I*. The actress sang "We Kiss in a Shadow," and "I Have Dreamed" with Carlos Rivas, and she did the narration for the ballet within the film "The Small House of Uncle Thomas." Jerome Robbins, who choreographed the ballet, urged her to audition for the part of María in the Broadway play *West Side Story*, but the young actress got cold feet.

Moreno appeared in few films between 1956 and 1960. In 1956 she portrayed Huguette in *The Vagabond King* and then, in 1957, played in *The Deerslayer*. She did not act in another film until *This Rebel Breed* in 1960. At that point, Moreno decided to return to theater and performed in the summer tour of *A View from the Bridge* by Arthur Miller. She received favorable reviews but could no longer cope with the frustrations that had plagued her career. Moreno made an unsuccessful attempt at suicide by overdosing on sleeping pills. When she awoke in the hospital, the actress realized life was worth living and made a full physical and emotional recovery.

Moreno's career was on the verge of skyrocketing when she left the hospital. When Robert Wise went looking for actors for the 1961 screen version of *West Side Story*, Jerome Robbins, who had not forgotten the young actress he had considered for the part of María, advised Wise to screen-test Moreno. She won the part of Anita in *West Side Story*, a Romeo and Juliet tale set against the backdrop of New York's West Side, with its gang warfares. She went on to give her most memorable performance, lighting up the screen with her dancing and singing of "America," a satire on life in the United States. *West Side Story* was a tremendous hit, winning ten Academy Awards, including an Oscar for Best Supporting Actress for Moreno.

Moreno had hoped that her Oscar would bring better roles, but her performance as Anita only reinforced her "Latin" image in Hollywood. After playing Rosa Zacharias in the 1961 film adaptation of Tennessee Williams's *Summer and Smoke* and appearing in the 1963 film *Cry of Battle*, she abandoned Hollywood for London. In 1964, she portrayed Ilona Ritter in Hal Prince's *West*

End production of the American musical *She Loves Me* and got excellent reviews, but British performance laws forced Moreno to return home. She landed the role of Iris Parodus Brustein in Lorraine Hansberry's play *The Sign in Sidney Brustein's Window*, which ran on Broadway. In 1968, Moreno won the Chicago Critics' Award for her role in a revival of *The Rose Tattoo*, in which she played Serafina.

In 1964, Moreno met Dr. Leonard I. Gordon, a cardiologist and internist at Mount Sinai Hospital in New York. In June 1965 they married, and in 1995 the happy couple celebrated a thirtieth wedding anniversary. They have a daughter, the actress and dancer Fernanda Luisa. With encouragement from Marlon Brando, Moreno reemerged on the Hollywood scene. She appeared in three 1969 motion pictures: *The Night of the Following Day*, *Marlowe*, and the comedy *Popi*, which won the applause of critics but was a box-office flop. In 1970 she played Sharon Falconer in the Broadway production *Gantry* and then starred in the Neil Simon comedy *Last of the Red Hot Lovers*. Moreno then gave a strong cameo performance as a prostitute in the 1971 landmark film *Carnal Knowledge* and garnered more favorable reviews. After a stint in children's television which brought her a Grammy Award for *The Electric Company Album* in 1975, Rita Moreno returned to theater in 1973 as the shoplifter in the play *Detective Story*. In 1973 and 1974 she played Staff Nurse Norton in Peter Nichols's *National Health* in New Haven, Connecticut, and in New York City.

In 1974, Moreno was invited to a performance of Terrence McNally's new play *The Tubs* at the Yale Repertory Theater in New Haven, Connecticut. She was surprised to find in the play the humorous character Googie Gomez, a Puerto Rican singer, whom she had developed on the set of *West Side Story* and had unveiled at a party McNally had attended. Although Googie Gomez may have offended Latinos in the audience, Moreno had created her with the intention of satirizing all the ethnic roles she had been asked to play, and McNally's interpretation of the character shared her vision. McNally asked Rita to play Googie Gomez when the play, retitled *The Ritz*, opened on Broadway. After fulfilling her obligations with *The National Health*, Moreno appeared in *The Ritz* in 1975. With her tour de force performances as Googie Gomez, she won a Tony Award for Best Supporting Actress. She played Googie Gomez again in the 1976 motion-

picture adaptation of *The Ritz,* but the screen version did not win
her the applause she had enjoyed onstage.

For her guest appearances on the *Muppet Show* in 1977,
Moreno was awarded an Emmy for Outstanding Continuing or
Single Performance by a Supporting Actress in Variety or Music.
The next year, she won another Emmy for Outstanding Lead
Actress for a Single Appearance in a Drama or Comedy Series for
her performance in an episode of *The Rockford Files.* Moreno was
then cast in the 1978 film *The Boss's Son.* Around the time she
created a nightclub act she has since performed in various cities
and on cruise ships. In 1980 appeared in the film *Happy Birthday,
Gemini* and costarred with Alan Alda and Carol Burnett in the
1981 comedy *The Four Seasons.* In 1982, Moreno starred on ABC's
situation comedy *Nine to Five,* receiving an Emmy nomination for
her effort. In 1985 she took to the stage again in Neil Simon's
comedy *The Odd Couple,* which received unfavorable reviews
despite its top-notch cast.

Although she has been performing for five decades, Moreno
still keeps a busy schedule. She has performed numerous times
with her daughter Fernanda Luisa in the productions *Steel
Magnolias* and *The Taming of the Shrew.* She has served on the
board of directors of Third World Cinema and the Alvin Ailey
Dance Company and on the theater panel of the National
Foundation of the Arts. In 1990, Moreno was honored with the
Hispanic Heritage Award in the performing arts. When she
began her career, there were no Latino role models. In fact, she is
one of the few Latino performers who has been able to cross over
to the mainstream audience. She told *Hispanic* magazine in 1989:
"Julio Iglesias has done it, but there are still very few, and I think
I was a pioneer. I guess that's why the Hispanic community is
proud of my accomplishments. I have crossed over, but never, not
for a minute have I forgotten where I came from, or who I am. I
have always been very proud to carry a badge of honor as a
Hispanic."

20

Geraldo Rivera

1943–

He was born Geraldo Miguel Rivera on July 3, 1943, in New York City. His father, Cruz Allen Rivera, was a native of San Juan, Puerto Rico, who worked as a cabdriver, a kitchen helper, and a dishwasher. His mother, Lillian (Friedman) Rivera, of Hungarian Jewish descent, worked as a waitress. Geraldo spoke about his parents to the *New York Times:* "I think that the most important thing I took from my parents was a sense of fair play, a sense of true belief in the American dream despite all my father's disappointment and despite the fact that he was truly victimized by racism in this country." As a way of protecting her son from the same racial prejudice his Latino name might attract, Lillian Rivera filled in Geraldo's birth certificate with the name "Gerald Riviera." In his 1991 autobiography *Exposing Myself,* Rivera describes his childhood as "a strange mix of whitefish and pasteles."

Geraldo's early years were spent in the decaying Brooklyn neighborhood of Williamsburg. As a boy, Geraldo exhibited physical frailties; he was underweight, asthmatic, and constantly ill. In 1950 the Rivera family moved to Babylon, Long Island, where, as a student at West Babylon High School, a more robust Geraldo participated in street-gang activities and athletics and paid little attention to schoolwork. His grades were so poor that after graduating from high school he returned to Brooklyn to live with an aunt while taking remedial courses in English and mathematics at New York Community College. He then enrolled in the Maritime College of the State University of New York, but eventually dropped out and did a two-year stint in the merchant marines. Upon returning to American soil, Geraldo tried his luck as a semiprofessional soccer player and worked briefly in a clothing store in Los Angeles.

Rivera then attended the University of Arizona, for what he called the unhappiest period of his life. Surrounded by WASPy classmates, he felt extremely self-conscious of his Latino roots and tried to pass as a WASP by calling himself Jerry Rivers. Upon receiving a B.S. degree in 1965, he entered Brooklyn Law School, working weekends and evenings at a department store and as a clerk for the Harlem Assertion of Rights and for Community Action for Legal Service. He earned a J.D. degree in 1969 and decided to concentrate on poverty law. After pursuing postgraduate studies as a Smith Fellow at the University of Pennsylvania, Rivera took a position with the Legal Services Program of the Office of Economic Opportunity. The stream of impoverished clients was unending, and Rivera realized after two years that as a poverty lawyer he could not vastly improve people's lives.

In 1970, WABC-TV in New York City was anxious to hire a bilingual person whom the station could put through three months of intensive training at Columbia's Graduate School of Journalism. WABC-TV selected Geraldo Rivera, and in September 1970 he joined the *Eyewitness News* team. At first Rivera was given routine assignments, like covering circuses and doing celebrity interviews. He soon stood out with his innovative brand of journalism that brought him face-to-face with his subjects. His fearless and passionate style won him recognition from the higher-ups at WABC-TV, who advanced him to hard news. One of his first special reports, "Drug Crisis in East Harlem," a look at

heroin addiction, moved Rivera to tears on camera and captivated viewers. For his efforts, he was honored by the Associated
Press Broadcasters Association with an award for general excellence of individual reporting. In 1971, Rivera married Edith
Vonnegut, Kurt Vonnegut's daughter, at the author's house on
Cape Cod. A few months later, by his own admission, he had an
affair with Marian Javits, and then he began to juggle several
relationships. His infidelity destroyed the marriage, and he and
Edith Vonnegut divorced in 1974.

One of Rivera's most highly publicized stories for *Eyewitness
News* aired in 1972. As part of his investigation of allegations of
abuse at Willowbrook State School for the Mentally Retarded on
Staten Island, Rivera took his camera crew on an inspection of
the site. He discovered children living unclothed in filthy conditions and for one week gave gripping daily reports from
Willowbrook. His reports prompted a swift response from New
York governor Nelson A. Rockefeller, who restored $25 million to
the mental-health budget. With $50,000 in unsolicited contribu-
tions, Rivera cofounded One to One, a charitable organization
dedicated to replacing institutions like Willowbrook with small
community-based facilities. Rivera hosted telethons and concerts
to raise money for One to One.

In 1972, ABC aired a ninety-minute special, *Willowbrook: the
Last Disgrace,* based on Rivera's reports for *Eyewitness News.* The
program gripped the nation. Rivera won numerous journalism
awards for *Willowbrook,* including the prestigious George Foster
Peabody Broadcasting Award for public service and Emmys for
excellence in individual reporting from the New York chapter of
the Academy of Television Arts and Sciences. He was also
swamped with television and film offers, and to honor his
achievements the U.S. Information Agency produced *Geraldo,* a
documentary of Rivera's life. In spite of all the publicity surrounding Willowbrook, Rivera's personal account, *Willowbrook: A
Report on How It Is and Why It Doesn't Have to Be That Way,*
published in 1972, experienced modest sales.

In 1973, Rivera worked on another riveting story for *Eyewitness News* about drug-addicted newborn babies. He visited New
York City hospitals to film babies in withdrawal and to interview
their addict mothers. In January 1973 the story was broadcast
prime time as a documentary entitled *The Littlest Junkie: A
Children's Story.* The program attracted so many viewers that it

received the highest rating for a news special in local television history. Many more *Eyewitness News* special reports followed, including *Migrants: Dirt Cheap,* on the hardships faced by migrant farmworkers; *Tell Me Where I Can Go,* on the plight of the elderly in New York City; and *Marching Home Again,* on the lives of Vietnam vets.

As a result of his superb reporting, in 1973, ABC gave Rivera the opportunity to host *Good Night America,* a ninety-minute news magazine, which became a regularly scheduled series in 1974. For *Good Night America* Rivera did a mix of celebrity interviews and well-researched news features on such controversial topics as the legalization of marijuana, homosexuality, and amnesty for draft dodgers. He continued to work for *Eyewitness News,* and in 1974 launched the "Help 7" Center, a consumer-action bureau. In 1975, Rivera signed on as a reporter with *Good Morning America,* where most of his stories concerned popular culture. *Eyewitness News* interpreted Rivera's move to *Good Morning America* as a violation of contract and dismissed the newsman. When ABC dropped *Good Night America* on June 9, 1977, Rivera protested so vehemently that he was fired from *Good Morning America.* Luckily, the new president of ABC News, Roone Arledge, made Rivera a newsman on the *ABC Evening News.*

In 1976, Rivera married Sherri Braverman, and the couple had a son, Gabriel, in 1979, but later divorced. In 1978, he became the chief reporter on *20/20,* the ABC news magazine, which premiered that year. He spent eight years with *20/20,* which, according to his autobiography, were "the richest, most productive years of my career." During his tenure with *20/20,* Rivera spent considerable time investigating stories overseas. On one assignment in Tripoli he risked his life to carry to safety a youth wounded in a blast as the cameras rolled. That evening, the footage was shown on *World News Tonight.* What Geraldo Rivera describes as his "finest hour" was a *20/20* report, "The Elvis Cover-Up," investigating the shaky facts surrounding the star's death, which became the most watched public-affairs program of the 1979–1980 season. In 1980, Ted Turner offered Rivera $500,000 a year and stock options to sign on with the fledgling Cable News Network (CNN). Rivera declined the invitation because CNN was not airing nationally at the time and parlayed Turner's offer into a raise at ABC, lifting his salary to the $1-million-a-year mark.

Rivera was fired from *20/20* on December 15, 1985, when he insisted on broadcasting a controversial report linking John F. Kennedy and Robert F. Kennedy to Marilyn Monroe at the end of her life. Between jobs in 1986 he hosted a live, syndicated special "The Mystery of Al Capone's Vault," covering the opening of the gangster's vault in a Chicago hotel. Rivera's worst suspicions that the vault might be empty were realized, and yet the program's ratings soared to 34.2 nationally, scoring a commercial coup. He then became a regular contributor to the syndicated program *Entertainment Tonight* and investigated stories in some way connected to celebrities, such as the dangers Hollywood stuntmen face and the tragedy of AIDS in the fashion industry. Rivera next did the special "American Vice: The Dope of a Nation," which aired on December 6, 1986.

In July 1987, Rivera married his fourth wife, C. C. Dyer, an associate producer of the *Geraldo* show. In September 1987, he launched *Geraldo,* his own daytime talk show, which features in-studio guests and an audience, who discuss contemporary issues and controversial topics, often dealing with sex. Soon after *Geraldo* debuted, Rivera made front page headlines when a brawl erupted in the studio between black activist Roy Innis and a group of neo-Nazis and his nose was broken by a chair thrown in the fight. In 1988, Rivera conducted an exclusive interview with Charles Manson as part of his special *Murder: Live From Death,* a commercial triumph that took third place on the all-time list of syndicated specials.

In 1989, Rivera and C. C. Dyer moved out of Manhattan and bought a riverfront mansion in nearby Locust, New Jersey. He commutes to Manhattan on the Highland ferry or by speedboat or helicopter. That year, Rivera "adopted" a class of eighth-graders at a junior high school in the barrio. He promised the kids that if they graduated from high school, he would subsidize their college tuition. In 1991, Rivera debuted as the host of a second syndicated series *Now It Can Be Told,* an investigative news magazine that deals with topical issues, such as airline safety and computer technology. In addition to anchoring *Now It Can Be Told* and hosting the *Geraldo* show, Rivera joined CNBC in 1994 to command *Rivera Live,* a program that explores topics in the news with a live panel of guests. With his comprehensive reporting and groundbreaking investigations, Geraldo Rivera has earned a position of excellence among journalism's greats.

21

Linda Chávez

1947–

Linda Chávez was born in Albuquerque, New Mexico, on June 17, 1947, to Velma Chávez, of Irish and English extraction, and Rudy Chávez, a conservative Spanish American descended from seventeenth-century Spanish colonists who settled in what is present-day New Mexico. The Chávez family prospered for four centuries in New Mexico until Linda's grandfather was jailed for bootlegging and their fortunes dwindled. Given this dismal state of affairs, Rudy Chávez was forced to quit school to help support his younger siblings. He made a living as a small contractor, while Linda's mother worked at the post office and then in retail.

When Linda was nine, the family moved to Denver. At age twelve, she suffered a great loss when her younger sister died from a kidney disorder. Rudy Chávez, a World War II veteran, instilled in Linda an appreciation of her Spanish heritage and a commitment to excellence in all her endeavors. She attended Catholic school, where she was a top student. In her youth Linda felt the effects of racial discrimination. Classmates called her a "dirty Mexican" and "*chiquita*," and some parents forbade their children to associate with her because of her Mexican roots. While in high school, she joined the NAACP and CORE and participated in a protest in front of a segregated Woolworth's. Chávez would later contend that civil rights demonstrations always made her uncomfortable and that she opposed the antiwar movement of the 1960s and favored U.S. intervention in Vietnam.

Chávez attended the University of Colorado in the late 1960s and began to shift slowly to the conservative camp. She tutored Mexican-American students in a remedial program and was ·dismayed to learn that they were pressuring the university to lower their minimum-grade requirements. After receiving her B.A. in 1970, she pursued graduate study at the University of California at Los Angeles (UCLA). She was enrolled in a Ph.D. program in English and Irish literature, but was pressured into teaching Chicano writing because UCLA was eager to start a Chicano studies program in the aftermath of the 1970 riots by Mexican Americans in East Los Angeles. Chávez contended that Hispanic literary works were too scant in number to draw up a syllabus for the course. When she insisted that students read the required course material, some refused, and she was forced to fail a number of them. The students retaliated by terrorizing Chávez and her family and vandalizing their property. Deeply discouraged, Chávez abandoned teaching in 1972 and went to Washington, D.C., to join her husband, Christopher Gersten. They married in 1967 and have three sons, whom they are raising in the Jewish faith.

In 1972, Chávez still considered herself a full-fledged Democrat and took a job that year with the Democratic National Committee, devising ways to counteract the Republicans' appeal to Hispanic voters. Chávez then worked on civil rights issues for Cong. Don Edwards. In 1974 she became a lobbyist at the National Education Association (NEA), a move she believes was a mistake because she was perceived as a minority representative.

She told the *Washington Monthly* in June 1985: "It was very clear to me they expected me to be the Hispanic lobbyist, to be their link to the Chicano caucus inside the NEA. I balked at that." Chávez then went to work for the NEA's rival, the American Federation of Teachers (AFT). For a brief time she was with the Department of Health, Education, and Welfare under President Jimmy Carter, then returned in 1980 to the AFT, where she took charge of writing the union's campaign literature endorsing Sen. Edward Kennedy instead of Carter in the Democratic primaries.

As an editor of the quarterly *American Educator,* Chávez wrote articles urging a return to "traditional values" in American schools, a decidedly conservative stance. Conservatives in Washington took notice, and in 1981, Chávez was hired as a consultant for the Reagan administration. Soon she was invited to become a member of the U.S. Commission on Civil Rights, a nonpartisan watchdog agency geared to monitoring the government's enforcement of civil rights laws. Chávez held out for a more influential position, and by 1984 she was appointed staff director of the agency. She created controversy by issuing a memo advocating the reversal of many traditional civil rights measures, such as racial hiring quotas. Her support of a study exploring the negative effects of affirmative action on minorities also caused quite a stir. As a result, many civil rights activists accused Linda Chávez of transforming the U.S. Commission on Civil Rights into an instrument of the Reagan administration. In 1984, Chávez approached White House officials to announce plans to change her party affiliation. To her surprise, Chávez was told she could contribute more to the party as a so-called Reagan Democrat.

Chávez's performance as director of the U.S. Commission on Civil Rights helped advance her career. In 1985 she was appointed director of the White House Office of Public Liaison, making her the highest-ranking woman in the Reagan administration. Chávez assumed this post despite her long affiliation with the Democrats. Chávez became an official Republican that year and worked to promote administration policy among members of Congress and interest groups.

In early 1986, Chávez left the Office of Public Liaison to begin campaigning for a U.S. Senate seat in Maryland on a conservative Republican platform. Chávez won the primaries but faced a tough race against Democratic representative Barbara Mikulski in only the second U.S. Senate race contested by two women. With two-thirds of the state of Maryland registered Democrat, Linda Chávez was clearly an underdog in the race. Her campaign was at even more of a disadvantage when she drew criticism for having changed her party affiliation and for being a relatively new Maryland resident. Her campaign tactics, which included calling the unmarried Mikulski "anti-male," brought accusations of mudslinging and hurt her bid for the office even more. In the end, Chávez lost the election in a landslide to Mikulski, who captured almost 62 percent of the vote.

After her defeat Chávez left politics in 1987 to become president of U.S. English, a nonprofit organization lobbying to make English the official language of the United States and considered by many as advocating racist policies. In late 1988 she resigned from the organization, citing its "anti-Hispanic" and "anti-Catholic" biases. She was then chosen the John M. Olin Fellow at the Manhattan Institute for Policy Research, a conservative think tank in Washington, D.C. In the early 1990s, Chávez became the director of the institute's Center for the New American Community, which studies the negative impact of multiculturalism on American culture.

In 1991 Chávez published *Out of the Barrio: Toward a New Politics of Hispanic Assimilation,* a detailed, conservative treatise on the assimilation of Latinos in the United States that has been the cause of much heated debate. In the book she argues for eradicating racial and ethnic preferences, yet she also endorses special programs to develop the skills of individuals from economically disadvantaged backgrounds. Chávez sums up her argument in this way in the closing passages of *Out of the Barrio:* "Discrimination against Hispanics, or any other group, should be fought, and there are laws and a massive administrative apparatus to do so. But the way to eliminate such discrimination is not to classify all Hispanics as victims and treat them as if they could not succeed by their own efforts. Hispanics can and will prosper in the United States by following the example of the millions before them."

22

Anthony Quinn

1915–

Anthony Quinn was born Anthony Rudolph Oaxáca Quinn in Chihuahua, Mexico, on April 21, 1915, to Frank Quinn, an Irish American, and Manuela "Nellie" Oaxáca Quinn, a Mexican of Aztec ancestry. Frank Quinn had been a soldier of fortune in the Mexican Revolution of 1910. As the fighting escalated, Frank Quinn and Manuela Oaxaca Quinn smuggled Tony across the border to El Paso, Texas. They worked as farm laborers and moved with the crops, harvesting walnuts in El Paso and eventually reaching San Jose, where the five-year-old Tony picked tomatoes and melons for five cents an hour. Not long after, the Quinns settled in the Mexican barrio of Los Angeles, where

Frank Quinn went to work as a cameraman and property man at the Selig studio. He launched his young son's film career by securing him a part as a juvenile Tarzan in a jungle film.

In January 1936, Frank Quinn was killed in a freak auto accident, a tragedy that had a profound effect on twenty-one-year-old Tony. He was forced to support himself in odd jobs as a shoeshine boy, newsboy, carpenter, trucker, and boxer while going to Belvedere Junior High School and, later, Polytechnic High School. At age fourteen, Tony worked as a foreman with the Camarillo Apricot Growers Association, and at sixteen he made money as a sparring partner for Primo Carnera. The teenage Tony and his sister Stella had to move in with their grandmother when their widowed mother married Frank Bowles and started a new life in another section of Los Angeles. In his 1972 auto-biography *The Original Sin,* Anthony Quinn writes that he never forgave his mother for the dissolution of the family and for marrying someone with his father's same first name.

When he started speaking English at age twelve, Tony discovered he had a speech impediment. While in school, he excelled at sculpture and playing the saxophone and studied basic architectural design. He decided to pursue a career as an architect and even showed his portfolio to Frank Lloyd Wright. At eighteen he worked as a janitor in a drama school, where a teacher, Mrs. Katherine Hamill, inspired him to pursue acting. Quinn gave up his plan to become an architect, underwent a tongue operation to rid himself of the speech defect, and then enrolled at Mrs. Hamill's school and joined a group called the Gateway Players.

While in the group, he learned that Mae West was searching for Latin types for a play she was producing in Los Angeles entitled *Clean Beds.* In 1936, Quinn made his professional stage debut in *Clean Beds* as an aging, drunken actor patterned after John Barrymore. Barrymore himself came to see the production seven times, befriended Quinn, and advised the budding actor to go to New York to appear on Broadway. While working in *Clean Beds,* Quinn got a bit part as a convict in *Parole,* a B movie at Universal Studios, which premiered at New York's Roxy Theater in 1936. It was the first of the many films the actor would appear in over the next six decades. He made a modest breakthrough when Cecil B. De Mille cast him as a Cheyenne warrior in the 1936 western *The Plainsman* and offered the young actor a contract. Quinn took the role, signing with Paramount. On the set of *The Plainsman,* Anthony Quinn met De Mille's daughter, Katherine, an actress in her own right. They married in Hollywood on October 21, 1937, and had five children; in 1941 their eldest son, Christopher, accidentally drowned on W. C. Fields's estate after wandering away from a party at the De Milles.

In the 1940s, Quinn played either the ignoble savage or the villain in countless action-packed melodramas, such as *Hunted Men* and *Television Spy.* Occasionally, Paramount gave Quinn a role in more expensive films, like the 1940 motion picture *Road to Singapore* with Bob Hope and Bing Crosby and, later, as Dorothy Lamour's suitor and the adversary of Hope and Crosby in the 1942 film *The Road to Morocco.* Quinn had a two-year stint at Twentieth Century-Fox, playing a one-eyed pirate in the 1942 epic *The Black Swan* and a Mexican who is lynched in the 1943 screen version of the bestseller *The Ox-Bow Incident.* After forty-six appearances in the movies, Quinn secured his first starring role in the 1947 motion picture *Black Gold,* based on a true story of a Native American couple who discovered oil and made millions.

In 1947, Quinn became a naturalized citizen, and later that year he left Hollywood to work on the stage. He made his Broadway debut on December 9, 1947, as a Greek American who gets himself elected to Congress by his shady dealings in *The Gentleman from Athens,* which folded after seven performances in New York. Elia Kazan, who had previously directed Quinn in Hollywood, offered the actor the part of Stanley Kowalski in the road company of Tennessee Williams's *A Streetcar Named Desire.* A year later, when the critics reviewed the play at City Center, they highly praised Quinn, who stayed with the part for nearly two years. Then came a few Broadway flops, and Quinn returned to the silver screen, only to be pigeonholed again as an "ethnic" actor. He landed one good role when Elia Kazan cast him as the eldest brother of the Mexican revolutionary Emiliano Zapata (played by Marlon Brando) in the 1952 film *Viva Zapata!* Quinn's performance won him an Academy Award for Best Supporting Actor, but the Oscar did not net him starring roles. Instead, he was cast in Technicolor potboilers such *Mask of the Avenger,* a 1951 swashbuckler from Columbia studios.

In the spring of 1953, Anthony Quinn decided to try his luck in Europe's burgeoning film industry. He put countless roles as ethnic heavies behind him and did creative interpretations, primarily of downtrodden, unfortunate, or misunderstood individuals. Quinn made five films in eleven months in Italy and emerged as an international star. American audiences forgot about Quinn until the release in 1954 of his fifth Italian movie, *La Strada*, a Fellini-directed picaresque tale of three strolling players, costarring Richard Basehart and Giulietta Masina. *La Strada* was a smash hit around the globe and won an Oscar in 1956 for Best Foreign Film, boosting Quinn's career.

Back in Hollywood the actor could now get star billing. He was cast in the 1956 film *Lust for Life,* playing Paul Gauguin to Kirk Douglas's title role as Vincent Van Gogh, for which Quinn was honored with a second Academy Award for Best Supporting Actor. In 1957, Quinn won an Academy Award nomination for Best Actor in *Wild Is the Wind.* That year he played Quasimodo, the hunchbacked bell ringer, opposite Gina Lollobrigida as the Gypsy girl, in Jean Delannoy's wide-screen rendition of the Victor Hugo classic *The Hunchback of Notre Dame.* After *The Hunchback of Notre Dame,* no major parts materialized, so the discouraged actor quit acting to direct. He made his directorial debut in the 1958 remake of *The Buccaneer* with Yul Brynner and Charlton Heston, but then returned to acting. In 1960, he took to the Broadway stage again, costarring with Laurence Olivier in *Becket.*

Anthony Quinn then went to Europe to star in three films: *Guns of Navarone* (1961), *Barabbas* (1962), and *Lawrence of Arabia* (1962). He gave first-class performances in *Guns of Navarone,* portraying a Greek officer, and in *Lawrence of Arabia,* playing a proud Arab chief, and both films made a big splash. While working on *Barabbas,* the biblical spectacular, Anthony Quinn met Jolanda Addolori, an Italian teacher turned wardrobe assistant. Soon she gave birth to a son by Quinn, who gave the baby his name and had him baptized. In April 1964, Jolanda had a second son by Quinn. The actor bought an Italian villa on his children's behalf, filling it with antiques, and paintings by Renoir and Degas. On January 21, 1965, Anthony Quinn and Katherine De Mille were divorced in Juárez, Mexico. Shortly after Christmas in 1965, Quinn married Jolanda Addolori at his agent's house.

After accumulating several more film credits, Quinn gave a stunning performance as Zorba, the wise and aging peasant, in the 1964 motion picture *Zorba the Greek.* The role established the actor as a superstar and won him a second Academy Award nomination for Best Actor. Many more films followed, including *Across 110th Street,* a 1972 police thriller set in New York. In 1978, Quinn gave a fabulous performance as Theo Tomasis, a wealthy, conniving, and influential tycoon in *The Greek Tycoon,* a thinly disguised interpretation of the Aristotle Onassis and Jacqueline Kennedy marriage. That year, Quinn also portrayed the struggling barrio paterfamilias in the Mexican film *The Children of Sanchez.*

In the 1980s, Anthony Quinn starred in scores of motion pictures, including the 1981 war film *Lion of the Desert,* bringing dignity and conviction to the part of Omar Mukhtar, the Libyan anticolonial hero. That year, he also played in the comedy–action thriller *High Risk* as the leader of ragged, corrupt revolutionaries in Colombia. On March 31, 1988, Quinn was honored for outstanding achievement at the New York Image Awards presented by the Hispanic Academy of Media Arts and Sciences. In February 1989, soon after shooting stopped on the NBC adaptation of Ernest Hemingway's *Old Man and the Sea,* the actor underwent quadruple bypass surgery and emerged with more energy than ever. During the 1980s, Quinn came to be regarded not only as an accomplished actor but also as a talented portrait painter and sculptor. He has exhibited his work throughout the United States.

Many more roles followed in the 1990s, including the portrayal of a wealthy sportsman in the 1990 motion picture *Revenge,* a tale of a doomed love triangle in lawless Mexico. In 1991, Quinn appeared in such motion pictures as the romantic comedy *Only the Lonely,* which saw Maureen O'Hara's return to the silver screen after a twenty-year hiatus; the violent action movie *Mobsters;* and Spike Lee's polemical film *Jungle Fever,* about contemporary race relations. Anthony Quinn's most recent credits include a part in the 1993 adventure movie *Last Action Hero,* about an alienated young boy who magically enters the world of his favorite big-screen hero. In early 1994, Quinn was hard at work with another Hollywood veteran, costar Katharine Hepburn, on a new film entitled *This Can't Be Love.* Even after seven decades of acting, Anthony Quinn keeps delighting moviegoers.

23

Chita Rivera

1933–

The third of five children, Chita Rivera was born Dolores
Conchita Figuero del Rivero to Pedro Julio Figuero and Ka-
therine (Anderson) del Rivero on January 23, 1933, in Wash-
ington, D.C. Dolores's mother was of Scotch-Irish and Puerto
Rican ancestry, while her father was Puerto Rican. Pedro Julio
Figuero played the clarinet and the saxophone in the U.S. Navy
Band, and performed with Harry James's orchestra, and the pit
orchestra for the Broadway musical *Lady Be Good*. When Dolores

was only seven years old, her father passed away, and her mother found a position as a government clerk to support the family. Having put aside her own ambitions to be a dancer in order to raise a family, Dolores's mother encouraged her young daughter's creative talents by providing her with singing, piano, and ballet lessons.

Dolores was particularly passionate about ballet, and she often performed in theatrical shows her brother Julio staged in the basement of the Rivero home. She demonstrated so much ability in ballet class that her instructor, Doris Jones, encouraged Dolores to audition for a scholarship to George Balanchine's School of American Ballet. Dolores won the prestigious scholarship in 1950, and she went to live with her uncle's family in order to attend the celebrated ballet school. Her dream was to one day dance with the New York City Ballet.

In 1951, Dolores graduated from Taft High School in the Bronx, and the next year, she landed her first professional part as a dancer by a stroke of luck. Just for fun she had accompanied a friend from the School of American Ballet to an open call for dancers for the national touring company of the musical *Call Me Madam,* the Ethel Merman vehicle choreographed by Jerome Robbins. As it turned out, Dolores was hired instead of her friend. She made her debut in *Call Me Madam* at the Imperial Theatre in 1952 and then toured the country with the musical as one of four principal dancers for almost a year. While on the road, Dolores discovered by accident that she could sing professionally when one of her cohorts sat her at a piano one night and made her carry a tune. Soon Dolores decided to return to New York City to replace Onna White as a principal dancer in *Guys and Dolls.*

After her Broadway debut in *Guys and Dolls,* the versatile and energetic Dolores had her pick of roles. In 1953 she appeared in the chorus of the original Broadway cast of *Can-Can* and a year later performed on television's *Imogene Coca Show.* In 1955, Dolores joined Ben Bagley's popular off-Broadway production *Shoestring Revue* and drew accolades for her performance. Bagley suggested she change her name, and Dolores settled first on Chita O'Hara, but three days later she decided on Chita Rivera. In May 1955 she was cast as Fifi, a French prostitute in the Broadway flop *Seventh Heaven,* and that same year she toured with the Oldsmobile Industrial Show.

In 1956, Rivera won the role of Rita Romano in *Mr. Wonderful*, a Broadway musical produced for Sammy Davis Jr. She soon began to make guest appearances on variety shows, among them the *Garry Moore Show*, the *Ed Sullivan Show*, the *Arthur Godfrey Show*, and the *Dinah Shore Show*, and in November 1957 she made the cover of her first *Dance* magazine. Chita Rivera parlayed her success in *Mr. Wonderful* into one of her best parts, that of Anita in the major musical *West Side Story*. After the musical's world premiere in Washington, D.C., the original production of *West Side Story* opened at the Winter Garden in New York on September 26, 1957. The musical received rave reviews and ran for 732 performances, and Rivera garnered her first Tony nomination. During the run, Rivera married Anthony Mordente, one of the dancers in *West Side Story*, and left the production when she became pregnant with their daughter, Lisa Angela Mordente. After the baby's birth, the couple performed again when *West Side Story* traveled to London in 1958, where the show was received with even more enthusiasm. They would later divorce.

Rivera held her own with costar Dick Van Dyke in her next role as Rose Grant in *Bye Bye Birdie*, which ran from 1960 to 1961. Her dynamic performance as "Spanish Rose" brought critical acclaim and another Tony nomination. In 1963 she played Athena Constantine in a short-lived play *Zenda*, and in 1964 she returned to England to act in a televised benefit with the immensely popular rock group the Beatles. In 1964, Rivera headlined for seven months in *Bajour* on Broadway, playing Anyanka, the Gypsy princess. Her spectacular performance won her a third Tony nomination, a Best Plays citation, and an invitation to be the official host of the World's Fair and Summer Festival Season in New York City.

In the mid-1960s, Chita Rivera decided to venture out on her own. She teamed up with her friends Fred Ebb, a lyricist, and John Kander, a composer, to develop a cabaret act. In 1966 the trio toured the United States and Canada with their act. Even though it was well received, Rivera was glad to return to the stage to perform as Linda Low in *Flower Drum Song* and as Jenny in *The Threepenny Opera*. In 1967 and 1968 she traveled across North America as the lead in the touring production of the Broadway hit *Sweet Charity*. In her screen debut in the motion-picture version of *Charity*, released in February 1969, Rivera played Nickie instead of Charity. The film experience made her realize she preferred the stage to the screen. In the early 1970s, Chita Rivera went on the road in a production of *Jacques Brel Is Alive and Well and Living in Paris,* and she starred as Katherine in *Kiss Me, Kate* with Hal Linden. In 1974, Rivera impressed critics with her intensity in *Father's Day,* in which she played the part of the divorcée at the request of the author, Oliver Hailey.

In 1975 she took her explosive cabaret act, "Chita Plus Two," on the road again. She returned to Broadway in June 1975 to play Velma Kelly in *Chicago* with Gwen Vernon and Jerry Orbach, earning a fourth Tony nomination. The musical was such a sensation that it ran for more performances than *West Side Story.* Nevertheless, Rivera left the production halfway through the run to tour again with the cabaret act, spending the late 1970s and the early 1980s on the road in Europe, Canada, and the United States. In 1980 the National Academy of Concert and Cabaret Arts bestowed upon Rivera its award for best variety performance.

During the early 1980s, Chita Rivera made frequent appearances on the stage. In March 1981 she played in the musical *Bring Back Birdie,* the sequel to *Bye Bye Birdie,* which closed after only four performances but earned Rivera a fifth Tony nomination. In 1983, Rivera's mother, to whom the actress was devoted, passed away. Rivera went on to star with Liza Minnelli in *The Rink,* which opened on February 9, 1984, at New York's Martin Beck Theater. Chita Rivera played the part of an Italian-American widow who wants to sell the family-owned rink to developers, an action her daughter, played by Minnelli, staunchly opposes. Rivera's performance won her a third *Dance* magazine cover and a much deserved Tony Award for Outstanding Actress in 1984. In 1984 the album *The Rink,* which Chita Rivera made with Liza Minnelli and the other singers from the musical, was released.

During the 1980s, Rivera also performed for the screen. In 1982 she appeared on the PBS special *Broadway Plays Washington: Kennedy Center Tonight* and in *Night of 100 Stars* as well as its sequel and in televised coverage of the Macy's Thanksgiving Day Parade. In 1985, she starred in *Jerry's Girls,* a revue devoted to the music of Jerry Herman of *Hello, Dolly!* and *Mame* fame. In the same year, Rivera was inducted into the Television Academy Hall of Fame. While appearing in *Jerry's Girls* in 1986, a speeding taxi collided with Rivera's car in Manhattan, leaving the actress with twelve fractures in her left leg. Doctors told her she might never walk again, but Rivera made a full recovery, which she attributes to the relentless discipline of dance.

After nearly a year of recuperation and physical therapy, Rivera started doing her nightclub act on cruise ships to test the waters. In the late 1980s she did both television and theater, appearing in *The Mayflower Madam* and *Can-Can* onstage and in such shows as *Celebrating Gershwin* and *Broadway Sings: The Music of Jule Styne* on television. In 1992, after more than forty years on the stage, Chita Rivera starred as Aurora, a vibrant glamour girl and a figure of death, in the Broadway production *Kiss of the Spider Woman—the Musical,* based on Manuel Puig's 1976 novel about a gay window dresser and a macho dissident who share a cramped prison cell. Rivera was excited to land the part, as she conveyed to *Dance* magazine in an article in the February 1994 issue: "Not since *West Side Story* have I felt that a show was as important as *Spider Woman.* This show deals with serious issues: politics, violence, sexuality, with the lot of people—the ones in Brazil and all over who just...disappear, because they think a different way, they look a different way, because of prejudice, or homophobia, or for whatever reason."

In 1993, Rivera won the Tony Award for Best Actress in a Musical for her role in *Kiss of the Spider Woman* as well as the Drama Desk Award, the Drama League of New York Award, the Fred Astaire Award for Achievement in Dance, and the National Hispanic Academy of Media Arts and Sciences Award, among other distinctions. In 1994 she was honored with the Mother Hale Award for Caring at a benefit for Hale House in Harlem, where abandoned and orphaned babies born to AIDS patients and drug addicts receive care.

24

Adolfo
1933–

Adolfo was born Adolfo Sardiña on February 13, 1933, in Havana, Cuba, to a well-to-do lawyer and his wife, who died in childbirth. Adolfo was raised by an elegant and eccentric aunt, María Lopez, who was fond of French couture and whose name graced most of the international best-dressed-women lists of the 1940s. When Adolfo was a boy, María Lopez used to tell him that when, in the 1920s, she came to Havana from Paris with her hair bobbed and donning short dresses, people used to stare at her in the streets. At an early age Adolfo took a keen interest in fashion, and his aunt cultivated his ambition to become a designer. Each year, María Lopez took the boy to Paris fashion shows and brought him along on appointments at the house of Balenciaga, her favorite couturier, before she switched to Chanel when Coco Chanel reopened her business in the 1950s. With his aunt, Adolfo met Chanel on four occasions, but he was too shy to engage in conversation with her.

Like the famous designer Halston, Adolfo began his career designing hats. At age seventeen he left Havana for Paris, where he immediately landed a job at the house of Balenciaga. Adolfo never saw the famous couturier or any of Balenciaga's dresses, but spent his days sweeping the floors or "picking up pins," as he described it. In utter despair he abandoned his apprenticeship with Balenciaga and then went to work at the house of Chanel for six months after María Lopez requested that her nephew be allowed to observe that operation. At Chanel, Adolfo was on the bottom rung and worked for no pay, but he gained a solid foundation in the making of hats. In 1948, Adolfo returned to New York and took a job as a millinery designer for Bragaard and then as an apprentice in the millinery department at Bergdorf Goodman. Around this time, he dropped his family name and became known professionally as Adolfo.

In 1953 he left Bergdorf Goodman to become the chief designer for Emme, one of the world's most prestigious milliners, which turned out both custom and ready-to-wear hats. In the 1950s, Adolfo was instrumental in making the hat a necessity for every well-dressed woman. In that decade he gained a reputation helping to make Emme into a trendsetter of the millinery business by designing fanciful hats with dramatic shapes in exotic furs and boldly colored fabrics and straws. As chief designer at Emme, Adolfo captured both a Neiman-Marcus Award and a Coty American Fashion Critics' Special Award in the 1950s. He was honored with the Coty in 1955 for his innovative technique of creating shaped hats without stuffing or wiring. In 1956 the young milliner received recognition as "Adolfo at Emme."

Despite the status he enjoyed at Emme, Adolfo dreamed of having his own millinery firm. After securing a $10,000 loan from Seventh Avenue designer Bill Blass and the remainder from assorted friends, Adolfo opened his own salon at 22 East Fifty-sixth Street in the summer of 1962. The young milliner's business thrived, and he was able to pay back the loan in less than a year.

The duchess of Windsor was enthusiastic about Adolfo's millinery designs, and she introduced him to Betsy Bloomingdale, Gloria Vanderbilt Cooper, and Babe Paley, who helped establish his career.

One reason for Adolfo's popularity was his ability to answer the needs of women who did not view the hat as a social necessity but were merely seeking unique headwear. He interested these clients in lynx or kit-fox hoods, kidskin bandannas, cloches, and jersey or velour visor caps. In his early collections Adolfo also incorporated fanciful evening wear, such as feathered head-dresses with long braids intertwined with garlic and flowers and attached to the wearer's tresses. For those who still preferred hats Adolfo turned out distinctive variations on familiar styles, like the beret, bowler, pillbox, and sailor. While his hats had long adorned the heads of the socially prominent women who crowded his salon, Adolfo received nationwide attention for the first time in 1965. That year, Lady Bird Johnson chose four of the milliner's hats for the presidential inaugural festivities, including two felt berets with grosgrain cockades and badger brushes to one side.

By the early 1960s, Adolfo was no longer content featuring only hats, and while the grandees of fashion mingled at cocktail parties in the evenings, he diligently studied dressmaking with the elegant Cuban designer Anna María Berrero, who had learned the ins and outs of couture in Paris. At first, Adolfo made simple dresses to offset his decorative hats; among his early designs was the 1962 off-white suede sleeveless dress with a low waist. As complicated hairstyles eliminated the need for hats in the mid-1960s, Adolfo's hats became simpler and his dresses more elaborate. By 1966 his long melton-cloth officers' coats with gold buttons and epaulets were dictating fashion trends, and in 1967 many of his choicest customers, bored with miniskirts, wore his calf-length wraparound felt skirts. In the late 1960s, Adolfo began to design knits inspired by Chanel's famous tweed suits. The designer has observed that his Chanel phase began in 1967 when *Harper's Bazaar* commissioned him to design a suit to be photographed on Gloria Vanderbilt. Adolfo liked the results so much that he continued throughout his career to incorporate Chanel motifs into his designs.

Adolfo was one of the first designers to answer women's call for costumes in the late 1960s, and for several seasons he created whimsical and romantic styles that enjoyed great popularity. In

1968, Adolfo's gingham dirndl skirts, bishop-sleeved cotton blouses, ribbon sashes, and floppy straw hats were the rage. He also made fashion headlines with his "bits and pieces" look, turning out Turkish harem pants, boleros, fringed jackets, scarves, sashes, and gold chains. In the summer of 1969, Adolfo showed elaborate patchwork skirts with matching scarves. That year, he received another Coty American Fashion Critics' Special Award for his innovative designs. In 1971 he abandoned costumes for the more body conscious, close fitting designs of the 1970s. By the fall of 1972 he was creating more subdued knits, in particular a closely worked crochet of silk and wool. With these materials Adolfo turned out long halter-necked dresses with cardigans for evening and jackets, vests, skirts, and pants with soft silk blouses for day.

In the 1980s, Adolfo operated out of his Fifty-seventh Street salon creating custom-made garments and designing an exclusive line of ready-to-wear clothes for Saks Fifth Avenue and Neiman-Marcus. As befitted a dressy decade, his 1980s designs included elaborate ball gowns as well as revealing cocktail dresses and Chanel-style knitted suits that were left unlined so that they fit closer to the body. In the 1980s, Adolfo earned the distinction of being the favorite designer of First Lady Nancy Reagan, and in 1982, Adolfo was honored with another Coty Award for his trendsetting designs.

In the early 1990s, Adolfo continued to feature clothes in the Chanel idiom. As in the past, his suits were nearly always made of some knit—even the plaids—and his jackets were usually un-lined. In 1991, Adolfo revived the caftan which he had made famous in the late 1960s. In June 1992 he celebrated his twenty-fifth anniversary as a designer, and the following March he announced that he would stop designing his custom and ready-to-wear clothing for women and would close his salon. By 1990, Adolfo had already licensed his name in exchange for royalties to manufacture more than thirty products around the world, in-cluding perfume, luggage, ties, and panty hose, and after his retirement from designing, he planned to concentrate his efforts on the licensing business.

Throughout his career, Adolfo won the praises of his clien-tele, who admired his ability to turn trends into flattering, wearable clothes, which became status symbols from the 1970s to the 1990s. His clients also appreciated the designer's hands-on approach to fashion and the utmost attention he paid to their predilections. Twice a year Adolfo traveled around the country for three months at a time, meeting the women he dressed. He has noted on many occasions that he derived inspiration for his designs from his clients rather than from works of art in museums. In an ironic reversal, Adolfo has stated that he outfitted his models to look like his clients. Three times a year, Adolfo visited France, Italy, and Switzerland to purchase fabric, and in January and June of each year he held fashion shows in New York. Since he never waited to show his clothes until after the official opening of the season, many of his excited fans gathered, a few donning identical outfits, to view the clothes they might already have ordered from Adolfo.

Roberto Clemente

1934–1972

One of seven children, Roberto Clemente was born to Melchor and Luisa (Walker) Clemente, on August 18, 1934, in Carolina, Puerto Rico. Roberto's parents were uneducated and impoverished: Melchor Clemente cut cane in the fields for a sugar company, while Luisa Clemente washed the owner's laundry. At home in the Barrio San Antón in Carolina, they stressed the value of education and hard work and sent Roberto and his siblings to the Fernández grammar school. When he was a boy, Roberto dreamed of owning a bicycle. Each day he lugged a heavy can of milk half a mile to a neighbor's house to earn one penny toward the bicycle. After three years he had saved enough to purchase a secondhand bike.

Roberto also developed a love for baseball at an early age. When he was three years old, his mother found the boy playing imaginary baseball against a wall because his family could not afford to buy him a ball. That day, Luisa Walker Clemente believed her son would be a great baseball player, and she made up her mind to do everything in her power to help him succeed. She often went without supper to provide food for her children so, as Roberto Clemente put it, they could "become strong to fight in the world." Roberto devoted as much time as he could to playing baseball and always carried a ball around with him. By age fourteen, thanks to his perseverance and his mother's constant encouragement, he was playing shortstop in San Juan's slow-pitch softball league and in a San Juan youth baseball league. At age seventeen he signed with the Santurce Crabbers in the Puerto Rican winter league for forty-five dollars a week.

Clemente impressed Pedrin Zorilla, the coach of the Santurce Crabbers, who also had connections with all the major league teams. In 1954, Zorilla brought Clemente to the attention of scouts from the Brooklyn Dodgers, who signed the young player. Even though the Dodgers' team managers realized the immensity of Clemente's talent, they sent him to their minor league farm club in Montreal because they already had four black players on the starting roster. They tried to hide him from rival scouts, but Clyde Sukeforth, a scout for the Pittsburgh Pirates, spotted Clemente in practice and urged the Pirates to sign him as soon as possible. The Pirates responded with a contract for Clemente at the end of the 1954 season.

Clemente played in the Pirates' outfield for the first time in 1955 and spent his entire major league career with the team, making baseball history and breaking records along the way. He had numerous opportunities to sign with more celebrated teams but Clemente felt enormous gratitude and devotion to the Pirates for having supported him when he was an unknown. When questioned about his decision to remain with one team throughout his entire career, Clemente answered: "Puerto Ricans, we are very loyal people." Clemente came to the Pirates after they had just suffered through three straight seasons of 100 losses and were the butt of jokes in baseball. Clemente was not an immediate star, although his superb fielding skills and powerful throwing arm were apparent from the start.

In the early 1960s, Clemente emerged as one of baseball's

best all-around right fielders. Among his countless distinctions, he won National League batting titles in 1961, 1964, 1965, and 1967. He paced the National League in hits (209) in 1967 and triples in 1969 (12), tied for the lead in hits in 1964 (211), and topped National League outfielders in assists four times, in 1959, 1960, 1966, and 1967. Clemente batted over .300 thirteen times in his career and became the eleventh major leaguer ever to reach the 3,000-hit mark. In 2,433 games, the baseball player batted .317 with 440 doubles, 166 triples, and 240 home runs. Except for 1968, Clemente played for the National League in every All-Star Game between 1960 and 1972. He led the Pirates to world championships in 1960 and 1971. His all-around talents earned him the National League's Most Valuable Player Award in 1966, and in 1971 he received the Babe Ruth Award.

Roberto Clemente brought enormous determination to the sport of baseball. He chased down every ball in range in the outfield, executing spectacular leaps and dives to make the play. On routine flies he relied on the basket catch made famous by his contemporary Willie Mays. Clemente always appeared uncomfortable at bat, stretching his back and rolling his neck, but once he took a swing, his talent at the plate became readily apparent. Standing deep in the box, Clemente would often pounce on inside pitches. The baseball player once remarked to a reporter that he always played mad: "The angrier I feel, the more determined I get."

But there was another side to Roberto Clemente. He was proud to be a Puerto Rican of African and Spanish descent. When Clemente married Vera Cristina Zabala in 1964, in allegiance to Puerto Rico, he insisted that the couple's three sons be born on the island and that the family spend the off-season there. Clemente was just as sensitive and outspoken about the discrimination he encountered because of race and language. "The Latin player doesn't get the recognition he deserves," he told a reporter, "and neither does the Negro unless he does something really spectacular."

Until the 1971 season Clemente did not receive the media attention he deserved. Then, in the 1971 World Series, when the Pirates played the Baltimore Orioles, all cameras were focused on him. In Pittsburgh's climactic Game Seven victory, Clemente played his heart out, chasing down fly balls, making incredible throws, and compiling a .414 batting average with 12 hits and 2 home runs to win the Series Most Valuable Player Award. The media kept a close watch on Roberto Clemente after that pivotal victory. He did not disappoint them. On September 30, 1972, Clemente drove a double off the New York Mets left-handed pitcher Jon Matlack at Three Rivers Stadium for career-hit 3,000, joining ten other players in the history of baseball who had accomplished the feat. That historic hit was also to be his last one in the regular season. The Pirates made it to the National League playoffs that year but ultimately were defeated by the Cincinnati Reds.

After the 1972 season Clemente returned to his native Puerto Rico, where he was considered a national hero. He was now an eighteen-year major-league veteran with a lifetime .317 batting average who looked forward to a few more years with the Pittsburgh Pirates. Late in December 1972 a disastrous earthquake hit Managua, Nicaragua. Clemente, guided by his humanitarianism, helped organize the Nicaraguan Relief Committee to gather food, medicine, and other supplies for the relief of victims. On New Year's Eve, 1972, in San Juan, Clemente boarded a DC-7 cargo plane headed for Nicaragua. Shortly after takeoff, the plane crashed, killing four passengers, including the great baseball player. It had been dangerously overloaded with supplies.

After his death Roberto Clemente was lauded by many as the "greatest ballplayer" baseball had ever seen. The Pittsburgh Pirates paid homage to their star player and retired his uniform, number 21. Roberto Clemente was also highly praised for his commitment to humanitarian causes. A fund was set up in his honor on behalf of earthquake victims in Nicaragua and to subsidize baseball clinics in Puerto Rico, which Roberto Clemente had planned to expand to help Puerto Rican youth. President Nixon memorialized the baseball player by writing a personal check for the fund "to be used for the relief of those he was trying to help." The Pittsburgh Pirates and the Richard K. Mellon Foundation each donated $100,000 to the fund, and various private individuals, banks, and businesses also made contributions. A few years later, the Roberto Clemente Sports City for underprivileged children was set up in Puerto Rico. Ruben Sierra, the Puerto Rican outfielder for the Oakland Athletics, got his start at Sports City and is the first product of Clemente's dream.

During the week of Roberto Clemente's death, the inauguration of the new governor of Puerto Rico, Rafael Hernandez Colón, was postponed as the island saluted its fallen son. Across America homage was paid to the distinguished baseball player. A park in Pittsburgh and a school in Harlem were named in Roberto Clemente's honor. On the day his plane crashed, a large neon sign high atop the city of Pittsburgh read ADIÓS, AMIGO. In the spring of 1973 the baseball world honored the memory of Roberto Clemente when the Baseball Writers Association of America held a special election and, waiving the five-year wait for induction, voted the legendary player the first Latino into the Baseball Hall of Fame. In 1994 a statue of Roberto Clemente, titled *The Great One,* was unveiled outside Three Rivers Stadium in Pittsburgh.

26

Lee Trevino

1939–

Lee Trevino was born in Dallas, Texas, on December 1, 1939, to Mexican-American parents who separated when he was two years old. He was raised in abject poverty by his grandfather, a Mexican immigrant gravedigger, and lived in a four-room shack without running water and electricity. The shack was situated in a hay field next to the fairway of the Glen Lakes Country Club, where Lee would make a few cents selling stray balls back to golfers. At age six, Lee cut a discarded club down to size and mimicked club members on a 2-hole course he dug in his backyard. He dropped out of school after seventh grade and became an assistant greenskeeper at a local pitch-and-putt course. Lee caddied whenever he got the chance and played a few holes when the course emptied. He played a full 18 holes for the first time when he was fifteen and shot a 77. Two years later, Lee Trevino joined the U.S. Marine Corps, where he was given a tryout on the green. He shot a round of 66 and from then on played with the colonels. During his four years in the Marine Corps, Trevino's golf game developed rapidly, and he turned pro in 1960 at the age of twenty-one.

After his discharge in 1961, Trevino got a job in El Paso as a golf assistant polishing clubs and shining shoes at Horizon Hills Country Club for thirty dollars a week. He played in local events and would also wager with wealthy players, often bringing in $200 a week. Just to increase the wager he would sometimes play with one club, a rusty 3-iron, and would allow his opponent handicap shots. In 1965, Trevino entered his first tournament, the Texas State Open, and won, earning $1,000 in prize money. He went on to his first U.S. Open in 1966, where he tied for fifty-fourth. In 1967, Lee's wife sent in his entry to the local qualifier for the U.S. Open, although the family could barely afford the twenty-dollar fee. Lee Trevino finished a respectable fifth that year at Baltusrol, won $6,000 in prize money, and was named Rookie of the Year. His victory was enough to convince him to join the Tour full-time. While most people in professional golf circles felt that Trevino would make a fine golfer, few believed that he was champion material.

Lee Trevino put all doubts about his future in golf to rest when he won the U.S. Open at Oak Hill Country Club in Rochester in 1968, beating Jack Nicklaus, who had captured the event the previous year. His victory was the biggest upset in the golfing world since Jack Fleck defeated Ben Hogan in a playoff in 1955. After three rounds at the U.S. Open, Trevino trailed 54-hole leader Bert Yancey by one stroke. Nicklaus was seven off the lead and never got closer than three shots to Trevino. In the final round Yancey missed putts and fell to 76 and third place. Trevino's last-round 69 held off Nicklaus, who closed with a 67 and finished four strokes behind the leader. After winning the coveted title, Trevino shouted: "I'm gonna play until I'm a hundred years old!"

With that victory, Lee Trevino, known as the "Merry Mex," became the first player in U.S. Open history to play four consecutive rounds in the sixties and in under par. He also matched the record score of 275, set by Jack Nicklaus in 1967.

Trevino finished out 1968 in sixth place on the money winners' list and was victorious at the Hawaiian Open, giving $10,000 in prize money to the family of a fellow golfer, Ted Makalena, who died in a surfing accident. In 1970, Trevino won two Tour events, emerged as the leading money winner, and was awarded the Vardon Trophy, given to the player with the lowest scoring average on the PGA Tour. He also finished tied for third in the British Open that year. By this time Lee Trevino had become not only the most gifted shotmaker on the Tour but also one of the most consistent players in the world. He posed a major threat to Jack Nicklaus, creating a rivalry between the players that has lasted to this day.

In 1971, Lee Trevino enjoyed an extraordinary winning streak and set records that still stand today. The U.S. Open at Merion Golf Club in Ardmore, Pennsylvania, will be remembered for the rubber snake Trevino tossed at Nicklaus on the first tee of the playoff, which Trevino won 68 to 71. Lee Trevino tied for first, with veteran Art Wall, at 275 in the Canadian Open at Richelieu Valley Golf and Country Club in Montreal; Trevino walked away the winner with a birdie at the first playoff hole. Then, in the British Open at Royal Birkdale, Trevino took a seven at the seventeenth hole and finished at 278, one stroke ahead of Lu Liang Huan. In 1971, Trevino also captured three other events on the PGA Tour and finished second on the money winners' list. He won the Vardon Trophy again and received such honors as PGA Player of the Year, *Golf* magazine's Player of the Year, and *Sports Illustrated*'s Sportsman of the Year. That year, Jack Nicklaus told Trevino: "I hope you never find out how well you can play because it will give the rest of us a chance to win."

Lee Trevino went on to retain the British Open title at Muirfield in 1972, beating local favorite Tony Jacklin. The turning point in the tournament came at the par-5 seventeenth hole. Trevino was leading Jacklin by a stroke when he duck-hooked his drive into a bunker and made a weak recovery. Out of anger, he hit the ball without planting his feet, and the chip went right into the hole. Jacklin missed his putt for a five, and Trevino regained the lead and finished with 278. This put him one stroke ahead of Jack Nicklaus, who was vying for a Grand Slam, having won the Masters and the U.S. Open. That year, Lee Trevino also fought to defend his U.S. Open title but finished fourth with a 78 in the final round. In 1972, Trevino won the Vardon Trophy for the third consecutive year. He would win it again in 1974 and 1980.

In 1974, Trevino seized his first PGA Championship at Tanglewood Golf Club in Winston-Salem, North Carolina. This tournament has gone down as one of the most dramatic confrontations in the annals of golf. Lee Trevino opened with a 73 but pulled ahead of the other players in subsequent rounds of 66, 68, and 69. When Trevino bogeyed the seventeenth, Nicklaus was within one shot. Nicklaus hit his approach about twenty feet from the final hole; Trevino, about twelve feet. Both players made par, and Nicklaus finished second, one stroke behind Trevino. Trevino repeated his performance in this tournament in 1980.

The year 1975 marked a low point in Trevino's career. That year, he and two other players, Jerry Heard and Bobby Nicholls, were struck by lightning during the Western Open at the Butler National Golf Club in Illinois and were rushed to the hospital. All the players made a full recovery, but late in 1976, Trevino underwent surgery for a herniated disc, which was probably caused by the lightning incident. He suffered from a weak back, which often prevented him from practicing on a regular basis, and in 1981 he had a nerve ending deadened to lessen the pain. In 1979, Trevino was inducted into the American Golf Hall of Fame, but it was not until 1984 that he relived his past glory on the golf course. He won his twenty-seventh Tour victory, his sixth major championship, and his second PGA title at the 1984 PGA Championship at Shoal Creek in Birmingham, Alabama. Trevino was in superb form, shooting four straight rounds in the sixties, surpassing Gary Player and Lanny Wadkins and winning by four strokes.

In 1983, Trevino married Claudia Bove, his third wife. It was also the year he published his autobiographical work *They Call Me Super Mex*. The year before, NBC hired him as their expert golf analyst. Trevino stayed with NBC for seven years but then devoted all his time to playing golf as his fiftieth birthday approached in 1989, making him eligible for the Senior Tour. Trevino was chomping at the bit to join the Senior PGA Tour and spent most of 1989 on a strict regime of physical conditioning and golf to prepare for the ninety Senior tournaments scheduled over the next three years. In 1990 he won seven events, including the U.S. Senior Open, where he finished two strokes ahead of Jack Nicklaus. Lee Trevino was number one on the money list with

$1,190,518, setting a record as the first Senior to earn more than the regular PGA Tour's leading money winner.

In June 1992 he ruptured ligaments in his thumb, which took him out of the running for another title for the rest of the year. Nevertheless, in 1992 he managed to win Player of the Year honors and to lead the Tour again in earnings. In December 1992, Trevino had surgery to repair his thumb. With a plastic brace under his glove and a few changes to his putting, he rejoined the Tour in March 1993 for the Gulfstream in Indian Wells, California. At the end of 1993, after three seasons on the Senior Tour, Lee Trevino had won sixteen tournaments, bringing his total to fifty-two titles and more than $7 million in earnings in the twenty-six years he has spent in pro golf.

At the height of his PGA career, Lee Trevino was one of the most accurate players in golf. Trevino's swing is distinct; his arc is solid and true, and he extends through the ball longer than any of his contemporaries. He has a strong grip, aims left, chases the blade at the top, then pulls through strongly with the left hand to fade the ball. Trevino is also a great putter and a genius at plotting strategies. His behavior on the course is almost as striking as his form. He possesses a buoyant, bubbly personality and is always chattering, making wisecracks, and smiling on the course, which sometimes annoys his opponents. Yet when the moment comes to concentrate, Trevino can channel all of his energy into the shot at hand. He is known for his iron nerves when a victory is at stake and for salvaging some incredibly difficult shots.

Despite the humor Lee Trevino brings to golf, he has never forgotten the poverty and prejudice he endured in his early years. On those occasions that he played in the Masters, Trevino always changed his spikes outside, underscoring the ostracism he suffered at country clubs in his early professional days in golf. In an article in the June 1992 issue of *Hispanic* magazine, he reflected on the absence of role models in his formative years: "Golf was not covered by the media, so even if there were any Hispanic golfers, I wouldn't have known about them." Despite all the obstacles Trevino faced, he has emerged as one of the greatest players in the history of golf. His experiences have also made him compassionate toward those less fortunate. Lee Trevino rarely leaves a tournament victory without donating a sizable sum to charity.

27

Gloria Estefan

1958–

She was born Gloria Fajurdo in Cuba in 1958 on the eve of Fidel Castro's Communist takeover. Her father, José Manuel Fajardo, a Cuban soldier, had been one of President Fulgencio Batista's bodyguards. When Batista fled the country and Fidel Castro seized power, the Fajardo family sought refuge in the United States. Upon their arrival, the CIA recruited José Manuel Fajardo as a member of the 2506 Brigade of Cuban refugees who took part in the failed 1961 Bay of Pigs invasion to topple Castro. Fajardo was captured by his own cousin during the botched invasion and spent eighteen months in prison. He went free after President Kennedy negotiated the release of prisoners taken by

Castro's forces. Back in Miami, Fajardo enlisted with the U.S. Army and later volunteered to go to Vietnam.

After returning from Vietnam, Fajardo was diagnosed with multiple sclerosis, contracted from his exposure to Agent Orange. While her mother worked and went to night school, Gloria, then a teenager, was left to care for her ailing father until he was later admitted to a VA hospital. In her childhood, Gloria had enjoyed writing poetry but had found guitar lessons boring. Now faced with the burden of caring for her family, she sought refuge in music and would often sit in her room singing Top 40 songs and teaching herself to play the guitar. In 1993, she spoke with *Billboard* magazine about the experience: "It was my release from everything....It was my way of crying."

In 1975, Gloria met keyboardist Emilio Estefan, who had fled Cuba with his family in 1966 after the Communists took everything they owned. When the two met, Estefan was working as a sales manager for the rum producer Bacardi and playing with a band called the Miami Latin Boys, whose members had also fled Castro's regime. As leader of the band, Emilio had been searching for a singer, and when he heard Gloria's voice, he decided she fit the bill. He asked her to sit in with the band, and soon after, he offered her the job of lead singer. Although she suffered from stage fright, she accepted the offer. She limited her singing to weekends in order to devote time to her studies at the University of Miami. Soon she committed herself full-time to performing. A year and a half after Gloria joined the band, the Miami Sound Machine, as the group was renamed, recorded its first album, *Renacer*, a selection of pop, disco, and original ballads in Spanish.

After several months of working together professionally, Gloria and Emilio Estefan were married, on September 1, 1978. Instead of holding a reception, the couple traveled to Japan, convinced that they would never have the opportunity to get away again. Their son Nayib was born in 1980, the same year that Estefan left his $100,000-a-year marketing job with Bacardi to devote all his efforts to the band. Estefan quickly parlayed the local success of the Miami Sound Machine into a contract with Discos CBS International, the Miami-based Hispanic division of CBS Records. From 1981 to 1983 the group recorded four albums in Spanish comprised of disco, pop, and even a few sambas. The Miami Sound Machine became a big hit in Latin America, and in the early 1980s the popular group packed soccer stadiums in Peru, Panama, Ecuador, and Guatemala but remained relatively unknown in the United States.

In 1984, Estefan convinced CBS to release the Miami Sound Machine's first album in English, *Eyes of Innocence*. The disco song "Dr. Beat" from the album became their first North American hit when it soared to the top of the European dance charts. This enthusiastic reception from the English-speaking world inspired the group to write more songs in English, some of which they included on their Spanish album *Conga*. The song "Conga" became the first single to make the pop, black, dance, and Latin charts of *Billboard* all at one time and enabled the group to break through to mainstream audiences. Gloria Estefan and the group, whose members have changed over the years, pride themselves on their unique blend of Latin rhythms, rhythm and blues, and mainstream pop. In 1986, the band released its all-English recording *Primitive Love,* which sold over a million copies and produced three hit singles: "Conga," "Bad Boys," and "Words Get in the Way," a song which made it onto the Top 10 pop chart of *Billboard*.

The Miami Sound Machine developed a unique approach to making music. Behind the scenes, three musicians, known as the "Three Jerks," wrote and arranged music and recorded albums with session players in the studio. Meanwhile, the band devoted itself to extensive concert tours. Gloria Estefan divided her time between the studio and concerts. The exposure from these tours, concerts in huge stadiums, music videos on MTV and VH-1, and the albums brought the group publicity. Estefan ultimately took center stage, and the group became known as Gloria Estefan and the Miami Sound Machine, or just Gloria Estefan. After releasing the 1987 album *Let It Loose,* with its number-one single "1-2-3," the Miami Sound Machine lost the "Three Jerks." Up until that time, their biggest hits had been fast dance numbers, but in the late 1980s, Gloria Estefan also incorporated ballads into the repertoire, which brought the group even greater popularity. The ballad "Anything For You," from *Let It Loose*, topped the charts, and the album went platinum. Suddenly, the Miami Sound Machine was making a splash.

Despite the fame the band has achieved in the United States, the Estefans are mindful of their Cuban heritage and are often at work on Spanish projects. The title of their 1989 album, *Cut Both*

Ways, is testimony of their desire to address both Spanish-speaking and English-speaking audiences. Gloria Estefan has also expanded her role in the band. For *Cut Both Ways* she not only was lead singer; she also contributed compositions and lyrics for many of the songs. Emilio Estefan eventually resigned as key-boardist with the Miami Sound Machine and channeled his managerial talent and energies into the highly successful Estefan Enterprises, a music production company. With Emilio off the tour, Nayib enjoyed the comfort and security of always having a parent at home. A close family, the Estefans often meet on the road.

On March 20, 1990, the band's tour bus was involved in an accident with a semi-truck on a snowy highway in Pennsylvania. Nayib and Emilio Estefan, who happened to be on board, suffered relatively minor injuries compared to Gloria, who had broken vertebra in her back and nearly severed her spinal cord. In a four-hour operation, surgeons implanted steel rods in her back to support her spine. Complete recovery seemed unlikely, and many questioned whether the singer would walk again. Estefan returned to her home on Star Island, near Miami, to begin her convalescence. With intensive physical therapy, the support of family and friends, and perseverance, she made a miraculous recovery. Less than a week after she was released from the hospital, she had already begun to write new material. Soon thereafter, her album *Into the Light*, with its powerful song "Coming Out of the Darkness," a celebration of her remarkable comeback, was released.

As her comeback appearance, Estefan performed on television's American Music Awards show on January 28, 1991, and two months later she began a year-long international tour to publicize *Into the Light*. She told *People* magazine in a February 1991 article how the accident had changed her: "It's hard to get me in an uproar about anything because most things have little significance compared with what I almost lost. And because of the fact that so many people got behind me and gave me a reason to want to come back fast and made me feel strong. Knowing how caring people can be, how much they gave me—that has changed me forever." In 1992 the Disney channel televised the special "Gloria Estefan—Going Home," which follows the pop singer and her Miami Sound Machine on the 1991 tour that marked her come-back from the bus accident.

In 1993, Estefan released her solo Spanish-language album *Mi tierra,* in which she replaces her Latin pop beat with the authentic sounds of mid-twentieth-century Cuba. In making the album, the Estefans engaged arranger-composer Joanito Marquez and mambo legend Israel "Cachao" Lopez, two musicians who were actually in Cuba creating the rhythms of that era. Estefan hoped that *Mi tierra,* a project close to her heart, would introduce younger Cubans to their musical roots and open doors for Latin musicians. By 1994 Estefan had seventeen Top Ten hits and had sold over 20 million copies of her albums.

Despite her busy schedule of recording and touring, Estefan finds time to contribute to many social causes. When Hurricane Andrew devastated South Florida in 1992, the Estefans organized relief centers in their studio-office complex and put together the Hurricane Relief concert with a star-studded lineup, raising $3 million for the victims of the disaster. They also released an inspirational ballad "Always Tomorrow," which Gloria Estefan had written, and donated the proceeds to hurricane aid. On April 27, 1993, Gloria Estefan took the stage with Aretha Franklin and other singers and actors in a benefit concert in New York City for the Gay Men's Health Crisis. In October 1993 the singer was honored for her contributions to Latinos at a benefit for the Casita María Settlement House, which serves Latino communities in the South Bronx and East Harlem.

28

Nancy López

1957–

Nancy López, the daughter of Domingo López, an auto-repair-shop owner, and Marina (Griego) López, was born on January 6, 1957, in Torrance, California. Her parents were hardworking and devoted much of their time and energy to their children. When Nancy was three the family moved to Roswell, New Mexico. Her parents took up golf to benefit her mother's health when Nancy was seven, and she often followed them around the Roswell public golf course. When she was eight, her father handed her a 4-wood and instructed her to hit the golf ball until it went into the hole. Nancy followed his advice, and in three years she was a better golfer than either her mother or her father.

Her parents saw the makings of a champion in Nancy and dedicated themselves to their daughter's career, ignoring their own needs to finance her golfing. Marina López realized that the family could not support three golfers, so she gave up the game so that Nancy could play. As Mexican Americans, they were ostracized by the golfing community in Roswell, and they could not afford to pay country-club fees so that Nancy could practice. The municipal courses of Roswell became Nancy's training ground, and her father became her coach. Despite these obstacles, Nancy captured the New Mexico State Women's Amateur Championship at age twelve. She went on to win the U.S. Junior Girls Title in 1972 and 1974, the Western Junior Girls Championships in 1972, 1973, and 1974, and the Mexican Amateur in 1975. Nancy López was the top-ranked amateur player in the world by the time she was sixteen.

López played on the all-boys golf team at her high school, Goddard High, leading the team to a state championship. While a senior at Goddard in 1975, López finished second in the U.S. Women's Open. Based on her outstanding performance on the green, she was awarded a $10,000 golf scholarship from Colgate-Palmolive to the University of Tulsa in 1976. That year, she won the Association for Intercollegiate Athletics for Women National Championship, the Trans, and the Western, and she finished second at the U.S. Women's Open. She also played on the winning U.S. team in the Espirito Santo and the Curtis Cup. An intercollegiate champion, Nancy López left college after her sophomore year to turn professional and joined the Ladies Professional Golf Association (LPGA) on July 29, 1977.

From the start, López astounded the professional golf world. In 1977, she played in six tournaments, finishing second at the Colgate European Open, her second tournament as a LPGA member. That first year, she went into a brief slump precipitated by her mother's premature death. In 1978, her first full season on the Tour, twenty-one-year-old Nancy López made a spectacular showing by winning a total of nine LPGA events, with a record five consecutive victories. She was named LPGA Rookie of the Year and Player of the Year for 1978, the only golfer to earn both distinctions in a single year. In addition, the Associated Press named Nancy López Athlete of the Year for 1978, and she was honored with the Vare Trophy for the lowest average on the pro tour, 71.76 strokes. She was the first player in LPGA history to average less than 72 strokes a round. In 1978, López set a new money-winning mark for women golfers with $189,813 in earnings.

The entire golf world was stunned by López's achievements, and after she won five consecutive tournaments, her popularity was so immense that attendance for the LPGA Tour tripled. The press was so taken by her that they nicknamed her "Wonder Woman." That she attracted crowds to women's golf and dominated newspaper headlines and television with appearances on such programs as the *Tonight* show gave the LPGA Tour the exposure it needed to enter the realm of big money by the 1980s. In 1975, before López turned pro, LPGA prize money hovered around the $1.8 million mark, while male players on the PGA Tour could earn $7.9 million. As fans by the thousands turned out to watch López, corporate sponsors flocked to the LPGA, and it was on its way to achieving parity with the PGA Tour.

López gave an impressive performance again in 1979, with eight victories out of nineteen events, making her the leading prizewinner of the season. Her stroke average of 71.20 won her a second Vare Trophy and set an all-time LPGA record until she lowered it again in 1985 to 70.73. She was also named LPGA Player of the Year for the second year in a row. In 1979 she married Tim Melton, a Pennsylvania television sportscaster, but the marriage proved detrimental to Nancy's career in golf, and the two parted in 1982.

On October 25, 1982, she married Ray Knight, best known as a 1986 World Series winner with the New York Mets and a baseball commentator for ESPN. The two are devoted parents of three daughters. López made sure that her busy golf schedule did not keep her away from the children by becoming the first woman pro to bring her family along on the tour. Although she cut back her appearances in the early and mid 1980s due to the births of her daughters, she still won an impressive twelve tournaments between 1980 and 1984, reaching $1 million in career earnings in April 1983, a feat only four women in golf had accomplished up until that time.

By 1985, López was back on the circuit full-time and enjoying a spectacular year. She finished in the top ten in twenty-one out of the twenty-five events in which she played and won five tournaments. López captured a second LPGA Championship by eight strokes and won the Portland Ping Championship, which was decided after a tense sudden-death playoff against Lori Garbacz. During the Henredon Classic in High Point, North Carolina, she set another astounding record in 1985 with a score of 268 (66, 67, 69, 66) for 72 holes, an extraordinary 20 under par. Her total of 25 birdies over the four rounds of the event also set a record. In 1985 she was again awarded the Vare Trophy for low scoring average and named LPGA Player of the Year. As the top money winner on the circuit that year, her earnings totaled over $400,000, the first time that mark was passed on the LPGA tour. Her 1985 earnings put her well on the way to a $2 million career total.

The year 1986 saw the birth of a second daughter, which restricted López's play that year. By 1987 she was back on the green, and on July 20, 1987, she became the eleventh golfer, and the youngest, to be inducted into the LPGA Hall of Fame after winning the Sarasota Classic, her thirty-fifth career victory. LPGA members also honored her contributions to golf with the Powell Award in 1987, and *Golf* magazine named her "Golfer of the Decade" for the years 1978 to 1987. In 1988 she was selected the LPGA Player of the Year for the fourth time in her career. By 1989, she had climbed to second place in career earnings on the LPGA Tour with over $2.5 million, only $100,000 less than all-time leader Pat Bradley. That year, she was inducted into the PGA/World Golf Hall of Fame. In 1992, the sports community bestowed on Nancy López the prestigious Flo Hyman Award, "given annually to a female athlete who exemplifies the dignity, spirit, and commitment to excellence of the great volleyball player." As of July 1993, Nancy López had enjoyed forty-six career victories, ranking her sixth in LPGA history, and had earned $3,708,470 in prize money.

Nancy López has an unusual swing, which over the years has attracted debate among golf purists and nonpurists. Among her faults, critics have targeted her strange habit of setting her hands low and then raising them as she brings the club back. In addition, her action takes the club to the outside, but then she compensates by attacking the ball from the inside on the down-swing. No matter how unorthodox Nacy López's swing may be, no one can deny it is a winner. Her marvelous putting stroke, aggressive approach, and amazing 240-yard drive combine to make her one of the most formidable players in the history of golf. With her impeccable track record, her tremendous poise under pressure, and charismatic personality, Nancy López has electrified women's golf like no other player since the legendary Babe Didrikson Zaharias. She has rightly earned the title bestowed upon her by the *New York Times* in 1993: "queen of the Ladies Professional Golf Association tour, the one the galleries cherish the most."

Young Latinos, in particular, cherish Nancy López. On the green she has always felt committed to representing the Latino community. In 1989, Nancy López told *Hispanic* magazine: "I've always felt like a role model for the Hispanic people. I hope that I stand for honesty." In addition, Nancy López has devoted herself to children's causes and has volunteered for such organizations as Aid to the Handicapped, which addresses the needs of children with a variety of illnesses.

29

Carlos Castañeda

1925–

Carlos Castañeda was born Carlos Arana Castañeda on Christmas Day, 1925, in Cajamarca, an ancient Inca town in Peru, to Cesar Arana Burungaray, a goldsmith and a watchmaker, and Susana Castañeda Navoa. Carlos attended the local high school in Cajamarca for three years. In 1948 the family moved to Lima, where Castañeda graduated from the Colegio Nacional de Nuestra Señora de Guadalupe and then entered the National Fine Arts School of Peru to study painting and sculpture. A fellow student at the art school once recalled that Carlos was a resourceful fellow who managed to live off gambling at cards, dice, and horses and that he was obsessed with moving to the United States. Susana Castañeda Navoa passed away when Carlos was twenty-four, and he was overwhelmed with grief at the loss of his mother. Refusing to attend the funeral, he retreated to his room for three days without eating. When he emerged he announced that he was leaving home.

U.S. immigration records reveal that Castañeda arrived in the United States in 1951, entering through San Francisco. Apparently, he corresponded with relatives back home at least until 1969. His cousin Lucy Chávez held on to his letters, which indicate that Castañeda served in the U.S. Army and left the military after an injury, or "nervous shock," but the Defense Department has no record of a Carlos Arana Castañeda. In 1960, Castañeda entered graduate school in anthropology at UCLA. After enrolling in the program, he frequented the Southwest and the Mexican desert, gathering information for a paper on southwestern native herbs. In his explorations Castañeda claims to have come upon an old Yaqui Indian sorcerer whom he calls Juan Matus, or Don Juan. He became an apprentice to Don Juan and soon found himself on a journey into an alien realm, a world so strange and engrossing that the best way to describe it was a "state of separate reality."

In 1961, Don Juan initiated Castañeda into Mexican indigenous sorcery, which has no connection to organized religion and is tied to the intricacies of the natural world. Castañeda learned that on rare, highly ritualized occasions sorcerers may use hallucinogenic drugs, such as peyote, to induce a state of illumination. With modern science as his guide, Castañeda viewed his discovery as another rational system which attempts to explain a uniform and objective reality. Then, under the influence of hallucinogenic drugs, Castañeda had terrifying but illuminating visions, which led him ultimately to the conclusion that the modern, scientific view of the world was not final. Don Juan always guided him throughout, reminding him that the purpose of these drug-induced states was to attain knowledge and power. Castañeda eventually began to gain access to nonordinary reality without the use of hallucinogens, which he found terrifying. "I had begun to lose the certainty, which all of us have, that the reality of everyday life is something we can take for granted," he would write in his first book. Overwhelmed by his discoveries, he withdrew from his apprenticeship in 1965.

Castañeda showed the results of his field research, in the form of a thesis, to sociology professor Harold Garfinkel, one of the founders of ethnomethodology. Garfinkel offered his criticisms, and Castañeda spent the next several years rewriting the thesis several times. All the while he lived off odd jobs as a cabdriver and deliveryman. In 1968 he published what became his master's thesis at UCLA, *The Teachings of Don Juan: a Yaqui Way of Knowledge,* in essence the story of how a European rationalist found a "separate reality" by practicing Yaqui Indian sorcery. The book offers lucid chronicles of the author's apprenticeship with the Yaqui Indian sorcerer and became not only a modern classic in anthropological literature but also a bestseller among the general reading public. The popularity of *The Teachings of Don Juan* may be attributed in large measure to the predisposition of the counterculture of the late 1960s to alternative, nonrational approaches to reality, derived from such means as meditation, Zen, yoga, divination, drugs, acupuncture, and ESP experiments. Many were intrigued by Castañeda's recorded experiences with psychotropic plants, such as peyote and magic mushrooms. Castañeda's Don Juan became a folk hero worshiped all the more by Americans because, unlike cult founders, he solicited no new followers.

In 1968, Castañeda went to Mexico to give Don Juan a copy of his book. Curiosity drew him back into the world of sorcery. He experienced more visions using hallucinogens, but his most astounding episodes were nonpsychedelic. He experienced numerous inexplicable events, which led him to abandon completely the rationale for a detached, objective view of reality. On one solitary journey in the mountains he heard mysterious sounds like slurps and squeals and felt paws touching his neck, which he could not explain through a rational view of the world. Don Juan revealed other phenomena that did not easily lend themselves to scientific explanations. Castañeda reported in his second book, entitled *A Separate Reality: Further Conversations With Don Juan* (1971), that the sorcerer caused a leaf to detach itself from a tree and fall, then repeated the pattern again and again.

In 1973, Carlos Castañeda was awarded his Ph.D. degree from UCLA after submitting his dissertation, which became his third book on Don Juan, the bestseller *Journey to Ixtlán: The Lessons of Don Juan,* published in 1972. In the earlier works, Carlos Castañeda focuses on comparing Don Juan's system of knowledge to his own and then describes the first steps in the destruction of his rational interpretation of the world. In *Journey to Ixtlán: The Lessons of Don Juan,* Castañeda changes course and explores the unique properties of the sorcerer's realm. The book also considers the second stage of illumination: attuning the whole body to the universe, without the use of hallucinogens, until a separate reality is perceptible. Before the publication of *Journey to Ixtlán,* a professor named John Wallace, at the University of California at Irvine, located a copy of the manuscript. He combined it with some lecture notes from Castañeda's seminar on shamanism and sold the text to *Penthouse* magazine. Castañeda was so angered over the incident that he went into hiding in Los Angeles and emerged only for a select few lecture engagements.

As Castañeda's reputation grew, so did doubts about whether Don Juan was real. No one has ever corroborated the existence of this sorcerer. Would-be disciples from the counterculture searched through Mexico for him, their task all the more difficult since Juan Matus is a common name among the Yaqui Indians, but they came up empty-handed. Many are convinced that Don Juan is a product of Castañeda's imagination, among them the writer Joyce Carol Oates, who remarked that Castañeda's writings seemed to her "remarkable works of art on the Hesse-like theme of a young man's initiation into 'another way' of reality.... There is a novelistic momentum, rising, suspenseful action, a gradual revelation of character." Whatever the truth of the matter may be, Carlos Castañeda is an authority on enlightenment, on a par with the Zen masters.

30

Linda Ronstadt

1946–

Linda Marie Ronstadt was born on July 15, 1946, in Tucson, Arizona, to Gilbert Ronstadt, of Mexican and German extraction, and Ruthmary (Copeman) Ronstadt, of Dutch ancestry. Linda grew up in a musical household, listening to anything she could tune into, such as Top 40, blues, country and western, and gospel beamed from a Mexican radio station just across the Texas border. She was particularly fond of her father's collection of recordings by the queen of mariachi, Lola Beltrán. Linda enjoyed harmonizing with her sister and two brothers and listening to her mother, who was fond of ragtime, play the ukulele and the piano. Her father, who owned a hardware store in Tucson, played the guitar and piano and sang Mexican songs like "La barca de Guaymas," which later inspired Ronstadt to make an album of her father's favorites. When Linda was six, she made the decision to become a singer. By the age of fourteen she had formed a trio with her brother, Pete, and sister, Suzie, called the New Union Ramblers, and they performed folk music at neighborhood pizza parlors and clubs and on local television shows.

In Tucson, Linda was enrolled at St. Peter and Paul Parochial School, where she rebelled against the nuns' strict discipline. Upon graduating from Catalina High School, she enrolled in the University of Arizona, but in 1964, after one semester, she dropped out to pursue her career. Eighteen-year-old Linda soon joined her musician boyfriend, Bob Kimmel, in Los Angeles and, with Kimmel and guitar player Kenny Edwards, formed the Stone Poneys, a folk-rock group in the style of the Lovin Spoonful and the Mamas and the Papas. The Stone Poneys played the region's club circuit, and then, in 1966, they signed a contract with Capitol Records and went on to record three albums together. In 1967 "Different Drum," a cut from their second album, *Evergreen,* made the charts, and the spotlight shone on Ronstadt for the first time. Despite their success, the Stone Poneys were discouraged by the pressures of touring, drug abuse, and the cool reception they got as openers for the Doors.

The Stone Poneys dispersed, and Ronstadt, who was always the group's number-one selling point, fulfilled her Capitol recording contract as a solo performer. Her solo career slowly got off the ground as she looked for a new direction to take. She teamed up with Nashville studio musicians on her 1969 album *Hand Sown...Home Grown* and her 1970 album *Silk Purse,* creating a singular country sound. *Silk Purse* brought Linda Ronstadt her first solo hit, the elegiac "Long, Long Time." As she would later recall, Ronstadt found these early days bleak, with endless touring, tumultuous relationships, cocaine use, and bouts of stage fright.

In 1973, Linda Ronstadt toured with Neil Young and then switched to Asylum Records. By 1974 she had chosen Peter Asher, who was largely responsible for James Taylor's hits, as her producer and manager. Under Asher's direction, Ronstadt's career would soon turn around. Together they set to work creating an updated canon of standards that combined the best of Motown, rock, country, and folk with the pre–rock music popularized by Billie Holiday, Ella Fitzgerald, and Frank Sinatra. They gathered these remakes in albums like *Heart Like a Wheel* (1974), *Simple Dreams* (1977), and *Living in the U.S.A.* (1978). *Heart Like a Wheel,* Asher's initial full production effort, was the first of five consecutive platinum albums for Ronstadt. Two smash hits evolved from the album: "You're No Good," a minor hit for Betty Everett in 1963, and Phil Everly's classic "When Will I Be Loved." Ronstadt followed up *Heart Like a Wheel* with her 1975 album *Prisoner of Disguise* and her 1976 album *Linda Ronstadt's Greatest Hits,* both of which went platinum.

Upon completing a six-month tour of Europe and America in December 1976, Linda Ronstadt had the honor of singing at President Carter's inaugural in January 1977. That year, the popular singer recorded her twelfth LP, *Simple Dreams,* which went platinum and yielded two smash hits, Roy Orbison's "Blue Bayou" and Buddy Holly's "It's So Easy." Ronstadt's 1978 album *Living in the U.S.A.* produced hits like Chuck Berry's "Back in the U.S.A.," Smokey Robinson's "Ooh, Baby, Baby," and "Just One Look," a major hit for Doris Troy in 1963. By the mid-1970s, Ronstadt had enjoyed so many recording successes that she was firmly established as rock's premier female star. She was honored with Grammy Awards for Best Female Pop Performance in 1975 and Best Female Pop Performer in 1976. In 1977, Ronstadt was awarded a Grammy for Best Female Vocal Performer for her recording of "Hasten Down the Wind."

In the 1970s Linda Ronstadt epitomized American pop rock, lending her voice to rock songs and ballads, new numbers and oldies. As the decade of the 1980s dawned, the singer steered away from rock and began to experiment with different musical genres, performing pop standards, Gilbert and Sullivan, opera, and mariachi songs. Ronstadt would continue along this road into the 1990s, even though she endured a commercial decline with her shift to less popular genres. In a 1984 article in the *Saturday Review,* Ronstadt acknowledges her father as a source of inspiration for her experimentation: "He really gave me a keen appreciation for every kind of music, always saying there is great music in everything."

In 1980, Ronstadt released *Mad Love,* a challenging album whose popular singles releases were "How Do I Make You?" and the oldies "Hurt So Bad" and "I Can't Let Go." That year, she shocked the music world by appearing in Joseph Papp's hit

Broadway production of Gilbert and Sullivan's *Pirates of Penzance,* in which she sang the demanding soprano part of Mabel in a stunning performance. Then, in 1984, she took the stage again as Mimi in an off-Broadway production of *La Bohème.* Her performance was received less enthusiastically by critics.

As if sensing her audience's longing for romance and nostalgia, Ronstadt returned to the business of remakes in 1983. This time she teamed up with Nelson Riddle, Frank Sinatra's veteran arranger and conductor, to produce three albums of vintage torch songs and pop standards: *What's New?* (1983), *Lush Life* (1984), and *For Sentimental Reasons* (1986). *What's New?*—which represented to the eighties generation the spirit of the new pop romanticism—soared up the charts and sold over three and a half million copies by 1992, revitalizing Ronstadt's career. She scored another big success with her 1986 album *Trio,* a country music project with Dolly Parton and Emmylou Harris, garnering several prestigious awards, including a Grammy Award for Best Country Performance in 1987 and the Academy of Country Music Award. In an article in the February 1990 issue of *Gentlemen's Quarterly,* Linda Ronstadt spoke of the satisfaction she derived from *Trio:* "It created something that was completely apart from me as an individual entity. It became its own individual entity. And that's a record that, if someone plays it, it never bothers me. I just love it. I'm real proud of it."

In more recent projects, Linda Ronstadt has roamed even farther from pop rock to explore her Mexican roots, in seeming defiance of record-industry wisdom. She collaborated with Ruben Fuentes, the maestro who regularly conducts Mariachi Vargas de Tecalitlán, to produce the 1987 album *Canciónes de mi padre,* a collection of the mariachi songs her father once sang. *Canciónes de mi padre* turned out to be harder than any album Linda Ronstadt had ever made, for she had to memorize songs in Spanish, a language she does not speak with confidence. In preparation, she listened to recordings by Lola Beltrán, and other singers like Miguel Aceves Mejia, Cuco Sanchez, and Lucía Reyes. Her efforts paid off when the album went gold, an enormous feat, since it was recorded in a language the majority of her fans do not understand. In 1989, Ronstadt released her masterpiece, *Cry Like a Rainstorm, Howl Like the Wind,* which includes marvelous duets with Aaron Neville and songs by Jimmy Webb. Another Spanish-language album *Mas canciónes,* filled with Mexican folk and mariachi music, followed in 1991 and also struck gold.

In 1991, Linda Ronstadt and Aaron Neville won a Grammy for Pop Performance by a Duo or Group with Vocal. That year, the singer also took the stage in an updated version of *La Pastorela,* a traditional Mexican holiday play, which aired on PBS's *Great Performances.* In 1992, Ronstadt released her album *Frenesí,* a collection of standards from Mexican international pop music, which, in the 1940s and 1950s, was heavily influenced by Cuban music. Several songs on the album, like "Quiereme Mucho," Ronstadt had heard on the radio on childhood vacations in Mexico. A year later, Linda Ronstadt won a Grammy for Best Tropical Latin Album for *Frenesí,* and she was also honored with a Grammy for Best Mexican-American Album for *Mas canciónes.* In 1994, Ronstadt spoke to *New Woman* about the significance of her Mexican records: "[They] made me able to go into that place where I am most authentically myself and tune myself up a bit, make myself stronger."

In 1993, Ronstadt released her first English-language pop album in four years, *Winter Light,* with country and new-age songs, a Spanish-language waltz, and vintage numbers, including a remake of a Carole King–Gerry Goftin song that was a hit for Maxine Brown in 1964. *Winter Light* bolstered her reputation as an accomplished classic-pop singer. While she has not ruled out doing more rock, Linda Ronstadt plans to follow her musical instincts. In an article published on September 9, 1992, in the *New York Times,* the singer spoke of her creative evolution: "…the least authentic stuff I do is rock-and-roll, which I came to late in my life. I was successful, and I wasn't going to argue about that. The success gave me a platform, and I learned something about singing American pop music, which I'm glad to know. Look, I didn't grow up in Tennessee, so Dolly Parton is more a stranger to me than Mexican singers. The stuff I sing with the most authenticity is the Mexican rancheras, which have always influenced my pop style."

31

Marisol

1930–

Marisol Escobar was born in Paris on May 22, 1930, to well-to-do Venezuelans Josefina (Hernández) Escobar and Gustavo Escobar, who made his money in the oil business. In Marisol's childhood, the family traveled constantly around Europe, Venezuela, and the United States, living out of suitcases instead of a home. Marisol told *ARTnews* in May 1989: "I thought everyone lived like this. But my only home is in art history." Her mother passed away when she was eleven years old, and Marisol took a vow of silence. She didn't talk for years except when necessary in school and at home. After her mother's death Marisol's father decided to move the family to the United States. They settled in Los Angeles, and Marisol was enrolled in the Westlake School for Girls.

In her teenage years Marisol experienced some unhappiness over the wild lifestyle her parents had led, and for two years she envisioned becoming a saint. Around this time, she began to study art in earnest and decided to become a painter. Her instructor, Howard Warshaw at the Jepson School, helped Marisol develop her talent. In 1949, with her father's encouragement, she left Los Angeles to study at the Ecole des Beaux-Arts in Paris. Upon her return to the United States a year later, she briefly attended the Art Students League in Manhattan, where she studied with Yasuo Kuniyoshi, and then, from 1951 to 1954, she was instructed by noted abstract expressionist Hans Hofmann at the New School for Social Research in New York and in Provincetown. In Manhattan, Marisol frequented the Cedar Tavern, where Jackson Pollock, Willem de Kooning, Philip Guston, and Franz Kline, future major painters, often gathered. De Kooning would become one of Marisol's early mentors.

As time went on, Marisol found herself less interested in traditional impressionism and expressionism and increasingly intrigued with pre-Columbian artifacts and South American folk art. She became fascinated with sculpture, which challenged her to experiment with drawing and painting in a three-dimensional context, and began to create figures of metal, wood, or terra cotta, which were first exhibited in a group show at a gallery on Tenth Street in Manhattan. Marisol's work impressed renowned art dealer Leo Castelli, and in 1957 he offered the artist her first one-woman show in his gallery. Marisol's pieces were met with critical approval for their energy and originality. By this time the artist had dropped her last name, which she thought was too masculine sounding.

In 1960, pop artists, who employed a common imagery found in comic strips, soup cans, and Coke bottles, were at the center of attention in the art world. Marisol found a kindred spirit in pop artist Andy Warhol, who included her in two of his early films and was later the subject of one of Marisol's first portrait sculptures. In the early 1960s pop artists were challenging the limitations of painting by abandoning the traditional canvas in favor of assemblage, putting together materials from popular culture, which were sometimes painted or sculpted. Marisol responded with huge carved figures comprised of a cube or rectangular block of wood onto which were added plastic, plaster, glass, metal, wire, old clothing, wigs, hats, and any other objects she could find on the street. For instance, Marisol turned a couch into a piece she called *The Visit,* to which she even donated her coat and purse for adornment.

Marisol worked late at night when most models were unavailable, so she began to make plaster casts of her own face and body and to photograph herself. She became intrigued with the surrealist and melancholy qualities these self-portraits lent to her art. Two pieces from 1962 illustrate the artist's use of self-portrait: *The Wedding,* in which Marisol appears as both the bride and the groom, and *Dinner Date,* in which two Marisols share TV dinners. Until 1976, Marisol employed her own image in her works, many of which offer humorous and biting critical commentary on the rituals of American political and social life. Later works relying on this technique include *The Party* (1966), which contains fifteen figures of society types, all bearing Marisol's features, and *Mi mama y yo* (1968), the artist's most personal sculpture and her favorite, which depicts a young Marisol protecting her vulnerable mother with a parasol.

By the early 1960s, Marisol's fame was growing, and she became increasingly involved in the New York art scene. Between 1960 and 1964 a stream of multi-media figures poured forth from her studio, and important exhibitions followed. Most notably, the Museum of Modern Art invited her to exhibit her work in its "Art of Assemblage" show in 1961, and in 1963 she was allocated space at its "Americans, 1963" show, where her work delighted the art world. In 1962, Marisol enjoyed instant recognition when she gave a solo show of humorous figures derived from pop and primitive art at New York's prestigious Stable Gallery. In 1962 prominent museums like the Museum of Modern Art, the Whitney Museum, and Buffalo's Albright-Knox Art Gallery began acquiring pieces of Marisol's art for their permanent collections.

While Marisol was gaining in popularity because of her artwork, the media, including *Vogue, Cosmopolitan,* and *Glamour,* were intrigued by her unique persona and lifestyle and focused attention on her looks, her clothes, and the parties she attended. In 1961, she stunned the art establishment when she arrived at an artists' panel discussion at the Museum of Modern Art wearing a white Japanese-style mask. By the end of the evening the audience was begging her to remove the mask. To everyone's surprise and amusement, Marisol's face was painted to resemble the mask. Out of her aura of cool chic, detachment, and mystery rose the myth of Marisol as the "Latin Garbo." Marisol, who did not intend to appear mysterious, was bothered by this myth because it diverted attention from the seriousness of her work.

The turbulence of the Vietnam War had an adverse effect on Marisol, as she told *ARTnews* in May 1989: "At the end of the '60s I was upset about many things. Student protesters said artists were phonies working for the system. Well, the minute someone buys, you are part of the system; we're all in the system unless you kill yourself. I went on a Vietnam protest march in Washington, D.C. and it was scary....So I decided to get away. I packed a suitcase and went around the world." In 1967, Marisol accepted an invitation from the *Telegraph Sunday Magazine* (London) to portray Prime Minister Harold Wilson and the British Royal Family, along with Charles de Gaulle, Francisco Franco, and Lyndon Johnson. Until 1973, Marisol traveled extensively in South America, India, the Far East, and the Caribbean, where she discovered scuba diving and underwater photography. Upon her return to the United States the artist began work on a series of fish sculptures with Marisol features, which drew a generally lukewarm response from critics when they were exhibited in 1973.

During the rest of the decade, Marisol worked on prints and designed sets for the dance companies of Martha Graham and Louis Falco. The year 1976 marked a turning point in her work when the artist discarded self-portrait. Of this process, she told *Smithsonian* magazine in 1984: "Originally, using my face was like a search for the self. I don't have to do that anymore because I know I'll never find it." Instead of offering sly and ironic commentary on American political and social life with her self-portraits, she now paid tribute to famous mentors by combining assemblage with celebrity portraiture. Throughout the 1970s and 1980s and into the 1990s she whittled crude and sophisticated portraits in weather-beaten wood of Georgia O'Keeffe, Louise Nevelson, Pablo Picasso, Martha Graham, Willem de Kooning, and numerous others. Marisol assembled many of these portraits in her New York show "Artists and Artistes" in 1981.

Marisol was also fascinated by the art of Leonardo da Vinci, who inspired such works as *Madonna and Child With St. Anne and St. John* (1978). At another New York show in 1984 Marisol's mammoth da Vinci–motivated piece *The Last Supper* was the centerpiece. It was purchased for $300,000 by a collector, who then donated it to the Metropolitan Museum of Art. In *The Last Supper,* the disciples are painted or drawn on cubes, and Jesus is made of stone salvaged from a demolished brownstone. The artist also incorporated into her work a disembodied hand holding a dagger, which represents deceit. Marisol noticed the unattached hand in da Vinci's original painting after years of studying various reproductions in which the hand had been painted out. Upon making this discovery, Marisol showed the original to her assistant, who gave out an ominous scream, as though he had witnessed a murder. In a strange twist, the assistant was stabbed to death in his apartment a year later. It took Marisol years to recover from the shock of his violent loss.

For the next five years, Marisol stayed away from the gallery scene and quietly devoted herself to carving figures at her studio in Tribeca in New York City. During this period, she completed a sculpture commissioned by New York City for La Guardia High School of the Arts. Marisol also won a competition sponsored by the American Merchant Mariners Memorial to design a monument honoring merchant seamen who lost their lives at sea, which is now perched on a breakwater off Manhattan. Marisol's works, including sculptures of Archbishop Desmond Tutu and Emperor Hirohito, appeared again in a solo show in May 1989 at the Sidney Janis Gallery in New York. In 1991, Marisol exhibited her sculptures at the National Portrait Gallery in Washington, D.C. That year, she also appeared as a defiant heroine advocating safe sex in a bilingual public-service comic strip posted in the New York subway.

Marisol continues to enlarge the scope of creative expression, but as she revealed to *ARTnews,* she has not always felt so unhampered as an artist: "Years ago there was no respect for the artist, and it was hard for me to say I was one. I did not feel that free. Now it's stamped in my passport: *artist.* You see, all life is a progression, and once you are free, there's no turning back."

32

José Limón

1908–1972

José Arcadio Limón was born to Florencio and Francisca (Traslavina) Limón on January 12, 1908, in Culiacán, the capital of the Mexican state of Sinaloa. In 1915, when José was seven years old, his family was uprooted by the Mexican Revolution of 1910 and fled to the United States, where they settled first in Arizona and then in Los Angeles. José attended parochial school in Los Angeles. Like his father, a musician and orchestra director, José was passionate about music. He also expressed an early interest in art, particularly painting, and later enrolled in the University of California at Los Angeles (UCLA) to pursue painting as a career. In 1928, after studying for several months at UCLA, he went to New York to attend the New York School of

Design. There he discovered that the painters who inspired him, such as El Greco, were not in vogue and that the students looked to the French modernist painters for inspiration. Greatly disillusioned by Limón abandoned art school and gave away his painting equipment.

Friends persuaded Limón to explore dance, but he was bothered by what he perceived as a lack of masculinity in the Mexican folk dances, tap dancing, and ballet he had seen. Finally, Limón was escorted to a performance by the extraordinary German modern dancer Harald Kreutzberg and was so impressed with what he called Kreutzberg's "dignity and towering majesty" that the very next day he signed up for classes at the Doris Humphrey–Charles Weidman Studio. Limón threw himself into dance. By 1930 he was performing on Broadway in the chorus of Norman Bel Geddes's modern rendition of *Lysistrata* and had danced in a duet, entitled *Études in D Flat Major,* with Leticia Ide at private recitals at the Humphrey-Weidman Studio. In 1931, Limón presented to the public his first choreographed composition, a solo to two preludes of Reginald de Koven.

Limón danced and studied under the tutelage of Doris Humphrey and Charles Weidman until 1940. In those years he evolved into a strong dancer and mastered the intricacies of choreography. He choreographed such works as *Canción y danza* and *As Thousands Cheer* in 1932 and *Life Begins at Eight-Forty* in 1934. As the decade drew to a close, however, Limón decided to turn his hand to concert dance and began to develop compositions based on Mexican and Spanish themes. He then formed the Little Group, a branch of the Humphrey-Weidman Company, which performed in several dance recitals. In 1937 he received a fellowship at the Bennington School of Dance in recognition of his promise as a choreographer. The award enabled him to complete his first group dance, *Danza de la muerte,* that summer, which premiered at the Vermont State Armory in Bennington.

From 1940 to 1942, Limón launched a West Coast tour and featured some of his works in a joint program with May O'Donnell, the former Martha Graham dancer. By mid-tour, dance critics were beginning to refer to him as one of the leading dancers in the world. On October 3, 1941, Limón married Pauline Lawrence, a former dancer with the Denishawn Company, who was a designer, manager, and pianist for the Humphrey-Weidman Company and the Limón Company for the rest of their career.

Upon completing the West Coast tour, Limón returned to the Humphrey-Weidman Company as a featured dancer in a well-received series of all-Bach concerts, in which the dancer performed his solo *Chaconne in D Minor*. Limón stunned the dance world in six performances with the Humphrey-Weidman Company the next spring and secured his place as one of the world's greatest modern dancers and choreographers.

This great moment in Limón's career was interrupted, however, when he was drafted into the U.S. Army. He spent two years in uniform, first driving a truck in the Quartermaster Corps and then directing and dancing in shows for Special Services. While stationed in Brooklyn at the end of the war, Limón founded his own dance company, the Limón Company, with Beatrice Seckler and Dorothy Bird. By then his mentors, Doris Humphrey and Charles Weidman, had gone in different directions, and Limón named Doris Humphrey artistic director of the company, which debuted in New York at the Humphrey-Weidman Studio Theatre on May 20, 1945. The concert showcased five Limón works, among them the *Vivaldi Concerto in D Minor*. Under the guidance of Doris Humphrey the company would feature Limón's and Humphrey's works for over a decade.

Doris Humphrey's first works for the Limón group, *Lament for Ignacio Sanchez Mejías* and *The Story of Mankind,* premiered in July 1946 at Bennington College. The company performed these works as well as the *Chaconne* and the *Vivaldi Concerto* at its Broadway debut at the Belasco Theatre in January 1947, in which guest artist Pauline Koner danced with the group for the first time. In 1946, Limón was granted American citizenship. In the summer of 1948 the Connecticut College School of Dance in New London opened its doors, and Limón was invited to join the faculty. The Limón Company was in residence at the college in the summers, when Limón taught dance and performed, until his death in 1972.

In 1950 the Mexican government invited Limón to bring his company to the Instituto Nacional de Bellas Artes in Mexico City. After the Mexican artist Miguel Covarrubias created the Ballet Mexicano, Limón set to work choreographing *Los cuatro soles, Tonanzintla*, and *Diálogos* for that group, which were danced at the Palacio de Bellas Artes in March 1951. Months later, Limón performed *El grito* with music by Silvestre Revueltas at the Palacio de Bellas Artes.

The years 1949 to 1968 were Limón's most prolific as a choreographer. He completed over thirty-five works for his company and for students at the Juilliard School in New York City, where he became a member of the dance faculty in 1953. Limón staged many of these works for the core group of performers in his company, including Lucas Hoving, Betty Jones, Pauline Koner, and Lavinia Nielsen. In a short season at the Ziegfeld Theatre in New York in the spring of 1949, Hoving and Limón danced opposite each other for the first time in the company's performances of *La malinche,* which is based on a Mexican legend. Their unique dance styles interacted magnificently in *The Moor's Pavane,* which was choreographed to music by Henry Purcell and premiered at the American Dance Festival on August 17, 1949, with Limón dancing the part of the Moor. The work, which places the story of Othello in the context of a courtly dance, has been in the repertory of many ballet and modern dance companies throughout the world. It captured the 1950 *Dance* magazine award for achievement in choreography.

In 1950 the American Dance Festival saw the premiere of another work Limón created for his performers, *The Exiles,* a duet on the flight of Adam and Eve from paradise. The Limón Company unveiled Doris Humphrey's *Night Spell* in 1951 and *Ritmo jondo* in 1953. Limón choreographed numerous works for an all-male group, including *The Traitor* in 1954, a dance on the betrayal of Christ, and *The Emperor Jones* in 1956, based on Eugene O'Neill's play and commissioned by the Empire State Music Festival. In 1958, the year Doris Humphrey died, Limón performed one of his greatest works, *Missa brevis,* which he called "an act of expiation" for the horror of war-ravaged Europe and a symbol of the endurance of the human spirit. *Missa brevis* marked the beginning of a series of works he choreographed for a large group of dancers. Some of his other important large works include *A Choreographic Offering,* the 1964 tribute to Doris Humphrey; *My Son, My Enemy,* a 1965 work commissioned by the Rockefeller Foundation; and *Psalm,* a 1967 work based on a theme from *The Last of the Just,* a novel by André Schwarz-Bart.

Limón's past work in Mexico led to important foreign engagements in the 1950s and 1960s. In the fall of 1954 the State Department–ANTA Cultural Exchange Program sponsored a South American tour of the Limón Company. Between 1957 and 1963 the State Department sent the Limón Company on tours to

Europe, Central and South America, and the Near and Far East. Limón's electrifying stage presence made these foreign tours an enormous success. He was honored with the *Dance* magazine Award for 1957 and the State Department's Capezio Award in 1964, owing in part to his outstanding work abroad. At the invitation of President John F. Kennedy and First Lady Jacqueline Kennedy, Limón and Pauline Lawrence attended a White House luncheon for President Jorge Alessandri of Chile in December 1962. President Lydon B. Johnson and Lady Bird Johnson invited the original cast of *The Moor's Pavane* to stage a special performance at the White House for King Hassan II of Morocco in February 1967.

In 1960, Limón received an honorary doctor of fine arts degree from Wesleyan University, and in 1964 he was named artistic director of the short-lived American Dance Theater. In February 1966 the Limón Company gave three performances of *Missa brevis* and *Choreographic Offering* at the Washington Cathedral in the nation's capitol. That year the National Council of the Arts awarded José Limón a $23,000 grant for choreography. In February 1968 the great dancer and choreographer returned to the Washington Cathedral for a week of repertory. In 1969, he performed for the final time as a dancer. He continued to choreograph new works for his company and to teach at the Juilliard School of Music in New York until his death from cancer on December 2, 1972.

33

Dolores Huerta

1930–

Dolores Fernández Huerta was born on April 10, 1930, to Alicia (Chávez) Fernández and Juan Fernández, in Dawson, New Mexico. Her mother was a second-generation New Mexican, and her father was the son of Mexican immigrants. When she was a toddler, Dolores's parents divorced, and her mother moved her and her brothers, John and Marshall, to Las Vegas, New Mexico, and then to Stockton, California. Alicia Chávez Fernández had trouble supporting her family in Depression-ravaged California and was forced to work in a cannery by night and as a waitress by day in order to feed and clothe her children. Luckily, Dolores's maternal grandfather, Herculano Chávez, followed the family to Stockton and took over the job of raising the children. Dolores forged a close relationship with her widowed grandfather, who created a happy, stable environment for his grandchildren.

Alicia Chávez Fernández's financial status improved during the war years when she ran a restaurant and then managed a hotel in Stockton with her second husband, James Richards. In the summer, Dolores and her siblings helped out in the family businesses, which catered to working-class people and farmers. Later, Dolores Huerta would speak admiringly of her mother's entrepreneurial spirit and the close relationship she forged with her children. After the birth of another daughter, her mother's second marriage ended in divorce, and in the early 1950s she wed her third husband, Juan Silva. This happy marriage saw the birth of another daughter and lasted until Alicia Chávez Fernández's premature death from cancer in 1962.

In her childhood Dolores seldom saw her father, a coal miner, but as an eleven-year-old she spent the summer crisscrossing New Mexico with him as he sold pots and pans door to door. Earlier Juan Fernández had worked in the coal mines and in the fields, harvesting beets in Colorado, Nebraska, and Wyoming to supplement his income. Faced with abysmal working conditions, low wages, and frequent accidents, he became a labor activist and served as secretary-treasurer of the CIO local at the Terrero Camp of the American Metals Company in Las Vegas. In 1938 he was elected to the New Mexico state legislature, representing San Miguel County, but served only one term in the statehouse due to his outspokenness. Through his efforts on behalf of laborers he became an inspiration to his daughter.

With her mother on a more secure financial footing, Dolores enjoyed a relatively middle-class upbringing in California and attended Lafayette Grammar School, Jackson Junior High School, and Stockton High School. Unlike most Latino women of her generation, she pursued a higher education and enrolled at Stockton College, but then temporarily interrupted her studies to marry Ralph Head. After the birth of two children, Celeste and Lori, the two divorced. With her mother's help in raising the children, Dolores returned to Stockton College, where she was awarded an A.A. degree. In those early years she held numerous jobs, including managing a small grocery store her mother owned and working as a secretary at the naval supply base and in the sheriff's office in records and identifications. Dissatisfied with her employment situation, she pursued a teaching career after obtaining provisional teaching credentials.

After World War II a wave of civic activism swept through New Mexico. Dolores, who was a registered Republican at the time, changed her party affiliation and became active in the civic and educational programs of the Community Service Organization (CSO), an agency geared toward helping poor communities throughout the United States. At the CSO she organized citizenship classes, registered voters, and pressed local government officials for improvements in the barrio. Based on her superb track record, she was hired to lobby in Sacramento for CSO legislative initiatives. During this time she met and married her second husband, Ventura Huerta, another activist in community affairs. The couple had five children, but the marriage dissolved after Ventura Huerta became disillusioned by Dolores's lack of commitment to domestic duties. During separations that ended in divorce Dolores's mother stepped in and supplied housing, baby-sitting, financial backing, and support for her daughter's CSO activities.

Dolores Huerta soon became embroiled in issues related to the exploitation of migrant farmworkers. She joined the Agricultural Workers Association (AWA), a northern California community-interest group founded by a local priest and his parishioners. The organization later merged with the AFL-CIO–sponsored Agricultural Workers Organizing Committee (AWOC); Huerta served as secretary-treasurer of AWOC, and in 1955, she met Fred Ross and Cesar Chávez, organizers of California chapters of the CSO. In 1958, when Cesar Chávez was appointed national director of the national CSO, Huerta became his principal assistant and helped expand the CSO to twenty-two chapters in California and Arizona.

Cesar Chávez and Huerta brought the plight of migrant farmworkers to the attention of the CSO and pushed for agricultural reform. The CSO advocated getting Latinos out of agricultural work altogether, but Chávez and Huerta knew that this was no solution. In 1962 they left the CSO and began organizing farmworkers from an office in Delano, California. They founded the Farm Workers Association (FWA), the forerunner of the National Farm Workers Association (NFWA), the first successful union of agricultural workers in the history of the United States. From the founding of the NFWA, Dolores Huerta was second in command and held many decision-making posts as an outspoken leader, executive-board member, administrator, lobbyist, contract negotiator, picket captain, and lecturer.

On September 8, 1965, the NFWA joined Filipino grape pickers, represented by the AWOC, in a strike against Delano grape growers protesting low wages. Within one year wine-grape growers in the region capitulated to the demands of the strikers, but table-grape growers held out. In the spring of 1968 the NFWA, which by then had merged with the AWOC to form the United Farm Workers Organizing Committee of the AFL-CIO (UFWOC), had no alternative but to take on the entire grape industry by organizing a national boycott of grapes. Dolores Huerta served as director of the table-grape boycott for New York City and was designated East Coast boycott coordinator in 1968. Through Huerta's initiatives in New York, the primary distribution center for grapes, Hispanic associations, unions, activists, peace groups, religious supporters, and concerned consumers were mobilized, which ultimately contributed to the success of the national boycott. A year later, California table-grape growers bowed to the pressure exerted on them by this grassroots coalition and negotiated the historic table-grape contracts of 1970.

As she rose through the ranks of labor reform, Dolores Huerta had to fight not only the aggressive California agribusiness but also gender and ethnic discrimination. In New York, during the table-grape boycott, Huerta came in contact with the nascent feminist movement through Gloria Steinem. As a result of this exposure to women who were fighting for equal rights, she began to incorporate a feminist sensibility into her human rights agenda. For her work toward gender equality, Huerta has been the recipient of numerous women's awards. She is an important role model for women, particularly Mexican-American women, in the United States.

In the 1970s, Huerta returned to New York to oversee the lettuce, grape, and Gallo wine boycotts, which culminated in the passage of the Agricultural Labor Relations Act (ALRA) in 1975, the first law to recognize the collective-bargaining rights of farm-workers in California. While dividing her time between boycotts, extensive travel, and speaking engagements, Huerta became romantically involved with Richard Chávez, Cesar Chávez's brother, and the couple had four children together. During the 1970s the United Farm Workers (UFW), a member union of the AFL-CIO, was formed, with Cesar Chávez as president. In the late-1970s, Huerta became director of the UFW's political arm, the Citizenship Participation Day Department (CPDD), and fought to win greater support for the new farm-labor law among legislators in Sacramento.

In the 1980s, Dolores Huerta's busy schedule of speaking engagements, fund-raising events, and labor initiatives continued unabated. She helped launch another UFW project, Radio Campesina, KUFW, the United Farm Workers' radio station. She also publicized the renewed grape boycotts of the 1980s and testified before state and congressional committees on numerous issues, including the health problems of field-workers, the hazards of pesticides, Hispanic political concerns, and immigration policy. In 1988, Huerta suffered a near fatal injury at a peaceful demonstration against the campaign platform of then presidential candidate George Bush. Police officers clubbed her with batons, and she had to undergo emergency surgery to remove her spleen. She received a record financial settlement for this personal assault. While recovering from her injuries in the early 1990s, Dolores Huerta gradually resumed her efforts on behalf of farmworkers. She has received numerous awards for her efforts and has inspired Chicano murals.

34

Federico F. Peña

1947–

Federico F. Peña was born on March 15, 1947, in Laredo, Texas, to Gustavo Peña, a broker for a cotton manufacturer, and Lucia (Farias) Peña. Federico enjoyed a comfortable childhood in Brownsville, Texas, with his five siblings, three of them triplets His parents encouraged the children to excel in school and in sports, and they stressed loyalty, perseverance, respect for others, and civic responsibility. All of the Peña boys, including Federico, were altar boys at the Sacred Heart Catholic Church in Brownsville and attended St. Joseph's Academy, a local high school.

By his own admission, Federico Peña had to work harder in school than his classmates to get good grades. Nevertheless, members of his St. Joseph's class voted him "most likely to succeed." After graduating with honors, he went on to the University of Texas at Austin, where he received a B.A. degree in 1969. He then entered the University of Texas School of Law and was awarded a J.D. degree in 1972.

After finishing law school, Federico Peña moved to Denver, where his brother Alfredo practiced law. When Federico passed the Colorado bar exam, the brothers formed a law partnership, Peña and Peña, in 1973. From 1972 to 1974, Federico Peña also worked as a staff attorney for the Mexican-American Legal Defense and Educational Fund (MALDEF), pushing for voting rights for Latinos and handling police-brutality cases. He then worked as a staff attorney for the Chicano Education Project (CEP), which sought to provide equal educational opportunities for Chicanos in Colorado. For four years Peña advocated bilingual education and better funding of public schools in Latino neighborhoods.

In 1977, as the CEP was drawing to a close, Peña campaigned for a seat in the Colorado House of Representatives, representing Denver's heavily Latino Northwest Side. He was successful in his bid for the seat, became a respected legislator, and was named outstanding Democratic freshman by the Colorado Social Action Committee. After his reelection in 1980 colleagues voted Peña minority speaker, and in 1981 they chose him as the outstanding legislator of the year. During his terms of office Peña belonged to the Chicano Caucus, comprised of elected officials from the Colorado legislature. Among the caucus members was a highly popular Latino legislator, the late Richard Castro, who would become one of Peña's closet friends and advisers and would prove indispensable to Peña's political success on two occasions. The first was just after Peña joined the legislature. Representative Castro, next in line for the post of assistant minority leader, stepped aside to make way for Representative Peña, who, as a result, gained recognition and admiration within the Democratic party.

In 1982, having served for four relatively quiet years in the state legislature, Federico Peña announced his intention to run for mayor of Denver in the 1983 election. He faced a formidable field of candidates, including the fourteen-year incumbent William McNichols Jr., at a time when much of the nation was enthralled with Reagan-style conservatism. When the young liberal attorney announced his candidacy, one poll reported that he had barely 3 percent of the electorate behind him. To political observers Peña's chances for victory seemed remote. Then, on Christmas Eve in 1982, a blizzard hit Denver, and the political climate of the city changed dramatically. More than three feet of snow fell before the mayor's Office of Emergency Preparedness was activated, making snow removal virtually impossible.

Outraged voters and business leaders considered the administration's languid response to the blizzard symptomatic of its political inertia. Voters began to notice the dynamic Federico Peña, with his campaign slogan Imagine a Great City and his vision of Denver as a major center of business and commerce. Peña persuaded diverse groups, such as mainstream liberals and moderates, the city's minorities, women's rights advocates, leaders of Denver's financial district, and local labor unions, to give him their vote. In the general election Peña and another candidate came out ahead, but neither carried more than 50 percent of the vote. A runoff election was held the following month, and Peña won with 51.5 percent of the vote. With this victory he became the first Latino to be elected mayor of a city without a large Latino voting bloc, Denver's first Latino chief administrator, and one of the nation's few Latino mayors.

The new mayor's efforts to get his ambitious expansion program off the ground were stymied by a troubled economy. As unemployment doubled in Denver and the vacancy rate in downtown commercial property skyrocketed, Mayor Peña's popularity plummeted. By the time he ran for reelection in 1987 his voter appeal was so low that in the primary election Peña got only 37 percent of the vote, finishing second to Denver attorney Donald Bain. Richard Castro, Peña's ally from the Chicano Caucus, came to his aid for the second time and won Latino voters over to the Peña camp. Peña garnered enough support in the Latino and African-American precincts of Denver to win him reelection on June 16.

With the economy on the mend during his second term, Mayor Peña could finally deliver on his major campaign promises. He completed many projects which would help transform Denver into a major trade and commercial center poised for the next century, among them a new $3.1 billion Denver International Airport and a new convention center. He also brought a National League baseball franchise to Denver, allocated $220 million for parks and recreation improvements, converted abandoned houses into habitable dwellings, and promoted the use of deoxygenated fuels to help reduce air pollution in Denver.

In his second term Peña regained his popularity, but he declined to seek a third term in 1991. He decided it was time to concentrate on increasing his income and to devote more time to his family. In May 1988, Peña had married Ellen Hart, a Harvard-educated lawyer, and the couple had two daughters, Nelia and Cristina. Upon stepping down as mayor, Peña founded Peña Investment Advisors, Inc., a corporate pension management company, for which he recruited top-notch Latino lawyers and business pundits. He also served as counsel for a prominent Denver law firm and as a member of a Colorado state commission that drew up a twenty-year plan to improve the public transportation system.

In 1992, Peña served on President Clinton's transition team, handling transportation issues. Although he said privately that a post with the new administration did not interest him, he accepted the president's invitation to become U.S. secretary of transportation. Clinton had been impressed with Peña's ability to win support for the Denver International Airport and wanted to appoint a second Latino to his cabinet. As U.S. secretary of transportation, Peña is responsible for allocating approximately $30 billion to highway repairs and the development of new environmentally friendly transportation systems.

In his first months in office, Secretary Peña was absorbed in issues concerning the beleaguered airline industry. In February 1993 he sanctioned the lodging of complaints against Australia and Japan for imposing restrictions on American airlines operating in their countries, acts in violation of agreements with the United States. On March 15 he approved Great Britain's bid to invest in the USAir Group, Inc. but warned that future investments hinged on greater access to Heathrow and other facilities for American aircraft. Peña also fostered the establishment of new carriers to compete with the major airlines in certain markets.

Federico Peña sits on the Colorado Board of Law Examiners and is an associate of the Harvard Center for Law and Education. He has been honored with the Grateful Appreciation Award of the Colorado Coalition for Persons with Disabilities and with the Jewish National Fund's Tree of Life Award.

35

Ellen Ochoa
1958–

Ellen Ochoa was born in Los Angeles on May 10, 1958, to Roseanne (Deardorff) Ochoa and Joseph Ochoa, a Californian of Mexican descent. Her parents divorced when she was in junior high school, and she lived with her mother, three brothers, and sister in the San Diego suburb of La Mesa, California. As Ellen was growing up, Roseanne Ochoa continually stressed academic achievement to the children. She viewed herself as a good role model for them when she started taking classes in 1959 at San Diego State University and twenty-three years later graduated with a triple major in business, journalism, and biology.

Her mother's commitment to education had a profound effect on Ellen, who devoted herself wholeheartedly to her schoolwork and showed a fine command of all academic subjects, with exceptional ability in math and science. Ellen was consistently at the head of her class, and in junior high school she was honored as outstanding seventh- and eighth-grade student.It was then that she discovered her special aptitude for mathematics. Although she watched all the *Apollo* moon landings on television in her childhood, she never dreamed that someday she would apply her strong math background to space travel. In the July 13, 1990, issue of *USA Today* she said: "Being an astronaut wasn't something I'd considered as a career or something I decided to do when I was 8. It's a way to use math in an interesting way." Ellen excelled in other subjects besides mathematics; at age thirteen she captured first place in the San Diego spelling bee championship. She also took an active interest in music and won praise as a flutist at Grossmont High School. Ellen was such a talented musician that in 1983 she was the student soloist winner at a competition sponsored by the Stanford Symphony Orchestra.

Ochoa was selected valedictorian of Grossmont High and went on to San Diego State University, where she was awarded a B.A. degree in physics and was again chosen valedictorian of her class. As an undergraduate she changed her major five times before finally committing to physics. For a while she considered pursuing the flute as a career but decided to enter a field that promised much greater financial stability. On July 23, 1990, she told the *Houston Post* of her quandary during her college days: "I was interested in a lot of things. I had no strong bent in one direction. I was thinking, 'What interests me? What is challenging?' And, of course, what could get me a job later."

Upon graduating from San Diego State University, Ochoa earned a master's degree and a doctorate in electrical engineering at Stanford University, where she was awarded a Stanford Engineering Fellowship and an IBM Predoctoral Fellowship. From 1985 to 1988, Ochoa worked as a research engineer in the Imaging Technology Branch at Sandia National Laboratories in Livermore, California. Before turning thirty-three, she developed an innovative process that implements optics for image processing normally performed by computer. As a result of her groundbreaking research, Ochoa holds three patents in optical processing.

While Ochoa enjoyed research, she was still deciding which direction to take in her career when, in 1985, she heard students at Stanford discussing the NASA space program. She realized that she met all the qualifications and submitted an application for the program that year. NASA rejected her application in 1985, but with fiery determination and confidence in her abilities, Ochoa resubmitted her application each year until 1987, when she was named one of the top 100 finalists and went to work for NASA. Ellen Ochoa developed a good reputation there as a researcher and later as chief of the Intelligent Systems Technology Branch at the National Aeronautics and Space Administration/Aimes Research Center at Moffet Field Naval Air Station in Mountain View, California. In 1989 she was awarded the Hispanic Engineer National Achievement Award for most promising engineer in government.

Ochoa progressed swiftly through the ranks at NASA; before long she was supervising a large group of scientists. Her greatest achievement was being chosen from a pool of 1,945 applicants, as a member of the astronaut class of 1990, consisting of eighteen men and four other women. She was elated to learn of her selection, since she had derived inspiration from the astronaut class of 1978, among whose members were the first six women ever selected for the program, and dreamed of one day joining their ranks. She told the *Houston Post* on July 23, 1990: "That hit home for a lot of people. We realized, 'Oh, it's really open to real people—not just an elite group of test pilots.'" Upon graduating with her astronaut class as a mission specialist in 1990, Ochoa became the first Latina chosen for the space-shuttle program. In July of that same year, the National Hispanic Quincentennial Commission in Washington bestowed upon Ellen Ochoa the Pride Award for her accomplishments.

In 1990, Ochoa married Coe Fulmer Miles of Molalla, Oregon, and then reported to the Johnson Space Center in Houston for astronaut training that included classroom preparation, shuttle simulation exercises, and instruction in survival. In late 1992, Ochoa was prepared to embark in March 1993 on her first flight as civilian missions specialist, following in the footsteps of Sally Ride, the first American woman in space. Before the flight Ochoa concentrated on fulfilling the mission and was not concerned about a possible mishap despite the fact that all seven crew members, had died in the *Challenger* shuttle disaster in January 1986 when the shuttle exploded shortly after takeoff.

In April 1993, when the space shuttle *Discovery* soared from its launchpad, Ellen Ochoa became the first Latina to travel into space. She was one of two scientists on the *Discovery*'s April 8, 1993, mission to study the composition of the earth's atmosphere and measure solar activity. On that mission, Ochoa was assigned the task of releasing and later retrieving Spartan, a satellite designed to study the sun's corona and the velocity and acceleration of the solar wind. On April 11, 1993, Ochoa successfully used the shuttle's robot arm to place the $6 million Spartan in a separate orbit. Two days later, as the *Discovery* sped over the South Pacific, Ochoa retrieved Spartan with the shuttle's arm and returned the satellite safely to its cradle in the ship's cargo.

36

Martin Sheen

1940–

The seventh of ten children, Martin Sheen was born Ramón Estévez on August 3, 1940, in Dayton, Ohio. His father, Francisco Estévez, emigrated from Vigo, Spain, by way of Cuba, and his mother, Mary Ann (Phelan) Estévez, came from Ireland. Ramón's mother passed away when he was eleven years old, and Francisco Estévez, a drill-press operator, feared he would have to split up the large family. With help from a local parish, the Estévez clan managed to stay together. As a boy, Ramón earned pocket money caddying at a local country club and collected empty bottles to pay admission to the Saturday movie matinee. He attended a parochial school run by the Sisters of Notre Dame, and every morning before classes, he was an altar boy at a traditional Latin mass.

At Chaminade High School, taught by the Marinist fathers, Ramón took a keen interest in drama, and by age seventeen he had acted in fourteen high school plays. Nearing his high school graduation, Ramón appeared on a local talent show, *The Rising Generation*, and gave a dramatic reading from the Book of Genesis, winning first prize—a trip to New York City and an audition at CBS Television. Francisco Estévez wanted his son to go on to college after finishing high school, but Ramón dreamed of an acting career. Rather than offend his father by refusing to pursue college, Ramón purposely flunked his college entrance exams, and with the bus fare given to him by a priest from his parish church, he left Dayton for New York City.

Ramón Estévez arrived in New York on February 1, 1959, and went to work as a night-shift stock boy at American Express, making the rounds of auditions by day. Fearing ethnic typecasting, Ramón soon assumed a more Anglo-sounding name. His first name metamorphosed into "Martin" in honor of Robert Dale Martin, the casting director at CBS who had encouraged the young hopeful, and "Estévez" became "Sheen" as a tribute to Bishop Fulton J. Sheen, a prominent Roman Catholic leader of the day. In New York, Martin Sheen became the quintessential struggling young actor. With no money for acting lessons, he and friends formed the Actors' Co-Op and performed showcase presentations. Barbra Streisand, another undiscovered actress, participated in the group. Before long Martin Sheen began work as a stagehand and property master for an avant-garde off-off-Broadway troupe, Julian Beck and Judith Malina's Living Theater, sharing the labor with another struggling actor, Al Pacino.

In 1959, Martin Sheen made his New York stage debut in the role of Ernie in the Living Theater's production of *The Connection*, Jack Gelber's controversial play about drug addiction. At a backstage party for the cast of *The Connection* in 1961, Sheen met Janet Templeton, a student at the New School for Social Research. He took her along when *The Connection* went on tour to London. They married in the United States on December 23, 1961. Sheen juggled casting calls and odd jobs to meet expenses, and in 1962, the Sheens' first of four children, Emilio (later known as the actor Emilio Estévez), was born; another boy, Ramón (who would also become an actor), followed. Martin delivered Ramón at home because the family could not afford medical care and nearly lost both mother and child in the difficult delivery. The couple would have two more children, Charlie and Renee, who both went into acting as well.

By 1963, Sheen's career was on the upswing. He landed a part in a segment of the television series *East Side, West Side*, starring George C. Scott. In 1964, Sheen made his Broadway debut in Jerry Devine's farce *Never Live Over a Pretzel Factory*, about three men trying to put together an art film in which an alcoholic Hollywood veteran stars. The play received mediocre reviews and closed after eight days, and Sheen went on to costar that year with Jack Albertson and Irene Dailey in *The Subject Was Roses*, Frank Gilroy's Pulitzer Prize–winning play. Sheen and Albertson were nominated for Tonys, and Albertson walked away with the coveted award. After this experience, Sheen would consistently withdraw his name from award nominations.

By the mid-1960s Martin Sheen was active in television as well as theater. In 1967 the actor landed the role of Jack Dawn on the daytime soap opera *As the World Turns*. He also appeared in productions of Joseph Papp's New York Shakespeare Festival, including a controversial, modern version of *Hamlet* in the 1967–68 season in which Sheen played the Dane as a Puerto Rican janitor and *Romeo and Juliet* in the 1968–69 season. While critics disapproved of the interpretation of Hamlet, they applauded Sheen's performance.

Meanwhile, Sheen had begun to make movies. In 1967, he won his first feature-film role, portraying a drunken hoodlum who terrorizes New York subway passengers in *The Incident*. As more roles began to materialize in the late 1960s, Sheen led a bicoastal life, regularly traveling between Los Angeles and his home in New York. He acted in a 1968 film version of *The Subject Was Roses* and won a minor part in the screen adaptation of Joseph Heller's surreal novel *Catch-22*, filmed in Guaymas, Mexico, and released in 1970. During shooting in 1969, he fell in love with warm weather and decided to relocate the Sheen clan to California, settling in Malibu. George C. Scott soon lured Sheen back to the New York stage for the 1969 Off-Broadway production of Athel Fugard's *Hello and Goodbye*. The play closed after only forty-five performances, and Sheen headed westward again.

Back on the West Coast, Martin Sheen came into his own in

several high-quality television movies and miniseries, including *Goodbye, Raggedy Ann* (1971), *Mongo's Back in Town* (1971), and *Welcome Home, Johnny Bristol* (1971). In 1972, he and Hal Brooks appeared as two gay men in *That Certain Summer,* television's first honest and compassionate portrayal of homosexuality. Although some of the press maligned the movie for its gay content, *That Certain Summer* was among the most celebrated films of 1972. Sheen was nominated for an Emmy Award for his performance, but as usual he withdrew his name from the list of nominees. His next projects included the 1972 motion picture *Rage,* costarring George C. Scott, and the 1973 low-budget film *Badlands,* in which the actor portrayed a mass murderer. *Badlands* enjoyed favorable reviews from critics but had a modest box-office turnout due to its violent content. In 1973, Sheen also starred in the film adaptation of Brian Moore's novella *Catholics,* and in 1974 he acted in the television movie *The Missiles of October,* NBC's reenactment of the 1962 Cuban Missile Crisis.

In 1974, Sheen was cast in two more television movies: *The Execution of Private Slovik,* the saga of the only American soldier shot for desertion since the Civil War, and *The Story of Pretty Boy Floyd,* also starring his brother Joseph Estévez. He later landed the role of Ben Willard in Francis Ford Coppola's 1979 film *Apocalypse Now.* The film was shot in the Philippines in grueling conditions, and toward its completion Sheen suffered a heart attack. He arrived at the hospital near death and asked for a priest to administer the last rites. His brother was flown in to act as his stand-in while he recuperated for three weeks in the hospital, surrounded by concerned family members. *Apocalypse Now* was a commercial and critical success and captured nominations for Academy Awards in eight categories, including one for Sheen for Best Actor.

After the filming of *Apocalypse Now,* Martin Sheen fell into a deep depression that lasted until 1981. For three months he lived apart from his wife and children and went on a drinking binge that led to his being sent to jail for swinging at a police officer. In spite of his emotional instability, he continued to act, and in 1980 costarred with Katharine Ross in *The Final Countdown.* In 1982, Sheen was cast in *Gandhi* as a Western journalist who traces Mahatma Gandhi's career during numerous visits to India. Sheen was struck by the spirituality and abject poverty of India, and the trip restored the faith he had lost in the 1960s. He began to practice religion again, mixing Roman Catholicism with his belief in reincarnation.

As his spirituality grew, so did his involvement in social and political issues. He donated his $100,000 salary for *Gandhi* to the charity Concern, which aids refugees in third-world countries. He returned his salary to the producers of the 1982 film *In the King of Prussia* and donated his services to the 1983 PBS production *No Place to Hide.* In the 1980s, Sheen took a stand on such issues as nuclear disarmament, rights for the homeless, American involvement in Central America, apartheid in South Africa, and AIDS, and his participation in protests frequently landed him behind bars. In 1986, Sheen had the opportunity to combine his activism and acting in the TV movie *Samaritan: The Mitch Snyder Story,* about the advocate for the homeless.

In 1991, Sheen took the stage again to play the hero in the National Actors Theater production of Arthur Miller's *Crucible.* That year he also directed sons Charlie Sheen and Ramón Estévez for the first time in the films *Cadence* and *Republic.* In 1991, Martin Sheen also filmed *Children of the Lie,* a public-service movie on domestic violence, and narrated the documentary *Children of the Cradle,* about Iraqi children who died in great numbers from severe malnutrition after the Persian Gulf War. In 1993 the actor played Robert E. Lee in *Gettysburg,* the cinematic re-creation of the battle that was the turning point in the Civil War.

Martin Sheen will undoubtedly grace the screen for years to come. In a *TV Guide* interview in 1975, he told Dwight Whitney: "People think acting is an accident. It's not. It's calculated, planned, scrutinized, rehearsed. A performer has to know what he's doing every instant, to invent and improvise, and feel, to bleed a little or else there's no growth....God, how I love to act!"

37

José Quintero
1924–

One of three children, José Benjamin Quintero was born in Panama City, Panama, on October 15, 1924, the day before Eugene O'Neill celebrated his thirty-seventh birthday and was poised to write the play *The Great God Brown*. Later, Quintero would make a habit of celebrating both October 15 and October 16. He was born into an upper-class family headed by Carlos Rivera, of peasant stock, and Consuelo (Palmorala) Quintero, who came from an aristocratic family. Carlos Rivera was in the cattle and brewery businesses and also held a high-ranking post in the Panamanian government. He was extremely disappointed at the birth of José; he had wanted a girl and was shocked that his son's skin was a shade darker than that of other family members. Quintero would later say: "From birth I was branded a disaster." Carlos Rivera tortured the young José with the knowledge that his birth was unwelcome, and the boy was stricken with fear upon finding it impossible to win his father's favor.

José attended LaSalle Catholic High School, where he disliked most of his subjects and often came home from school with his clothes covered with ink stains. While at LaSalle he displayed a talent for decorating altars and gravitated toward the priesthood. He began to read religious texts such as the *Lives of the Saints,* and *Quo Vadis,* but his attention was diverted by the Bette Davis films that made their way to Panama City. He changed direction and upon graduating from LaSalle High School in 1943, convinced his sullen father to send him to Los Angeles City College. Carlos Rivera expected his son to study medicine, but José had no interest in the field and spent his time watching films and studying acting. In Los Angeles, José saw his first play, *Life With Father,* though he only understood one word: "God." When his English had improved, he went to see Emlyn Williams's *Corn Is Green* every night during its two-week run in Los Angeles. After two years at Los Angeles City College, Quintero returned to Panama to look for a job and ran into trouble because his work identity card listed his color as "brown," which barred him from certain white-collar jobs. His infuriated father stepped in to rectify the situation.

Having failed at a number of jobs, Quintero returned to the United States, where he enrolled at the University of Southern California to pursue acting. Soon he received a letter from his father containing $500 and a note with a warning not to ask for another cent and the vitriol words "I once had a son whose name was the same as the one you bear, but as far as I am concerned, he is dead." Abandoned, but freed from his father's stranglehold, Quintero graduated with a B.A. degree in 1948 from the University of Southern California and went on to the Goodman Theatre Dramatic School in Chicago. There he met the budding actress Geraldine Page, whose performance in a school production of *The Sea Gull* he found impressive. In the summer of 1949,

Quintero accompanied other drama students as they journeyed east to Woodstock, New York. At the Woodstock Summer Theater he directed his first plays: *The Glass Menagerie* by Tennessee Williams and *Riders to the Sea* by John Millington Synge. The group made a profit by the end of the summer, and with a leap of faith they decided to continue as the Loft Players in New York City.

In 1950, with about $7,500 they had raised from philanthropic friends, the group took over the padlocked Greenwich Village Inn, a nightclub near Sheridan Square that had shut down. When they christened the theater Circle in the Square, little did they know it would become Off-Broadway's most important stage. The Loft Players were comprised of fourteen members, among them Emilie Stevens, Jason Wingreen and Ted Mann, and each took part-time jobs so that they could devote time each day to performing. Beginning in 1950, Quintero was invited to observe the open classes of Martha Graham, whom he considers not only a dancer and a choreographer but one of our greatest directors

As their debut, the Loft Players decided to revive the Berney-Richardson musical fantasy *Dark of the Moon*. The night before they were to begin rehearsals, no one had volunteered to direct, and to resolve the problem, the group bought a bottle of wine. After drinking its contents, they played spin the bottle to choose a director. The bottle pointed at Quintero, and the rest is history. In an article published in the *New York Times* in 1988, Quintero spoke of that first directorial experience at Circle in the Square: "The young director had no recourse but to initiate a fearful journey inward, an exploration of the world within him, where he begins to find the materials of his real identity. Daily, he comes to rehearsals; filled with shame and terror at first, he reveals a raw piece of himself, whose texture matches, and therefore illuminates, a patch of reality of the play." *Dark of the Moon,* a theater-in-the-round production, opened in February 1951 and ran for eight weeks, reaping plaudits from critics and winning four Off-Broadway awards.

That first year, Quintero directed numerous productions, including *The Bonds of Interest* by Jacinto Benavente, *The Enchanted* by Jean Giraudoux, and *Yerma* by Federico García Lorca. In the spring of 1952 the Loft Players produced *Burning Bright* by John Steinbeck. Quintero then cast Geraldine Page in the lead in his

1952 revival of *Summer and Smoke* by Tennessee Williams. Top Broadway drama critics applauded the Off-Broadway production, firmly establishing the reputation of Geraldine Page and giving birth to the Off-Broadway theater movement in New York City. Theaters began popping up all over Greenwich Village and lower Second Avenue, and Off-Broadway thrived.

In the early 1950s, Quintero mainly directed the works of such prominent American writers and dramatists as Tennessee Williams and Truman Capote. In 1953, Quintero revived *The Grass Harp* by Truman Capote to the accolades of the critics and the public, and the production fared better than it had on Broadway. In November 1953 the Loft Players produced *American Gothic*, a dramatization by Victor Wolfson of his novel *The Lonely Steeple*, and the production ran until early 1954. Meanwhile, Quintero was hard at work directing Jane Bowles's *In the Summer House*. He was asked to step in when the play was already in rehearsal and had just three weeks to get it ready for a Broadway opening in December 1953. At the same time, Quintero was directing the dramatization of Alfred Hayes's novel *The Girl on the Via Flaminia*, which received many favorable reviews for direction when it opened in February 1954.

Then, in 1956, three years after Eugene O'Neill's death, Quintero decided to revive the neglected playwright's *The Iceman Cometh*. First he had to secure the rights to the play. He approached O'Neill's widow, Carlotta Monterrey O'Neill, who was her husband's sole heir and literary executor. During their meeting she took out four hatboxes and asked Quintero to choose the one he most fancied. With a high sense of drama she carefully opened the boxes individually and paraded each hat as Quintero, in deep concentration, rejected one after the other. Finally, Carlotta O'Neill removed the fourth hat from its box and placed it on her head. Quintero declared it his favorite, and Carlotta O'Neill responded that the rights to produce *The Iceman Cometh* were his, for he had selected the hat she had worn at her husband's funeral. The production of *The Iceman Cometh* won resounding applause and the Vernon Rice Award for the director, establishing Quintero's reputation and restoring Eugene O'Neill's status as a major American playwright.

Carlotta O'Neill was so pleased with Quintero's work that she broke Eugene O'Neill's twenty-five-year seal and granted Circle in the Square permission to stage *Long Day's Journey Into Night*.

O'Neill had wanted all of his parents' friends and relatives to be dead before his agonizing family saga was produced. *Long Day's Journey Into Night* opened on Broadway in November 1956, starring Fredric March, and garnered the *Variety* Award and a Tony Award for its director. After *Long Day's Journey Into Night*, Quintero forged a close relationship with Carlotta O'Neill and gained much intimate knowledge of O'Neill's life from the widow. In the ensuing years the director and Circle in the Square presented more productions of O'Neill's plays than any other theater in the world.

In the 1960s, Circle in the Square was moved to Bleecker Street and Quintero produced new plays like Jean Genet's *Balcony*, Athol Fugard's *Boesman and Lena*, and *Plays for Bleecker Street*, which Thornton Wilder wrote specifically for Circle in the Square. In 1961, Quintero and Ted Mann opened the Circle in the Square School where, for many years after, Quintero conducted classes in directing. In 1961, Quintero, whose closest bonds had been with men, began a long relationship with a former advertising executive named Nick Tsacrios. Tsacrios sacrificed his future in advertising to help Quintero handle the business end of his career. In 1963 the Loft Players staged a revival of *Desire Under the Elms* with Colleen Dewhurst and George C. Scott.

In 1966, having directed six O'Neill plays, Quintero went to Mexico to work on a production of *Camille*. For years he had directed productions in a half-drunken state, for, like O'Neill, Quintero suffered from alcoholism. The producer of *Camille* was the husband of the Mexican star who played the lead, and he did not like the way Quintero, who was a little drunk, demonstrated for the actor playing Armand how Camille should be embraced. The following day, Quintero was arrested outside the theater and driven to police headquarters. After Nick Tsacrios made a telephone call to the Panamanian embassy, Quintero was released with no explanation, and the production was terminated. He felt guilty over the episode, and as repentance he drove to the site of the shrine of the Virgin of Guadalupe, where, in keeping with custom, he crawled on his knees up the long flight of stairs to the shrine as Tsacrios walked at his side. Quintero had padded his knees with cloth, but they were bloodied.

In 1967, Quintero returned to New York to direct the unfinished O'Neill play *More Stately Mansions*. Though he had reservations about the play, his drinking had worsened, and he needed the money. He was able to convince Ingrid Bergman to star as Deborah Harford. The production failed, and Quintero's drinking became more destructive. Around this time, the director was also profoundly affected by the mental and emotional collapse of Carlotta O'Neill. Upon his return from Mexico, he found her in a mental hospital, and in her final years she had terrifying conversations with O'Neill's ghost for having broken the seal on *Long Day's Journey Into Night*. In 1970, Carlotta O'Neill died, and Quintero was devastated by the loss.

In 1972, Circle in the Square moved to Broadway. A year later, José Quintero staged O'Neill's *Moon for the Misbegotten*, with two of his favorite stars, Colleen Dewhurst and Jason Robards Jr. It was a successful revival, which Quintero called the "resurrection company," for the director felt a sense of rebirth. For his effort Quintero was honored with a Tony Award and Drama Desk Awards in 1973 and 1974. Before rehearsals began, he had been freed from his drinking habit with the help of Vincent Tracy, a layman who had invented a treatment for alcoholism. After the success of *A Moon for the Misbegotten*, Quintero and Nick Tsacrios moved to San Juan, where they enjoyed the quiet, the year-round gardening, and the gambling. In 1974, Quintero published a memoir entitled *If You Don't Dance, They Beat You*. In 1977, he directed his tenth O'Neill play and the last remaining challenge of the O'Neill repertory, *A Touch of the Poet*, which had been a disappointment when it premiered on Broadway in 1958. Quintero's revival was an overwhelming success.

In 1980, Quintero directed Tennessee Williams's play *Camino Real* at Circle in the Square. In 1986 he started a three-year project to translate Eugene O'Neill for radio, which grew out of his displeasure with previous radio productions of O'Neill's plays in which actors were made to stand and speak into the microphone. Quintero allowed his actors to move about; his productions of *The Hairy Ape* and *S.S. Glencairn: Four Plays of the Sea* for National Public Radio garnered applause when they aired in 1989. In 1987, Quintero was diagnosed as having throat cancer and had to have his vocal chords removed. Upon hearing the news, he thought first of O'Neill, who in the last ten years of his life suffered from a nervous disorder preventing him from writing, which essentially meant the end of his creative output. Quintero's fate was not O'Neill's, and with an instrument to magnify his voice, he returned to directing.

In 1988, Quintero continued his all-consuming explorations of O'Neill and directed his seventeenth production of O'Neill's plays, a revival of *Long Day's Journey Into Night* for the centennial of the playwright's birth. It opened to high critical acclaim and played in repertory at the Neil Simon Theatre as part of the first New York International Festival. Concerning the production he told the *New York Times*: "You are more prone to loud statements when you are younger. I think I have grown toward greater simplicity."

38

Richard Rodriguez

1944–

 One of four children, Richard Rodriguez was born on July 31, 1944, in San Francisco, California, to Leopoldo Rodriguez, a dental technician, and Victoria (Moran) Rodriguez, a clerk typist. Richard was born just a few years after his working-class parents emigrated from Mexico to the United States. When he was three years old, the family moved to Sacramento, where they settled in a primarily Anglo neighborhood. Richard spoke only Spanish at home as a small child and was keenly aware that his family was different from those on his street. Wishing to fit in, six-year-old Richard once tried to scrape the brown off his skin with his father's razor. But he would soon find a one-way ticket to the American mainstream in the classroom. When Richard, barely able to speak English, entered a Catholic grade school in Sacra-

184

mento, the tough-minded Irish nuns—the Sisters of Mercy— gave him strict lessons on how to navigate in English, thus opening wide the doors of assimilation. The nuns even insisted that Richard's parents speak English at home to ease the boy's linguistic burden. Richard learned those American lessons so well that he became alienated from his parents' comfortable Spanish world.

A superb student, Richard stood out from his peers at Bishop Armstrong High School. He was admitted to Stanford University in Palo Alto, where he was not held to the same standards as the white students and was pigeonholed as the Spanish-speaking student, the disadvantaged one, by his college teachers. Rodriguez earned a B.A. degree from Stanford in 1967. Although his grades were not outstanding, the country's top graduate schools beckoned him to enroll, and Rodriguez entered the master's program in philosophy at Columbia University, where he received his M.A. degree in 1969. With his master's in hand, he went on to the doctoral program in English at the University of California at Berkeley. He spent four years at Berkeley and then one year at the Warburg Institute in London on a Fulbright fellowship, working toward his degree. While on the Fulbright, he visited Ireland, the native land of the Sisters of Mercy, and felt that he had come home. After he returned to Berkeley, Rodriguez completed his dissertation on English Renaissance literature.

Disconsolate over the loss of ethnic identity he had suffered as part and parcel of his inevitable Americanization, he chose not to submit the dissertation. He also turned down several offers, extended due to affirmative action, for university teaching posts, including an an invitation from Yale University. He could not bear the irony of being considered a minority when he had striven successfully to assimilate into mainstream America and become one of the majority. He informed the universities of his decision in letters to the chairs of all the English departments that had selected him, believing they had filled the quota set by affirmative action. Rodriguez turned his back on the relatively secure life of an academic for a riskier career doing freelance writing and working on his autobiography. The National Endowment for the Humanities awarded him a fellowship, which helped him through the first year of writing the autobiography, entitled *Hunger of Memory: The Education of Richard Rodriguez.*

Published in 1982, *Hunger of Memory* chronicles Rodriguez's voyage through the American educational system to acculturation, which produced both painful alienation from the Spanish language, Mexican culture, and his immigrant parents, and resulted in liberation and power derived from full access to public life. In the book he writes: "If I rehearse here the changes in my private life after my Americanization, it is finally to emphasize the public gain. The loss implies the gain: The house I returned to each afternoon was quiet.... Once I learned the public language, it would never again be easy for me to hear intimate family voices." In *Hunger of Memory*, Rodriguez criticizes bilingual education for depriving children of the lessons they need to succeed in mainstream society. In an interview in *Publisher's Weekly* in 1982, Rodriguez elaborated on the hazards of bilingual education: "To me public educators in a public schoolroom have an obligation to teach a public language.... For Mexican-Americans it is the language of *los gringos*. For Appalachian children who speak a fractured English or Black children in a ghetto, the problem is the same, it seems to me.... My argument has always been that the imperative is to get children away from those languages that increase their sense of alienation from the public society."

For his views on bilingual education and affirmative action, Rodriguez received much criticism, particularly from the university educated of the Left, who accused him of being a "Tio Tom" and an "ethnic self-hater." As he spoke at universities and colleges across the nation, the writer was heckled and shouted down for his controversial views. *Hunger of Memory* also stirred rage in many Latinos, particularly Mexican Americans, who, as Richard Rodriguez told the *Los Angeles Times*, "thought the book was about self-hate and shame at being Mexican. I thought it was about social class: What does it mean to have parents who are unable to read the books you are reading in high school, who are unable to share your thoughts?"

Rodriguez's haunting memoir elicited praise from many others, particularly for its insightful examination of the impact of language on the individual, its repudiation of the prevailing ethnic ethos, and its endorsement of Americanism. For *Hunger of Memory*, Rodriguez was awarded a Gold Medal for nonfiction from the Commonwealth Club in California in 1982 and in the same year was named the recipient of the Christopher Award for autobiography and the Anisfield-Wolf Award for Civil Rights from the Cleveland Foundation. In 1982, Rodriguez embarked on a national lecture tour for the English-Speaking Union, and in 1984 he was selected as the Perlman lecturer at the University of Chicago. In the 1980s he became a journalist with the *Los Angeles Times* and the Pacific News Service, a newspaper syndication group based in San Francisco.

In 1992, President Bush bestowed on Richard Rodriguez the Charles Frankel Humanities Award from the National Endowment for the Arts. The next year, the writer published *Days of Obligation: An Argument With My Mexican Father,* a collection of loosely related essays that appeared in different form in *Harper's,* the *Los Angeles Times Sunday Magazine*, the *New Republic*, and other publications. In *Days of Obligation*, Rodriguez explores the Mexican and Californian sensibilities, touching on the themes of race and ethnicity, education and religion, introduced in *Hunger of Memory.*

In *Days of Obligation*, Rodriguez shifts his narrative continuously from the present to the past, from youth to age, as he ranges over the philosophical landscape of California and Mexico. The "argument" of the subtitle makes reference to a conversation between a man, who sides with Mexico in the belief that fate inevitably triumphs, and a boy, who is certain that California, with its endless promise and optimism, will prevail in the end: "Kodachrome, drive-in California—freeways and new cities, bright plastic pennants and spinning whirligigs announcing a subdivision of houses; hundreds of houses; houses where there used to be fields. A mall opened on Arden Way and we were first-nighters. I craved ALL-NEW and ALL-ELECTRIC, FREE-MUGS, and KOOL INSIDE and DOUBLE GREEN STAMPS, NO MONEY DOWN, WHILE-U-WAIT, ALL YOU CAN EAT." As the storyteller grows older, he feels a greater affinity to Mexico, a place steeped not in American optimism but in tragedy: "Tragic cultures serve up better food than optimistic cultures; tragic cultures have sweeter children, more opulent funerals. In tragic cultures, one does not bear the solitary burden of optimism. Now that I am middle-aged, I incline more toward the Mexican point of view, though some part of me continues to resist the cynical conclusions of Mexico."

In a poignant chapter entitled "Late Victorians" in *Days of Obligation,* Rodriguez, who makes his home in San Francisco, addresses the AIDS crisis, which has deflated the dreams of those gay hopefuls who flocked to that city "to become someone new at the edge of the sea." He also speaks of his Catholicism in *Days of Obligation*: "As a gay Catholic I am more Protestant than Catholic: I'm assuming the legitimacy of my conscience as a guide. But as a Catholic I believe in the prophetic role of the community.... The testimony of what I have learned as a gay Catholic is that suffering can redeem us."

After completing a book tour promoting *Days of Obligation*, Rodriguez returned to writing for various newspapers, including the *Los Angeles Times* and the *New York Times*. In 1994, Rodriguez wrote numerous articles published in the *Los Angeles Times*, most notably a piece on sports and morality in America in which he claims that athletes are not intrinsically moral, as Tonya Harding proved, and a story on gay men and the military in which he contends that the outcry over allowing gays to serve stems from the insecurity of heterosexual men. Rodriguez continues to write for the Pacific News Service, is a contributing editor of *Harper's* magazine, and makes frequent guest appearances as a TV essayist on the *MacNeil/Lehrer Newshour*.

39

Dennis Chávez

1888–1962

The third of eight children, Chávez was born Dionisio Chávez at Los Chávez, a small community west of Albuquerque, New Mexico, on April 8, 1888. At the time of his birth, New Mexico was still part of the U.S.-Mexican territory; not until twenty-four years had passed would it be admitted to the Union as the state of New Mexico. Dennis grew up in an impoverished Spanish-speaking household headed by his father, David Chávez, and his mother, Paz (Sanchez) Chávez, both Mexican Americans. The Chávez family moved to Albuquerque when Dennis was seven years old, affording him the opportunity to attend school, where his name was changed to Dennis.

David Chávez died when Dennis was still a boy, and after seventh grade Dennis was forced to forgo his education to work driving a grocery wagon. One day he discovered workers on a picket line at the Santa Fe Railyard. In an early demonstration of his sympathy for the downtrodden, he refused to cross the picket line and subsequently lost his job. He educated himself by reading history books and biographies at the Albuquerque library in the evenings. Early on, he joined the Democratic party, in part because his hero Thomas Jefferson was the party's founder. Later, he taught himself surveying and in 1905 left his job with the grocery wagon to join the Albuquerque Engineering Department as a highway worker. At this job he realized how desolate New Mexico was, particularly the region in the northern part of the state, where roads were poor or nonexistent, an issue he would later take up in the Senate.

In 1915, Chávez left the Albuquerque Engineering Department, and in 1916 he served as a Spanish interpreter for the Democratic candidate Andrieus Jones during his successful campaign for the U.S. Senate. As a reward, Jones secured a clerkship in the Senate for the ambitious young Chávez. While clerking in 1918 and 1919, Chávez studied law at Georgetown University with the support of his wife, Imelda Espinosa, whom he married in 1911. Since he had never attended high school, Chávez had to pass a special entrance examination to study law. In 1920, he returned to Albuquerque to set up a law practice and before long had parlayed his experience in labor law, into a political career.

Among his reasons for entering the political arena was a desire to rid New Mexico of practices detrimental to the poor and working class. In the 1920s, New Mexico was run according to a patronage system, adhered to by Anglo and Latino Republicans, which funneled resources into the wealthy sections of the city and state. Dennis Chávez campaigned hard and won a seat in the state legislature in 1922. One of his first acts in the New Mexico House of Representatives was to sponsor a bill to provide free textbooks to children in poorer schools.

In 1930, Chávez was elected to the U.S. House of Representatives, easily defeating the incumbent Republican New Mexican congressman Albert Simms. In 1932 he won reelection on the Franklin D. Roosevelt ticket. But Chávez had always had his sights set on the U.S. Senate, and in 1934 he fought a hard campaign for the Senate seat of Democrat Bronson F. Cutting, a politically powerful, Harvard-educated easterner. Chávez was narrowly defeated after a confusing and bitter campaign, but he did not give up the fight.

Chávez and others challenged the legality of Cutting's reelection, carrying their case all the way to the floor of the Senate, where, in 1935, they filed a petition charging voter fraud. While the case was still pending, Cutting was killed in a plane crash, and Governor Tingley appointed Dennis Chávez to fill the vacant seat until the next election, in 1936. Despite some Democratic opposition, Chávez was in the Senate nominated and elected in 1936, defeating the popular Republican contender Miguel Otero.

Once in the Senate, Chávez became a fervent New Dealer and supporter of President Franklin D. Roosevelt's social legislation. In 1937 he defended Roosevelt's much-maligned plan to enlarge the Supreme Court in order to make it more liberal. That same year, the senator supported the Navajo Indians, who were protesting the cut in grazing stock that had been proposed for the purpose of conservation. In the late 1930s, Senator Chávez also got involved in issues pertaining to Latin America. In 1938 he made the news with the Chávez-McAdoo bill, which proposed that a federal radio station be put in operation to compete with Nazi and Fascist broadcasts to Latin America. In 1939 he also championed the benefits of closer economic ties with Latin America long before the ratification of the North American Free Trade Agreement (NAFTA). As the only Spanish-speaking senator at the time, Chávez represented the U.S. government in negotiations with Panama regarding the Panama Canal and the proposed Pan-American Highway, an international thoroughfare that would extend from the southern border of the United States to Panama.

With his hard work in the Senate, Chávez was easily re-elected in 1940 for six years on Roosevelt's third-term ticket. After his reelection, he again proved himself to be an independent thinker in foreign affairs by initially opposing the president's Lend-Lease program of 1941 to aid the Allies in World War II, in favor of neutrality, but then reversed himself on the issue. During the early 1940s, Senator Chávez also looked beyond the American mainland to Puerto Rico. In 1942, Chávez won Senate approval for a $5,000 investigation of the social and economic problems plaguing Puerto Rico, and as a result, he was nicknamed "Puerto Rico's Senator." Before the end of the year Chávez reported that

the island's problems were caused by overpopulation and the
strain of the war, and he suggested that English, rather than
Spanish, be the official language in Puerto Rican schools. School
administrators and the media in Puerto Rico opposed the English-only rule but appreciated Chávez's interest in Puerto Rico.

In the 1940s some of Senator Chávez's votes supporting
liberal social legislation displeased many constituents, but he
stuck firmly to his beliefs. One issue in particular that caused a
stir was Chávez's cosponsorship in 1943 of the Equal Rights
Amendment, which the senator advocated based on the knowledge that "wherever the common law, unmodified by statute,
exists, there injustice for women exists."

Despite the disagreements that arose among his New Mexican supporters and serious attempts to unseat him, Chávez was
reelected in 1946 and 1952. Another social issue of the 1940s that
incited much controversy and perhaps ushered in Dennis
Chávez's greatest contribution to America was civil rights. In
1947, he cosponsored a bill, the Fair Employment Practices Act,
which would prohibit discrimination on the basis of race, color,
national origin, or ancestry. The bill was defeated by southern
filibusters, but many believe that it set the stage for the passage of
the Civil Rights Act of 1964.

Another of Chávez's great triumphs in the Senate was his
successful passage of the Federal Highway Act of 1952. With his
appointment in 1947 as chair of the Senate Public Works Committee, Dennis Chávez gained control over all matters related to
federal spending on highways, which he regarded as important
links of commerce and defense. In 1952, he introduced the
Federal Highway Act, the most comprehensive bill to date on
highway improvement and over the next decade oversaw $50
billion in spending for interstate highway construction. As chair
of the Senate Public Works Committee, Chávez also obtained
funds for Forest Service and National Parks access roads, farm-
to-market routes, and highways across Native-American reservations in the West. He also obtained extensive federal funds for
New Mexico to channel into reclamation, irrigation, and flood
control.

Senator Chávez also wielded great influence in the area of
defense. Early in 1960 Chávez was selected as chair of the Defense
Appropriations Subcommittee. In this key position the senator
oversaw the spending of some $40 billion annually. He worked

vigorously in support of a billion-dollar increase in Eisenhower's 1960 defense budget. Chávez commanded the attention of the military by virtue of New Mexico's Los Alamos National Laboratory, the nation's premier weapons research and design facility and test site of the first atomic bomb. His control over these military dollars meant personal contacts with presidents which then turned into friendships, giving him even greater clout in Washington.

As one of his last acts, Chávez campaigned for President Kennedy, bringing out the Hispanic vote throughout the Southwest despite a battle with cancer that took his life in 1962. President Kennedy once said of Senator Chávez: "I came to admire him as a leading advocate of human rights and for his intense interest in the defense capability of our nation." A statue of Senator Chávez stands in the U.S. Capitol Building in tribute to his lasting achievements, and he has been lauded as a "great American" on a U.S. commemorative postage stamp.

40

Joseph M. Montoya

1915–1978

Joseph M. Montoya was born on September 24, 1915, in Peña Blanca, a small town in Sandoval County, New Mexico, to Thomas O. Montoya and Frances Montoya, descendants of eighteenth-century Spanish immigrants. His father was Sandoval County sheriff and afforded the family a modest lifestyle. Upon graduating from a predominantly Mexican-American high school in nearby Bernalillo in 1931, Joseph enrolled at Regis College in Denver, Colorado. He received his college degree in 1934 and then went on to Georgetown University Law School in

Washington, D.C., working part-time as a clerk in the Department of the Interior in order to cover his tuition and living expenses. In 1936, during his second year in law school, Montoya was elected to the New Mexico House of Representatives after a campaign conducted during summer vacation. At twenty-one years of age, he was the youngest representative in the state's history.

In 1938, Montoya was awarded an LL.B. degree from Georgetown University and was reelected to his seat in the New Mexico legislature. He was also named Democratic majority floor leader, the youngest ever, and served in that post in 1939 and 1940. In 1939 he was admitted to the New Mexico bar and decided to practice law in Santa Fe. Viewing political posts as stepping-stones to greater power, Montoya chose to run for a seat in the state senate in 1940. He became its youngest member and began to serve in that body in 1941. He twice was reelected to the post, serving until 1946, by which time he had attained the positions of senate majority whip and chair of the influential Senate Judiciary Committee. In 1946, Montoya ran for lieutenant governor, was elected, and served two terms, from 1947 until 1950. He did not seek reelection to any post in 1950 due to the two-term limit.

By 1952, after a two-year absence, Montoya was eager to reenter the political arena. He was elected state senator and served in that post in 1953 and 1954. In 1954 he was again elected lieutenant governor and was reelected to the post in 1956. That same year, the opportunity arose for Montoya to seek election to the U.S. Congress. Congressman Antonio Fernández, in his eighth term in office died suddenly, leaving a full-term seat vacant in the Congress. The New Mexico legislature held a special election to fill the vacancy, and Joseph Montoya, who had long aspired to serve in Congress, ran for the seat. Considered the natural replacement for Congressman Fernández, Montoya, then forty-two years old, was elected to the first of four consecutive terms in the U.S. House of Representatives in April 1957. He went immediately to Washington, where he adapted swiftly to the ways of Congress and established a reputation as a hardworking legislator and a loyal Democrat.

Montoya's efforts in Congress paid off when he was named a member of the influential House Appropriations Committee. Among his greatest accomplishments in the House were his sponsorship of the Vocational Education Act of 1963 and legislation establishing numerous wilderness preserves in the nation under the Wilderness Act of 1964. In November 1962, after being relected to a fourth term in the House of Representatives by loyal constituents in New Mexico, Congressman Montoya received word of the death of Dennis Chavez on November 18, 1962. Montoya was the natural successor to Dennis Chavez in the Senate, but he was challenged by Republican governor Edwin L. Mechem, who resigned his post so that his lieutenant governor, who subsequently became governor, could appoint him to the U.S. Senate. Mechem won Dennis Chavez's senate seat in 1962, but Joseph Montoya refused to acknowledge defeat and launched an intensive campaign for the post in 1964. He was able to convince the state legislature to pass legislation adopting the preprimary convention, which ensured that the party organization would certify candidates for the primary election. By doing so, Montoya discouraged opposition in the 1964 Democratic party. With a united party to back him and adequate financial resources, he posed a threat to incumbent senator Mechem and won the election by a clear margin.

Elected to serve in the unexpired term of Senator Chavez as well as in a separate term commencing on January 3, 1965, Montoya assumed office the day after the election, on November 4, 1964. Thus, he had the advantage of seniority and tenure over the senators elected in 1964. He quickly involved himself in committee work in the Senate and was appointed to the Senate Agriculture Committee, where he backed consumer protection legislation; he was soon considered the expert on the packing, inspection, and regulation of meat. Senator Montoya authored and sponsored legislation that was instrumental in improving the unhealthy practices in meatpacking houses, including the Wholesome Meat Act of 1967, the Wholesome Poultry Act of 1968, and the Clean Hot Dog Act of 1974. He also pushed for other agriculture-related legislation, such as the Screw Worm Eradication Bill of 1973.

In the 1970s the senator was appointed to the Public Works Committee and chaired the Economic Development Subcommittee, which sponsored the legislation that created the Economic Development Administration, a source of federal assistance for many underdeveloped areas of the nation. In terms of civil rights Montoya sponsored the Congressional Youth Political Participation Act of 1974. He was a fervent supporter of the Voting Rights

Act of 1965, the open-housing legislation of 1968, and the voting-rights amendments of 1970 and 1975. A friend of the elderly, Montoya supported Medicare, Medicaid, and several other bills providing health care to senior citizens. He also advocated measures to help Native Americans and in 1971 sponsored the Indian Education Act.

Montoya worked hard to end discrimination against Latinos and improve their quality of life not only in the Southwest but all across America. Senator Montoya ardently supported legislation to expand educational opportunities to Latinos, such as the Bilingual Education Act of 1968 and amendments to it in 1974. He authored and sponsored the bill establishing the Cabinet Committee on Opportunities for the Spanish-Speaking, another for the training of bilingual persons in the health professions, and one that created a Commission of Alien Labor in 1974. In addition, Montoya proposed legislation creating National Hispanic Heritage Week. He was committed to preserving the cultural, linguistic, and ethnic heritage of Hispanics across America. Since Montoya was the only Spanish-speaking member of the U.S. Senate, the White House often requested that he represent the United States at international conferences. During his tenure in the Senate, Montoya served as a delegate at several annual Mexico–United States Interparliamentary Conferences and played a crucial role in strengthening relations between the two nations.

By 1976, when he sought a third term of office, Montoya already wielded a great deal of power on Capitol Hill and was on his way to becoming one of the most influential senators in Washington. He was both a member of the powerful Senate Appropriations Committee and the third-ranking member of the Public Works Committee. He was poised to become vice chairman of the Joint Committee on Atomic Energy, of vital importance to the senator, since there were atomic-energy programs at Los Alamos and Sandia Laboratories in New Mexico. Through participation in various committees and subcommittees he could exert influence on a specific program or proposal from various angles.

Despite his increasing power in the Senate, Montoya's popularity waned in the mid-1970s, and he was defeated for reelection in 1976 by the former astronaut Harrison Schmitt. In part, Montoya was a victim of the anti-Washington sentiment sweeping the nation in 1976 in the aftermath of the Watergate scandal. Furthermore, the media in New Mexico had waged an aggressive anti-Montoya campaign, accusing the senator of conflict of interest in his personal business investments, which inflicted extensive damage to his political career. As Joseph Montoya would later state, the defeat was a defeat for the people of New Mexico. After leaving office his health rapidly declined, and he was diagnosed with a rare liver disease. On June 5, 1978, Joseph Montoya died of liver and kidney failure.

41

Julio Iglesias
1943–

Julio Iglesias was born Julio José Iglesias de la Cueva on September 23, 1943, in Madrid, Spain. His family was headed by his father, Dr. Julio Iglesias Puga, a prominent gynecologist, and his mother, María del Rosario de la Cueva Perignat. His mother's lineage can be traced to Cuba, Puerto Rico, and Andalusia, while his paternal forebears came from Galicia in northwestern Spain. The Iglesias family settled in the upper middle class Argüelles district of Madrid, and Julio and his younger brother Carlos were enrolled at the nearby Roman Catholic school, Colegio del Sagrado Corazón. Julio performed poorly in school and was not

199

chosen for the choir, but became adept at soccer. At age sixteen he joined the junior reserve squad of the Real Madrid Club de Fútbol, Spain's premier professional soccer team. Many felt Julio had a future in the sport, but his parents insisted that he concentrate on academics.

After completing his secondary education, Julio Iglesias went on to study law, intending eventually to join the Spanish diplomatic service. He played soccer avidly until his sports career came to an abrupt end in the summer of 1963 when the car he was driving was involved in a near-fatal accident that left him paralyzed from the chest down. When his father brought a wheelchair into his hospital room, Julio became determined never to use it and to regain the full use of his limbs. He endured three years of convalescence, never veering from his goal to walk again. During his long hospital stay a nurse presented Julio with a guitar to take his mind off his disability. When he successfully replicated the tunes he heard on the radio, he realized that he had musical talent and began to compose his own songs. In 1967, while still convalescing, he watched a broadcast of "Festival de la Canción," a national singing competition held in Benidorm, Spain, and announced to his parents that someday he would win the competition.

With the help of his family and their loyal chauffeur, José Luis, Iglesias made a dramatic recovery. Shortly after, his parents sent him to Cambridge, England, for three months to practice his English. Iglesias spent the evenings in Cambridge singing traditional Mediterranean love songs in pubs. At some point during his English sojourn he wrote his first song, the ballad "La vida sigue igual," which he sang in the 1968 Benidorm Festival de la Canción, held on the Spanish Mediterranean coast. His victory in the competition propelled him on the road to international fame. For more than a year after winning at Benidorm, Julio did little singing and committed himself to studying law, as he had promised his father. Around this time, he composed many songs. One of his most popular songs was "Guendoline," which he wrote for the music contest at the 1970 Eurovision Festival in Holland. Although Iglesias lost the contest, the song became a smash hit, winning him name recognition across Europe.

Having established a reputation in Europe, Julio Iglesias ventured to Chile and Guatemala, where he launched an extraordinary Latin American career that has witnessed his albums on the top ten charts year after year. Iglesias soon took his music to the Caribbean and Eastern Europe. In 1971 he married Filipino socialite Isabel Preysler. The couple had three children, but their union ended in 1978, and their marriage was annulled in 1979 by a liberal Catholic tribunal in Brooklyn. In the early 1970s, Julio Iglesias was cast in two Spanish-language films, *La vida sigue igual* and *Todos los días,* but proved to have little acting ability. He told *People* magazine in 1988: "They're the worst films you can ever see. I was the most ridiculous actor." In the 1970s, Iglesias recorded numerous albums under the Alhambra label, including *Como el álamo al camino* (1972), *Julio Iglesias* (1972), *Soy* (1973), *A Mexico* (1975), *El amor* (1975), *America* (1976), *A mis 33 años* (1977), and *Emociónes* (1978). His music career picked up momentum, and by the time he won first place at the Eurovision Festival in 1972, his albums were the rage not only throughout Europe and Latin America but in Arab nations and in Japan.

In the late 1970s, Richard Asher, head of the International division of CBS Records, signed Julio Iglesias to an exclusive contract. Under the CBS International label, Iglesias recorded the 1981 album *De niña a mujer,* dedicated to his daughter, along with the 1982 LP *Momentos.*

Although Iglesias had achieved popularity among Latinos in the United States, it took him a few years to reach mainstream American audiences by way of England. British tourists vacationing in Spain were struck by his sound, and they started taking the singer's records back to England, where they caught on with disc jockeys. As a result, in 1981, Iglesias became the first Spanish singer with a bestselling single in England when his hit song "Begin the Beguine," a Spanish rendition of the Cole Porter classic, hit the top of the British charts. Another single, a version of "Yours," a hit years earlier with Vera Lynn, was also a bestseller in Britain for Iglesias.

Optimistic over his popularity in England, in 1983, CBS and the singer embarked on a quest to conquer America. Iglesias studied English and watched American television, then set to work on his first English-language album. Also planned was a huge media blitz, orchestrated by the prestigious public relations firm of Rogers & Cowan. Before long Julio Iglesias made appearances on major American talk shows, like David Letterman and Johnny Carson, and performed at celebrity events across the nation. In March 1983, Kirk Douglas and his wife,

Ann, introduced Iglesias to big names in Hollywood at a celebrity bash at Chasen's restaurant. That same month, the singer took the stage before sold-out audiences at Radio City Music Hall in New York, the Universal Amphitheater in Los Angeles, and the M-G-M Grand Hotel in Las Vegas.

In September 1983 Julio Iglesias celebrated his fortieth birthday at parties thrown in New York and Paris, with international celebrities in attendance. In Paris, Mayor Jacques Chirac bestowed on Iglesias the Medaille de Vermeil de la Ville de Paris. Iglesias was also the recipient of the first Diamond Disc Award of the *Guinness Book of World Records* as the bestselling singer in the world, with over 100 million albums sold. That year Iglesias sang at an NBC-sponsored gala birthday party for Frank Sinatra. After President Reagan and First Lady Nancy Reagan heard Iglesias at an outdoor concert, they invited the singer to the White House on several occasions. In 1982, Iglesias performed at a White House salute to Bob Hope, and in December 1983 he starred with the Reagans, Andy Williams, and Leslie Uggams on the NBC special "Christmas in Washington."

By the time Iglesias released his first English-only album, *1100 Bel-Air Place*, in 1984, he already enjoyed celebrity status in the United States, and the album had a sale of a million copies in five days; *1100 Bel Air Place* covers the whole musical gamut, from upbeat Latin numbers to duets with Diana Ross, the Pointer Sisters, and the Beach Boys. In the spring of 1984, Iglesias signed a multi-million dollar contract with the Coca-Cola Company. The singer would promote Coca-Cola and Diet Coke in commercials aired in 155 countries in exchange for sponsorship of his seven-month world tour that kicked off in June 1984 with a benefit at the United Nations.

In 1988, Iglesias recorded the English-language album *Non Stop*, with its socially conscious duet with Stevie Wonder, "My Love," and the dance song "Ae, Ao," which became a hit single. The LP had taken nearly three years to make and had cost $3 million in studio time. Iglesias sold over 3 million *Non Stop* records worldwide and an impressive 1.2 million in the United States, but these sales figures disappointed the singer, who was used to selling a higher volume. Furthermore, the sales were evidence that he still had not achieved his goal of being admitted to that pantheon reserved for America's most beloved music stars, such as Frank Sinatra and Barbra Streisand. In 1989, Iglesias launched *Only,* his signature perfume line, in sixty countries, including the United States. Overnight he sold a million bottles worldwide. That year, he was also appointed goodwill ambassador for UNICEF.

Julio Iglesias's greatest fear is that his fame might fade, and to prevent such a scenario, he tours incessantly. He is superstitious to the point of obsession, leaving the room if salt is spilled, refusing to wear yellow, and forbidding whistling in his presence. Furthermore, he always sings onstage with pants cut too short, like the ones he wore the night he won the Benidorm competition in 1968. Iglesias is convinced that he derives strength from the sun and sunbathes each day for two hours. Among his other idiosyncrasies, the singer always insists on being shot by the camera from the right side; when he appeared on CNN's *Larry King Live*, he was the first guest to switch chairs with the host. Another key to staying in top form is remaining single, as Julio Iglesias told *People* magazine in 1988: "If you commit your brains and heart to another, you can no longer fight, and I need to fight."

Raúl Julia

1944–1994

The eldest of four children, Raúl Julia was born Raúl Rafael Carlos Julia y Arcelay in San Juan, Puerto Rico, on March 9, 1944, to Olga Arcelay and Raúl Julia, a successful restaurateur who introduced pizza to Puerto Rico. Raúl attended an elementary school managed by American nuns, and as a first-grader he portrayed the Devil in a class play and discovered he had a gift for acting. In his childhood, he performed in as many school productions as possible. His parents often took underprivileged children into the household to live with the family, and this cultivated Julia's sense of a moral obligation toward humanity. Upon graduating from San Ignacio de Loyola High School, Julia went on to the University of Puerto Rico, where he studied psychology, premed, and law. His parents wanted him to pursue a career in law, but Julia's heart was in acting.

At the University of Puerto Rico, Julia sang baritone solos and did comedy as a member of the Lamplighters, a cabaret act, who performed at El Convento, a hotel in San Juan. After receiving his B.A. degree in liberal arts, he worked with local theatrical troupes and occasionally performed in nightclubs. The American comedian Orson Bean spotted Julia in a nightclub performance and advised him to go to New York City to study acting under Wynn Handman, a talented drama coach and the artistic director of the American Place Theatre. Julia had planned to go to Europe to pursue acting, but he took Orson Bean's advice and headed to New York in 1964. Just as he was about to leave Puerto Rico, his younger brother was killed in a car accident, and the tragedy had a profound effect on Julia for years to come. Once in New York, Raúl Julia signed up for lessons with Handman and made the rounds of casting calls and theatrical producers' offices. Weeks later he made his New York stage debut in a Spanish-language production of Calderón's *Life Is a Dream (La vida es sueña)*.

Raúl Julia's family supported him during his first year in New York, but as soon as he got his Equity card after playing in *Life Is a Dream*, he severed those financial ties. He was so poor in those early days that he survived on chicken backs while searching for work in the theater. Julia soon joined Phoebe Brand's Theater in the Street, which staged Spanish and English productions in New York's ghettos. On many occasions Julia had to duck Coke bottles and eggs tossed by ungrateful spectators. In 1966 he met producer and director Joseph Papp, who was instrumental in launching his career. That year, Papp cast the young actor as Macduff in the New York Shakespeare Festival's Spanish-language, mobile-unit production of *Macbeth*, which toured the boroughs, bringing theater to those who had little opportunity to enjoy the arts. Later, in 1966, Julia landed the role of Luis in René Marques's *Ox Cart*, the story of a Puerto Rican family's difficult adaptation to life on the mainland.

In the summer of 1967, Julia returned to the New York Shakespeare Festival when Joseph Papp cast him as Demetrius in *Titus Andronicus* after the actor brought down the house with his reading at a Puerto Rican poetry festival. In 1968 he portrayed the clerk in Vaclav Havel's satire *The Memorandum* at Joseph Papp's New Public Theater. That year, Raúl Julia also played Cradeau in a 1967 Off-Broadway revival of Sartre's *No Exit*, and in 1968 he took the stage in the Off-Broadway musical *Your Own Thing*. Between acting jobs, Julia had a difficult time keeping afloat financially, so he worked part-time tutoring students in Spanish and selling *Life* magazine subscriptions. Finally, he sought help from Joseph Papp, who immediately made him house manager for a new production at the Public Theater.

In September 1968, Julia made his Broadway debut as the servant Chan in Jack Gelber's *Cuban Thing*, a drama about Fidel Castro's revolution, which folded after only one performance. In 1969, Julia played in two one-act plays about urban violence, *Paradise Gardens East* and *Conerico Was Here to Stay*. A few months later, in Washington, D.C., he was cast in three roles in a revised version of *Indians*, Arthur Kopit's play about the genocide of Native Americans. *Indians* moved to Broadway in October 1969, but despite critical acclaim, the play closed in January 1970. Within weeks Julia was rehearsing his role as a Persian elder in the limited-run Off-Broadway production of *The Persians*. Julia earned the plaudits of critics for his strong portrayal of a fugitive Latin revolutionary in Mel Arrighi's comedy *The Castro Complex*, which opened in November 1970.

In a dry period, Julia accepted small parts in three motion pictures released in 1971: the thriller *The Organization* about an international drug-smuggling syndicate; *Been Down So Long It Looks Like Up To Me*, an adaptation of Richard Farina's underground classic; and Jerry Schatzberg's *Panic in Needle Park*, a sobering view of young drug addicts in New York City. A turning point in Julia's career came in 1971 when Joseph Papp invited the young actor to play the lead role of Proteus in a musical version of Shakespeare's romantic comedy *The Two Gentlemen of Verona* that ran in Central Park in the summer of 1971. The play was such a smash hit that it moved to Broadway that winter and garnered a number of Tony Award nominations, including one for Julia as Best Actor in a Musical. For several weeks in the summer of 1972, Julia juggled both the part of Proteus in *The Two Gentleman of Verona* and Osric in the last act of the New York Shakespeare Festival's production of *Hamlet*.

Impressed with Julia's performance in *The Two Gentlemen of Verona*, Peter Hall cast the actor in the space-age musical *Via Galactica*. In the summer of 1973, Julia returned to the New York Shakespeare Festival to play Orlando in *As You Like It* and Edmund in *King Lear*. In 1974, upon the recommendation of a friend, Julia signed up for a rigorous workshop on est, the experiential process of enlightenment and self-awareness, led by Werner Erhard, est's founder. Julia once said that he derived most of his energy from practicing est. For many years he was involved with the Hunger Project, a group Erhard founded to end world hunger by the year 2000. In 1974, Julia was also cast in the pilot *Aces Up*, a proposed CBS comedy series. In his next effort, he appeared in Off-Broadway productions of *The Emperor of Late Night Radio* and *The Robber Bridegroom* before opening in December 1974 in the revival of the Frank Loesser–George Abbott musical *Where's Charley?* In *Where's Charley?* Julia portrayed Charley Wykeham, a role that won him a second Tony nomination.

Julia gave spectacular performances in 1976 as Mack the Knife in the New York Shakespeare Festival's production of *The Threepenny Opera*. On June 28, 1976, Raúl Julia married Merel Poloway, an actress and dancer; the Indian guru Baba Muktananda presided over the wedding at his ashram in the Catskills. That year, Julia starred as an amorous Italian race-car driver in the chase and destruction comedy *The Gumball Rally*. In 1977, he portrayed Lopakhin in Chekhov's *Cherry Orchard* and then appeared in mid-1978 as a vampire in a road-company production of the 1977 Broadway hit *Dracula*. Theatergoers raved about Julia's Dracula, and after Frank Langella, the originator of the part on Broadway, stepped down, Julia was selected as his replacement. In his next project he portrayed Petruchio in the New York Shakespeare Festival's production of *The Taming of the Shrew* in the summer of 1978. In his next big-screen effort, he starred in the 1978 suspense film *The Eyes of Laura Mars*. The following summer, Raúl Julia played the title role in *Othello* at the Delacorte Theatre, and in January 1980 he returned to Broadway to perform in Peter Hall's production of *Betrayal*.

In his next stage effort, in 1982, Julia was cast as a film director in a midlife crisis in the Broadway musical *Nine*, based on Fellini's semiautobiographical film *8½*. *Nine* received twelve Tony Award nominations, one for Julia's performance, and the play won five Tony's, but Julia lost to Ben Harney of *Dreamgirls*. He went on to star as a villain in the 1982 adventure film *The Escape Artist* and an elegant Latin waiter in the 1982 romantic comedy *One From the Heart*. Julia then played Kalibanos, a lecherous Greek goatherd who inhabits a cave outfitted with a

Sony Trinitron television in Paul Mazursky's 1982 film *The Tempest*. In one of his most powerful cinematic performances, Julia portrayed Valentin Arregui, a Marxist journalist who shares a jail cell with an apolitical gay man (William Hurt) in the deeply moving film *Kiss of the Spider Woman* (1985). In preparation for filming, he conducted research, as he always did for serious roles, interviewing Brazilians who had been tortured by the military. For his portrayal in *Kiss of the Spider Woman*, Julia was one of the recipients of the Best Actor Award from the National Board of Review.

After *Kiss of the Spider Woman*, he received a deluge of movie scripts and decided to concentrate primarily on his screen career. In the mid-to-late 1980s he played in numerous motion pictures, most notably *The Morning After* (1986) as Jane Fonda's villainous ex-husband; *La gran fiesta*, the first full-length film out of Puerto Rico; and *Moon Over Parador* (1988), as the unsavory neo-Fascist chief of secret police. He also starred in *Tequila Sunrise* (1988), as a cocaine kingpin; *Trading Hearts* (1987), as a baseball pitcher dropped from the major leagues who falls in love; and *The Penitent* (1988), as a man called upon to be Christ in the annual tradition of reenacting the Crucifixion. In what he deemed one of his most important roles, Julia portrayed Father Oscar Romero in the 1989 independent film *Romero*, which chronicles the life of the priest who rose from anonymity to become a leader of the people in politically troubled El Salvador. Julia once acknowledged that making the film became an experience for personal conversion. In preparation for the part he listened to Romero's taped diaries and sermons, and gradually Romero's faith drew him back to Catholicism.

In his next big-screen project, Julia played the lead, a Buenos Aires nightclub entrepreneur, in the 1988 film *Tango Bar*, about the reunion of friends who over a decade ago had staged a popular tango revue. Julia then starred in the title role of Macheath in the 1990 film *Mack the Knife*. He gave an extraordinary screen performance as Alejandro "Sandy" Stern, the Argentine-born lawyer who defends the prime suspect in a murder in the 1990 box-office hit *Presumed Innocent*. Julia spent days with a top criminal lawyer and saw court cases to get Sandy Stern's character down pat. That year, he also portrayed an anti-Batista "freedom fighter" in *Havana*, a splendid film set against the Cuban revolution, the leader of a car-theft ring in the high-speed action-adventure *The Rookie,* and the legendary Dr. Victor Frankenstein in Roger Corman's *Frankenstein Unbound.* In 1990, Julia also played the lead in *Macbeth* as part of a Shakespeare Marathon at the New York Public Theater.

In another highly memorable screen part, Raúl Julia played Gomez Addams opposite Anjelica Huston as Morticia in the 1991 motion picture *The Addams Family,* inspired by the wicked cartoons of Charles Addams. Millions of American filmgoers mourned the sudden death of Raúl Julia, who succumbed to complications from a stroke on October 16, 1993.

43

Gloria Molina

1948–

The oldest of ten children, Gloria Molina was born on May 31, 1948, in Montebello, a suburb of Los Angeles, California, to Mexican Americans Leonardo Molina and Concepción Molina. Leonardo Molina was born in Los Angeles but raised in Mexico, and he returned to the United States with his wife under a bracero program in 1947. Gloria attended El Rancho High School in Pico Rivera, southeast of Los Angeles, and after graduating, she enrolled in Rio Hondo College in Whittier, where she majored in fashion design. In 1967, Leonardo Molina was hurt in an industrial accident, and nineteen-year-old Gloria had to take a full-time job as a legal secretary to keep the family afloat. She took night classes and earned a degree from East Los Angeles College in 1968 and then went on to California State University at Los Angeles, where she studied until 1970. A year later, Molina took a position as a job counselor at the East Los Angeles Community Union, a corporation concerned with economic development.

Molina first heard the call for social equality for Latinos during the Chicano movement of the 1960s. In the 1970s she decided to do something to better the lives of Latinos and became deeply engaged in community affairs. As an expression of her newfound activism, she served on the board of United Way of Los Angeles and was involved in the Latin American Law Enforcement Association. In 1973 she was selected founding president of the Comisión Femenil de Los Angeles, an organization founded by Chicana activists and dedicated to working for better child care and job training for Latinas in the community. During her tenure as president, Molina contributed to the development of many social programs to ease the burden on Chicanas in Los Angeles. From 1974 to 1976 she served as national president of the Comisión Femenil. She also cofounded Hispanic American Democrats, the National Association of Latino Elected and Appointed Officials (NALEO), and Centro de Niños, an organization geared toward aiding children.

Molina first met with political success when, in 1972, she urged then governor Ronald Reagan to appoint a Latina to the California Commission on the Status of Women. In 1974, Molina's political career got off the ground when she took the position of administrative assistant to California State assemblyman Art Torres. In 1977, President Jimmy Carter appointed Molina director for region nine of Intergovernmental and Congressional Affairs in the Department of Health and Human Services. After her stint in Washington she returned to California in 1980 to assume the post of chief deputy to the speaker of the California State Assembly, Willie Brown. In 1982, Molina learned that Torres was running for the state senate, leaving his assembly seat vacant. She decided to make a bid for the California State Assembly, the lower house of the California legislature. She then had a rude awakening when she went to pick up her membership card in the legislative club and it was stamped "men only." Then local Chicano politicians warned her that she lacked the necessary qualifications to run for a state assembly seat, insisting that the community would not back a woman and that funding would go to another candidate.

Molina was infuriated by the politicians' patriarchal attitudes, and in the spirit of egalitarianism, she vowed to combat the Establishment, as she told *Hispanic* magazine in an article in its July 1991 issue: "I was shaking in my boots, but I had to tell them, 'I will have all those things,' otherwise I would have folded. I had reservations about a good deal of it, but I wasn't going to let them deny me the opportunity." In the aftermath of this confrontation Molina organized a dynamic grassroots campaign. Women were instrumental in mobilizing the campaign, contributing or raising 75 percent of the $194,000 Molina spent. Even though her opponents had more campaign funds, clout, and endorsements, Molina won the seat and became the first Latino in the California State Assembly.

The going was rough for Molina during her two terms as an assemblywoman, for as a political maverick with a commitment to minorities, women, and progressive issues, she encountered many obstacles. Nevertheless, she was successful in getting two laws passed that improved the quality of life in her district: One outlawed discrimination against immigrants in auto insurance, and the other made notifying a neighborhood mandatory if it is to be sprayed to combat agricultural pests. Although she is a liberal Democrat, Molina once sponsored a bill to make work a requirement for welfare, believing the measure would help people get jobs. In recognition of her achievements in the California State Assembly, the Mexican American Opportunity Foundation bestowed upon Gloria Molina its Woman of the Year Award in 1983. That year, she was also chosen Hispanic of the Year by *Caminos* magazine and Democrat of the Year by the Los Angeles County Democratic Central Committee. In 1984, *Ms.* named her Woman of the Year for being a symbol of excellence.

In 1986, Molina put a stop to plans by California governor George Deukmejian to build a new state prison in a Chicano residential area of East Los Angeles. She took a leadership position in the fight to bench the construction plans and reassured voters that she would continue to fight the prison proposal even after she left the assembly. In 1987 a new Latino city council seat was created as part of a settlement reached by the city of Los

Angeles and the Mexican-American Legal Defense and Education Fund (MALDEF) on a gerrymandering suit. The settlement also called for a special municipal election to fill the seat. Molina decided to run. While most political observers expected a runoff since four candidates were vying for the seat, Molina captured 57 percent of the vote, becoming the first Latino elected to the Los Angeles City Council. As a city councilwoman she worked to provide a better environment for her constituents. She sought to take back the streets from drugs and crime by confronting drug dealers and donated $75,000 from her office budget to establish MASH-LA (More Advocates for Safe Homes), an organization devoted to teaching people how to improve their neighborhoods and rid them of gangs, crime, and drugs. She also helped to develop public and private partnerships to make more affordable housing available and create more parks in the community.

In 1990, Molina ran in a special election for a seat on the conservative, five-member Los Angeles County Board of Supervisors, the most powerful locally elected governing board in the United States. The Los Angeles County Board of Supervisors helps to oversee a county, which includes the city of Los Angeles, with a population of 9 million and a budget of $12 billion. MALDEF had sued the Los Angeles County Board of Supervisors for gerrymandering, and in June 1990, Judge David V. Kenyon of the federal district court ruled that the all-white board had intentionally diluted the voting power of the county's 3 million Latino residents and ordered that the districts be remapped so that one would have a majority of Latino constituents. Nine candidates, five of them Latino, entered the race for the seat for the newly created district. In a January vote no candidate won a majority, so on February 19, 1991, a runoff was held. Molina defeated her rival and former boss, State Senator Art Torres, when the votes were counted. Her election to the post was a historical milestone, since she became the first woman ever elected to the Los Angeles County Board of Supervisors and the first Latino elected to serve since 1875. Furthermore, she tipped the balance in favor of the liberals on the board.

At a news conference to discuss her election, she said: "I can't go into the board of supervisors and start acting like them. I did not get elected to meet their needs. I was elected to meet the needs of the people in the First District." From her first weeks as a county supervisor, Molina challenged the way the board conducted business, criticizing the way it handled the budget process, arguing against a pay increase for herself and the other supervisors, and trying unsuccessfully to get them and their staff to take an unpaid two-day leave so that more funds would be available for health-care programs. She moved aggressively to reaffirm her reputation as a strong advocate for minority and women's rights. In her first eight months as a supervisor, Molina fought to pass a measure that would offer $300 million in county contracts to businesses owned by women or members of minorities.

Molina also helped hire additional employees to cut the waiting time at welfare offices and at an AIDS clinic. Furthermore, Molina worked to make it possible for people, in a county where 30 percent of the population speaks Spanish, to testify in Spanish at board hearings. In her first six months as a county supervisor she proposed about forty motions, and fewer than five were rejected. Molina had no qualms about grilling members of the county bureaucracy or polemicizing with her fellow board members. On one occasion she confronted oil-company officials who had neglected to inform citizens about a drilling project in the district. In the widely publicized debate over whether bleach kits and condoms should be distributed to drug users, a measure public health officials advocate to combat the spread of AIDS, Molina accused a conservative supervisor who opposed the measure as talking "absolute nonsense."

Molina's achievements in Los Angeles did not go unnoticed by the national Democratic leadership. In the summer of 1992 then Democratic presidential candidate Bill Clinton appointed Molina cochair of his national campaign, and she joined Mickey Kantor and Cong. Maxine Waters in the campaign hierarchy. Gloria Molina never hid her aspirations to one day run for mayor, and she was considered an early favorite in the 1992 mayoral race in Los Angeles. However, on November 17, 1992, Molina announced that she would not run for mayor of Los Angeles because she was committed to her responsibilities as a Los Angeles County supervisor and was worried that Governor Pete Wilson would appoint a conservative Republican to replace her on the board. She could not abandon the women, Latinos, and other minorities of Los Angeles.

Gloria Molina is married to Ron Martinez, a businessman, and has a daughter named Valentina.

44 *Ramón Novarro*

1899–1968

One of ten children, Ramón Novarro was born José Ramón Gil Samaniegos in Durango, Mexico, on February 6, 1899, the son of a dentist. The family's fortunes were wiped out by the Mexican Revolution of 1910, and one by one the Samaniegos left Mexico. In 1917, Ramón and his brother Mariano slipped across the Mexican border and into the United States with ten dollars in their pockets. The rest of the family remained behind in Mexico until the brothers could afford to transport them to the United States. Now one of the family's breadwinners, Ramón found a job in a grocery store and later worked as a theater usher, piano teacher, and singing waiter. A dance impresario caught his singing act and hired him for a vaudeville show. Samaniegos went

215

to New York for rehearsals, which did not pay a salary, so to make ends meet, he got a job as a busboy in the Horn & Hardart Automat in Times Square. In 1917, he broke into the young movie industry as an extra, which was more in keeping with his ambitions to become a screen actor. He is known to have appeared on-screen as an extra in *The Women God Forgot* (1917), *The Hostage* (1917), *The Little American* (1918), *Joan the Woman* (1918),and *The Goat* (1918).

For four years, Ramón Samaniegos made the rounds of Hollywood studios, living in near starvation as he waited for his big break. Several established actors took an interest in him, and he auditioned for D. W. Griffith and Sam Goldwyn, but no parts followed. In 1921 the vaudeville dance director Marion Morgan, in whose troupe Samaniegos had danced since 1919, helped him land a role performing a novelty dance in the full-length Mack Sennett comedy *A Small Town Idol,* with Ben Turpin and Phyllis Haver. Hollywood applauded Samaniegos's comedic mimicry in the film, but no studios offered the budding actor a contract. However, Sam Goldwyn cast him in a small part with his first billing, in the 1922 film *Mr. Barnes of New York.* In the same year, he was chosen to play the lead in a small independent production, *The Rubaiyat of Omar Khayyam,* directed by Ferdinand Binney Earle. No company would take on *The Rubaiyat of Omar Khayyam* for release, and the film languished in a vault until 1925, when it was released under the title *A Lover's Oath.* After the disappointment of *Omar Khayyam,* Samaniegos returned to work as an extra and danced with his sister Carmen in vaudeville acts.

The brother and sister team tangoed together as unbilled extras in the background of Rex Ingram's 1921 production *Four Horsemen of the Apocalypse.* Meanwhile, Ingram, then a major Hollywood director, was one of the few to see *The Rubaiyat of Omar Khayyam* before it was packed in mothballs, and he was impressed with Samaniegos. Ingram cast the actor in a feature role—the dashing Rupert of Hentzau in Metro Company's (later M-G-M) 1922 popular swashbuckler *The Prisoner of Zenda*—at seventy-five dollars a week. Samaniegos sent fifty dollars of his salary to Durango to pay for a brother's transportation to Los Angeles. The critics and the public applauded Samaniegos for *The Prisoner of Zenda* and hailed him as a new find and an original type, the first of the Latin lovers. Ingram signed the actor to a $125-per-week personal contract and made him change his name. Samaniegos immediately chose a surname from his maternal side of the family, and overnight he became Ramón Novarro. It was the beginning of a star-studded career that lasted until the advent of cinematic sound, over a decade later.

Ingram cast Novarro as the tragic lover opposite Barbara La Marr and Lewis Stone in *Trifling Women* and then assigned him roles in three pictures, which were to make him a Hollywood star. The first was *Where the Pavement Ends,* in which Novarro plays a South Seas island boy in love with a missionary's daughter. In the original version the boy drowns in a waterfall at the end of the movie. Audiences were up in arms that their matinee idol could meet such a cruel fate, so Ingram filmed a new ending in which the boy discovers he is a Caucasian with a sunburn and can therefore marry the missionary's daughter. The two other Ingram films that were pivotal in Novarro's success were the cheerful romantic adventures *Scaramouche* (1923), set in French Revolutionary times, and *The Arab* (1924), which was filmed in North Africa. After shooting *The Arab,* Rex Ingram and his wife chose to remain in North Africa and sent Novarro back to Hollywood, where his $500-per-week Ingram contract was translated into $10,000 a week with Metro-Goldwyn.

Novarro went on to do three films in 1925: *Thy Name Is Woman,* with Barbara La Marr; *The Red Lily,* with Enid Bennett; and *The Midshipman,* filmed at the Naval Academy in Annapolis. He then starred in the 1926 masterpiece *Ben-Hur,* the role for which he is invariably best remembered. The film was a box-office triumph, raking in $9 million worldwide. With *Ben-Hur,* Novarro's popularity reached new heights despite the fact that some critics thought his portrayal lacked masculinity. Novarro was such a big hit that the letters which poured into post offices addressed to Mr. Ben Hur easily found their way to the actor. After *Ben-Hur,* Novarro returned to less epic projects, such as the 1927 motion picture *Lovers?,* a tale of how gossip can become reality, costarring Alice Terry, and the 1927 film *The Student Prince in Old Heidelberg,* with Norma Shearer.

Since these films did not increase his popularity, M-G-M cast about for a project that might bring Novarro greater success. The studio chose the 1929 film *The Flying Fleet,* in which Novarro plays one of six men training for the navy air corps. He spends most of the film exposing his garters—M-G-M's attempt to attract women to the box office. Novarro then starred in the highly commercial

1929 film *The Pagan,* which boasted a musical score, and the all-talkie *Devil May Care.* He played a Spanish troubadour opposite Dorothy Jordan in both *In Gay Madrid* (1930) and *Call of the Flesh* (1930), later renamed *The Singer of Seville.*

Once the talkies became a fact of life, Novarro's career waned. In the early 1930s rumors abounded that the actor would retire and take up opera singing or enter a monastery. Novarro continued, however, to appear in films, starring in the 1931 elegant romantic fable *Daybreak,* about an Austrian guardsman who falls in love outside his class. The film was unpopular with the public and the critics, but Novarro's career got a boost when he was cast with Greta Garbo in one of his favorite films, the 1932 *Mata Hari,* about the famous woman spy of World War I. M-G-M then Novarro to a new seven-year contract to act and direct. He landed a role in the 1932 film *Huddle,* a would-be serious class drama that flopped, and then starred with Helen Hayes in the 1932 motion picture *The Son-Daughter,* about true love among the Chinese of San Francisco.

Novarro was then cast in a 1933 remake of *The Arab* entitled *The Barbarian* in which he plays a potentate in the Middle East who woos an American lady who is passing through. None of these roles reinvigorated Novarro's career, but the studio persevered and cast him opposite Jeanette MacDonald in the 1934 lightweight musical comedy *The Cat and the Fiddle.* He then starred as an Indian brave in love with an outcast maiden (Lupe Velez) in the absurd 1934 melodrama *Laughing Boy* and as a European archduke in love with a ballerina in the 1934 musical *The Night Is Young.* In 1935, Novarro's film career screeched to a halt, which the actor once attributed to the fact that M-G-M would not allow him to grow up, insisting that he accept juvenile roles, such as a Yale football player in a college picture.

Novarro had always wanted to be an opera singer, so after making *The Night Is Young,* he devoted himself to music and concert appearances. However, his few operatic attempts, which he himself backed financially, fizzled. In semiretirement from films, Novarro also managed, his real estate holdings; during the years when he made $5,000 a week, Novarro had invested in land in the San Fernando Valley and in Mexico. He lived alone, never marrying, but entertained quite frequently in his house in the Hollywood Hills, complete with a full-size theater. In 1935, Novarro acted in and produced the musical *A Royal Exchange,* but critical reviews and audience opinions were scathing. In Hollywood he wrote, produced, and directed *Contra la corriente* (1936), a Spanish feature film, and then was signed by Republic for a comeback in the 1937 film *The Sheik Steps Out*, about a modern sheik who has a riotous time in the big city. The studio liked the film well enough to sign the actor to four more films, but after shooting the 1938 motion picture *A Desperate Adventure*, Novarro asked to be released.

In 1940, Novarro began to work in Rome on a French film *La comédie de bonheur*, but when Italy entered World War II, the project was abandoned. Later, the director, Marcel l'Herbier, managed to complete the film, but the results were mediocre, for some of the negatives had been burned and two members of the cast had died. In Mexico, Novarro made the 1942 film *La virgen que forjo una patria*. Toward the end of the 1940s, Novarro tried his hand at character acting. He portrayed a Cuban rebel leader in the 1949 downbeat adventure story *We Were Strangers*; a Mexican police chief in the 1949 comedy melodrama *The Big Steal*; a grinning gunman in the 1950 western *The Outriders;* and a police chief in the 1950 suspense film *Crisis* with Cary Grant and José Ferrer.

In 1958, Novarro played a character role in Walt Disney's ten-part television miniseries *The Nine Lives of Elfego Baca*, which relates the exploits of Elfego Baca, a sheriff, in Socorro County, New Mexico, during the 1800s. In January 1960, Novarro was one of fourteen stars interviewed on the NBC special "Hedda Hopper's Hollywood." The actor was not seen on the big screen again until he starred as a villain opposite Sophia Loren in his last film, *Heller in Pink Tights*, the 1960 spoof of westerns which recounts the adventures of a dramatic company touring the West in the 1880s. In 1961, Novarro appeared in Alfred Hitchcock's thriller *La Strega*. In 1962, the actor made his Broadway debut in the featured role in *Infidel Caesar*, Gene Wesson's rendition of Shakespeare's *Julius Caesar*. One of Novarro's last appearances was in a 1965 episode of the popular television series *Bonanza*.

For the last year and a half of his life the actor concentrated on writing his autobiography. The book was never finished. On October 30, 1968, Ramón Novarro was found bludgeoned to death in his Hollywood home. Two young men were implicated in the crime and sentenced to life in prison.

45

Lou Piniella

1943–

Piniella was born Louis Victor Piniella on August 28, 1943, in West Tampa, Florida, to Louis Piniella, a tobacco and candy distributor, and Margaret Piniella, a secretary and later a bookkeeper. Lou's maternal grandparents, who emigrated from Spain, and his uncles lived in the family home in one of Tampa's Spanish neighborhoods. As a young boy, Lou was often left in the care of his grandparents, and as a result, he spoke only Spanish until he started school, where the nuns taught him English. On weekends the entire family got together to play sports. His father and uncles played in a men's amateur baseball league, and as a small child Lou was a batboy for his father's team. His mother was also a great athlete who excelled on the softball field.

In the summer of 1956, Lou played baseball for the West Tampa Pony League and proved to be a superb hitter. That year, the team made it to the national championship in Ontario, Canada. During a sightseeing trip in Ontario to the top of Mount Baldy, Lou slipped on a loose rock and tumbled two hundred feet down the mountain. Miraculously, he survived the fall, breaking only his ankle and suffering a minor concussion and severe bruises. Lou attended Jesuit High School in Tampa, where he exhibited natural ability in his favorite sport, basketball, and made Catholic all-America, averaging thirty-four points a game. His ankle, however, would never be the same after the fall in Ontario, which ultimately prevented him from seriously pursuing basketball.

Lou was quite a prankster in school, and his coaches often had to bail him out of detention. He was also terribly hotheaded, and this impeded his progress in sports. In his senior year minor league scouts talked with his baseball coach about signing Lou as a pitcher after graduation. Lou refused to pitch a game early in the season and was dropped from the baseball team. As a result, the scouts passed him by. After graduating from high school, Lou went into the American Legion summer program and hit a strong .500. He signed a letter of intent to play basketball and baseball at the University of Tampa and made the varsity basketball team as a freshman guard. In a key game Lou missed four free throws in a row, and that ended his basketball hopes.

In 1962, Lou arrived home from college one afternoon to find a scout for the Cleveland Indians waiting inside with an offer to play professional baseball. Lou immediately signed the contract for $25,500, and two days later, he was off to Selma, Alabama, the home of the Cleveland Indians' Class D farm team. He altered his stance at the plate and batted .270 with Selma that year. Lou's temper got the best of him during one game that year in which he struck out with the bases loaded. He threw his glove into a rain barrel, and it sank to the bottom. When he reached inside to retrieve the glove, he fell in the barrel and had to be pulled out. In November 1962, Piniella was drafted by the Washington Senators and sent to the Senators' Class B team in the Carolina League in 1963, where he performed well and was named best rookie in the league.

At the end of the season the Senators were poised to call Piniella up to Washington, but his major league debut was postponed when he accidentally put his left arm through a glass door at a party and required thirty-seven stitches. He went home to mend, and later that year the Senators sent him to play winter ball in Nicaragua. In 1964 the National Guard then ordered Piniella to serve a brief stint of active duty, and he missed spring training. That summer, the Senators traded the young player to the Baltimore Orioles, who sent him down to the Class C club in Aberdeen, South Dakota. After he hit .270 in twenty games for Aberdeen, the Orioles called up Piniella but in four games he batted only once. At the end of spring training in 1965, he was sent to the Orioles' minor-league headquarters in Georgia.

In 1966, the Cleveland Indians drafted Piniella again and tried unsuccessfully to make a catcher out of him. He was then sent back to the minor leagues, this time with Cleveland's Triple A Portland, Oregon, club, a step away from the major leagues. He worked on hitting the curveball and the slider and raised his batting average from .289 in 1966 to a strong .317 in 1968. On April 27, 1967, Piniella married Anita García, a former Miss Tampa. The couple has three children. In October 1968 the Seattle Pilots acquired the unprotected Piniella in the American League expansion draft, but several months later they traded him to the Kansas City Royals. In his major league debut with the Royals, Piniella led off for the first time in his career. He finished the 1969 season batting .282 with 11 homers and 68 RBIs in 135 games. Kansas City fans nicknamed him "Sweet Lou," and the American League elected him Rookie of the Year.

In 1970, Piniella improved his performance with a batting average of .301, with 11 homers and 88 runs batted in, but the following season his average fell to .279 due to a thumb injury. After the 1971 season he played winter ball in Venezuela and had a brilliant year in 1972, batting .312, second best in the American League and leading the league in doubles with 33. That season, Piniella was named to the All-Star team for the first time in his career as the fourth-highest vote getter in the American League. Under the Royals' new manager, Jack McKeon, with whom he was at odds, Lou Piniella had a bad year in 1973, with his lowest full-season batting average—.250. On December 7, 1973, the New York Yankees acquired him in a trade, and Piniella joined one of the most famous and successful teams in sports history. Despite having to uproot his family from Kansas City, Lou looked forward to wearing Yankee pinstripes.

Piniella would spend the rest of his career with the Yankees, playing with such extraordinary teammates as Bobby Murcer, Thurman Munson, and Graig Nettles. In a game on May 27, 1974, Piniella made three assists in a single inning, tying the major league record. That season he had a solid batting average of .305 and helped the Yankees along in their quest for the American League Eastern Division title. Piniella had a tough season in 1975 as a result of a punctured eardrum, with only 199 at-bats and a woeful .196 batting average. He made a comeback in 1976 and helped the Yankees clinch their first pennant in a dozen years. In Game One of the World Series against the Cincinnati Reds, Piniella became the first designated hitter in World Series history when he led off the second inning.

Piniella had his most spectacular season in 1977, hitting .330. The Yankee made it to the World Series again that year, this time trouncing the Los Angeles Dodgers for the world championship. Piniella made an enormous contribution to the team by batting .333 in the Series. He had a phenomenal season again in 1978, batting .314, and in one crucial play he enabled the Yankees to advance to the World Series. It happened in the ninth inning of the decisive playoff game against the Boston Red Sox, when Piniella made a clutch play, "the greatest defensive play" George Steinbrenner had ever witnessed, thus clinching the pennant for the Yankees. The Yankees advanced to the World Series in 1978, where they repeated as champions by defeating the Dodgers four games to two.

In 1979 the Yankees finished fourth, and Lou Piniella was the team's leading hitter and the most reliable player offensively and defensively. Piniella became a designated hitter in 1981 after Dave Winfield was installed in the outfield. That year, Piniella played in only sixty games, batting .277. As always, he was a spectacular performer in the playoffs and World Series, hitting .387 in thirteen postseason games and .438 in the World Series. In recognition of his contributions to the team, the Yankees signed Piniella to a new three-year contract stipulating a salary of over $350,000. While the Yankees finished fifth in the American League East in 1982, Piniella batted .307. In August 1982, Steinbrenner asked Piniella to act as batting coach and to help in the decision making about players and trades.

In 1983, Piniella was plagued by an injured left shoulder, but managed to bat .291. After 15 years in the major leagues, he retired from play in June 1984, still batting above .300, and was named the Yankees' first-base coach. On October 27, 1985, he signed a one-year contract to succeed Billy Martin as the fourteenth manager in George Steinbrenner's thirteen-year reign as the franchise's Yankee's owner. Piniella was a hot-tempered player turned hot-tempered manager, and he often surrendered to his emotions on the field. During the 1986 season he smashed furniture in the clubhouse after the Angels defeated the Yankees in Anaheim Stadium. He also exhibited tremendous warmth and a fine sense of humor among the players and was extremely popular with the fans, who chanted "Loo-oo" whenever he appeared. In 1986, Piniella won ninety games as a rookie manager and the Yankees rewarded his efforts with a two-year contract worth an estimated $600,000.

With little support from George Steinbrenner, Piniella resigned from the Yankees in 1988 to work in the broadcast booth for a year before a managing post opened up with the Cincinnati Reds. In 1990, Piniella's Reds breezed through the playoffs and swept Oakland in the World Series. Piniella's relationship with the Reds soured in a game against San Francisco in August 1991 when the temperamental manager lashed out at Gary Darling, the home-plate umpire, who had reversed a ruling by another umpire, thus depriving the Reds of a home run. After the game Piniella accused Darling of discriminating against the Reds. Two months later, Darling and the Major League Umpires Association filed a $5 million defamation suit against Piniella. Marge Schott, the Reds' owner, did not come to Piniella's defense or pay for his lawyer, as might have been expected. Piniella found Schott's lack of support quite disturbing, and in October 1992 he rejected an extension of his three-year contract with the Reds.

On November 9, 1992, Lou Piniella was named manager of the Seattle Mariners, the ball club with the worst record in the American League in the 1992 season. He joined the club with the hope to instill in them a winning tradition. With Piniella at the helm, things quickly began to look up for Seattle. In 1993 the team had a winning season for only the second time in its sixteen-year history. In June 1993, Piniella told *Sport*: "Hopefully, this will be my last stop. I see myself staying here for the long haul." With his outstanding track record as both a player and a manager, Piniella has proved that he has just what it takes to eventually lead the Seattle Mariners to the World Series.

46

Tito Puente

1923–

Tito Puente was born Ernest Anthony Puente Jr. on April 20, 1923, in Brooklyn, New York. His parents had just arrived on the mainland from Puerto Rico. His father, Ernest Anthony Puente, was from Aguadilla, Puerto Rico, and worked as a foreman in a razor-blade factory; his mother, Ercilia, was from Coamo, Puerto Rico. Ercilia Puente was the first to recognize Tito's musical talent, and she signed him up for piano lessons when he was seven years old. In a childhood spent in Spanish Harlem, Tito also went to dancing school, and in the early 1930s he and his younger sister Anna performed as a song-and-dance team. Tito dreamed of being a dancer until he suffered an injury, which abolished all thoughts of a dancing career. In childhood, he also sang with a schoolboy quartet at parties and on street corners.

Drawn naturally to percussion at an early age, Tito worshiped Gene Krupa and formally studied the drums. He grew up listening to boleros and rumbas with one ear and big-band music with the other and was particularly impressed when he heard Miguelito Valdes sing "Dolor cobarde" with Orquesta Casino de la Playa. Later, the works of Benny Goodman, Artie Shaw, and Duke Ellington sparked his interest in the emerging tradition of improvisational jazz. In his early teens Tito became a semiprofessional percussionist and performed regularly with a combo called Los Happy Boys at the Park Palace at 110th street and Fifth Avenue and with Noro Morales at the Stork Club. Los Happy Boys was Tito's training ground in percussion, and he picked up many tips from the group's Cuban drummer. Enthralled by music, Tito dropped out of Central Commercial High School to join José Curbelo's band. In 1941, Puente got his first big break when the regular drummer in Machito's famous big band was drafted. Puente took over on the drums and broke with custom when he played standing up rather than seated. In another innovation, Puente brought the timbales, the twin Cuban metal drums on a stand, with two tuned cowbells and often a cymbal, to the front of the bandstand for the first time in Latin music.

Puente ended up spending three years in the U.S. Navy during World War II. He served on an aircraft carrier in the South Pacific, entertaining the sailors on the sax and drums in a big band and tooting bugle calls in the early morning. When he was discharged in 1945, Puente studied on the GI Bill at the prestigious Juilliard School of Music in New York City, where he gained a greater knowledge of theory, orchestration, and conducting. At around this time he also worked as an arranger for Machito, José Curbelo, Pupi Campo, Frank Martí, Miguelito Valdes, and Marcelino Guerra. His early compositions included "Cuando te vea" and "Pilareña," with lyrics by Machito. Puente formed his own band in 1948, which he called the Picadilly Boys, a play on *picadillo*, a Caribbean dish of ground beef and special seasonings. He began recording on the Tico label, doing such early singles as "Abaniquito" and "Picadillo." Tito Puente played both Latin music and jazz and searched for ways to combine the two styles.

By the early 1950s the Picadilly Boys, by then renamed the Tito Puente Orchestra, had quite an enthusiastic following on the Latin music scene in Los Angeles, Philadelphia, and New York.

At that time, the mambo, a fast, staccato Afro-Caribbean dance from Cuba, derived from Congolese religious dance, was the craze in ballrooms across America. Puente and his orchestra helped popularize the mambo at the Palladium at Fifty-third Street and Broadway in Manhattan, the mecca of Latin music, where they rivaled Tito Rodriguez and his Mambo Devils as headliners. By the mid-1950s, Puente established himself as a talented Latino musician who could cross over and please Anglo audiences. In 1956, RCA Victor released Puente's hit album *Puente Goes Jazz*. In May 1956 the New York daily *La Prensa* voted Puente "King of Latin Music"; he won over Perez Prado as the most popular performer of the mambo.

RCA Victor released Puente's bestseller *Dance Mania* in 1958 and cut its sequel, *Dance Mania II*, in 1959, although that album did not hit the shelves until 1963. By then Puente had returned to Tico Records. In the mid-1960s, Chicano rocker Carlos Santana turned one of Puente's popular 1950s songs "Oye, como va" into a Top 40 hit, and the King of Mambo won enthusiastic new audiences. At around this time Puente teamed up on numerous occasions with the outstanding Cuban vocalist Celia Cruz, known as the Queen of Salsa. Together they recorded eight albums on the Tico label in the 1960s, including *Cuba y Puerto Rico son, El quimbo quimbunbia, Alma con alma,* and *Algo especial para recordar*.

In 1968, Puente had the honor of serving as grand marshal of New York City's Puerto Rican Day parade, and in 1974 his Latin compositions "Picadillo," "Para los rumberos," and "Oye como va" were played by marching bands in New York's Saint Patrick's Day parade. After the journalist and television personality Felipe Luciano criticized the organizers of the Newport Jazz Festival in 1974 for excluding Latin groups, Puente got an invitation to perform and dazzled the crowds with his invigorating rhythms. In March 1977, Puente joined Carlos Santana, who had enjoyed a huge success with Puente's compositions "Oye como va" and "Para los rumberos," for a concert and dance at Roseland in Manhattan. In 1979, Jimmy Carter invited Puente, as the official "Goodwill Ambassador of Latin American Music," to perform at the White House, and his became the first Latin orchestra to play for a president. Puente would later perform at President Ronald Reagan's inaugural ball. In 1978 Puente was honored with his first Grammy Award for the number "Homenaje a Beny More," a collaboration with Celia Cruz.

The 1980s and 1990s found Puente forging the best of Latin music and jazz into his unique style. In 1983 he won a Grammy for "On Broadway" and in 1985 for "Mambo diablo." In 1990, Puente won his fourth Grammy Award, this one in the Tropical Latin Performance category for his composition "Lambada timbales" from his ninety-ninth album, *Goza mi timbal*. He told *Down Beat* magazine in May 1991, "Sometimes jazz can be boring, but I give it a new twist. Latin music can be boring too, because it's only tonic and dominant. [You take an] exciting progressive melodic line, then combine it with exciting rhythms—like Dizzy did years ago with Chano Pogo on Manteca: that's the marriage we're after. You gotta know about jazz to play these things." In 1991, Puente was named the recipient of a Golden Eagle Award, which recognizes the achievements of Latinos in the entertainment industry.

In 1992, Puente played himself in the film *The Mambo Kings*, based on the Pulitzer Prize–winning novel by Oscar Hijuelos about struggling Latin musicians. He contributed several songs to the motion picture soundtrack of *Mambo Kings*, sparkling with his twenty-one piece orchestra in "Ran Kan Kan" and stealing the show with "Para los rumberos." Years before, Puente portrayed a Xavier Cugat–like Latin American bandleader in Woody Allen's *Radio Days* (1987), a richly nostalgic movie about growing up in Queens in the 1940s, interspersing vignettes of family life with scenes about radio performers in that medium's golden age.

In 1992, Puente also released his 100th album, entitled *Mambo King: the 100th LP*, which marks the performer's return to a more traditional Latin style. On February 15, 1992, Puente was toasted at a concert at Madison Square Garden by his peers, including singing sensation Celia Cruz and bandleaders Oscar D'León, Tito Nueves, Ismael Miranda, and José Alberto. In the 1990s, Puente took note of the influx of Latin music into the mainstream pop and rock scene, as in the music of Gloria Estefan and the Miami Sound Machine, and once commented that this phenomenon had opened up more doors for him as a Latin performer. After the release of his 100th album, Puente was already poised for the next album. He told the *New York Times*: "Bill Cosby...said he liked album No. 86, you know he said it as a joke. I'm just looking to the next 100 records. I have to make a living." In 1994, Puente passed the 100-album milestone with the release of *Tito Puente's Golden Latin Jazz All Stars "In Session,"* an album assembled with a crew that included Mongo Santamaría,

Dave Valentín, Hilton Ruíz, Charlie Sepúlveda, and Giovanni Hidalgo.

When he is not making music or movies, Puente contributes time and energy to numerous humanitarian causes. In 1979 he set up the Tito Puente Scholarship Fund, which provides annual support to New York City's music students. In 1989 he raised $150,000 to aid victims of Hurricane Hugo in Puerto Rico.

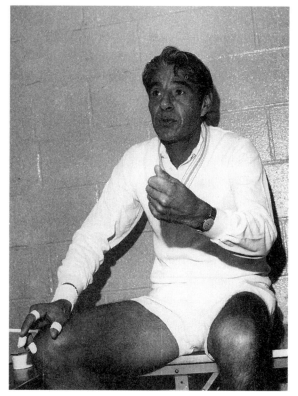

Richard "Pancho" Gonzáles

1928–1995

The oldest of seven children, Pancho Gonzáles was born Ricardo Alonzo Gonzáles on May 9, 1928, in Los Angeles, California, to Mexican-born parents of modest means. His father was a housepainter and his mother a seamstress, and together they provided their children with a stable home life. Ricardo was a restless boy who always had to be on the move. At Edison Junior High School he vented some of that energy on the playing fields and was awarded certificates in football and basketball. In 1940 his mother gave the twelve-year-old Ricardo a fifty-cent tennis racket bought at a drugstore as a Christmas present, partly to divert his interest from contact sports.

Ricardo took to tennis the minute he hit the court and soon befriended a high school tennis player named Charles Pate. Pate nicknamed him "Pancho," and in return for help on his newspaper route he gave Ricardo some tennis balls and taught him the game's fundamentals. Gonzáles never took formal lessons; he learned by watching others play and by practicing. He won his first tournament in 1939 while still at Edison Junior High. That same year, his name was mentioned in a column in the *Los Angeles Times* entitled "Southern California—Cradle of Tennis Champions." Pancho was on his way to becoming a legendary tennis player.

By age fifteen Gonzáles had become a California champion. He was ranked number one among young male players in Southern California, having defeated junior champion Herbie Flam, considered the rising star in tennis, in four straight matches in 1943. Gonzáles's performance in the first of these matches caught the attention of Perry Jones, secretary of the Southern California Tennis Association. Jones wanted to bring Pancho into the junior development program, but the boy was ineligible due to his poor academic performance and truancy record. He did not respond well to discipline and was frequently absent from the Manual Arts High School. A boy of Pancho's background was also not welcome at exclusive country clubs, so he resorted to practicing on public courts.

Gonzáles soon dropped out of school, devoted himself entirely to tennis, and rose steadily in the amateur ranks until he enlisted in the navy in the fall of 1945. After his discharge in January 1947 he returned to the tennis court, reaching the finals in the Southern California Championships that May. That same year, the Southern California Tennis Association financed his first cross-country trip to the eastern grass-court circuit. In the second round of the U.S. Championships, Gonzáles kept Gardnar Mulloy on the court for five sets before acknowledging defeat. In the Pacific Southwest Tournament in 1947 he electrified the tennis world when he defeated tennis stars Jaroslav Drobny, Bob Falkenburg, and Frank Parker, before losing in the final to national champion Jack Kramer.

In March 1948, Gonzáles married Henrietta Pedrin. That year, he won the California and New Jersey State championships and lost the TriState at Cincinnati. He was also victorious at the Western Championships in Indianapolis and captured his first national title by defeating Nick Carter in the National Clay Court finals in straight sets. While it was apparent that Pancho Gonzáles was a gifted young player, few expected the twenty-year-old to beat former champion Frank Parker, the top-seeded player, 8–6, 2–6, 7–5, 6–3, in the singles at the U.S. Championships at Forest Hills in September 1948. When Pancho Gonzáles served and volleyed his way to the final, in which he polished off the South African player Eric Sturgess, the tennis world was stunned.

Pancho's game faltered in 1949 because he trained poorly, put on weight, and lost his competitive edge. He began to lose crucial matches and was seeded second at the 1949 U.S. Championships. Despite these setbacks, Gonzáles played extraordinary tennis at Forest Hills. In the final he faced Ted Schroeder, the favorite in the match, and before thirteen thousand fans defeated him. What Gonzáles appreciated most about winning that match was seeing himself on the cover of *American Lawn Tennis*, his wife, Henrietta, at his side. In 1949, Gonzáles also helped the United States capture the Davis Cup by winning both his matches in the challenge round against Australia. That year, with Frank Parker, he also won the men's doubles titles at Wimbledon and the French Open.

In 1949, Gonzáles turned pro. He was not allowed to play at Wimbledon because the delegates of the International Lawn Tennis Federation had not yet voted in favor of open tennis, which would allow professionals to compete with amateurs in the world's premier tennis tournaments. Open tennis would not come to Wimbledon until the summer of 1968. Many in tennis agree that if major tournaments had been open to all players when Pancho Gonzáles was at his peak, he would have captured many titles on grass either at Wimbledon or Forest Hills.

When Pancho turned pro, he was still too undeveloped a player to compete against tennis great Jack Kramer, who won twenty-two of their twenty-six matches. Gonzáles faded from view for several years, until Kramer retired from tennis. In 1954, he emerged as Kramer's successor, dominating play with his majestic and accurate high-speed service, excellent footwork, superb defensive shots, and cunning tactics. For the next decade

Gonzáles reigned as king of the professional tennis court. The only way a promoter could ensure a big turnout at a match was to feature the star tennis player. In the 1950s, Gonzáles monopolized such tournaments as the London Professional Championships, capturing the title in 1950, 1951, 1952, and 1956.

In the 1960s, with Ken Rosewall and Rod Laver dominating tennis, Gonzáles continued to play in major tournaments and was a challenge to younger rivals. From 1963 to 1967 he was the coach of the Davis Cup team. In 1964, his last serious bid for a ninth U.S. pro title, Gonzáles advanced to the finals, where he was bested by Rod Laver in four hard sets. In 1968, at age forty, he reached the quarterfinals of the first U.S. Open by defeating second-seeded Tony Roche in a spectacular first-round match. That same year, Gonzáles was inducted into the International Tennis Hall of Fame. He would still find glory on the tennis court at an age when most tennis players had long since retired from competitive play.

In 1969, Gonzáles stunned the spectators at Wimbledon by defeating Charlie Pasarell, ranked number one in 1967, in the tournament's longest match in history, 112 games in five hours and twelve minutes, until Michael Chang and Stefan Edberg beat the record by fourteen minutes at the 1992 U.S. Open. This first-round duel took two days to complete, beginning one afternoon and ending the next evening. With that match Pancho Gonzáles managed, in the twilight of his career, to dazzle fans on center court at Wimbledon, the world's cathedral of tennis, an opportunity denied him for so long due to his professional status. Later that year, Gonzáles trounced John Newcombe, Ken Rosewall, Stan Smith, and Arthur Ashe in succession to win a tournament in Las Vegas.

In 1970, in the opener of a series of $10,000 winner-take-all matches leading to a grand final, Gonzáles was victorious over Rod Laver, who was then ranked number one in the world. That same year, he won the Howard Hughes Invitational, the Tucson Dunlop Classic Doubles with Roy Emerson, and the Paris Open Indoor Doubles with Ken Rosewall.

Three months before his forty-fourth birthday, in 1972, Gonzáles became the oldest player to capture a tournament title in the open era, beating Georges Goven in Des Moines, Iowa. As late as 1972, he was ranked ninth in the United States. He was the oldest player to be ranked so high and tied Vic Seixas's American longevity record as a member of the Top 10. In 1972 the veteran Gonzáles teamed up with Jimmy Connors to win the Pacific Southwest Open doubles title and the Buckeye Classic doubles. Beginning in 1973, Gonzáles was a consistent winner on the Grand Masters tour for over-forty-five champions. Between 1950 and 1972 Gonzáles earned $911,078 on the court, and as a Grand Master he reached the million-dollar mark in earnings.

Pancho González died in Las Vegas on July 3, 1995 of cancer.

48

Luis Valdez

1940–

The second of ten children, Luis Valdez was born on June 26, 1940, in Delano, California, to farmworkers Armida and Francisco Valdez. The family migrated with the California crops, and by age six Luis was working in the fields. As a child he took a keen interest in puppet theater and by age twelve was already producing shows. He attended numerous schools throughout the San Joaquin Valley and, despite the constant interruptions in his education, graduated from James Lick High School in San Jose, where the Valdez family had finally dropped out of harvesting. In 1960 Valdez entered San Jose State College (now University) on a scholarship and majored in mathematics and English. In college his theatrical talents unfolded, and he completed his first full-length play, entitled *The Shrunken Head of Pancho Villa*, about

Mexican Americans trying to find themselves in society. The Drama Department at San Jose State College produced the play in 1963. Shortly after, Luis Valdez won a regional playwriting contest with his one-act play *The Theft*.

Upon graduating from San Jose State College in 1964 with a B.A. degree in English, Valdez joined the San Francisco Mime Troupe at a moment when it was involved in "agitprop" theater, condemning U.S. intervention in Vietnam and other so-called breaches of world peace. The lessons in presentational and popular theater that Valdez learned in the several months he spent with the mime troupe served him well when he returned to Delano in October 1965, after a cultural-exchange trip to Castro's Cuba. In Delano, Valdez aided Cesar Chavez in his efforts to organize farmworkers into a union to fight for the end of exploitation in the fields by California growers. Valdez created a farmworkers' theater, El Teatro Campesino, as a means of dramatizing the workers' plight and garnering public support for their unionizing efforts.

In 1967, after spending two years with the farmworkers union and on a national fund-raising tour, Valdez took his El Teatro Campesino to Del Rey, California, where he organized a cultural center, Centro Campesino Cultural, and incorporated other themes about the grassroots Mexican American into his scripts. His new direction gave birth to *Los vendidos* (1967), an allegorical play which explores Chicano stereotypes, such as "the standard farmworker," within a political context. PBS aired the play nationally in 1972, and it won several awards, including an Emmy. *Los vendidos* is invariably the Chicano play that has been staged most by theaters across the nation. In 1967, El Teatro Campesino launched a national tour and earned a reputation for innovation and political commentary—and for drawing large audiences.

In 1968, El Teatro Campesino produced Valdez's play *The Shrunken Head of Pancho Villa*, which was awarded an Off-Broadway Obie Award. Other plays from the late 1960s include *La conquista de Mexico* (1968), a puppet show exploring the Spanish conquest of the Aztec, and *No saco nada de la escuela* (1969), a satire on the injustices perpetrated by schools on minorities. In 1969, Valdez relocated El Teatro Campesino to Fresno, California, to take its message to a larger audience. That year, El Teatro Campesino was honored with the Los Angeles Drama Critics

Circle Award, and Valdez presented some of his work at the Théâtre des Nations, an international festival at Nancy in northern France. Valdez also produced a film entitled *I am Joaquin* and founded Tenaz, a national organization of Chicano theater groups in the Southwest. During this period he also joined the faculty at Fresno State College, helping to organize the La Raza Studies Program from 1968 to 1970.

Valdez taught at the University of California at Berkeley and at Santa Cruz from 1971 to 1974. In 1971 he had produced *La gran carpa de la familia Rascuachi,* which captures the essence of the *corridos,* or folk ballads, as well as the humor and pathos of the Mexican *pelado,* the poor man. By 1974 the play had take on epic proportions, exploring such themes of Chicano life in America as birth, death, unemployment, welfare, labor exploitation, and assimilation. A scene in a later version of *La gran carpa,* in which the Virgin of Guadalupe is deified alongside Jesus Cristo—Quetzalcóatl, precipitated loud protest from antireligious Latin American and Chicano theater companies at the Quinto Festival de Los Teatros Chicanos Primer Encuentro Latinoamericano in Mexico City in 1974. This controversy quickly led to El Teatro Campesino's break with the Chicano theater movement. In 1976 and 1977, El Teatro Campesino adapted *La gran carpa* for PBS and entitled it *El Corrido.* In 1976, the group also embarked on a tour of eight European countries, with Valdez acting in the role of Jesus Pelado Rascuachi in *La gran carpa,* to critical acclaim.

In the late 1970s, El Teatro Campesino took a more commercial direction. Valdez made his Hollywood debut, writing the screenplay and acting with El Teatro Campesino members, in the 1977 motion picture *Which Way Is Up?,* an Americanization of Lina Wertmuller's *Seduction of Mimi,* starring Richard Pryor. Valdez then turned his attention to Broadway. In 1978, he was named the recipient of the prestigious Rockefeller Foundation Playwright-in-Residence Award, which allowed him to write and produce the musical drama *Zoot Suit,* a mixture of fact and fantasy, based on the infamous Los Angeles Sleepy Lagoon case of 1942 and the Zoot Suit riots of 1943. *Zoot Suit* first ran in Los Angeles theaters in 1978 to critical acclaim and public applause, drawing Chicanos to the theater in large numbers for the first time in history. The play captured the Los Angeles Critics Circle Award for Distinguished Productions and eight Drama-Logue Awards for Outstanding Achievement in Theater.

With its premiere at the Winter Garden Theater in New York in 1979, *Zoot Suit* became the first work written and produced by a Latino to appear on Broadway. The play received mediocre reviews from New York critics and theatergoers, which Valdez attributed to Eurocentric attitudes among Anglos—"the white man's sense of arrogance and belief that the truth lies in Western European culture." Despite *Zoot Suit's* troubles in New York, a film version of the play was produced in 1981, making Valdez the first Chicano to write and direct a film for a major studio. It enjoyed moderate box-office success. In 1982 the Hollywood Foreign Press Association nominated the film for a Golden Globe Award, and that year it captured first place at the Cartagena Film Festival in Colombia.

After launching his Hollywood career, Valdez divided his attention between the stage and screen. In 1981, El Teatro Campesino established its first playhouse in San Juan Bautista, where that year it staged *Bandido! The American Melodrama of Tiburcio Vasquez, Notorious California Bandit*, Valdez's historical play based on the exploits of Tiburcio Vásquez, a California outlaw. In 1982, El Teatro Campesino produced Valdez's *Corridos*, an exploration of the poetic and psychosexual themes in Mexican folk ballads, with songs in Spanish and dialogue in English, which fueled the feminist debate over Valdez's sexist treatment of women. *Corridos* enjoyed such critical acclaim on the stage that it was produced on video in 1987 and was aired as a special on PBS in the fall of 1987, featuring Linda Ronstadt dramatizing Mexican ballads.

In 1983, President Reagan's Committee on the Arts and Humanities honored Luis Valdez's accomplishments, and a year later he was named Regents' lecturer in theater at the University of California at Irvine. In 1985, Valdez completed the play *I Don't Have to Show You No Stinking Badges,* a story of assimilation and generational conflict among Chicanos yearning to be middle class. While he was rehearsing the play, he wrote and worked on the production of his 1987 big-screen hit *La Bamba,* a tribute to the 1950s rock singer Ritchie Valens, whose life ended in tragedy just months after he had risen to fame. The film made history for its simultaneous distribution in Spanish-language versions in American cities with large Latino populations. With *La Bamba* Valdez earned the reputation as a talented filmmaker in both mainstream and Latino markets. On March 31, 1988, he was lauded for his great achievements at the New York Images Awards, presented by the Gotham chapter of the Hispanic Academy of Media Arts and Sciences.

After *La Bamba*, the demands and pressures of his Hollywood career hampered Valdez's playwriting. He told *American Theatre* magazine in 1992: "The playwright in me is a little frustrated because the screenwriter is too busy to pay much attention to writing new plays.... I persist in film because it's such a powerful medium...." In 1992 he began work on the production of *Frieda and Diego*, a screenplay he collaborated on with his wife, Lupe, about the life of the famous Mexican painter Frieda Kahlo. Valdez's choice of Italian-American Laura San Giacomo to play Kahlo was a source of controversy in the Chicano theater community, prompting the screenwriter to postpone temporarily both the project and the world premiere of *Bandido! Bandido!* finally debuted at the end of 1992, and in 1993, Valdez was back at work on *Frieda and Diego*. In 1994, Valdez's screen version of *The Cisco Kid*, filmed entirely in Mexico, aired on TNT.

Ricardo Montalbán

1920–

The youngest of four children, Montalbán was born Ricardo Gonzalo Pedro Montalbán Merino on November 25, 1920, in Mexico City to Castilians Jenaro and Ricarda Montalbán. His parents moved from Spain to Veracruz, Mexico, where Jenaro Montalbán opened a men's shop. A Cervantean scholar, Ricarda Montalbán was highly educated and could even converse freely in Latin with the priests. When Ricardo was quite young, the family moved to Torreón, in northern Mexico, where Jenaro Montalbán managed a dry-goods store. The Montalbán household was harmonious. Ricardo and his older siblings were dressed in fine clothes and enrolled in the best schools. Religion was an important facet of family life, and the children attended mass every

Sunday. In his youth Ricardo spent summers on a cattle ranch with his best friend's family and swam, climbed mountains, rode horses, and played at fighting bulls.

Ricardo attended the Alfonso XIII Grammar School for three years and was then sent to Colegio de la Paz, where he excelled in mathematics, grammar, and logic. Due to his Castilian Spanish and style of dress, which his parents insisted the family preserve, he was often taunted in school. The only source of amusement in Torreón was the movies, and young Ricardo was enthralled by Andy Hardy pictures and Fred Astaire and Ginger Rogers. After completing grade school, Ricardo went to Mexico City to study with the Maristas priests, but a government crackdown on religious schools brought an end to his stay after only one year. Ricardo was soon enrolled in the Academia Comercial Treviño, a business school, to study to become a certified public accountant. He found the discipline dreary and his future uncertain, so he went to work in a dry-goods store. His brother Carlos soon relieved him of the drudgery and brought him to Los Angeles.

Ricardo entered Fairfax High School in Hollywood, where he debuted in the school play *The Whole Town's Talking* and then performed the lead in *Tovarich*. An M-G-M talent scout saw him and offered him a screen test. Instead, Ricardo went with Carlos to New York to broaden his scope as an actor onstage. In 1941 he made his professional film debut in a three-minute movie for a jukebox "soundie" called *The Latin From Manhattan: Introducing Ricardo*. After haunting the offices of agents and producers, his opportunity came when he was cast in a small summer-stock role in *Her Cardboard Lover*, starring Tallulah Bankhead. Ricardo then played bit roles in several Broadway productions and again was spotted by an M-G-M talent scout. This time his screen test landed him a small role in *Tortilla Flat*. However, news arrived that his mother was gravely ill, and Ricardo turned down the part to rush to her side.

After his mother recovered, Montalbán headed south to Mexico City, where, in the midst of the golden era of Mexican film, he swiftly moved from bit player to lead. After playing a bit part in the unsuccessful *Hostages*, he was soon cast as the Gypsy bullfighter in the 1942 remake of the classic *Santa*, directed by Hollywood's Norman Foster. At around this time Foster's wife showed Ricardo a picture of her sister Georgiana Young, a fashion model in New York, whom, it turned out, he had seen in a bit in *Alexander Graham Bell*. Enamored of the model, he had been carrying her photo around for months, and once he had even trailed her. Before starting his next film, he flew to Los Angeles for a blind date with her. They fell in love and within three weeks were married in a civil ceremony in Tijuana.

Montalbán then starred in two more Mexican films and then returned to Los Angeles to be with Georgiana, who was seven months pregnant with their child. They arranged a quiet church wedding in 1944, and then the actor returned to Mexico to star as a bullfighter in *La hora de la verdad* (1944). After finishing the film *Pepita Jimenez* (1944), Montalbán rushed back to Hollywood for the birth of the first of four children. Jack Cummings, an M-G-M producer in search of a Mexican actor to play a bullfighter, saw *La hora de la verdad*, and M-G-M called Montalbán to audition for the part. He had planned to return to Mexico, where he had made thirteen films in four years, but he won the part of the reluctant matador opposite Esther Williams in the 1947 musical *Fiesta*, his American feature-film debut. In *Fiesta*, Montalbán also teamed up with Cyd Charisse, M-G-M's hottest new dancing star. Film critics declared that Montalbán was a promising young actor, and Cummings put him under contract with M-G-M—to play "Latin lover" roles.

After *Fiesta*, Montalbán starred in three more musicals: *On an Island With You* (1948), with Esther Williams and Cyd Charisse; *The Kissing Bandit* (1948), again with Cyd Charisse; and *Neptune's Daughter* (1949), in which the actor sang Frank Loesser's "Baby, It's Cold Outside." Montalbán was then cast as a Mexican American in William Wellman's *Battleground* (1950). In *Right Cross* (1950) he played an antisocial middleweight champion who in the end "learns" that the discrimination he faces as a Mexican American is a product of his own paranoia. On the set of the 1951 western *Across the Wide Missouri*, he suffered a bad fall from a horse. Though he was in excruciating pain, he finished filming the picture. His left leg never returned to normal, and years later the actor consulted a Los Angeles Rams physician, who determined that he had suffered a pinprick hemorrhage in the spine and that had it been larger he would have been paralyzed.

In 1953, Montalbán starred with Cyd Charisse in *Sombrero*, the romantic adventure of three bachelors in a small Mexican village. After portraying the dashing rancher in pursuit of a rich girl, played by Lana Turner, in *Latin Lovers* (1953), M-G-M dropped Montalbán's contract. Films slowly came his way as a freelancer. His first film was the dreadful *Courtesan of Babylon,* which he made in Italy. After Montalbán starred in a few more mediocre Italian movies, Warner Brothers hired him to portray Nakamura-san, an elegant kabuki actor in *Sayonara* (1957), a story of romance in occupied Japan. Montalbán went to Kyoto to learn and rehearse the intricate movements of Japanese actors, but most of his scenes ended up on the cutting-room floor. He then joined the cast of the musical play *Jamaica* (1957), starring on Broadway with Lena Horne.

In 1969, Montalbán cofounded Nosotros, an organization devoted to solving what it called "the injustices and problems involved in the hiring of Spanish-surnamed actors, actresses and technicians in the motion picture and television industry." As a founder and first president of the organization, Montalbán sought to eliminate the stereotyped Latino image, what he called the "laggard, lover or bandit"; put an end to the practice of excluding actors from consideration for a part simply because they have a Latino surname; and to better train the organization's members. He suffered backlash from his involvement with Nosotros and did not work on a film in Hollywood for four years.

Montalbán did, however, break into television, which allowed him the opportunity to demonstrate a wider acting range. By 1970 his television credits included varied guest spots in such vintage series as *Playhouse 90, Wagon Train,* and *Ben Casey.* He told *TV Guide* that year: "…it is to TV that I owe my freedom from the bondage of the 'Latin lover' roles. Television came along and gave me parts to chew on. It gave me wings as an actor." In the 1970s he appeared in numerous television movies, including 1972's *Return to the Planet of the Apes.* In the 1970s, he returned to the theater, participating in three highly acclaimed national tours of a dramatic reading from G. B. Shaw's *Don Juan in Hell,* under the direction of Agnes Moorehead and John Houseman.

In the 1970s, Montalbán acquired a national reputation, which he owes in part to his appearances on Chrysler commercials. Chrysler Motors had originally hired the actor because they needed a front man with Spanish roots who fit the name of their luxury car, the Cordoba. Montalbán pitched Chrysler's upscale models with such gentlemanly flair and polish that the company kept him as a spokesman for two decades. He also owes his national reputation to his role as Mr. Roarke, the mysterious host endowed with powers to make dreams come true for a price on ABC's long-running series *Fantasy Island*. He landed the role in 1978 and stayed with the highly successful program until it went into reruns in 1984. The part not only made him a household name among all generations of Americans but an international television star when *Fantasy Island* was aired around the globe.

In 1979, Montalbán won an Emmy Award for his portrayal of Chief Satangkai in *How the West Was Won: Part II*. He also won the plaudits of critics for his portrayal of the bare-chested, maniacal Khan in the 1982 space adventure *Star Trek II: The Wrath of Khan*. In 1986 and 1987, Montalbán played the unsavory Zachary Powers on the *Dynasty* spinoff *The Colbys*. He landed the starring role in the 1988 motion picture *The Naked Gun*, playing Vincent Ludwig, a shipping magnate who smuggles heroin and is pursued by a detective, played by O. J. Simpson. The film was a box-office hit, raking in $9.3 million in the first few days after its release. On June 14, 1992, Montalbán cohosted "A Salute to Our Hispanic Heritage," a celebration of Latino culture held at Ford's Theatre to raise money for the theater and for the National Hispanic Scholarship Fund. In May 1993, Montalbán underwent back surgery after losing strength in his legs from a condition caused by his 1949 accident.

For his contributions to film and Latino culture, Montalbán has been awarded many honors in Mexico and the United States. In 1987 he was named the recipient of the Nosotros Lifetime Achievement Award. In 1992 he was honored with the Desi Entertainment Award for Lifetime Achievement, and in 1993 he received the twenty-ninth Screen Actors Guild Achievement Award for fostering the finest ideals of the acting profession.

50

Bobby Bonilla

1963–

Bobby Bonilla was born Roberto Martín Antonio Bonilla on February 23, 1963, in the Bronx, New York, to Roberto Bonilla, an electrician, and Regina Bonilla, a social worker. Life was not easy for a boy from the projects in the South Bronx, one of the toughest neighborhoods in the nation, where drug abuse, shootings, gang violence, and other criminal activities are an everyday occurrence. When Bobby was a child, the Bonilla family was forced to move seven or eight times to avoid confrontations with violence. However, there was no real escape from crime, and even routine trips to the grocery store were fraught with danger. Leaving home one day at age twelve to play basketball with his friends, Bobby encountered a man running down the street brandishing a .22. The children ducked under a car to get out of the line of fire and emerged unscathed, but terrified, from the incident.

Bobby's parents divorced when he was eight years old, and he and his siblings lived with their mother, although Roberto Bonilla continued to take an active role in his children's lives. He encouraged Bobby to excel in sports and took him along on jobs so that he could spend more time with him. Roberto Bonilla kept a close eye on his children. Every evening between eight and nine o'clock he would drive by their apartment building and honk the horn, a signal for all the children to gather at the window so he could check that they were home safely. As a child, Bobby was adept at sports, particularly baseball, and would often go to Yankee Stadium to watch his heroes play. He played organized games for school teams and sandlot baseball on the playgrounds, where he worked hard to replicate the swings of his favorite players, such as Willie Randolph and Graig Nettles. Bobby practiced his swing so much that he grew into an accomplished switch-hitter. As a child, Bobby slept with a baseball bat in his bed, and if he awoke in the middle of the night, he would jump up and take a few swings.

When Bobby was a youngster, his mother was working toward a master's degree in social work at Columbia University. At home she stressed the value of education to her children. She jumped at the opportunity to enroll Bobby, made eligible by his good grades and fine character, at Lehman High School, a predominantly white, middle-class school located an hour away by bus. At Lehman High, Bobby met with racist attitudes and had to defend himself from the taunts of other boys. The baseball coach at Lehman, Joe Levine, saw the makings of a star in Bonilla and took the young player under his wing. The baseball team played a light schedule, and in one season Bobby participated in only thirty-three games.

Bonilla would have been drafted by a major league team while still in high school, but scouts avoided the inner city, and so he graduated from Lehman in 1981 with no future prospects in baseball. When Joe Levine learned that an eastern U.S. high school all-star team was scheduled to go to Scandinavia that summer, he filled out an application on behalf of his star player and got Bonilla on the team. Another team member was Jim Thrift, whose father, Syd Thrift, joined the boys on the tour. It was Syd Thrift, a former Pittsburgh Pirate scout and later Pittsburgh's general manager, who brought Bobby Bonilla into the major leagues by highly recommending him to the Pirates.

The Pittsburgh Pirates signed Bonilla as a nondrafted free agent in 1981 and sent him to their rookie-league team in Bradenton, Florida, where he hit a mediocre .217 his first year. Bonilla performed poorly because he had not played in as many games in high school as the other rookies. With an uncertain future ahead in baseball, Bonilla attended a trade school in order to become a repairman. Bonilla batted only .228 in his second minor league season, but because he was a switch-hitter who showed promise, the Pirates kept him on the roster. He was tutored intensively by former Pirate great Willie Stargell and other fielding and batting instructors, and by 1983, Bobby Bonilla had raised his average to .256. When Bonilla was playing winter baseball in Puerto Rico, his childhood sweetheart, Millie Quiñones, paid a visit, and the two decided to get married. They were so broke that a player on the team had to pay for their wedding license.

In 1985, Bonilla's career with the Pittsburgh Pirates was just taking off when he broke his right leg in a collision with Bip Roberts during spring training. The break was so bad that the Pirates did not think that Bonilla would play baseball again, and they shipped him to the low minors. That winter, Bonilla was left off the Pirates' roster and was picked up by the Chicago White Sox. Bonilla broke into the major leagues with Chicago in 1986, but four months later, Syd Thrift brought him back to Pittsburgh in exchange for pitcher José DeLeón. Bonilla became a starter for the Pirates in mid-1987.

In his five seasons with the Pittsburgh Pirates, Bonilla achieved stardom. He helped guide the Pirates to two National League East championships and was voted a member of the National League All-Star team every year from 1988 to 1991. Highlights from his career with the Pirates include an upper-deck home run, the seventh in Three River Stadium history, which Bonilla hit on July 12, 1987. That year, the powerful switch hitter had a career-high batting average of .300. In 1988, Bobby Bonilla led the National League in home runs and RBIs in the first half of the season, then slowed down and finished with 24 home runs and 100 runs batted in. In 1990 he enjoyed a superb season with the Pirates, hitting .280, with 32 home runs and 120 runs batted in.

The Pirates offered Bobby Bonilla little financial reward for his spectacular play that season, and he grew disenchanted with the team. In the winter of 1990 the player took the team to salary arbitration and lost. The Pirates then presented Bobby Bonilla with such salary contract offers as $16.8 million for four seasons, but Bonilla knew that based on his performance, he was worth more. In 1991, Bonilla had a stellar year, finishing third in the voting for the league's Most Valuable Player and helping the Pirates to advance to the National League Championship Series. He informed the baseball world that at the end of the 1991 season he would be a free agent. As a result, Bonilla was deluged by contract offers. The New York Mets won the fierce bidding war that ensued. The Mets' general manager, Al Harazin, signed the twenty-eight-year-old Bonilla to a five-year, $29 million contract, then the biggest salary in baseball. Harazin chose Bonilla in hopes of reviving the Mets' pennant chances in 1992.

Bonilla was excited by the thought of playing baseball in the city that feels like home to him. But he carried an enormous weight on his shoulders going into the 1992 season, for the Mets organization and the New York fans pinned their pennant hopes on their newly acquired star player. Bonilla was impervious to the pressures of fulfilling his promise with the Mets. In the October 14, 1991, issue of *Sports Illustrated,* he claimed that he doesn't feel pressure on the field: "You talk about pressure in baseball. Pressure is growing up in the South Bronx. We're talking about houses burning and people starving...." Bonilla endured a difficult first season in New York, but it was not due to the anticipation of the Mets franchise and New York spectators. For most of the 1992 season he suffered from a an ache in his right shoulder and underwent arthroscopic surgery to repair a torn bicep tendon. He still performed well during his debut with the Mets, hitting 2 home runs in St. Louis on opening night and leading the team in home runs and coming in second in RBIs for the season.

Despite his injuries and the disappointments of that year, Bonilla was pleased to play in New York and was sure that New York fans were glad to have him on the team. He told the *New York Times* in September 1992: "I am embraced by the black and Latin communities. Just to say I'm playing with this team, it's important to some people. I played at Lehman High School, at St. Mary's Park, at Throgs Neck. That means a great deal to a lot of New York fans." Bonilla anticipated a great comeback during his second season with the Mets in 1993. However, toward the end of the year, he was again plagued by a shoulder injury that required surgery. On September 7, 1993, in Houston, Bonilla ruptured ligaments in his left shoulder while rounding second base. Despite his injuries, Bobby Bonilla concluded the 1993 season with a personal best of 34 home runs, 87 runs batted in, and a .265 batting average, with the prospect of a brilliant season in 1994.

Bobby Bonilla spends time off the baseball diamond contributing to the lives of those less fortunate and helping to alleviate the suffering of the human spirit. He often makes the rounds of hospitals, nurturing the hopes of children.

51

Jaime Escalante

1930(?)–

Jaime Escalante was born in the early 1930s in La Paz, Bolivia, the son of an elementary-school teacher. He attended San Andrés University in La Paz, where he earned his teaching credentials during the political unrest plaguing that country in the late 1940s. At the age of twenty-two, he secured his first teaching post at Nacional Bolivar High School and then taught at Colegio Militar, a military academy. He soon won a national reputation as an outstanding teacher. For five consecutive years, high school students whom he taught at a school in San Calixto won top prizes in math and physics. In 1959, Escalante, a progressive educator, organized the first national symposium of physics and mathematics for Bolivia's high school teachers.

The military and economic troubles brewing in Bolivia in 1963 led Escalante and his wife, Fabiola, to emigrate to the United States with their son. They settled in California, where life presented myriad difficulties for the highly acclaimed teacher. He spoke no English, and his Bolivian teaching credentials were worthless in the United States, so he was forced to work in a coffee shop while he learned English. He then landed a job testing computers for the Burroughs Corporation, but he found little satisfaction in this line of work and longed for the classroom. For seven years he took night courses toward a degree in math from California State University. Upon receiving his teaching certification, Jaime Escalante gave up his higher salary working on computers and joined the faculty at Garfield High School in the 1973–1974 school year. He was originally hired by Garfield High School to teach computer science, but by the time of his arrival the school still had no computers, so he ended up teaching math instead.

Escalante came to Garfield High at a time when the school's progressive administrators had had enough of the status quo and were pushing for academic achievement from a student body that was 98 percent Latino and over 50 percent first-generation American. In the mid-1960s, Garfield High's accreditation had been threatened. Order and discipline had disintegrated to such an extent at the school that teenage gang members were allowed to set up turf boundaries on the campus. The threat to accreditation awakened administrators of the Los Angeles Unified School District to the school's dire straits. Escalante's initial experiences at Garfield High School were daunting. He found a school in an East L.A. neighborhood beset by drugs, crime, and gang violence. Despite the progress administrators had made, the kids still had many fights inside the school, too many were gang members, most were not motivated to learn, and, sadly, some had no school supplies.

In his early days at the school Escalante wavered between returning to his computer job or instilling a sense of respect and responsibility in the students—and then quitting. He decided to remain at Garfield High School, and little by little he made inroads with the students and began to turn their lives around in the classroom. In the late 1970s he submitted a proposal for advanced placement (AP) calculus. The principal of Garfield High at the time, Henry Gradillas, and the AP coordinator were determined to strengthen the school academically, and they supported Escalante's program. In 1979, Escalante held his first calculus class with an enrollment of five students. Four of his five students achieved outstanding results and passed the AP test that first year.

With those students and subsequent classes, Escalante used an innovative team approach to teaching, as he told *Educational Leadership* in an interview in its February 1989 issue: "I make them believe that we have a team which is going to prepare for the Olympics. And our Olympics is the advanced-placement calculus exam." He built the students' self-confidence, making them believe in themselves and showing them that the way to a bright future was through education. Once the students were confident and thinking like a team, he began to direct all their energy to the study of math and pushed, cajoled, irritated, and praised them for results. At times he whispered to keep their attention focused on the topic at hand or spoke in a booming voice. If students dozed off, Escalante socked them with a red velvet pillow. As a way to encourage excellence, he also kept in contact with parents, and over the years, because of such community involvement, parents began to expect that the children would go on to college.

With each year the number of students at Garfield High interested in advanced calculus doubled, and with each class Jaime Escalante proved that Latino students could transcend their disadvantaged background and the gangs and drugs of East L.A. and excel academically. Within three years after the AP calculus program was launched, Escalante's students were scoring the highest possible grade, five, and almost all were receiving at least a three, the passing grade, on the challenging AP test in calculus. A score of three and higher entitles a student to receive course credit at most colleges and universities across the nation. With their self-esteem bolstered, students began to set their sights on college, and many envisioned attending some of the top colleges and universities in America.

In 1982, Escalante suffered a mild heart attack. That same year, controversy arose when the Educational Testing Service (ETS), which administers the AP tests, questioned the validity of the scores of eighteen of Escalante's students. The suspicions of ETS officials had been aroused by a pattern of corresponding incorrect answers, and they accused two Garfield High students of cheating. The ETS issued an ultimatum: Either all the students take a new, more difficult test, or their scores would be invalidated. Escalante denied the accusations and then encouraged the students to take the test over. Twelve agreed, and they all passed. The grades were positive proof of the effectiveness of Escalante's teaching methods.

By 1988 the dropout rate at Garfield High School had fallen to 14 percent, whereas it had stood as high as 55 percent a decade earlier. By the mid-1980s only six public schools in America prepared more students for the AP calculus test than Garfield. In 1987, 75 percent of Garfield High's graduating seniors had made provisions for college, and a number of students were recruited by the best colleges and universities. The Foundation for Advancement in Science and Education provided funds to help send the students to college, and the teachers also hunted for scholarships for the students.

The 1982 incident concerning the ETS and Escalante's AP calculus students had received much attention from the media, and the publicity over the story piqued the interest of film producer Tom Musca and director Ramón Menendez. The were convinced that the students' scores would never have been questioned if they had not been predominantly Latino or from Garfield High School. Menendez and Musca approached Escalante about making a film of his achievements in the classroom. While he had little time for such a venture, Escalante ultimately granted the actor Edward James Olmos, originally from East L.A., permission to accompany him eighteen hours a day for one month in preparation for the principal role of Escalante in the film.

The 1988 film *Stand and Deliver* was applauded by film critics and audiences across America. After its release, Escalante was praised for his achievements by President Ronald Reagan, who invited the teacher to the White House. Vice President Bush, who visited Garfield High School in the spring of 1988, singled out Escalante as one of his heroes during the second presidential debate. The publicity that Escalante garnered from the film attracted $750,000 that year in corporate contributions to Garfield High School. He went on to host a PBS series on math, science, and careers which included the special *Math...Who Needs It?!* The series won a Peabody Award and twenty-one other

broadcasting and education awards. It seemed as though Escalante would spend the rest of his teaching days helping students
excel at Garfield High School.

However, shortly after the release of *Stand and Deliver,*
Escalante found many of the teachers at Garfield envious of his
fame, and he began receiving death threats and prank phone
calls. Then the school's math teachers voted to remove him from
the chair of the math department, a post he had held for over a
decade, and a feud with the teachers' union ensued. It became
impossible for Escalante to remain at the school. In the summer
of 1991, Escalante left Garfield High School and his San Gabriel
Valley home for Sacramento's Hiram Johnson High School. At
Hiram Johnson, only six students had passed the AP calculus
exam in 1990, and Escalante faced the same kinds of challenges
that he had overcome at Garfield High School. With his innovative approach, he set to the task of turning the students of Hiram
Johnson High School into winners and continued his lifelong
pursuit of excellence.

52

Rafael Chacón

1833–1925

Chacón was born on April 22, 1833, in Santa Fe, then the territory of New Mexico under Mexican rule, to Doña María Refugio Secundina Lopez de Chacón and Albino Chacón. Rafael's father, descended from early Spanish settlers, enjoyed the luxury of an education, a certain sign of affluence, and later held various important posts in the Mexican government.

Rafael Chacón was baptized at Santa Fe Cathedral on April 26, 1833, as José Rafael Sotero. As a child held in the arms of one of the family's servants, Rafael witnessed the bloody executions of the ringleaders of the Rebellion of La Cañada in 1837. In early childhood, he listened attentively to accounts of the family's

255

genealogy. Out of these early experiences grew his keen desire to keep a record of historical events which he could pass on to the next generations. In 1841, he was enrolled in the Beginners School run by Doña Mariquita, and then he went to the school of Don Serafin Ramírez. After Ramírez whipped the boy severely, Albino Chacón sued him and placed Rafael with Teacher Pacheco, a devout Catholic who was not terribly learned but was a perfect mentor for small children. In six months Rafael had learned everything he could from Pacheco, and he was able to recite the sacred ritual from the *Introibo ad altare dei* to the end of the mass and the entire catechism. Albino Chacón, who was then a secretary to General Armijo, took Rafael into his office and taught him writing and the rudiments of grammar and mathematics.

When Rafael was eleven years old, he was sent to military school in Chihuahua, Mexico, even though the age of acceptance was fourteen. Albino Chacón supplied his son with all the necessities as well as a letter of introduction. Soon after he arrived at the school, some cadets who were inveterate gamblers stole all of Rafael's belongings and money, leaving the boy penniless and without food. One day, as Rafael sat weeping over his desperate condition, a letter from his father arrived enjoining him to recite the *Salve Regina* in honor of the Blessed Virgin Mary and to go to church to hear mass. As Rafael walked toward the Church of Saint Francis, he found nine pesos and stale pieces of bread scattered in the sand. He kept the money in a belt tied around his waist and made the storekeeper from whom he bought food promise to tell his unruly comrades that all of his purchases were on credit so that they would not rob him again.

Soon a Cap. Don Miguel Gomez took pity on Rafael and invited the boy to live in his home and gave him a new supply of clothes. Father Don Antonio Gomez, the captain's brother, lived in the household and instructed Rafael in religious matters. From 1844 to 1846, Rafael resided in the Gomez household and attended the military school, studying military ordinances, manuals of arms, arithmetic, and elementary geometry and participating in drills, gymnastic exercises, and training in pieces of artillery. In August 1846, General Armijo ordered Albino Chacón to call out all the militia to fight American battalions, led by Gen. Stephen W. Kearny, that were advancing on New Mexico to capture the territory in the Mexican War. As a cadet, Rafael was subject to duty, but since he was only thirteen years old, Albino Chacón asked General Armijo to excuse him from fighting. However, Rafael, a young subaltern, joined his father in a battle against the Americans. In the end, General Kearny's "Army of the West" conquered the territory of New Mexico, which was ceded to the United States by the Treaty of Guadalupe Hidalgo in 1848.

By 1855, Rafael Chacón was a loyal American citizen, and that year he enlisted under Kit Carson as a first sergeant in Company B of St. Vrain's Ballatón. Soon after, he took part in punitive expeditions against the Muacho Ute and Jicarilla Apache Indians, who had massacred the inhabitants of a trading post at Fort Pueblo. As a result of the campaign, the Utes and the Apaches agreed to remain on a reservation and gave up all territorial claims. On July 31, 1855, Chacón received an honorable discharge, and between stints of military service over the next six years, he led a peaceful life as a farmer and trader. From 1856 to 1859, Chacón was involved in international commerce, trading the goods he acquired from the Native Americans to Mexicans for a huge profit. From 1857 to 1858 he also served as justice of the peace in the precinct of El Chamizal.

In April 1858, Chacón married Juanita Paez, an uneducated noble woman, and the couple settled down in Santa Fe, where Chacón secured a government position copying legislative bills. He also engaged his wife and his mother in a tailoring business he ran on the side, and the threesome turned out several pairs of pants each day. By May 1859, Chacón had saved enough money from all of his enterprises to build and furnish a house. However, in August 1861, his comfortable domestic life came to an end when the Confederate army in Texas threatened to invade New Mexico in hopes of capturing a large portion of the Southwest for the secessionists. Juanita Paez and the couple's children went to live with his parents, while Chacón formed a company of soldiers whom he led to Fort Union to be sworn into the volunteer service of the United States to fight in the Civil War. Chacón's company was designated Company K of the First Infantry Regimen and was almost totally Spanish speaking. After long months of waiting, the army of Texans marched toward Fort Craig. Chacón's troops emerged victorious at the Battle of Valverde. As fought in New Mexico, the Civil War was of short duration and resulted in a Union victory.

After the expulsion of the Confederates from New Mexico, Chacón's company was assigned to garrison Fort Wingate, south of Grants, New Mexico. In 1864 he joined Union troops to round up the Navajo Indians and force them to live on reservations. Later, as commander of Fort Stanton, he fought the Mescalero Apaches. In 1866, Chacón, practically penniless, took his family northward to settle near present-day Trinidad, Colorado. With his industry and grit, he rebuilt the family's fortunes through agriculture and ranching. In the early 1870s, Chacón set to work on his memoirs with the guidance and support of his lawyer-son Eusebio. Never having totally mastered English, Chacón wrote in Spanish. He toiled for six years on the manuscript, which he hoped would someday be published.

After completing the manuscript, Eusebio Chacón had three copies typed and bound, with the intention of having the manuscript printed. He kept one copy for himself and gave one to a daughter. The third copy of the manuscript was given to Juanita Paez. In 1925, Chacón died, and his widow handed over her copy to Felipe Chacón. This proved to be a fortuitous gesture, for the handwritten manuscript and two of the typewritten copies were later lost. Only Felipe Chacón's copy of the Chacón memoirs was preserved. It was later handed down to Felipe Chacón's eldest daughter, Herminia Chacón de Gonzales of El Paso, Texas, who safeguarded it for many years. Seventy years after Rafael Chacón wrote his memoirs, they were finally translated by Felipe Chacón's second daughter, Vera Chacón de Padilla of Albuquerque, New Mexico, who acquired the manuscript from her sister. Her translation served as the basis for a book on Chacón published in 1986 by Jacqueline Dorgan Meketa. Thus, Rafael Chacón's eyewitness accounts of life before and after the arrival of the Anglos in New Mexico became a valuable tool in "revising" the historical record in order to better represent the experiences of the Hispanos.

53

Sandra Cisneros

1954–

Sandra Cisneros was born in Chicago in 1954 to a Mexican father and a Mexican-American mother. She was the only girl out of seven children. During childhood, her six brothers shunned her company, so Sandra spent a lot of time alone and became a shy and introverted child. She also became a keen observer of the world and the personalities around her, a skill that would benefit her in her future literary career. Sandra and her six brothers were raised in poverty in the Chicago barrios, and as a child she developed a fear of mice, which she attributes to her anxiety over life in the underclass. The family often escaped the Chicago barrios for Mexico City to quell Sandra's father's longing for that city. They returned each time from their pilgrimages to Mexico to settle in a different Chicago apartment. This constant moving about brought enormous upheaval to Sandra's life, further exacerbating her feelings of separation.

Sandra Cisneros attended Catholic schools in Chicago, where she says the nuns ignored her experiences as a member of an ethnic minority. Rather than reveal her creativity to her teachers, she wrote in secrecy at home until high school, when she began to read her poems in class. In her sophomore year a teacher recognized a burgeoning talent and encouraged her to work on a literary magazine, of which she was eventually named editor. After graduating from high school Cisneros enrolled at Loyola University. Her father consented to her decision to pursue higher education so that she could find a suitable husband. In a November 1990 article in *Glamour* magazine, she wrote of the positive aspects of her father's sexist attitude: "In retrospect, I'm lucky my father believed daughters were meant for husbands. It meant it didn't matter if I majored in something like English. After all, I'd find a nice professional eventually, right? This allowed me the liberty to putter about embroidering my little poems and stories without my mother interrupting...."

From Loyola University, Cisneros went on to the Iowa Writers' Workshop, where she received a master's degree. Her race and class set her apart from the other students, and she often felt alienated. This alienation reached a critical point at a seminar on Gaston Bachelard's "Poetics of Space," when students described the posh houses of their childhood, in stark contrast to hers in the Chicago barrio. Cisneros had a sudden revelation during that seminar that her unique experiences as a Latina gave her a raison d'etre for her writing. She set to work on her first book, *The House on Mango Street,* in which she describes the home of her imagination in the novel's opening pages: "They always told us that one day we would move into a house, a real house that would be ours for always so we wouldn't have to move each year. And our house would have running water and pipes that worked. And inside it would have real stairs, not hallway stairs, but stairs inside like the houses on T.V."

Published in 1984, *The House on Mango Street* is comprised of vignettes told by Esperanza Cordero, a creative Chicana girl growing up in a Chicago barrio. Esperanza longs to escape the poverty-stricken neighborhood of the barrio and then to return someday "for the ones I left behind. The ones who cannot get out." By the end of the book she has been sufficiently empowered to embark on her quest. *The House on Mango Street* crisscrosses two cultures and is peppered with Spanish words and phrases. Cisneros told *Newsweek* in 1991 that she is grateful for her bicultural experience, which provided her with "twice as many words to pick from...two ways of looking at the world." In 1991, *The House on Mango Street* was reissued by Vintage to critical acclaim. It is widely read by students from junior high school to graduate school, and Stanford University, among others, has included the book in its curriculum.

After receiving her master's degree, Cisneros returned to Chicago, where she taught literacy skills to high school dropouts and worked as a college recruiter. She lived alone despite her father's pleas that she move back home and pursued her writing at the kitchen table at night. In 1986, Cisneros received a Dobie-Paisano fellowship which took her to Texas. That year she completed a book of poetry, *My Wicked, Wicked Ways*, which was published in 1987. Critics applauded the collection, and in 1992 it was rereleased in hardcover by Turtle Bay Books.

After her fellowship ended, Cisneros wanted to remain in Texas but was unable to make a living there. In the throes of depression, she accepted a guest lectureship at California State University in Chico. Soon after, she was awarded the first of two National Endowment for the Arts fellowships in fiction she would receive. The fellowship helped her out of a financial quagmire and restored her self-esteem. She then contacted literary agent Susan Bergholz, whose telephone number she had been carrying around for months. With Bergholz's help she signed a contract with Random House for *Woman Hollering Creek*, which was published in 1991. The novel launched Cisneros on the road to literary fame.

Woman Hollering Creek is a series of often witty and always honest and compassionate stories exploring the lives of girls and women on both sides of the Texas-Mexican border. Like *The House on Mango Street*, it is written from a feminist perspective and offers a stark portrayal of the reality of women's experience and their relationships with men. The path her characters follow veers dramatically from the author's own life experiences. As Cisneros told *Hispanic* magazine in 1993, she refused to follow the traditional path of marriage her female characters choose: "I have been able to be a writer because I had no one to think of but myself. Art is my husband." *Woman Hollering Creek* was well received by literary critics.

The hard times Sandra Cisneros experienced in her early career have molded her into an activist. She is a highly visible spokesperson for Latinos and defends their interests at every opportunity. For example, Cisneros refused to appear in an Annie Leibowitz ad for The Gap, claiming that the store showed a lack of commitment to the Latino community. She champions the rights of working class Latinos and insists that Latino writers deserve greater representation in library collections. She told Mary B. W. Tabor of the *New York Times*: "I'm a translator. I'm an amphibian. I can travel in both worlds. What I'm saying is very important for the Latino community, but it is also important for the white community to hear. What I'm saying in my writing is that we can be Latino and still be American." Sandra Cisneros has been recognized for her work on behalf of the Latino community. In 1993 she was one of three winners of the 1993 Anisfield-Wolf Book Awards for *Woman Hollering Creek,* given annually for works dealing with racism and ethnicity.

Sandra Cisneros's political convictions also embrace causes beyond the Latino community. For instance, she was an outspoken critic of the war in the Balkans. In a March 14, 1993, article in the *New York Times,* adapted from a speech she gave for the March 7 International Women's Day Rally in San Antonio, Cisneros demanded that President Clinton and world leaders resolve the conflict in the former Yugoslavia. Cisneros writes from a personal perspective of her Bosnian friend Jasna, who traveled to the United States to translate Cisneros's stories into Serbo-Croatian but speaks for all the victims of the war: "She's in there. Get her out, I tell you. Get them out. They're in that city, that country, that region, that mouth of hell, that house of fire, get her out of there, I demand you."

54

Cesar Romero

1907–1994

One of four children, Cesar Romero was born Cesar Julio Romero on February 15, 1907, in New York City, the son of distinguished Cuban émigrés. His father, Cesar Julio Romero, was a machinery exporter and his mother, María Mantilla Martí, enjoyed a career as a concert singer under the stage name María Mantilla. Cesar's maternal grandfather was the Cuban revolutionary poet and patriot José Martí, who planned the Cuban war of independence and died fighting for freedom in 1895. Cesar attended P.S. 166 on Manhattan's West Side before entering Collegiate School in 1922, where he was voted best dancer and handsomest student upon graduation in 1926. Though not

among the top academic achievers, he distinguished himself with
his enthusiasm and theatrical talent.

When the Cuban sugar market collapsed in 1922, Cesar's
father, whose company did business exclusively with Cuban sugar
interests, lost over half a million dollars, leaving the family with
plenty of finely tailored clothes but no money. Young Cesar took
to dressing elegantly and charmed his way into dinner parties
and Broadway shows. In 1931, his father found him a job as a
teller in a Wall Street Bank. He found the work boring, so when
Lisbeth Higgins, an heiress, suggested that they become a dance
team and go onstage, he agreed to the idea, although he had no
formal training. The popular duo performed in Manhattan
nightclubs of that era. Throughout his life Romero was regarded
as Hollywood's most desirable dancing partner at parties as well
as on the stage and screen.

In his search for a Latin who spoke flawless English for the
hit stage comedy *Strictly Dishonorable*, producer Brock Pemberton
discovered Cesar Romero in the Montmartre nightclub in Manhattan. Soon Romero landed a part as a dancer in the 1927 New
York production *Lady Do* and made his Broadway debut as Ricci
in the 1932 play *Dinner at Eight*, which ran for more than three
hundred performances. While he was appearing in *Dinner at
Eight*, Metro-Goldwyn-Mayer (M-G-M) offered the budding actor
a contract. Cesar Romero made his screen debut as the gigolo
Jorgensen in M-G-M's 1934 motion picture *The Thin Man*. While
he was often cast as the "other man" or a gigolo, Romero was still
given the label "Latin lover" at the beginning of his Hollywood
career. In 1984, he commented on this phenomenon: "When I
started in motion pictures in 1934, they said I was going to be the
next Valentino. I was never a leading man, and very seldom did I
do a picture where I got the girl. But I was saddled with the label
because I had a Latin name."

After lending the actor to Warner Brothers for a film, M-G-M
canceled Romero's contract. In the mid-1930s, Universal signed
him to a three-year contract and cast him in such films as the 1935
comedy *The Good Fairy*, starring Margaret Sullavan; 1935's *Diamond Jim;* and the 1936 romantic comedy *Love Before Breakfast*.
Darryl F. Zanuck, of Twentieth Century, borrowed Romero for
several films when Universal declined to raise his salary. His
performance as Koda-Khan in the 1937 Shirley Temple film *Wee
Willie Winkie* led Zanuck, who by then had merged his company

with Fox, to offer Cesar Romero a fourteen-year contract. Romero often made five or six films a year for Twentieth Century-Fox. Among such films, he was cast in the 1939 Shirley Temple picture *The Little Princess* and with Sonja Henie in the 1938 romantic musical *Happy Landing* and the 1943 ski film *Wintertime*.

After filming *Wintertime*, Romero's work with Twentieth Century-Fox was interrupted by World War II. The young actor enlisted in the U.S. Coast Guard, attaining the rank of chief boatswain's mate, the highest uncommissioned rank in the service. In the three years he served, Romero was stationed in the Pacific theater of war and frequently worked as a spokesperson publicizing the war effort. After the war he landed more light comedy roles, such as in the 1947 musical *Carnival in Costa Rica*, played Hernán Cortés in *Captain From Castile* (1947), and starred in the 1948 musical comedy *That Lady in Ermine* and in the 1948 family film *Deep Waters*.

Fox cast Romero in the leading role in the successful Cisco Kid Western serials, beginning in 1939 with *The Cisco Kid and the Lady*. In 1940 and 1941, Romero starred in six Cisco Kid adventures. However, Fox was forced to drop the series when Latin America took offense that Cesar Romero, a quintessential Latin lover, was playing the Kid as a dandy. An international incident erupted over the casting, and diplomatic cables whizzed between Latin America and the U.S. State Department. In the end, Zanuck was ordered by the State Department to either change Romero's style or stop making the series altogether. Zanuck ceased filming. In 1942, Romero starred opposite Ginger Rogers in *Tales of Manhattan*, comprised of separate stories of a tail coat which passes from owner to owner.

After leaving Fox, Cesar Romero worked as a freelancer in the 1950s, appearing in such films as the 1954 western melodrama *Vera Cruz*, the 1951 musical *Happy Go Lovely*, 1953's *Prisoners of the Casbah*, the 1955 western *The Americano*, and the large-scale classic *Around the World in 80 Days*, with its forty-four cameo stars. Romero was the urbane, mysterious foreign courier in the 1954 television series *A Passport to Danger*. His film career continued well into the 1960s with such films as the 1960 caper comedy *Ocean's Eleven*, the 1965 clumsy comedy *Sergeant Deadhead*, and the dismal 1965 comedy *Marriage on the Rocks*. In the 1950s and 1960s, Romero also was a popular guest on various television shows. He appeared occasionally in variety series starring Milton Berle, Martha Raye, Dinah Shore, Betty Hutton, Red Skelton, and James Stewart. He also played guest roles in drama series, such as *The Zane Grey Theater* and *Playhouse 90,* and in westerns like *Wagon Train,* and *Stage Coach West.*

To younger audiences, the enduring and versatile Romero is most familiar as the malevolent Joker in the television series *Batman,* which first aired in the mid-1960s and then went into reruns. While Romero did not mind forsaking his looks for the career-revitalizing part, he was distressed when producers ordered him to shave off his mustache. *Batman* star Adam West once reminisced about the mustache: "It was as if he'd be losing all those wonderful movies he made when he was the dashing Latin Romeo." The producers backed down and told Romero to conceal the mustache with makeup, but apparently it was still discernible through the greasepaint.

In 1984, in honor of his fiftieth year in films, Cesar Romero received the Career Achievement Award at the Hollywood International Celebrity Awards Banquet. That same year, he earned a Nosotros Golden Eagle Award for his success as a Latino in the entertainment industry. In 1991, Romero accepted the Imagen Hispanic Media Award for lifetime achievement, and in 1992 he was honored by the Beverly Hills Chamber of Commerce with its Will Rogers Memorial Award.

A bachelor all his life, he once said of his single status: "I have no regrets." Cesar Romero was active in the community up until his death. In November 1993 he lent a hand at the Los Angeles Mission on Skid Row, serving Thanksgiving dinner to the homeless. On the celebrity guest list, Romero was expected to attend the opening night of Andrew Lloyd Webber's *Sunset Boulevard* on December 9, 1993. Romero died of complications from a blood clot on New Year's Day, 1994, in Santa Monica, California.

José Feliciano

1945–

The second of twelve children, José Feliciano was born José Monserrate Feliciano on September 10, 1945, in Lares, Puerto Rico. He was blind at birth from congenital glaucoma. His father worked as a farmer, but he could barely support the family on his low wages. In 1950 the family relocated from Lares to New York City, first to Spanish Harlem and later to the Lower East Side, where José's father found work as a longshoreman. José faced poverty and racial discrimination in his childhood, but these hardships were tempered by his love for music, which enabled him to block out harsh reality.

Very early on José showed signs of enormous musical talent. As a three-year-old, he first accompanied his uncle on a tin soda-cracker can, and at age six he taught himself to play the concertina simply by listening to records and practicing. By age nine he had mastered the guitar. That year, he performed in public for the first time at El Teatro Puerto Rico in Spanish Harlem. José practiced the guitar so intensively that his mother had to take the instrument away from him to get him to go to bed. He was determined not to let his blindness deter him from pursuing his aspirations, and he went on to master the banjo, bass, mandolin, bongo drums, harmonica, timbales, kazoo, piano, and harpsichord. Feliciano is completely self-taught except for brief classical guitar training.

Feliciano attended Charles Evans Hughes High School on West Eighteenth Street in Manhattan, where he performed frequently in talent shows and assemblies. In those early days, his favorites were the songs of such rock-and-roll singers as Fats Domino, Elvis Presley, and Chuck Berry, and he was most influenced by Ray Charles and Sam Cooke. While still in high school, he began performing at Greenwich Village coffeehouses, playing folk, flamenco, and pop guitar. By the age of sixteen he was contributing to the family income, and at age seventeen, with his father out of work, he dropped out of school to perform full-time and support his family. In 1963 the young singer accepted his first professional job at the Retort Coffee House in Detroit. Back in New York that summer, he played an engagement at Gerde's Folk City in Greenwich Village and was such a hit that he received bookings at the Bitter End and the Gaslight in Greenwich Village. Feliciano met Hilda Perez, the manager of one of the spots where he performed, and they married on October 19, 1963. The couple later divorced.

In 1964, Vanguard Records recorded Feliciano's performance at the Newport Jazz Festival, and that year an RCA Victor executive heard him at Gerde's and arranged an exclusive recording contract. Feliciano soon released "Everybody Do the Click," a gimmicky debut single, before recording his first album, *The Voice and Guitar of José Feliciano,* released in the summer of 1965. Both the single and the album failed to make it onto the U.S. music charts, but they caught on with disc jockeys and were played regularly over the air. In January 1966, Feliciano released another English-language album, *A Bag Full of Soul.* Two cuts in particular from the album, "Goin' to Chicago" and Bob Dylan's "Masters of War" drew the attention of critics: That June, the singer debuted on the New York concert stage at Town Hall.

Feliciano enjoyed his first success among Spanish-speaking audiences. He achieved recognition through Spanish concert tours in the United States and Latin America and through three Spanish-language albums produced by RCA International in 1968, *Una voz, una guitarra*; *Mas exitos, de José Feliciano;* and *La voz y la guitarra de José Feliciano.* "La copa rota" and "Amor gitana," two singles from *Una voz, una guitarra,* made it onto the Latin America pop charts that year. Around this time, the singer performed in television programs syndicated to Spanish-language stations in Latin America and the United States.

At the same time, Feliciano made every effort to gain a foothold with English-speaking audiences. In the spring of 1968, the singer released *Feliciano!,* which was his first album to hit the charts, reaching number two. With its impassioned arrangements of recent hits, *Feliciano!* was also his biggest seller and his first album to go gold. The single from the album, "Light My Fire," was a smash hit, rising to the number-three spot on the U.S. pop charts and selling more than a million copies. Feliciano transformed this Doors 1967 hit, with his Latin style and acoustic guitar, to create a singular sound.

In 1968, Feliciano followed up "Light My Fire" with a version of Tommy Tucker's rhythm-and-blues standard "Hi Heel Sneakers," another hit which made it to number twenty-five on the charts. His popularity soared, and in September 1968, he played at the Greek Theater in Los Angeles. In October of that year he was invited to Tiger Stadium in Detroit to sing "The Star-Spangled Banner" before Game Five of the World Series. His Latin-jazz rendition of the national anthem insulted traditionalists, who booed Feliciano during the performance, stirring a nationwide controversy, which the singer took advantage of by releasing a live recording of the anthem. In December 1968, Feliciano appeared with Chuck Berry, Marvin Gaye, the Grateful Dead, Joni Mitchell, and others before a crowd of 100,000 at the Miami Pop Festival in Hallandale, Florida.

In early 1969, the singer was honored with two Grammy Awards, one for Best New Artist of 1968 and the other for Best Contemporary Pop Vocal Performance for "Light My Fire." On April 27, 1969, the singer made his first television special, *Feliciano—Very Special,* with guests Andy Williams, Glen Campbell, Dionne Warwick, and Burt Bacharach.

His smash hit "Feliz Navidad" ("I Wanna Wish You a Merry

Christmas") became one of his hallmarks when it was released on the 1971 album *José Feliciano*. That year, with wife and manager Hilda Perez, Feliciano also wrote the song "Rain," which became a British hit for Bruce Ruffin. In 1974, Feliciano recorded the theme song to the enormously popular television show *Chico and the Man* and included the number on his album *And the Feeling's Good*. Despite these successes, Feliciano's popularity waned among English-speaking audiences in the United States in the mid-1970s, and RCA turned to promoting the Spanish-language material. In an effort to win back American fans, Feliciano left RCA in September 1976 and signed with various recording companies, including the Private Stock label.

While Feliciano has a small but devoted group of fans in the United States, he has enjoyed consistent sales overseas, earning forty gold and platinum albums internationally by 1993. His albums marketed for Spanish-speaking audiences in the 1980s drew applause from music critics. The singer captured Grammy Awards for Best Latin Pop Performance for his 1983 album *Me enamore*, his 1986 song "Lelolai," his 1989 song "Ceilito lindo," from the album *I'm Never Gonna Change,* and for his 1990 song "Por que te tengo que olvidar." At the first annual Latin Music Expo in 1991, Feliciano was honored with a Lifetime Achievement Award. In the early 1990s the singer's high school in Harlem was christened the José Feliciano Performing Arts School.

56

Rosemary Casals

1948–

Known affectionately by her fans as "Rosie" and "Rosebud," Rosemary Casals captured over ninety titles during her tennis career, which began in 1966. She is considered one of the best doubles players in the history of the game. Casals was a powerful and acrobatic player who hit a sizzling overhead smash and an unorthodox behind-the-back shot. Off the court, Casals was a constant critic of the tennis establishment for its rampant class discrimination, which she experienced firsthand. Casals also helped revolutionize the sport by battling rampant sexism and

271

gender inequality, thereby setting the stage for women's tennis to flourish as a popular national sport in the 1980s and 1990s. She declared: "I go through the same headaches trying to live and play tennis as the men do. I'm for equal pay for equal play."

Great-niece of the master cellist Pablo Casals, Rosemary Casals was born on September 16, 1948, in San Francisco, California, to poor immigrants from El Salvador. Her great-uncle and great-aunt, Manuel Casals and María Casals, took Rosemary and her sister, Victoria, into their home when their parents could no longer care for the children. Manuel Casals, who owned a modest vending-machine business, taught Rosemary to play tennis at Golden Gate Park when she was eight years old. Later, he would assume the role of her only tennis coach. Rosie was a natural, and by age nine she was competing in local tennis tournaments. By age sixteen she was ranked number one in both juniors' and women's levels in northern California.

Rosie's family could not afford the top-of-the-line equipment and clothes of players at country clubs, then tennis's chief milieu. Casals was ostracized by fellow players at the clubs, and her needs were often overlooked by the well-to-do tennis establishment. At one junior event ten-year-old Rosie had to sleep for several nights in the family's 1949 Studebaker because the sponsor of the event failed to provide a promised room. She commented on the effect this had on her self-esteem in the May 31, 1982, issue of *People*: "It was a rude awakening. The other kids had nice tennis clothes, nice rackets, nice white shoes and came in Cadillacs. I felt stigmatized because we were poor." Despite the hardships she endured at the event and the advantages her opponents enjoyed, Rosie walked away with the trophy.

Casals worked hard to overcome another disadvantage she faced in tennis. Standing five feet two inches, she was well below the average height of a competitive female player. As compensation for her short stature, early on she developed incredible speed, lightning-fast reflexes, and a vast repertoire of shots, including a ferocious volley, lob, and smash. By age sixteen she was competing nationally, and at the tender age of seventeen, in 1965, she was ranked eleventh in the country. That year, she won the Women's Hard Court singles title and made it to the women's singles semifinals at Forest Hills in an exciting match against tennis great María Bueno. Rosie lost the Bueno match at Forest Hills but won the favor of spectators with her aggressive style of play. When Casals was eighteen, Harry Hopman, the legendary Australian coach, described her as one of the best junior prospects in the world.

Casals proved Hopman right. During the early years, she teamed up with Billie Jean King, and the duo was virtually invincible in doubles. With their furious and charismatic play, they took the staid tennis world by storm and lured the media, new spectators, and corporate sponsors, to women's tennis, which would ultimately make it possible in the 1980s and 1990s to attract the big crowds that men's tennis enjoyed. Among other titles, the dynamic pair won the U.S. hard-court and indoor tournaments in 1966 and reached the quarterfinals at Wimbledon. Having gained experience in national and international play, Casals and Billie Jean King would dominate doubles play in the years that followed. Among their many victories, they captured the Wimbledon doubles title in 1967, 1968, 1970, 1971, and 1973; the U.S. Championships doubles title in 1967; the U.S. Open doubles title in 1971 and 1974; and the Italian doubles title in 1970. Casals was also a formidable singles player, and in 1966 she advanced to the semifinals at Forest Hills. Highlights of 1967 include a women's singles title for Casals at the Wills Invitational tournament in Auckland, New Zealand. In 1969 she was a semifinalist in singles play at Wimbledon and the U.S. Open.

In the late 1960s a battle over prize money in tennis was raging; lines were drawn according to class. Wealthy players, whose livelihood did not have to depend on their game and who feared prize money would taint tennis, challenged players who wanted to turn pro and earn money legitimately rather than take under-the-table payoffs to fund their play on the circuit. Players who admitted their professional status paid the price when major tournaments, such as Wimbledon, refused to admit them into competition. This changed in March 1968 when the International Lawn Tennis Federation (ILTF) voted to allow amateurs and professionals to compete against each other for prize money in what is called open tennis. Rosemary Casals, Billie Jean King, Françoise Durr, and Ann Jones seized the day and became the first women touring professionals in the history of tennis.

With the advent of prize money in tennis, men earned substantially more than women on the court. Equal prize money for women tennis players was the next hurdle pioneers like Rosie Casals faced. The turning point came in 1970, when women players protested that in the season's last major tournament, the Pacific Southwest Open, the men's winner would receive $12,500, while women quarterfinalists would split the lowly sum of $7,500. The United States Lawn Tennis Association (USLTA) ignored the protests. The women found a strong leader in Gladys Heldman, editor of *World Tennis* magazine, who with corporate sponsorship from Philip Morris organized a women's tournament, the Virginia Slims Invitational, in Houston to coincide with the Pacific Southwest Open. Seven U.S. women tennis players boycotted the Pacific Southwest Open to participate in the first Virginia Slims Invitational, among them Casals, who won the first prize of $1,600. She would capture eight more Virginia Slims titles, from 1970 through 1978.

The success of the Virginia Slims Invitational prompted Casals to join the newly formed women's professional tennis circuit. In the first year, Casals emerged as one of the top money winners among the sixteen women who participated. In 1973, she collected $30,000, the largest prize ever awarded in women's tennis at the time, by defeating Nancy Richey in the finals of the Family Circle Cup tournament. That year, Rosie Casals also won the Wimbledon mixed doubles, as she had in 1971, and was a finalist in the Virginia Slims Championship doubles. In 1974, Casals was fifth among leading women money winners, with earnings of $72,389, and in 1977 she ranked eighth, with a grand total of $126,139.

In 1973, Casals again challenged sexism in tennis. She was a commentator for ABC-TV during the much-publicized Billie Jean King–Bobby Riggs match at the Houston Astrodome in late September, billed the "Battle of the Sexes." Before a crowd of 30,000 and 59 million television viewers, King easily defeated Riggs, who was overweight and way past his prime. At the time, Casals spoke candidly about sexism in tennis and in the King-Riggs match. She told *Sports Illustrated* that she did not see why women had to prove themselves against "an old, obnoxious has-been like Riggs, who can't hear, can't see, walks like a duck, and is an idiot besides."

The Riggs-King match roused the nation's interest in tennis, which led to another innovation in the sport, namely, World Team Tennis (WTT), in which tennis players played on teams representing different cities in the same way other professional sports are organized. In the mid-1970s, Casals played for the Detroit

Loves and the Oakland Breakers and coached the Los Angeles Strings, in addition to playing in regular tennis tournaments. From 1976 to 1980 she was a member of the Federation Cup team, and in 1977, 1979, and 1980 she was a member and coach of the U.S. Wightman Cup team. This frantic schedule took its toll physically on Casals, and in June 1978 she had to undergo knee surgery, which cost the tennis player her Top 10 singles ranking and forced her to cut back on tournaments. In the aftermath of her surgery Casals paired up with Wendy Turnbull to form a powerful doubles team. They advanced to the doubles finals at Wimbledon in 1980 and at the U.S. Open in 1981, and in 1982 they captured the U.S Open doubles title. By 1982, however, Casals had reduced her time spent on the circuit to fewer than twenty-six weeks a year.

From the institution of open tennis in 1968 to the end of her career on the professional tennis circuit, Casals boasted 528 match victories, making her one of the top players in tennis. Along the way she picked up over ninety titles and helped the U.S. team win four Wightman and four Federation Cups. Despite numerous singles victories, she made it into the record books as the best player of that era who did not win a major singles title. Even after her retirement from professional tennis, Casals was still making stunning court appearances. In 1990, she again teamed up with Billie Jean King to win the U.S. Open Seniors' Women's Doubles title in an exciting finals match.

Off court, Rosie Casals remains a committed spokesperson for women in tennis. In 1981 she formed Sportswomen, Inc., a company which promoted a Women's Classic tour for over-thirty female players and was an agency for new players. She has taken a stand on such issues as an age requirement in women's tennis, advocating that girls under sixteen be barred from professional play, since the majority of young players are plagued with injuries stemming from overwork on the court. When she is not shaping the future of women's tennis, Casals occupies herself with myriad pursuits, including golf, television, and singing. In the early 1980s she exercised her musical talents as a backup singer on Pattie LaBelle's first solo album and also launched Midnight Productions, a television company.

57

Orlando Cepeda
1937–

The youngest of two brothers, Orlando Manuel Cepeda was
born in Ponce, Puerto Rico, on September 17, 1937, to Pedro
Cepeda and Carmen (Pennes) Cepeda. His father was a professional baseball player and such a great slugger that he was called
Puerto Rico's Babe Ruth. Pedro Cepeda never played in American major league baseball (only Caucasian players did in his
heyday), but he was a hero on the island. Orlando, who was
nicknamed "Peruchín" or "little Pedro" excelled at basketball at
the Baldorioty de Castro school in San Juan, but his father
pushed him to play baseball.

276

Orlando's athletic potential was compromised by his bowed legs, one of which was shorter than the other. When he was fifteen years old, he underwent an operation on his knee, spending two months in the hospital and five more hobbling on crutches. Under his father's tutelage Orlando developed fine baseball skills and attracted the attention of Pedrín Zorilla, the coach of the Santurce Crabbers, who had connections with the major leagues and had launched such players as Ruben Gomez, Juan Pizarro, and Roberto Clemente. In 1954, Cedpeda graduated from the Baldorioty de Castro school and in early 1955, under instructions from Zorilla, reported to the Giants' minor league training camp at Melbourne, Florida, for a tryout. The Giants gave him a $500 bonus and sent him to their minor-league farm club in Virginia, the Salem team in the Class D Appalachian League.

The day before Orlando Cepeda's first game in the 1955 season, his father, age forty-eight, died of malaria. Orlando rushed home to attend his funeral, which he paid for with his bonus money. The loss of his father and a severe case of homesickness, combined with difficulties speaking English, rampant race discrimination, and discord with his manager, made Cepeda's first months as a rookie dismal. He spoke of those early days with *Sports Illustrated* in 1991: "I was only seventeen, and it was tough. I lived in the black part of town, and on Sunday mornings I'd hear the people singing gospel music in the church across the street. I'd sit by the window in my room listening, and I'd cry from misery and loneliness. I don't know how I ever got through that time, but I know now that you've got to go through hardships when you're young to make your life meaningful later on." With Zorilla's intervention, Cepeda was transferred to the Kokomo, Indiana, team in the Mississippi–Ohio Valley League, which turned out to be a happier arrangement.

Cepeda played third base with Kokomo in the ninety-two games left in the 1955 season, compiling 21 home runs and 91 runs batted in and leading the league with a .393 batting average. Cepeda then moved up to the St. Cloud farm club in the Class C Northern League in 1956, where he played first base primarily and led the league in all three major hitting categories, with 26 home runs, 112 runs batted in, and a .355 batting average. Cepeda's performance on the diamond earned him a promotion in 1957 to the Giants' Triple A farm team, the Minneapolis

Millers, in the American Association. With Minneapolis, Cepeda played third and first base as well as the outfield, compiling a .309 average, with 25 home runs and 108 runs batted in.

In 1958, the same year the Giants moved from New York to San Francisco, Cepeda was called up to the big leagues. In his rookie year with the Giants he played in 148 games, attained a .312 batting average, hit 25 home runs, and drove in 96 runs, with a league-leading 38 two-base hits. For his spectacular performance Cepeda was unanimously voted National League Rookie of the Year by the Baseball Writers' Association, and the *Sporting News* honored him with its National League Rookie Player of the Year Award for 1958.

By the time the 1959 season rolled around, it looked as though Cepeda would be playing first base forever. Then, in July, Willie McCovey, a first baseman, joined the Giants and had a remarkable debut. Both sluggers wanted to play first base, and Cepeda was switched to left field, which hurt his pride and caused quite a stir in the dugout. Fellow players told him to demand that the management allow him to play first base. Despite the controversy Cepeda played in 151 games in the 1959 season, compiling a .317 average with 105 runs batted in, 27 home runs, 35 two-base hits, and 23 stolen bases, an even better record than he had in his rookie year. As a result of his stellar performance, the *Sporting News* named Orlando Cepeda the first baseman on its 1959 National League All-Star team.

In 1961 Cepeda injured his right knee in a home-plate collision, but he continued to play for the next three years despite terrible pain. In December 1964 the player underwent knee surgery and as a result spent most of the 1965 season on the disabled list. That season, Cepeda went to bat only thirty-three times and had a feeble .176 average; in his absence, Willie McCovey took over as the regular first baseman and hit 39 homers. Despite his impressive statistics Cepeda had fallen out of favor with Giants' manager Alvin Dark, who felt he was not playing up to his potential and failed to take into consideration the injured knee. In the 1966 season Orlando Cepeda had to earn his stripes all over again if he hoped to make his way back into the lineup, but he gained no recognition from the Giants' new manager, Herman Franks. Even though he loved San Francisco, Cepeda asked to be traded, and on May 8, 1966, the Giants swapped Cepeda to the St. Louis Cardinals for Ray Sadecki.

Cepeda had a good year with the Cardinals in 1966, hitting .301 and winning the National League's Comeback of the Year Award. In 1967 he compiled a .325 batting average, hit 25 home runs, and led the league with 111 runs batted in. Cepeda then led St. Louis to a pennant victory and the World Series championship in seven games over the Boston Red Sox. In November 1967, Cepeda was unanimously chosen the National League's Most Valuable Player of the Year, the first National League player to win the distinction unanimously since Carl Hubbell in 1936. That year, the *Sporting News* named Cepeda National League Player of the Year, and again elected him first baseman on its National League All-Star team.

In 1974, Cepeda's playing days came to an end, and he retired from baseball. A year later, he returned to Puerto Rico with plans to build a health spa, launch youth baseball camps, and hold baseball clinics. Cepeda experienced difficulty coping with his new life without baseball and began drinking in excess. While he was conducting a baseball clinic in Colombia in 1975, he bought, for his personal use, some marijuana from a cabdriver. Cepeda went to the San Juan airport on December 12, 1975, to retrieve two packages of marijuana flown in from Colombia, and was promptly arrested for importing an illegal substance. He was tried in federal court in 1976, and was convicted and sentenced to five years in prison. On the island where his father, Puerto Rico's Babe Ruth, was adored, Orlando Cepeda was ostracized.

After serving ten months, Cepeda was released from prison, but at that time, Puerto Ricans could not forgive him for his sin, and the isolation and humiliation he felt ultimately drove him from the island. In 1984, Cepeda moved to Los Angeles and briefly operated a baseball school. He wrote his autobiography, entitled *High & Inside,* but sales were poor. His second wife divorced him, and the friends he had on the Los Angeles Dodgers were discouraged from fraternizing with him. Cepeda told *Sports Illustrated* of this dismal time in his life: "In L.A., nothing worked. I was clean and trying to do better in life. I had made one mistake, and I suffered for that. I had hurt myself, my family, my friends. I was going through a kind of hell. I was depressed, angry."

Then, one night in Los Angeles in 1984, Cepeda's world completely turned around. The retired baseball player joined a friend at a meeting of a Buddhist sect, the Nicheren Shoshu. In

Buddhism he found a philosophy that restored balance and tranquility to his life, and he began chanting regularly and practicing its tenets. Cepeda soon met his future wife, Miriam, a Puerto Rican from New York. In 1986 a publisher by the name of Lawrence Hyman was interviewing former Giants for a story and tracked Cepeda down in Los Angeles. Hyman persuaded Orlando Cepeda to attend a game at Candlestick Park, where the fans remembered him with fondness. Cepeda had not visited the ballpark since the Giants had traded him two decades before. As soon as he walked through the gate at Candlestick Park, fans cheered him.

In 1987, Cepeda met the Giant's vice president, Pat Gallagher, who asked him if he'd be interested in coming back to work for the team. In January 1989, Cepeda was hired as a special assistant for player development, but he evolved into a goodwill ambassador, representing the Giants at various social functions. In Game Three of the 1989 Championship Series, the first playoff game in the series at Candlestick, Orlando Cepeda had the honor of throwing out the first ball. He stood on the mound, tears streaming down his face. He told *Sports Illustrated*: "I was crying because I knew I was where I belonged. Oh, it was so beautiful to be wanted again."

Orlando Cepeda is highly regarded for his community service. He has campaigned extensively against drug abuse and has worked on behalf of numerous charitable organizations. In 1990, Cepeda was inducted into the Bay Area Sports Hall of Fame. Due to the drug incident of 1975, the Baseball Writers Association of America has refused thus far to induct Orlando Cepeda into the Baseball Hall of Fame. In 1993, Puerto Rico finally forgave its native son and named Cepeda to the island's Baseball Hall of Fame.

58

Piri Thomas

1928–

The first of seven children, Thomas was born John Peter Thomas in New York City on September 30, 1928, to Dolores Montañez and Juan Thomas. Dolores Montañez came from Bayamón, Puerto Rico, while Juan Thomas was born in Oriente Province, Cuba. Piri's parents met in New York City and married in 1927. During the Depression, Juan Thomas labored as a digger for the WPA, while Dolores Montañez worked in a needle-industry factory and did piecework at home. The Depression years in which Piri grew up brought abject poverty and hopelessness to the barrio. Life was made even more difficult for the boy by his uncertainties over his identity. The Thomas household identified itself as Puerto Rican, and Piri's parents cultivated their children's emotional ties to the island. While the other Thomas children were lighter-skinned, like their mother, Piri inherited his father's darker color. He often felt that his father gave preferential treatment to the other children due to their lighter skin. Furthermore, society perceived of Piri as black. To make matters worse, young Piri also felt uncomfortable at school, where his heritage and the Spanish language were dismissed and values he found foreign were instilled.

As a young teenager, Piri moved with his family to the Italian neighborhood of East Harlem, where he had to learn the way of the streets to survive. Although he worked hard at odd jobs, his pay was low, and he suffered discrimination. As time went on, Piri became estranged from society, joined a youth gang, and resorted to petty theft. As World War II drew to a close, Juan Thomas's employment prospects brightened, and he worked in a Long Island airplane factory. In 1944 he pooled all the family savings and his salary and purchased a little house in a white middle-class neighborhood in Babylon, Long Island, so that the family could enjoy good schools, fresh air, and an easier way of life. In Babylon, Piri felt further alienated from his family, who he felt had adopted white middle-class values. He was also taken aback by the blatant racism he encountered in the Babylon schools. One positive event at school that profoundly affected his life was when an English teacher became his mentor. She was impressed by one of Piri's compositions and wrote on the back: "Son, your punctuation is lousy; your grammar is nonexistent. But if you want to be a writer, someday you'll be."

Searching for a sense of belonging, Piri left home at age sixteen and returned to the barrio, where he sold drugs on the street for a living. He was consumed by issues of identity and wondered whether he should consider himself a Puerto Rican because of his language and ancestry or accept society's label of black. With an African-American friend, he traveled to the Deep South, where he experienced segregation firsthand. As he told *Publisher's Weekly* in a May 21, 1967, interview: "I wanted to find out who I was. I mean, in my relations as a human being. I got so damn mad, I said: 'Damn, white man! What's your value on skin? Man, we're humans, too'! I felt this cry in my heart." Thomas then joined the merchant marines, and traveled to the West

Indies, South America, and Europe and came to the conclusion that blacks faced discrimination the world over. He returned to New York, where his mother lay dying. After she passed away, Piri found solace in heroin and sold the drug to support his habit. After getting off heroin, he turned to armed robbery to make a living.

In 1950, Piri Thomas was arrested and convicted of attempted armed robbery and assault after a holdup and a shootout in a Greenwich Village nightclub. He was sentenced to five to fifteen years of hard labor in a maximum-security prison. After recovering for six weeks at the prison ward of Bellevue Hospital, he was transferred to the Bronx Tombs, to Sing Sing, and to Great Meadows, a maximum-security prison in Comstock, New York, where he spent seven years. In prison, Thomas discovered a world much like the one on the streets. He faced not only racism but the dehumanization of being reduced to a number, deprived of making independent decisions, and totally confined. But the difficult experience of prison turned his life around.

Thomas began to examine his inner resources, and his compassion for others grew immensely. In Comstock he studied hard and obtained a high school equivalency diploma, trained in brickmasonry, and frequently read and wrote. During his last four years behind bars, he began to work on his autobiography. In Comstock, Thomas also had a religious awakening and began to study various faiths, including Islam, which had a profound effect on him. As he told *Publisher's Weekly*: "I'll never forgot the quiet dignity of those Muslims in Comstock. And I feel if any man practices his religion, no matter what, with sincerity, he can't help having dignity, pride, and a sense of harmony with himself. Like, for me, God in any language means love—not hate."

At age twenty-eight Thomas was paroled, and he returned to his old neighborhood a changed person. He moved in with an aunt, a principled woman, who helped her nephew convert to Pentecostalism. Thomas underwent a frustrating search for work. He was barred from joining the brickmasons' union because of his prison record, but he finally found work as a handyman and then joined the bakers' union. At church Piri Thomas met a Puerto Rican woman, Daniela, who had recently arrived on the mainland; they married and had a child. They moved to Long Island to be near Thomas's family but later lost their home through the persistent efforts of bigoted neighbors. During this time Thomas turned to community service and worked in a church youth center, helping kids steer away from drugs and crime and providing for them a forum to vent their frustrations. When he was in his early thirties Thomas traveled to Puerto Rico, where he worked with Dr. Efrem Ramíriz, director of the Hospital of Psychiatry in Rio Piedras, Puerto Rico, to establish a rehabilitation program called Nueva Raza. The program called for pairing drug addicts with recovered addicts who could help guide them to recovery.

In 1961 and 1962, Thomas worked in gang rehabilitation and appeared in and provided the narration for *Petey and Johnny*, a film about rehabilitation work in East Harlem. The film was released in 1964 and subsequently won first prize at the Festival Dei Populi in Florence, Italy. At around this time Thomas considered writing a book and told a CBS executive, who suggested that he find a ghostwriter. Thomas decided to write the book himself, and through a connection he met Angus Cameron, an editor at Alfred A. Knopf. Two months later, out of his talk with Cameron, he received a grant from the Louis M. Rabinowitz Foundation to fund his writing. *Down These Mean Streets*, the first of Piri Thomas's autobiographical narratives, was published in 1967 and garnered a great deal of publicity for its groundbreaking content.

Down These Mean Streets is a forceful and compelling account of the author's adolescence and early adult years. At its heart is the crisis of identity of a dark-skinned working-class Puerto Rican growing up in America. It essentially chronicles the author's journey from a dehumanizing world overwrought with racial strife, poverty, drugs, and crime, through the penal system and a spiritual cleansing, to a place of harmony, dignity, community, and creative productivity. After the publication of *Down These Mean Streets,* Thomas appeared on a variety of television and radio shows and was featured in myriad articles in major newspapers and magazines. He was also chosen as writer and narrator of the film *The World of Piri Thomas,* a television documentary exploring street life in the barrio.

In 1972, Thomas published the sequel to *Down These Mean Streets,* entitled *Savior, Savior Hold My Hand,* in which he concludes that "to us people of the Barrio, the ghetto is our church, and the only way we're gonna make heaven out of this hell is by getting together." In 1974 he published *Seven Long Times,* his third autobiographical narrative. In the book he asserts that crime in America is rooted in racial and economic injustices that breed frustration, anger, and despair. He also condemns the oppressive atmosphere in America's penal institutions, which claim to re-habilitate prisoners but in reality degrade them mentally and physically.

While writing his three autobiographical narratives, Thomas continued to do community service and traveled to schools, colleges, and community centers to speak with young people about his life and works and the issues facing ethnic minorities in America. He advocated spiritual unity unfettered by race and party affiliation and condemned a society that allows its children to turn to crime. In 1978 he abandoned autobiography and published *Stories from El Barrio,* a collection of eight short stories exploring the lives of Latino children who grow up in New York's boroughs. One tale recounts with humor the exploits of three urban youths who venture to the marshes of New Jersey on a Boy Scout trip; another explores the rich and complicated fantasies of a crippled child. In the last two decades Thomas has also authored numerous articles on minorities in the United States that have appeared in such publications as the *New York Times Magazine* and the *Saturday Review.*

59

Oscar De La Hoya

1973–

Oscar De La Hoya was born on February 4, 1973, into a poor Mexican-American family in the East Los Angeles barrio. Oscar's father, Joel De La Hoya, worked in the warehouse of an air-conditioning company, and both he and Oscar's grandfather, Vincent De La Hoya, had spent time in the ring in their youth. When he was a small child, Oscar would often fight in the street and get beat up. He liked fighting so much that his father took him to Pico Rivera Sports Arena and taught him jabs and feints. In his first bout, at age six, Oscar knocked out his opponent in the first round. Starting at age ten, he worked out at the

Resurrection, a church turned athletic club in East Los Angeles, where he diligently punched bags, skipped rope, and shadowboxed. Oscar kept going to the gym and resisted the lure of drugs and gangs in his neighborhood. While in junior high school, he officially launched his amateur boxing career. In 1988, at age fifteen, the young boxer reigned as the national Junior Olympic champion.

In 1989, De La Hoya clinched the Golden Gloves 125-pound title and the 125-pound division at the U.S. Championships, his first national title. As the youngest boxer in the competition, he won a gold medal at the Goodwill Games in 1990 and was heralded as one of the world's most promising young fighters. Oscar's mother, who was sick with breast cancer, skipped radiation treatments to see her son win the gold. She died at age thirty-nine in October of that year. On her deathbed she asked Oscar to fulfill one wish, to win the gold medal for her at the 1992 Olympics in Barcelona. On his way to Barcelona, De La Hoya captured his second consecutive national title at the U.S. Championships in March 1990. A year later, De La Hoya was the U.S. Amateur Boxing's 132-pound national champion and the USA Boxing 1991 Boxer of the Year. He graduated from Garfield High School in May 1991 but missed his prom. That evening, he was beating two-time world champion Julio Gonzalez in the U.S.-Cuba dual meet at Fort Bragg, North Carolina.

De La Hoya was the country's strongest hope for a medal in boxing going into the 1992 Olympics in Barcelona. In July 1991 he had won the gold medal in the 132-pound division at the U.S. Olympic Festival in Los Angeles. His first bout at the Olympics was anticipated to be his toughest, since he faced Julio Gonzalez, the four-time World Amateur Junior Lightweight champion from Cuba. De La Hoya confounded Gonzalez with his amazing footwork, dizzying uppercuts, and sharp jabs, and in what was the biggest boxing upset in Barcelona he won a 7–2 decision, to the crowd's amazement. In his second-round match, he faced the Korean champion, who was said to have an edge over the American. It was a close fight, but De La Hoya emerged triumphant, 11–10. He went on to the gold-medal fight, defeating Marco Rudolph of Germany. De La Hoya clinched the gold medal in the 132-pound division at the 1992 Olympics, the only U.S. fighter to capture gold.

In celebration of his Olympic victory, De La Hoya circled the ring with an American flag in one hand and a Mexican flag in the other. According to the fighter: "The American flag was for my country; the Mexican flag was for my heritage. Besides, I felt sorry for Mexico, which hadn't won any medals in the Olympics to that point." The world was moved by the story of this young man who had fulfilled the promise he made to his mother before she died. De La Hoya returned to the United States a hero. He made appearances in public and on such television talk shows as *Arsenio Hall* and the *Tonight* show. De La Hoya was a sensation when he told Jay Leno all about his visit to the White House after he won the gold medal. The young boxer also lectured in schools on the dangers of drugs and gangs and became the idol of every Latino kid who dreamed of escaping the barrio through glory inside the ropes.

As an amateur boxer, De La Hoya amassed 225 wins and only 5 losses, with 153 knockouts, including his gold medal at the 1990 Goodwill Games and the 1992 Olympics and two U.S. championships in the 132-pound class. His amateur career came to an end shortly after the Olympics when he signed with Robert Mittelman, a New York booking agent, and Steve Nelson, a New York mortgage banker, who presented him with a management contract of over $1 million, the biggest deal in amateur boxing history. De La Hoya then turned pro and went after mass-market endorsements. Since September 1992 he has been a TV spokesman for many commercial companies.

De La Hoya made his professional debut at the Forum in Inglewood, California, on November 23, 1992, wearing a sombrero into the ring and waving his trademark American and Mexican flags. He stopped his opponent, Lamar Williams, with a knockout in only 1:42 of the first round, thus earning $200,000 in 102 seconds. In his dressing room after the bout, De La Hoya told reporters: "It was all over so fast. I feel like I waited for this moment all my life. I tried to make it last." By November 1, 1993, De La Hoya's professional record was 11–0, with 10 knockouts. A month later the boxer complained of injuries and pulled out of a bout scheduled for December 9 at the Paramount in New York City. He then sacked his managers, Mittelman and Nelson, claiming they tried to take over completely, and designated himself manager, put together the team that had helped him win the gold medal in Barcelona, including his cook, and linked up with fight promoter Bob Arum's Top Rank organization.

Despite the risk that a young boxer poses, Arum quickly negotiated a $21 million deal with HBO to televise De La Hoya's next twenty-five fights. HBO stipulated that De La Hoya would fight exclusively against champions to attract big crowds. In his first bout under Arum, in February 1994, Oscar De La Hoya vied for the World Boxing Organization's junior lightweight title held by Denmark's Jimmi Bredahl. To prepare for the bout, the fighter went to a training facility at Big Bear Lake in California, where each day he endured two hours of boxing with sparring partners in a gym deliberately heated to 95 degrees to simulate the heat from the lights and the crowd in a real arena. The championship bout was held at the newly revamped Olympic Arena in Los Angeles, where De La Hoya's grandfather and father boxed decades before. During the much-publicized fight, De La Hoya showed remarkable stamina as he went into the tenth round of the scheduled twelve round bout. The fight was called in the tenth round by a ring physician who determined that Jimmi Bredahl could not go on, and De La Hoya earned a technical knockout. With the victory, De La Hoya clinched his first championship and improved his record to 12–0, with 11 knockouts.

On July 30, 1994, De La Hoya met Jorge Paez at the M-G-M Grand Garden in Las Vegas to battle for the World Boxing Organization's lightweight championship, his first fight at 135 pounds in the lightweight division. Going into the fight, the boxer felt he had to win the hearts of Mexican fans who had expressed adoration for Paez. Since the Paez bout was considered the biggest challenge of his career, De La Hoya also felt that by winning he would put an end to the criticism about dodging big-name fighters that had hounded him all year. De La Hoya lost the coin toss earlier that week and had to make his grand entrance into the ring before Paez, an irritating factor, since he prefers to be last. He did not let it get to him once the match began, and he felt the added power and confidence of his extra five pounds. Thirty-nine seconds into the second round of the fight, De La Hoya astounded Paez, the crowd, and the boxing world with an incredible knockout.

De La Hoya still lives at home with his father, his older brother Joel, his younger sister Ceci, and his grandmother Candelaria. With the boxer's prosperity, the family moved from the East L.A. barrio to a large house in Montebello, California.

When he is not in the ring, De La Hoya dreams of eventually going to college and becoming an architect. He also hopes to parlay his own Olympic gold medal into several title belts and top-dollar deals with advertisers, à la Sugar Ray Leonard, whom he idolized as a boy. As he gets older, De La Hoya will almost certainly grow into the welterweight and middleweight classes, and he may get even heavier. As he grows, he will take on many world champions, and with his marvelous hand speed, a superb jab, and a devastating left hook, De La Hoya has a long career ahead.

60

Oscar Hijuelos

1951–

Oscar Hijuelos was born in New York City on August 24, 1951, to Pascual Hijuelos and Magdalena Hijuelos, Cubans from Oriente Province, the easternmost province in Cuba and home to Desi Arnaz, Fidel Castro, and Fulgencio Batista. His ancestors have been traced back to Galicia, in Spain. Pascual Hijuelos's family owned two farms in Cuba, while Magdalena Hijuelos's parents, who hailed from Barcelona, ran two factories on the island. Although Oscar's father came into a small inheritance, he had a penchant for drinking and was overly generous, and the inheritance dwindled. In 1943, Oscar's parents left Cuba and settled in New York, where Oscar grew up on West 118th Street on the Upper West Side. At home the boy spoke only Spanish, and until age four he knew no English.

In 1954, when Oscar was three years old, the family visited Cuba, the only trip he has taken to his parents' homeland. He tried to visit the island in later years, but the Castro government refused to issue him a visa because of his association with the exiled poet Heberto Padilla. Upon returning to New York, Oscar came down with a fever, chills, and back pains and was diagnosed with nephritis. The prognosis was grim, and he was admitted to a hospital in Connecticut for terminally ill children, where doctors expected he would die. He spent the next two years at the hospital isolated from his parents, who were only allowed to communicate with him from a distance.

Oscar was eventually released from the hospital, but throughout his childhood he was plagued by the fear that he would die young, and he had nightmares about the illness for three decades. After his recovery, Magdalena Hijuelos sheltered her son, and as a first-grader, Oscar spent only eight weeks in the classroom. He told *New York* magazine in March 1, 1993: "I used to think of the household as a country in itself. I literally thought of the street as some kind of a river and you needed a passport to cross it. I was a very quiet, crazy kid. To this day, if I'm dysfunctional, it's because I think of life as solitary."

As he got older, Oscar began to defy the geographic parameters his mother had set and ventured into the outside world. In his teens and early twenties he played the guitar in a band in the South Bronx whose members were mostly Puerto Ricans. Their repertoire consisted mainly of Top 40 tunes and some Latin numbers. Oscar also played on an all-black softball team called the Harlem Ravens. When he was seventeen years old, his father passed away. Later, the writer attempted to recapture his father's amiability and warmth in prose. After attending Catholic and public schools, Hijuelos went on to Bronx Community College and then transferred to City College. Upon receiving his B.A. degree, the future author enrolled in the graduate writing program at City College. Donald Barthelme, whose works Hijuelos much admired, became his mentor there. For a brief time in 1975, Hijuelos was married to a singer.

One of Hijuelos's classmates in the graduate writing program was Karen Braziller, who was launching Persea Books at the time. She asked Hijuelos to submit some of his work to Persea for possible publication, and from the four or five manuscripts he submitted emerged his first novel, *Our House in the Last World,* published in 1983. An autobiographical tale, *Our House* offers a portrait of émigré life in America in which the characters view their homeland of Cuba as the first and ultimate world, a paradisiacal land accessible only in death: "The sunlight, *el señor sol,* a friendly character who came out each day. Nightingales, dirty hens, sparrows, doves, chicks…Cuba, Cuba…Cuba, Cuba." The *New York Times* heaped praise on *Our House in the Last World* for its "warmth and tenderness."

At the time of the novel's publication, Hijuelos was doing inventory control full-time for Transportation Display, Inc., a company that posts advertisements in New York's mass transportation system. The writer was dismayed when his novel did not appear on the shelves of major bookstores, and he realized that small presses tend to suffer from poor distribution. Determined to drum up publicity for *Our House in the Last World,* Hijuelos obtained permission from Transportation Display, Inc. to display an advertisement he designed for his book next to ads for novels by Danielle Steel. A paperback editor for Washington Square Press happened upon one of the ads and, surprised that a small press would funnel so much into advertising the novel, interpreted it as a winner and purchased the paperback rights for $1,500.

In 1985 the American Academy of Arts and Letters named Hijuelos the recipient of the prestigious Rome Prize, and the National Endowment for the Arts bestowed on him its highly coveted fellowship. These awards enabled Hijuelos to leave his job and travel the world, seeking inspiration for future literary projects. He immersed himself in archaeology, and on several trips to Italy he joined digs in the Temple of Vesta in the Roman Forum. Soon after the trips to Italy, Hijuelos set to work on *The Mambo Kings Play Songs of Love,* a spirited tale of two brothers, Cesar and Nestor Castillo, Cuban immigrant musicians, who leave Havana and come to New York City in 1949 to strike it rich. The brothers, whose musical and amorous escapades take them from Latin dance halls to bustling kitchens and cheap hotels, write a romantic bolero, "Beautiful Maria of My Soul," which is a hit and lands them on *I Love Lucy,* the wish fulfillment of every Cuban immigrant of that era.

All the while, the plot of *The Mambo Kings Play Songs of Love* defies convention and wanders, with little regard to chronology, through the characters' encounters with love, death, pain, and sex. Hijuelos described the novel's structure to *Publisher's Weekly* in July 21, 1989: "The formal idea was sort of like having a record going round and round. You know how sometimes when you listen to music and the song cuts off and you're into another feeling?" Upon this narrative frame Hijuelos erects his meditations on sexuality, immortality, and memory: "I intended a little bit of parody of the super-sexual virility that men are obsessed with in the macho cultures. I was having fun with it. Also, for me, it's a play on mortality, and on the body and how one can be hyperphallic...and it won't make any difference to the ultimate issues of love or family or death."

Upon finishing the novel, Hijuelos concentrated his efforts on promoting *The Mambo Kings Play Songs of Love,* which was published in 1989, and made a hundred tapes of Latin music to distribute to the sales division at Farrar Straus. The novel made the bestseller list, and won Oscar Hijuelos a Pulitzer Prize in literature in 1990, the first Latino writer ever to receive this literary honor. In 1992 the motion picture *Mambo Kings* was released to mixed reviews. After the publication of the book, Hijuelos was forced to deal with several frivolous lawsuits. In one case, ultimately thrown out of court, a Long Island woman, who had belonged to a 1950s group called Glorious Gloria Parker and her All Girl Rumba Orchestra, sued the author for using her name in the novel and stated in the affidavit that she had become "the subject of ridicule and small talk at the Syosset Village Association's annual tree-lighting ceremony where I was to perform." With profits from the book, Hijuelos traveled and collected antiquities, such as Egyptian funeral masks from the Ptolemaic period and a portion of an Egyptian sarcophagus panel.

In early 1993, Hijuelos began to jot down notes for his next writing project, and later that year he published his third novel. Hijuelos told *New York* magazine in 1993 about his inspiration for the book: "I wanted to do a thing about this other America I never really participated in....*Mambo Kings* defined the process by which Latino literature gets published. *Mambo Kings* said it was okay to be a Latino writer if you were gritty....This is all rubbish—all these tags! Now *Fourteen Sisters* says it's okay for

Latino writers to write about America." Told from a woman's perspective and tinged with magic realism, *The Fourteen Sisters of Emilio Montez O'Brien* chronicles in vivid snapshots the lives of fourteen daughters and one son of a Cuban mother and an Irish father in America as the twentieth century dawns. As in *The Mambo Kings Play Songs of Love*, sexual encounters abound, even among the elderly.

Although his intent was to imbue the novel with "a pure appreciation of the *female* principle of life," as he told *New York* magazine, Hijuelos spends far fewer pages fleshing out the sisters' lives than he does the life of their brother Emilio, whose exploits in Italy during World War II, Greenwich Village in the postwar era, and in Hollywood B movies are recounted in detail. This may be partly due to the sheer number of sisters. However, according to critics who have pointed a finger at Hijuelos's machismo, it also reflects the author's view that women's lives revolve primarily around men. Nevertheless, the novel unlocks in the reader fond memories of a bygone era.

When he is writing, Hijuelos completely submerges himself in his text, working day and night. In 1993 he was still living near the Upper West Side neighborhood of his childhood, the place where he derives most of his inspiration. After receiving the Pulitzer Prize, Hijuelos moved from a one-bedroom apartment to a two-bedroom in the same building, and despite his friends' insistence, he refuses to move to a nicer place.

61

Emilio Estévez

1962–

Emilio Estévez was the first child born to Martin Sheen, of Cuban and Irish descent, and Janet (Templeton) Sheen. He was born in Manhattan on May 12, 1962, and spent his early years on the Upper West Side. At age six, he was mugged in the lobby of the family's apartment building, and the Sheens began to consider leaving New York City. In 1968, the family moved to California, where Emilio and his siblings, the actors Ramón Estévez, Charlie Sheen, and Renee Sheen spent their childhood surrounded by Hollywood names and the Pacific surf. Once in California, young Emilio began to write short stories and poems. At age eight, he submitted an original episode to Rod Serling's *Night Gallery* television series. Although he received a rejection slip for his effort, it did not deter him from writing.

In his childhood, Emilio had numerous opportunities to travel with his father, for Martin Sheen made movies around the globe. In his early teens, Emilio spent time in Rome, where his father was on the set of the film *The Cassandra Crossing* and then in the Philippines while his father acted in *Apocalypse Now*. Sheen had a heart attack while shooting *Apocalypse*, and amid the havoc, Emilio landed his first acting job as an extra in that film.

While not globetrotting, Emilio attended school in Santa Monica, California. He was a well-rounded student, earning mostly A's and B's and acting in the plays produced in his junior high school. There he got his first taste of the cinematic process shooting Super 8 films with his brother Charlie and friend Sean Penn. In senior high Emilio steered away from film, but in his final year he shifted his attention back to acting. He objected to the high school's stage production that year, so he wrote and starred in his own play, entitled *Echoes of an Era*, which Sean Penn directed. The play was based on the experiences of a Vietnam vet whom Emilio had befriended in Manila during the filming of *Apocalypse Now* and was well received by both students and faculty.

Upon graduating from high school, Emilio chose to become an actor and took Martin Sheen's original Spanish surname, Estévez, as his professional tag. In 1980 he starred with his father in an episode of *Insight*, the syndicated television program produced as a minisermon by the Catholic Paulist order. Estévez made his motion-picture debut in the 1982 Disney Studios film *Tex*, an adaptation of a 1979 teen novel by Susan E. Hinton. *Tex* was a stepping-stone to his role in the 1983 motion picture *The Outsiders*, Francis Ford Coppola's adaptation of another popular Hinton novel geared toward adolescents. Between the shooting of these films Estévez starred in several TV movies, including the NBC-TV thriller *Nightmares*, in which he portrayed a video-game addict, and the 1982 ABC-TV movie *In the Custody of Strangers*, in which he played a teenage drunken driver who is charged with assault, arrested, and imprisoned. In the movie Martin Sheen, as Emilio's fictional father, faces a forty-day ordeal to get his son released from prison.

With the release of *The Outsiders* in 1983, Emilio Estévez became one of the screen's most popular young actors. He also achieved critical recognition in his next feature project, the 1984 comedy *Repo Man*. In this cult classic of the 1980s he portrays a young Los Angeles punker who becomes the protégé of a car repossessor played by Harry Dean Stanton.

In 1981, during the filming of *Tex*, Estévez set to work writing a screenplay of the teenage novel *That Was Then...This Is Now* by Susan E. Hinton, who had given the young actor rights to the property. In 1984, Estévez's option had run out, and he still had not secured studio financing for the project. He had luck finding financial brokers in the Midwest to back the film, and with director Chris Cain, he set to work revising the screenplay. After starring in John Hughes's *The Breakfast Club*, Emilio filmed *That Was Then...This Is Now*, casting himself as Mark Jennings, a lonely youth anxious to get through his adolescence. In its first four weeks of release in 1985, *That Was Then...This Is Now* grossed $7.6 million, more than repaying its financial backers.

Estévez was next cast as Kirbo Krager, a law student working as a part-time waiter, in the 1985 motion picture *St. Elmo's Fire*, a film about recent college graduates facing a confusing world. The film met with moderate commercial success but was scorned by critics. In the six months following the shooting of *St. Elmo's Fire*, Estévez wrote three screenplays, including *Wisdom*, which marked his debut as a producer-director in 1986. Before filming *Wisdom*, Estévez went to North Carolina for the shooting of the 1986 thriller *Maximum Overdrive*, the directorial debut of novelist Stephen King, in which modern-day machinery runs amok and lawnmowers chew up homeowners and electric knives plunge into waitresses. Then, on the set of *Wisdom*, Estévez played opposite Demi Moore and gave an impressive performance as a young man obsessed with robbing the rich and giving to the poor. Despite his valiant efforts, *Maximum Overdrive* and *Wisdom* were failures at the box office and flops with the critics.

Estévez reestablished his commercial appeal when he and Richard Dreyfuss played a pair of detectives in the highly popular 1987 comedy *Stakeout*, which received favorable reviews. In 1988, Estévez gave a superb performance as Billy the Kid in *Young Guns*, in which he appeared professionally for the first time with his brother Charlie. In 1990 Estévez again teamed with Charlie Sheen, as writer-actor-director of *Men At Work*, a low-brow comedy about two garbage men who dream of opening their own surf shop. In 1990, he portrayed Billy the Kid in *Young Guns II*, aging seventy years on-screen. That year Estévez also played Alex Furlong, a young race-car driver who is pursued by a bounty hunter and crashes into the year 2009 in the action-packed thriller *Freejack*. In 1992, Estévez was cast in the family-oriented comedy *The Mighty Ducks*. In February 1992, Estévez announced his engagement to Paula Abdul, the pop-music star, and on April 29, 1992, the couple were married. Estévez is the father of two children from an earlier relationship with the model Carey Salley.

In 1993, Estévez and Richard Dreyfuss were joined by Rosie O'Donnell in the sequel to *Stakeout,* entitled *Another Stakeout.* That year, Estévez also appeared in the chase film *Judgement Night,* playing a suburbanite who winds up in the middle of a murder scene while on his way to a boxing match with his buddies and spends the remainder of the film fleeing from the killers. In 1994 the actor played in *D2: The Mighty Ducks,* the sequel to *The Mighty Ducks,* in which a peewee hockey team heads to Los Angeles.

62

Raquel Welch

1940–

She was born Raquel Tejada to Josephine Sarah (Hall) Tejada, an American of English and Scottish descent, and Armand Tejada, a Bolivian immigrant of Castilian extraction, on September 5, 1940, in Chicago. When she was two years old, the family moved to La Jolla, a coastal resort town in Southern California, where Armand Tejada worked as a structural engineer in a General Dynamics plant. At a young age Raquel was drawn to music; she loved to listen to 1940s tunes and was particularly fond of Al Jolson. When she was chosen at age five to recite "The Night Before Christmas" at the local church, Raquel discovered she enjoyed performing. Two years later, she was cast in a tiny part as a boy in a San Diego Junior Theater production of *The Princess and the Caterpillar*.

At La Jolla High School, Raquel, or "Rocky" to her friends,

was a member of the dramatics club, a cheerleader, and vice president of her senior class. She also studied ballet under a local instructor, Irene Clark, and entered beauty contests, winning her first title at age fifteen. Raquel would go on to become Miss La Jolla, Miss San Diego, Miss Contour, and Maid of California. After she graduated from high school in 1958, she pursued an acting career but met with no success. She found a job broadcasting the weather for a local television station and took acting classes at San Diego State College. On May 8, 1959, she wed her high school sweetheart, James Westley Welch, and the couple had two children before they divorced in 1964.

After the divorce Welch left the children with her parents in California and went to Texas, where she worked as a model for Neiman-Marcus and as a cocktail hostess to raise money for cosmetic surgery on her nose; she believed the surgery was necessary to make a splash at the movie studios. She soon returned to California, fetched her children, and settled down in Hollywood. In pursuit of her big breakthrough she made the rounds of the studios, and by the end of 1964, Welch had secured a few minor parts. First she landed a regular spot on the weekly ABC-TV variety show *Hollywood Palace* as a "Billboard Girl" who introduced the stars and the acts. Next she got her first film break, a small role in Joseph E. Levine's production of *A House Is Not a Home*. Welch then landed a bit part in the Elvis Presley movie *Roustabout* and was on the threshold of a lively career. In October 2, 1964, *Life* magazine featured a story on Hollywood stars in the making, among them Raquel Welch.

Soon after *Life* printed that feature story, Raquel met the publicist Patrick Curtis, an enterprising former child actor who was working at the public relations firm Rogers & Cowan. When Curtis realized Welch's potential, he left Rogers & Cowan to launch his own firm, Curtwel Productions, with Welch. Curtis set to work immediately promoting what was perceived to be Raquel Welch's main asset, her voluptuous figure. It wasn't long before Welch won a modest role in the 1965 motion picture *A Swingin' Summer*, and the critics took note. Twentieth Century-Fox then signed her and custom-designed a role for her in the 1966 sci-fi film *Fantastic Voyage*, about a team of scientists who are reduced to microscopic size in order to enter the bloodstream of an ailing man and save his life. Welch's appearance in the film in a wet suit, rather than her performance, captivated audiences.

By 1966, Raquel Welch was on the road to becoming America's premier sex symbol and an international celebrity without even appearing in a single important film. That year, Twentieth Century-Fox loaned the actress to Hammer Film Productions for their motion picture *One Million Years B.C.*, a B drama about love in the Stone Age. Welch was cast as Loana Shell, a cave woman who prances around in a chamois-leather bikini and has a vocabulary of only three words. Welch had reservations about the film; she knew her physical features won her the part, not her talent. Her performance delighted audiences in Europe, and Welch, the darling of the *paparazzi*, was featured on more than ninety European magazine covers. Enthusiasm over Welch spread to the United States, where she appeared on at least sixteen magazine covers and became an instant celebrity.

On Valentine's Day, 1967, Welch and Patrick Curtis married in Paris. Curtwel Productions turned the wedding into a publicity frenzy by having the bride appear in a loosely crocheted white minidress before hundreds of photographers at city hall. Soon after the wedding Welch was cast in a number of low-budget films with European producers, including the unsuccessful *The Biggest Bundle of Them All*. The only film in which she appeared that was not panned by critics was the 1967 British comedy *Bedazzled*, a reworking of the Faust legend. In *Bedazzled* she starred as one of the seven deadly sins, Lillian Lust, clad in a silver bikini. Curtwel Productions then returned to the United States, where, between 1968 and 1970, Raquel Welch won numerous parts; producers and investors knew that her beauty and sex appeal would entice moviegoers to the box office.

In 1969, Welch went to Spain to work on a film for Fox, the controversial *100 Rifles*, the story of an Indian uprising in Mexico in 1912. In the film Welch plays Sarita, a Mexican Yaqui Indian, whose lover is a black man, played by Jim Brown. Their interracial love affair on-screen, the first in a major motion picture, got so much publicity that viewers flocked to movie theaters. In 1969, Welch was cast as a nightclub dancer pursued by a demented killer in the raunchy suspense film *Flare-Up*, and she caught the critics attention with her dance sequence at the Pussy Cat À Go-Go Club in Las Vegas. In 1970 she played a cameo role in *The Magic Christian* as a slave driver commanding a galley filled with bare-breasted oarswomen. That year, she also appeared in *Myra Breckenridge*, a film based on Gore Vidal's controversial bestseller about homosexuality, transsexualism, and Hollywood. In the film the actress was cast as Myra, the mannish female alter ego of the transsexual Myron, played by Rex Reed. *Myra Breckenridge* flopped with the critics for its "filthy language" and "the gamiest cast of the season," according to writer Howard Thompson of the *New York Times*.

Welch met with a positive response that same year for her first television special, the CBS spectacular *Raquel*, which aired on April 26, 1970. It was given one of the biggest budgets ever for a single show, netting Raquel Welch a rumored $400,000.

September 1971 saw Welch's divorce from Patrick Curtis, and from 1971 to 1974 she appeared in innumerable films, including *Fuzz* (1972), costarring Burt Reynolds, and *Bluebeard* (1972) costarring Richard Burton. Welch and Burton had an affair on the set, and their liaison continued for months by mail after filming. Welch then was cast in one of her most challenging roles as a roller-derby star in the 1972 motion picture *Kansas City Bomber*. In preparation for the part she endured months of training on roller skates, which left her bruised, and during the shooting of the film she fell and broke her wrist.

In 1974 Welch costarred with Richard Chamberlain, Faye Dunaway, and Charlton Heston in *The Three Musketeers*. For her performance as Constance Bonancieux in the lusty action film, she was named Best Actress in a Comedy or Musical at the 1974 Golden Globe Awards. Later that year, Welch starred in *The Four Musketeers*, the perfunctory sequel to *The Three Musketeers*, and made another successful television special for CBS, *Really Raquel*, in which she sang, danced, and told jokes. In the 1975 film *The Wild Party*, about a silent-film comedian on the skids, Welch could finally put her acting talent to work, delivering what has been called the best performance of her life (though the movie failed).

In 1977, Welch costarred with the leading French actor Jean-Paul Belmondo in *L'Animal*. Welch is quoted in the February 1985 issue of *Redbook* as saying that the filming of *L'Animal* in Paris "...was one of the best things I ever did because I met André." André is the French screenwriter and producer André Weinfeld. It was love at first sight on the set of *L'Animal*, and immediately after filming, Welch and he traveled together to Sardinia. In 1979, Welch starred in a film aired on television, *The Legend of Walks Far Woman*, and on July 5, 1980, Welch and Weinfield married in Mexico. During the next two years the two were inseparable, and Welch looked to Weinfield for advice on her career. He collaborated with her on her next television special, *From Raquel With Love,* which ABC-TV broadcasted shortly after their wedding and which received high ratings. The couple separated in 1989.

In December 1980, Welch's career hit a low when Metro-Goldwyn-Meyer (M-G-M) replaced her with Debra Winger after production had already begun on the film *Cannery Row.* M-G-M claimed that Welch had behaved unprofessionally on the set, while the actress countered that she was let go to cut the film's production costs. She filed a $20 million lawsuit against M-G-M and was awarded $10.8 million by the court, but this decision was later overturned. Life took a turn for the better when producers of the Broadway show *Woman of the Year* phoned Welch to offer her a part in the production. Raquel Welch replaced Lauren Bacall for two weeks in the 1981 hit Broadway musical. Longing to be respected for her acting talent, Welch was delighted when critics lauded her performance. When Bacall later took a six-month break from the show, she was invited back as her replacement. On January 2, 1983, Welch took the stage for the final performance at the Palace Theatre on Broadway, having proved she was not just a sex symbol; she was a serious actress.

Despite applause from the media for her talent, Welch could not escape her sex-symbol association in the 1980s. She capitalized on this reputation as the fitness craze raged in America by publishing *The Raquel Welch Total Beauty and Fitness Program,* a bestseller that sold 100,000 copies by the end of 1985. In the 1980s she made numerous home-exercise videos, including *Raquel— Total Beauty and Fitness, Raquel—Lose Ten Lbs. in Three Weeks,* and *Body and Mind—Total Relaxation and Stress Relief Program.*

In 1987, Welch won praise for her role as a woman dying from Lou Gehrig's disease in the made-for-television movie *Right to Die.* That same year, she also released a pop single in Europe, "This Girl Is Back in Town," and promoted it on a continental tour. In 1988 she won plaudits from critics for her performance in the television movie *Scandal in a Small Town.* In 1990 the Los Angeles Hispanic Women's Council named Raquel Welch "Woman of the Year."

63

Andy García

1956–

A Hollywood heartthrob and a formidable actor, Andy García has appeared on the screen since the late 1970s, when he took up residence in Hollywood in anticipation of his big break. In the December 1990 issue of *American Film,* García summed up the acting style that has earned him high critical acclaim in this way: "I don't try to pick it apart. It becomes a kind of spiritual thing for me. You have a master plan, but to get to the core of the starfish you have to come at it from every angle—even the most sinister characters are capable of laughing and crying."

The youngest of three children, Andy García was born on April 12, 1956, in Bejucal, Cuba, into a conservative Catholic family. Details about his childhood are sketchy because the actor rarely grants interviews and has refused to talk at length about his personal life. It is known that his father, René García, was a prominent lawyer and landowner, with a successful produce business in Havana, and that his mother, Amelia García, taught English. When Fidel Castro came to power, Cuba's banks were nationalized, and private property was confiscated. Having lost everything, the García family fled Castro's Communist regime and settled in Miami when Andy was five years old.

The family had little money, and René García had to work long hours as a jobber in a hosiery company to support the family. Andy García alluded to his sense of estrangement and his longing to return to Cuba during those early days in Miami in an article printed in the November 22, 1992, issue of the *New York Times*: "We were not immigrants. We were in political exile in Miami." English did not come easy to Andy, and his struggle with the language left him alienated from the other children in school. In the *New York Times* article García also spoke about the difficulties of learning a foreign language: "When you struggle with a foreign language, you're surrounded by people who don't know what you are saying, and you don't know what they're saying. So you are in isolation. That probably has a definite impact on your point of view."

García entered the world of acting relatively late in life. In high school he was an avid basketball player who planned to make a career of the sport, but after a bout of mononucleosis and hepatitis in his senior year, his level of play declined. While attending Florida International University, he pursued his new interest, acting, and majored in theater. While in college, García met his future wife, Marívi, short for María Victoria, whose family fled Cuba at the same time as the Garcías. Marívi, a distinguished photographer, devotes a great deal of time to the couple's three daughters.

Before long, García landed parts in regional-theater productions in Florida and made a low-budget film in Spanish. In 1978 he moved to the seedy side of Hollywood, and like the stereotypical actor waiting for a break, he worked at odd jobs by day and as an actor at night. In 1980, a casting agent spotted him while he was performing with an improvisational group at the Comedy Store in Los Angeles. With the agent's intervention, García landed his first screen role as a gang member in the pilot of the TV series *Hill Street Blues*. He was finally on the road to success.

García was determined from the very outset to accept only those roles he believed in, and so his early acting career was limited. In 1983 he had a minor part in the baseball movie *Blue Skies Again,* and in 1985 he was cast in a small role as a police detective in the tropical thriller *The Mean Season,* starring Kurt Russell and Mariel Hemingway. He began to appear more frequently on the screen, mostly in urban-crime thrillers, after giving an electrifying performance in the 1986 motion picture *8 Million Ways to Die,* playing Angel Maldonado, a mercurial cocaine kingpin and the leader of the villains. The film was a commercial disappointment, but García won critical raves for his performance. Perhaps more importantly, he caught the attention of Brian De Palma, who then offered the actor the role of a sadistic hit man opposite Kevin Costner in his upcoming gangster movie *The Untouchables* (1987), based on the memorable television series of the 1950s about Al Capone. García convinced De Palma to give him a good-guy role in *The Untouchables,* and as the upright FBI agent, García held his own among a formidable cast, which included such major actors as Kevin Costner, Sean Connery, and Robert De Niro.

García's commanding screen presence in *The Untouchables* won him widespread recognition and attracted major-studio notice. In 1988 the actor was cast in *American Roulette,* a spy thriller, and in *Stand and Deliver,* in which he portrayed a slick bureaucrat. He then won a role as Michael Douglas's partner in *Black Rain,* a 1989 thriller about two New York City detectives on the trail of a vicious Japanese gangster. In 1990 he played Raymond Avila, a young detective who uncovers a web of police corruption in the drama *Internal Affairs.* García also starred in *A Show of Force* (1990), a motion picture loosely based on an actual political scandal in Puerto Rico in which two pro-independence youths were fatally shot.

The part García needed to achieve full-fledged movie-star status materialized in 1990. García beat fierce competition for the part of Vincent Mancini, the illegitimate heir who takes the torch from the now-aged don in the 1990 sequel *The Godfather, Part III.* García's performance earned him strong critical acclaim. For his portrayal of Vincent Mancini in *The Godfather, Part III,* García won an Academy Award nomination in 1991 for Best Supporting Actor and a 1991 Golden Globe Award nomination for Best Costar.

In the aftermath of *The Godfather, Part III*, García became an in-demand actor. In 1991 he portrayed a bad-tempered, chain-smoking newspaper reporter in the romantic mystery *Dead Again*. His next project was the 1992 motion picture *Jennifer 8*, with Uma Thurman and John Malkovich, which opened to mixed reviews. He was next cast in the 1992 film *Hero*, costarring Dustin Hoffman and Geena Davis, about a man who rescues people from a plane crash and an imposter who claims responsibility for the heroic deed. García plays the imposter, a down-and-out Vietnam vet who discovers in the end that he, too, has heroic qualities.

García is extremely proud of his Cuban roots and vows to lead a life in both America and Cuba once democracy is restored on the island. He told *American Film* in 1990: "No one is more Cuban than me. And you can ask any of my friends and they'll tell you. My culture is the basis of my strength. I would be a nonentity without my culture." García has effectively incorporated Cuban culture, music, and literature into his professional life. In 1992 he was at work producing a documentary in Spanish about Israel (Cachao) Lopez, a Cuban forefather of the mambo. He also commissioned the famous Cuban novelist Guillermo Cabrera Infante to write a screenplay, *The Lost City*, for García to direct. *The Lost City* is set in Havana on the eve of the revolution and is about a young man who runs a cabaret and ultimately realizes that he must flee his homeland. García told the *New York Times*: "It's all about that man's eventual exile, the end of an era, a loss of culture, a city, a way of life. And finding solace in exile with the one thing that's never betrayed him—which is the music." García would love the opportunity to shoot the film in Cuba, but he refuses to go back as long as Castro is in power.

García has always felt nostalgic about his lost homeland of Cuba. As a way of quelling his longing for its culture, he has forged close ties with the Cuban community in Miami, where he owns a house. García cherishes his family in Florida and he and Marívi try to spend several months a year there to immerse their three daughters in the Cuban atmosphere so that they may develop a sense of cultural identity. In a show of support for South Florida, which has the largest Cuban population in the United States, García cohosted the Hurricane Relief benefit to help victims of Hurricane Andrew, which hit Florida in 1992. On January 16, 1993, the actor participated in another benefit, which drew him close to Cuban culture. He performed with Cachao and his Mambo Orchestra at a "Celebration of Cuban Music" at Radio City Music Hall to benefit Boys Harbor, the Harlem youth-services agency.

Although he wholeheartedly embraces his Cuban heritage, García believes it is discriminatory to categorize him as a Latino actor. He told *American Film*: "In order to stop the racism, in order to stop the stereotyping, we all have to be considered—all of us—actors first. And may the best actor for the part get the part. Not the best Hispanic actor. Because if not I shouldn't be playing an Italian in *The Godfather....*"

64

Dolores Del Rio

1905–1983

Dolores Del Rio was born Lolita Dolores Martinez Asúnsolo y Lopez Negrete on August 3, 1905, in Durango, Mexico, to Jesús Asúnsolo and Antonia (Lopez Negrete) de Asúnsolo. Jesús Asúnsolo, descended from Spanish Basques, was the director of the Bank of Durango when Dolores was a small child. He fled to the United States during the Mexican Revolution of 1910, leaving his wife and the young Dolores behind with relatives in Mexico City until his return in 1912. Dolores grew up in Mexico City and attended the Convent of Saint Joseph, an exclusive French private school, where, as a proper young lady of the aristocracy,

310

she studied Spanish dancing in addition to other subjects. Later, she claimed to have been presented at the Spanish royal court at age fourteen.

In 1921, at age sixteen, Dolores left school and married Jaime Martínez Del Rio, a wealthy lawyer educated in England and France, and the couple went to Europe on a two-year honeymoon. As they traveled through Spain, Del Rio danced for Spanish soldiers returning from the Spanish-Moroccan War. She drew plaudits from Alfonso XIII and took an instant liking to the spotlight. After the long honeymoon the couple returned to Mexico City, where they mixed with intellectuals and studied literature, classical music, and archaeology. Their placid existence changed forever when a visiting friend introduced them to the American movie director Edwin Carewe, who was scouting for a "female Valentino." Carewe was so impressed by Del Rio that he invited her to Hollywood.

In 1925, Carewe offered Del Rio a bit part in the United Artists motion picture *Joanne*, launching her film career. Del Rio and her husband were excited about her new career in Hollywood because they longed to get away from the economic uncertainties of Mexico, where, in 1924, their investments in agriculture had suffered serious losses. *Joanne* would be the first of fifteen silent films Del Rio played in between 1925 and 1929. In keeping with the established American tradition of labeling Latin American actors cast in "good guy" roles as "Spanish," Del Rio was touted as a "Spanish actress." She was cast in such memorable films of the silent era as *All the Town Is Talking* (1925), *What Price Glory?* (1926), *Resurrection* (1927), *Ramona* (1928), and *Evangeline* (1929).

In *What Price Glory?*, the second-bestselling film of 1926, Del Rio plays Charmaine, a coquettish French peasant girl. The entire film world was stirred by her performance and awaited a fundamental work to confirm her talent. In her first leading role in the film *Resurrection*, an adaptation of the Tolstoi novel, Del Rio won the respect and admiration of the American public. Her performance in *Ramona*, in which she played a character of Mexican descent for the first time, marked Del Rio's second great success and drew accolades from film critics and the studios of United Artists, which awarded the actress a private bungalow on the company lot. After the release of *Ramona*, United Artists sent its new star to appear in person at the opening nights of the film throughout the United States and Europe. Del Rio needed police protection in every city, since crowds surrounded her, seeking a glimpse of the Mexican star.

Del Rio was fortunate to appear on the Hollywood scene during the silent-film era, for in those early days she did not yet know English. By the time sound was introduced Del Rio had already established herself, and therefore her accent did not relegate her to the "bad guy" roles many Latino actors were forced to play at the time. Filmgoers first heard her voice in the 1929 film *Evangeline,* a silent film based on the Longfellow poem, into which three ballads she sang in French were edited before its release. In 1930, when many actors with accents had been left by the wayside, Del Rio starred in her first film with sound and went on to enjoy as successful a career in talkies as she had in silent films.

In 1930, Del Rio's first husband, whom she had divorced earlier, died, and the actress married Cedric Gibbons, an art director with Metro-Goldwyn-Mayer who had designed the Academy Award "Oscar." The couple settled down in a house in Santa Monica, California, built in the art moderne style. Gibbons worked a grand staircase with a landing into his design for Del Rio to command at parties, stunning guests with her beauty and style. Her marriage to Gibbons would last eleven years, or the remainder of her career in American movies. After the marriage ceremony, the actress then signed a contract with United Artists, which had agreed to pay her $9,000 a week. However, United Artists backed out when she suffered a serious illness, and so, upon recovery, Del Rio signed a contract with RKO Studios.

In 1932, Del Rio was cast in the hit film *Bird of Paradise* as a near-topless Polynesian who throws herself into a volcano. In 1933 she starred in the musical *Flying Down to Rio,* which is best remembered as the film that featured Fred Astaire and Ginger Rogers on-screen for the first time. In *Flying Down to Rio,* Del Rio plays a beautiful Brazilian who dances a tango with Fred Astaire. Few know, however, that it was she who taught the famous dancer the steps of the Argentine dance, which she had learned from Valentino. With *Flying Down to Rio,* the actress also had the honor of introducing to American audiences the two-piece bathing suit.

A turning point came in Del Rio's career when she starred in Orson Welles's *Journey into Fear,* released in 1943. The relationship she had with Welles precipitated her divorce from Cedric Gibbons in 1941. Del Rio and Welles then made plans to marry, but he met Rita Hayworth around that time and forgot all about Del Rio. In 1942, she sold her house in Hollywood and returned to her native Mexico. In an interview for the February-March 1981 issue of *Modern Maturity*, the actress spoke about the reasons behind her return to her native land: "...by 1940 I knew I couldn't build a satisfying career on glamour, so I came home. My father had died, and I felt a need for my country, my people. Also I wanted to pioneer with our beginning Mexican film industry." She acquired an old place in Coyoacán which she gradually converted into a mansion and filled with countless objects, including pre-Columbian artifacts, a crimson oil by Frieda Kahlo, and the oil portrait Diego Rivera had painted of the actress.

With Del Rio's appearance in two noteworthy Mexican films released in 1943, *Flor sylvestre* (Wild Flower) and *María Candelaria* (known in English as *Portrait of Maria*), Mexican cinema came of age. *Flor sylvestre* was Del Rio's first Mexican-made film, and the actress selected Emilio Fernández as director-writer, Gabriel Figueroa as cameraman, and Pedro Almendariz as leading man. Backed by this trio, Del Rio's career reached new heights, and she won the Arieles, the Mexican equivalent of the Academy Award, for Best Performance in a Leading Role in *Flor sylvestre*. *Portrait of Maria* was the actress's second Mexican feature, for which she was again supported by her trio. The film won the Golden Palm at Cannes in 1946, establishing Del Rio as the leading actress of the Mexican cinema and the first of the big international stars of the 1940s.

Throughout the 1940s and 1950s, she continued making films in Mexico and also ventured to other countries. According to one source, Del Rio was barred at this time from entering the United States because she "aided anti-Franco refugees from the Spanish Civil War." In 1947, Del Rio played her last American part until the 1960s, when she returned to the United States. She was cast as an unwed Native-American mother in the film *The Fugitive*, which John Ford made in Mexico. The film also starred Henry Fonda as an alcoholic priest.

Long known as the "First Lady of the Mexican Theater," Del Rio occasionally appeared in theatrical productions throughout her career. In the late 1950s, Lewis Riley, an American theater producer and director, invited Del Rio to perform on the Mexican stage in his production of *Lady Windermere's Fan*, Oscar

Wilde's comedy filled with paradoxes and epigrams. Around this time, the actress also took the stage in Henrik Ibsen's drama *Ghosts*. In 1956, Del Rio toured New England with the stage production *Anastasia*. Del Rio and Lewis Riley married on November 24, 1960, and settled down in an affluent suburb of Mexico City.

In the 1960s and 1970s, Del Rio cut down on her creative output. From 1960 to 1978 she took to the stage on only a few occasions and appeared in only five films in Mexico. She returned to Hollywood in 1960 to star in the western *Flaming Star* as Elvis Presley's full-blooded Kiowa Indian mother. In 1964 she played a Spanish woman in director John Ford's last film, *Cheyenne Autumn*, which Ford himself described as his apology to the Native Americans he had portrayed as one-dimensional in his previous westerns. In 1966, Del Rio acted in the Spanish film *La dama del alba* and in the television show *Dolores Del Rio's Mexico*, aired in 1968. The actress then went to Italy to appear in a Carlo Ponti film starring Sophia Loren and Omar Sharif, *C'era una volta* (1967), known popularly in the United States as *More Than a Miracle*.

In 1970, Del Rio retired from the stage and screen and immersed herself in charitable work. With financial backing from the government and the Mexican Actors Association, she opened the Estancia Infantil, a day-care center for the children of Mexican actors. She administered the nursery and could frequently be found there interacting with the children. Del Rio came out of retirement in 1978 to costar with Anthony Quinn in what would be her last film, *The Children of Sanchez*, a U.S.-Mexican production. Dolores Del Rio died of chronic hepatitis at her home in Newport Beach, California, on April 11, 1983.

65

José Villarreal
1924–

José Antonio Villarreal was born on July 30, 1924, in Los Angeles, California, to parents Felícitaz (Ramírez) Villarreal and José Heladio Villarreal, from Zacatecas, Mexico. During the Mexican Revolution of 1910, José Villarreal Sr. spent seven years fighting in Pancho Villa's army. In 1921, two years before his birth, José's parents immigrated to the United States to work as farm laborers, moving with the crops in California. José spent his childhood migrating with his parents as they harvested crops in the fields, and as a little boy he came to know only the close-knit and secure world of the *campesinos*. Like the other migrant workers, the Villarreal family lived in tents pitched in the fields, and in the evenings José would fall asleep listening to the tales the migrants told of Mexico. He was enchanted by these tales, as he told *Bilingual Review* in an interview in the spring 1976 issue: "And every camp was different, none existing for more than six or seven weeks, then off we would go to the next harvest, where new people would gather and there would be new tales to be told and heard. I knew when I was six years old that the one thing I most wanted from life was to be a storyteller."

Finally, in 1930, Villarreal's parents found steady employment and settled in Santa Clara, California, where the boy was immediately enrolled in the first grade. In school he began to learn English from his first-grade teacher, Miss Uriell, who spoke no Spanish but somehow managed to communicate with her pupil. By the end of the year Miss Uriell had taught José to read in English, and by the third grade the boy was writing short stories and poems in his newfound language. That year, the principal, recognizing his genius, promoted the boy to fourth grade. Up until he graduated from high school, Miss Uriell would give him books as Christmas gifts. Villarreal once commented that he looks back on those early days of learning and on his teacher with great fondness. Those days, however, were not without pain and hardship, for he grew up *pocho*, between two cultures, with parents who forbade him to speak English at home, a language they had not made any effort to learn. Little by little, José's parents accepted English in their home. In addition, he had to contend with the harsh reality of racism as he sought to assimilate into American society.

Villarreal graduated from high school and joined the navy in 1942 just as the United States was poised to enter World War II. After his discharge, he enrolled at the University of California at Berkeley, where he was awarded a B.A. degree in English in 1950. Villarreal then entered a graduate program at the University of California at Berkeley and at Los Angeles, but then decided to write rather than accept a literary scholarship. During the 1950s, Villarreal traveled about the United States and began to work on his first novel. He married Barbara Gentles in 1953, and between 1954 and 1958 the couple had three children. Villarreal took many jobs to provide for his new family, and for a long stretch of time he worked as a technical writer and editor. At one point the family lived in the San Francisco Bay area, where Villarreal took a position as an editor and translator at the Stanford Research Institute.

While he was visiting Mexico in 1956, Villarreal completed another version of an autobiographical novel, *Pocho,* he had been working on. It was published in 1959. Villarreal's experiences growing up between cultures in the Santa Clara Valley of the 1930s are at the core of the novel. The young protagonist, Richard Rubio, caught between cultures and generations, struggles to assimilate into the American mainstream and is forced to confront racism, cultural conflict, linguistic confusion, and conformity, just as the author did in his childhood and youth. From 1960 and 1968, Villarreal was employed as a senior technical writer at Lockheed Aircraft Corporation. In 1963, his father decided to return to Mexico. Eight years had passed since the death of Felícitaz (Ramírez) Villarreal, and José Villarreal Sr. longed for the comfort of his homeland.

After leaving Lockheed in 1968, Villarreal went to work as a supervisor for technical publications at Ball Brothers Research Corporation in Boulder, Colorado. In 1970 an Anchor paperback edition of *Pocho* was published. Americans were so struck by the novel that Villarreal was soon inundated with offers of teaching positions, guest lectureships, and editorial posts. Villarreal went on to teach at the University of Colorado, the University of Texas at El Paso, Santa Clara University, the Universidad Nacional Autónoma de México, the University of the Americas, and the Preparatoria Americana of the American School in Mexico. While *Pocho* enjoyed immense popularity with mainstream American readers in the 1970s, Villarreal became the center of controversy during the Chicano movement of the late 1960s and 1970s when he stated on numerous occasions that he neither identified himself as a Chicano writer nor was convinced of the existence of a Chicano literature. Around this time, student activists at the University of Colorado confronted the writer for what they perceived as his anti-Chicano stance.

In 1973, Villarreal gave up his U.S. citizenship and became a Mexican citizen. Doubleday published Villarreal's second novel, *The Fifth Horseman,* in 1974, five years after the writer had completed the first draft of the work. An epic of the 1910 Mexican Revolution written with wide brush strokes, *The Fifth Horseman* opens on a hacienda as Mexico is teetering on the edge of revolution. The novel then proceeds to chronicle the brutality and terror of the fighting that shook the country to its foundation and sent many of its citizens scrambling across the Rio Grande.

The novel essentially ends where *Pocho* begins. Villarreal has commented that his second novel is superior to the first, and literary critics praised *The Fifth Horseman* for its fine structure, strong story line, historical veracity, and the use of Spanish syntax in English dialogue so that it seems as though the characters are speaking Spanish. Nevertheless, the novel was ignored for the most part by the press and the reading public and subsequently went out of print.

While teaching at the University of Texas at El Paso, just across the border from Júarez, Mexico, Villarreal had the opportunity to observe the people on the streets of these border towns. He was particularly fascinated by the Mexican street urchins who hustled to survive, and one of these boys was transformed into the literary character Ramón Alvarez, later Clemente Chacón, of Villarreal's third novel, *Clemente Chacón,* published in 1984. While Villarreal quickly informs the reader that "he, Clemente Chacón, was Horatio Alger, even if he was Catholic and brown," the novel is no ordinary, sentimental rags-to-riches story and explores not only success but the sacrifices and conflicts the immigrant must face in America to get ahead. Villarreal provides shocking details of Ramón's life in a desperate Mexican border town, where he is forced to survive as a shoe-shine boy, pimp, and drug dealer. The character ultimately crosses the Rio Grande and at the expense of his Mexican past assumes a new identity as Clemente Chacón and becomes a successful American insurance executive. By the book's end Clemente Chacón is able to integrate his split identity and fuse the past and the present, declaring: "I am a Mexican and I am an American, and there is no reason in the world why I can't be both."

José Villarreal has commented that *Clemente Chacón* is his most successful work. The writer planned two more novels to accompany *The Fifth Horseman* and *Pocho* in a tetralogy, but the books have yet to be published.

66

Ritchie Valens

1941–1958

The second of two boys, Ritchie Valens was born Richard Steve Valenzuela on May 13, 1941, in Pacoima, California, to Joseph Steve Valenzuela, a Mexican American, and Concepción (Reyes) Valenzuela. Ritchie's father was a tree surgeon, and his mother had been working at a munitions factory before he was born. At a young age, Ritchie exhibited a natural talent for music. His mother recalled how at age three Ritchie tried to make a toy guitar from a can and rubber bands and how, at age five, the boy made a guitar from a cigar box with the help of an uncle. When he was around three years old, his parents split up, and Ritchie went to live with his father; his brother Robert stayed with his mother. Joseph Valenzuela often spoiled Ritchie, but he was also strict and insisted that the young boy develop his musical gifts. In his youth Ritchie enjoyed singing country-and-western songs, and his heroes were the "singing cowboys" Roy Rogers and Gene Autry. The boy also played trumpet and guitar, the instrument of choice of his cousin "Dickie," who exposed Ritchie to Latin songs.

In 1951, when Ritchie was ten, his father died suddenly. Ritchie stayed briefly with uncles in Norwalk and Santa Monica, California, where he attended the Carmelita School before joining his mother and siblings at his father's house and returning to Pacoima Elementary. While he was a student at Pacoima Junior High School, he became absorbed in the guitar. He practiced the instrument for hours on end in a quiet room in the family house and constantly played for his fellow students during recess, at lunchtime, and at school functions. In those days, Ritchie was shy, and friendly to everyone regardless of race, which led other Mexican-American students to label him *falso,* meaning "hypocritical."

In the mid-1950s, Ritchie began performing with a group of mostly Mexican-American musicians who called themselves the Silhouettes. His repertoire consisted mainly of Little Richard songs and other popular hits of the late 1950s, as well as some Latin numbers, such as *corridos,* traditional Mexican folk ballads often employing contemporary themes. A charismatic singer, Ritchie won loud applause during performances at private parties throughout the San Fernando Valley. In 1956 his family was forced to move to a smaller house because they could no longer meet the mortgage payments on his father's house. With the Silhouettes, Ritchie held a dance at the Pacoima Legion Hall to raise money to cover the first mortgage payments on the new house. The dance proved to be a turning point in Valens's life, for a representative of Bob Keane, who ran Del-Fi Records, was in attendance. Ritchie was invited to audition at the basement studio in Bob Keane's house in the Hollywood hills. Some of his friends from the Silhouettes attended the audition and were nearly arrested, since Mexicans were not allowed in the Anglo neighborhood. Ritchie made a strong impact with his repertoire of Little Richard and rhythm-and-blues numbers. Bob Keane signed the budding star and changed his name to Ritchie Valens.

In early 1957, Ritchie's maternal grandfather passed away, and on the day of the funeral, disaster struck at Pacoima Junior High when a jet collided with a navy plane over the school's athletic field, killing eight. After that incident Ritchie had a fear of flying. Later that year he entered San Fernando High School, but his attendance waned in proportion to his fame, since he spent more and more time on the road. At San Fernando High, Valens met Donna Ludwig, the girl who later inspired the Top 10 song "Donna." The two became fast friends but did not date, since Donna's father forbade her from associating with a Mexican American. During this time period the teenage singer never formally split with the Silhouettes, even after establishing himself as a solo act.

Valens's recording career was launched with the Del-Fi release of the lively country-rock song "Come On, Let's Go." Curiously, Valens never sang the song the same way twice, even after it was commercially recorded. His exposure to traditional Mexican music, with its variations in melody, influenced the singer's style. By August 1958, Keane began promoting "Come On, Let's Go" through the Los Angeles radio stations, and the song enjoyed considerable air play in the western states, where it became a regional hit. By September it made the national charts; on September 1, 1958, "Come On, Let's Go" was the "Pick of the Week" in *Billboard* magazine. On October 6, 1958, Ritchie Valens performed the hit song on *American Bandstand* in Philadelphia. The young star subsequently appeared on Alan Freed's television show in New York, the *Buddy Deane Show* in Baltimore, and the *Milt Grant Show* in Washington, D.C.

Shortly after, Valens wrote, recorded, and released two songs that would make him a national name and one of rock's biggest rising young stars. One was the Top 10 "Donna." This plaintive ballad, a classic of early rock music, shot up to number two on the charts by January 1959 and would become Valens's biggest hit. "Donna" inspired other songs, such as Dion's 1963 hit "Donna, the Primadonna," which was resurrected in the mid-1970s by Donny Osmond and Freddy Fender. Its flip side, "La Bamba," a lively rock song featuring lyrics entirely in Spanish, also met with an enthusiastic reception. "La Bamba" is a traditional Mexican wedding song from the region of Veracruz. Initially, Ritchie Valens did not want to include the song in his repertoire in an effort to preserve the dignity of his culture. In December 1958, "La Bamba" first made it onto the *Billboard* charts, and in ensuing decades the song was resurrected by such folk musicians as the Kingston Trio, Joan Baez, and Harry Belafonte.

Valens also wrote and cowrote other songs, which would appear on albums released posthumously, and recorded versions of hits like "Bluebird Over the Mountain" and "Paddiwack," a variation of the "Children's Marching Song" his mother used to sing to him. In December 1958, Valens gave a concert and a short interview during the morning assembly at Pacoima Junior High. The school principal recorded the event over the PA system, and in 1960 the tape was released on an album of unfinished songs Valens had written. That month, the young teen idol also performed in *Alan Freed's Christmas Jubilee,* a spectacle which ran from Christmas week to New Year's.

Upon his return to Los Angeles after the holidays, Valens starred along with such singers as Chuck Berry, Jimmy Clanton, Eddie Cochran, and Jackie Wilson in the Hal Wallis film *Go, Johnny, Go,* the last of the rock-and-roll films Alan Freed promoted. On January 11, 1958, Ritchie performed in the first rock-and-roll prime-time television series *The Music Shop,* as the featured guest for the first time in his career. This television appearance, during which he sang "La Bamba" and "Donna," would be his last. That month, Valens signed a long-term contract with General Artist Corporation (GAC), a booking agency which put together rock-and-roll packages for performers. GAC had organized an "extensive buildup" for Ritchie Valens, which included a "Winter Dance Party" tour with other musicians, including Buddy Holly and the Big Bopper (J. P. Richardson).

Before departing on the tour, which would cover the Midwest during the treacherous winter months, Valens held a farewell party with family and friends at a house he had just purchased. The tour proved to be a hardship from the start; the musicians' bus, which was barely heated, kept breaking down. At some point it became clear that the group would not make it to their gig in Fargo, North Dakota, with enough time to shower and rest before a long performance. On February 3, 1958, Buddy Holly, tired of the cold, crowded bus, decided to charter a small plane from the municipal airport in Mason City, Iowa, to get himself and his band members to Fargo hours ahead of the bus. Ritchie asked Buddy Holly's guitarist, Tommy Allsup, for his seat. They flipped a coin, and Valens won, and thus the seventeen-year-old musician found himself on the ill-fated flight. Soon after takeoff the plane crashed in a cornfield in Clear Lake, Iowa, killing all on board.

Valens was buried at the San Fernando Mission Cemetery in San Fernando, California, on February 7, 1958. A bar of notes and the song title "Come On, Let's Go" are engraved on his headstone. On February 21, 1959, the singer's first album, entitled *Ritchie Valens,* was released posthumously. Demand for more recordings intensified, and in October 1959, *Ritchie* was released. In December 1960, *Ritchie Valens in Concert at Pacoima Junior High* filled the shelves. Musicians such as Herschel Almond, Benny Barnes, and Waylon Jennings commemorated the performers who lost their lives in the crash with songs. In his 1971 elegiac hit "American Pie," Don McLean paid homage to the fallen singers by calling the tragedy "the day the music died."

In the aftermath of the tragedy Valens's life and achievements were overshadowed to a great degree by the attention given Buddy Holly, a musician who had been longer in the limelight. That came to an end in 1987 with the release of *La Bamba,* a film memorializing Valens. *La Bamba* was written and directed by Chicano Luis Valdez and produced by his brother Danny Valdez, who viewed Valens's life as an "inspirational story" for all youth, no matter their ethnicity. Latino artists Los Lobos and Carlos Santana made cameo appearances in *La Bamba,* and some of Valens's relatives, including a sister, were cast in the film.

Although it was generally unknown that Ritchie Valens was of Mexican origin until after his death, the young singer was the first to marry Latin rhythms with rock and roll. In so doing, Valens set the stage for the explosion of Latino sounds in mainstream American music and fostered a greater awareness and appreciation of the contributions Latinos make to American culture.

67

Pancho Segura

1921–

One of nine children of mixed Spanish and Incan blood, Pancho Segura was born Francisco Segura Cano on June 20, 1921, in Ecuador, aboard a steamboat bound for Guayaquil, the country's main port. Pancho's legs were deformed by premature birth and diseases he contracted in childhood, and he was called *pata de loro*, or "parrot foot," for his funny gait. The Segura family lived in a humble sugarcane house with an earthen floor on the outskirts of Guayaquil. Pancho's godfather, Juan José Medina, was one of the wealthiest men in Ecuador and ran Guayaquil's only tennis club, all of whose members were upper class. In 1927, Pancho's father, Domingo Segura, left his job as a foreman for an American export firm to work as the caretaker of the tennis club. Medina decided that tennis might help the ailing Pancho, so he allowed the boy to play on the courts after hours. Pancho eagerly practiced hitting balls with a paddle his mother had fashioned out of balsa wood. He also earned a little pocket money working as a ball boy at the club. The constant exercise on the courts and the swims he took in the Guayas River strengthened his legs.

At age eight, Pancho began attending public school and earned money for the family by running errands for club members and helping his father keep the grounds in order. When he was eleven, he acquired his first real tennis racket, a worn Top Flight, from a visiting Brazilian player. Still weak from a double hernia he suffered a year earlier, Pancho could not handle the racket with one hand, so he adopted a two-fisted forehand and backhand, probably the first tennis player to do so. When his godfather allowed him to use the club's rowing machine, Pancho rowed constantly to build up his body. Soon he was strong enough to swing the Top Flight racket with one hand, but by then his two-fisted grip was so effective that he never reverted to a one-handed stroke.

As a teenager, Pancho fell ill with malaria, and a doctor advised that he leave the tropics. A family moving to Quito, the capital of Ecuador, situated in the mountains, offered to take Pancho along as a companion and tennis partner for their children. In 1937 he returned to Guayaquil, with superb tennis skills and in top form. A year later, it was suggested that Pancho play on the Guayaquil club team in the tournament against the Quito tennis club for the Pichincha Cup, Ecuador's most prized athletic trophy. The class-conscious members of the Guayaquil tennis club were horrified at the thought of having a player of mixed blood, known in Ecuador as a *cholo,* on the team. The club's president threatened to resign if Pancho was forbidden to play, and the members backed down. On the train ride to Quito, Pancho was forced to sit alone. In Quito he won all of his matches, enabling Guayaquil to capture the Pichincha Cup. Now a prized player, Pancho was allowed to sit with fellow teammates on the trip home.

That same year, the Ecuadoran Olympic Committee, after heated debate, entered Pancho in the Bolivarian Olympics at Bogotá. Once again Pancho confronted class discrimination when other countries, led by Peru, tried to bar the young player from participating on the grounds that he was a professional. Segura won his matches, defeating Carlos Acuna, the Peruvian champion, to capture the singles title. With that victory, Segura established himself as Ecuador's number one player and earned a hero's welcome upon his return to Guayaquil. A region of the city was renamed Borough Segura, and the street the player lived on was christened Calle Pancho Segura in his honor. His name appeared on signs all over the city, and his picture was printed on a fifty-centavos postage stamp.

In 1940, Segura was sent to the United States to participate in the U.S. Championships at Forest Hills. He first played at the Southampton Invitation in Long Island, wearing long pants, which had gone out of fashion on American tennis courts in 1929. In his first match, Segura was defeated in less than twenty minutes. He had never before encountered the high-bouncing twist serve in vogue among American players, and he lacked a power serve, volley, and lob and any notion of tactics or pace. At Forest Hills, Segura advanced to the second round but was defeated by Frank Parker. In the winter of 1940, Segura studied English at a public school and practiced diligently on indoor courts. In May 1941 he won his first major American tournament, besting Ladislav Hecht at the Brooklyn Championships. At the U.S. Championships at Forest Hills that year, Segura again went down in defeat in an exciting second-round match against Bryan Grant. Tennis great Gardnar Mulloy, then coach at the University of Miami, saw Segura play and after the match offered the young player a scholarship.

Pancho Segura enrolled at the University of Miami that fall as a member of the freshman class and was coached on the court by Mulloy. Representing Miami, Segura won the singles of the U.S. Intercollegiate National Championships in 1943, 1944, and 1945 as the only male player in this century to win three straight intercollegiate titles. In 1944, Segura also defeated Bill Talbert, 6–3, 2–6, 7–5, 6–3, to win the singles of the U.S. Clay Court Championships in Detroit. Teaming up with Talbert, Segura went on to capture the U.S. Clay Court doubles title that year. In 1945 the duo successfully defended their title. In 1946 he teamed up with Tom Burke to capture the U.S. Intercollegiate doubles crown. That March Segura prevailed in singles at the U.S. Indoor Championships, upsetting Don McNeill, 1–6, 6–3, 6–4, 7–5.

In June 1946, Segura won the title by besting top-seeded Dinny Pails in a surprise upset at the London Grass Court Championships. A few days later, at his debut at the All-England Tennis Championships at Wimbledon, Segura was defeated in the third round by unseeded Tom Brown. At the French National Championships that year he lost to Marcel Bernard in the third round. However, Segura teamed up with Enrique Morea to advance to the men's doubles final in Paris; the pair went down in defeat after five sets to Bernard and Yvon Petra. For eight frustrating years, from 1940 to 1947, Segura tried desperately to win the U.S. Championships at Forest Hills and attain the number one amateur ranking in the United States. However, he was no match against Bill Talbert during the war and when Frank Parker and Jack Kramer returned from the service, Segura rarely advanced to the quarterfinals of the tournament. The highest ranking he ever attained in that eight-year period was number three in 1943.

Having failed to reach the top of the amateur ranking, Pancho Segura turned pro in 1947. He signed a contract to participate in Jack Kramer's first professional exhibition tour, which guaranteed him a minimum salary of $20,000. In an exhausting series of one-nighters around the country, Jack Kramer and Bobby Riggs headlined, while Pancho Segura and Dinny Pails played in the secondary matches. Segura always put his all into a match, as if British royalty were watching, and with his fine sense of humor, he was in charge of bolstering morale in the group.

In 1947 he married Virginia Spencer Smith of Forest Hills, and in June 1948 he took time off from the exhibition tour to participate in the U.S. Championships at Forest Hills but lost in the third round to Frank Kovacs. Segura and Jack Kramer captured the doubles crown at Forest Hills after defeating the defending champions Bobby Riggs and Don Budge. Segura then rejoined the exhibition tour that played overseas for the 1948–1949 season.

In the fall of 1949, Bobby Riggs organized another exhibition tour headlining Jack Kramer and Pancho Gonzales, while Pancho Segura played Frank Parker in the preliminary singles. As he gained experience on the professional tour, Segura mastered his strokes and developed extraordinary agility and a large shot selection. That season, he played Frank Parker, who had once run him off the court as an amateur, and by the end of the 1949–1950 tour, Segura had won fifty-seven of his matches against Parker. With his winnings, Segura bought his mother an apartment house in Guayaquil, and he brought six siblings to the United States to attend school. His tennis improved rapidly, and at the 1950 U.S. Professional Championships in Cleveland, Segura beat Jack Kramer in the semifinals and then went on to defeat Frank Kovacs in the final to clinch the title. As the U. S. professional champion, Segura became the first player of South American origin ever to capture one of the world's major men's singles titles.

Segura's victory earned him top billing with Jack Kramer on the 1950–1951 exhibition tour, and he won twenty-nine of the ninety-seven matches against Kramer. At the U.S. Professional Championships in 1951 and 1952, Pancho retained his title by defeating Pancho Gonzales in the finals two years in a row. In 1948 and 1955 he won the doubles of the U.S. Professional Championships with Jack Kramer and in 1954 and 1958 with Pancho Gonzales. In 1958, at the Masters Round Robin Championship in Los Angeles, Segura, then nearing his fortieth birthday, overwhelmed Pancho Gonzales, Rex Hartwig, Tony Trabert, Lew Hoad, and Ken Rosewall in successive matches, to make it to the finals.

Open tennis came too late for Pancho Segura, and he entered only one open tournament, the men's doubles of the first open Wimbledon in 1968, at age forty-seven. Segura and doubles partner Alex Olmedo won the longest doubles match of Wimbledon's open era, ninety-four games, defeating Abe Segal and Gordon Forbes, 32–30, 5–7, 6–4, 6–4, in the second round. The first set was the longest in Wimbledon history. After retiring from the game in the late 1960s, Segura concentrated on teaching tennis as the resident pro at the Beverly Hills Tennis Club until 1972 and then at the LaCosta Resort in Carlsbad, California, beginning in 1973. From the late 1960s to the mid-1970s, he coached Jimmy Connors. In the late 1970s, Segura participated in the Grand Masters Over-35 tournaments, and in 1982 he and partner Fred Stolle won the U.S. Open Senior Men's Invitational doubles title at Flushing Meadow.

In 1946, Ecuador awarded Pancho Segura a decoration of merit in recognition of the prestige he brought to the country. In 1984 he was elected to the Tennis Hall of Fame.

68

Gary Soto

1952–

Gary Soto was born on April 12, 1952, in Fresno, California, to parents of Mexican descent. Gary's grandparents had been born in Mexico and later crossed the Rio Grande to earn a livelihood in the factories and fields of America. Gary spent his childhood in the barrio in Fresno, and although he heard Spanish constantly in the Soto household, he never received formal lessons in the language. When Gary was five years old, his father was involved in a fatal, work-related accident that left him in a coma. Soto would later translate this heart-wrenching experience into poems such as "Spirit" from his collection *The Elements of San Joaquin*: "But it was you father/Who sent me across/A dry orchard/Where I pointed/To a thin cloud/And thought/Beyond/That cloud/You lived in Limbo/God's Limbo/And were watching/And soon for/The first time/You would come to me/Calling *son son*."

Gary attended the local schools in Fresno and then enrolled at Fresno City College, convinced that he did not stand a chance of being admitted to California State University. At Fresno City College Soto majored in geography but soon gave up the subject and concentrated on poetry. He had read Edward Field's poem "Unwanted," and the theme of alienation in the poem's lines had struck a chord in him. Henceforth, he harnessed his intellectual powers and was soon excelling academically. Soto transferred to California State University at Fresno, where for two years he studied under the poet Philip Levine. He was at the top of his class at California State University, graduating magna cum laude in 1974. He then enrolled in a graduate program at the University of California at Irvine, where he was named Graduate Student of the Year in Humanities.

Not long after he began graduate studies, Soto submitted some of his work to various literary journals and soon saw his poetry in print. In 1975 he was published in *Entrance: 4 Chicano Poets*, a collection of poetry by four Mexican-American poets. That year Soto won the first two of the many awards of his career when he was named the recipient of the Academy of American Poets Prize and the *Discovery* Nation Award. On May 24, 1975, Gary Soto married Carolyn Oda. In 1976 he received an M.F.A. degree in creative writing from the University of California at Irvine. After obtaining his degree, Soto took a trip to Mexico City and then spent the 1976–1977 academic year as a writer in residence at San Diego State University. In 1976 he was also honored with the United States Award of the International Poetry Forum. That year, Soto published his first poetry collection, *The Elements of San Joaquin*, comprised of snapshots from his childhood in the bleak Fresno barrio. The final poem of the first section of the book, entitled "The Morning They Shot Tony Lopez, Barber and Pusher Who Went Too Far, 1958," is emblematic of the horror and hostility that his Chicano characters come face-to-face with in Fresno.

Soto accepted a teaching post in the Chicano Studies Department at the University of California at Berkeley beginning in 1977. That year, *Poetry* magazine bestowed upon him the Bess Hokin Prize, and *Nuestro* magazine selected his poetry. Gary Soto's second collection of poems, *The Tale of Sunlight*, was published in 1978 to an enthusiastic reception by literary critics. Throughout the collection Soto makes frequent references to

Latin America, and in one poem, "The Map," in the opening section, the poet traces his birth to all of Latin America. "How an Uncle Became Gray," the final poem in the second section, is dedicated to the literary genius Gabriel García Marquez. In fact, Soto once said with regard to García Marquez that *The Tale of Sunlight* is "a poem in praise to him." The collection was a finalist for the Lenore Marshall Poetry Award, and in 1978, Soto was nominated for the Pulitzer Prize and the National Book Award for *The Tale of Sunlight*.

Soto was the recipient of a Guggenheim Fellowship in 1979 and spent a year writing in Mexico City. In 1980 he published the chapbook *Father Is a Pillow Tied to a Broom*, filled with poems previously published in literary journals, and 1981 saw the publication of *Where Sparrows Work Hard*, filled with somber and sobering stories of the hard lives of working-class Chicanos in California trapped in the culture of poverty. Soto was awarded a National Education Association Fellowship in 1981, and in 1984 *Poetry* honored him with the Levinson Award. The year 1985 saw the publication of Soto's poetry collection *Black Hair* in which the themes of death and childhood reverberate. In the closing poem of the collection, "Between Words," Soto reminds the reader to live for the day: "Remember the blossoms/In rain, because in the end/Not even the ants/Will care who we were/When they climb our faces/To undo the smiles."

In 1985, Soto shifted from poetry to prose with the publication of a collection of autobiographical essays *Living Up the Street: Narrative Recollections*, the first in a series of prose works that are linked thematically. In *Living Up the Street*, Soto records tragic, painful, comic, and triumphant moments from his childhood, adolescence, and young adulthood in Fresno. He provides little analytic content in the book, leaving it to the reader to draw conclusions about these remembrances. *Living Up the Streets* won a Before Columbus Foundation American Book Award in 1985. Soto then wrote *Small Faces* (1986), a continuation of his narrative recollections, in which major events, some painful, from the writer's life are recounted. He then set to work on the third book in the autobiographical series, entitled *Lesser Evils: Ten Quartets* (1988). In a departure from *Living Up the Streets* and *Small Face*, *Lesser Evils: Ten Quartets* is a meditation on the larger themes of life rather than a chronicle of events. Soto has commented that the book essentially deals with his Catholicism. In *Lesser Evils* the writer also abandons anger and reaches a point of reconciliation and harmony. In the spring of 1988, Soto was named Elliston Poet at the University of Cincinnati.

In the 1980s, Soto began to focus on writing for children, and in 1987 he published *The Cat's Meow,* in which eight-year-old Nicole, who is part Mexican, is astounded when her cat Pip begins to speak Spanish. In 1990 he penned his first book for young readers, *Baseball in April,* and 1991 saw the publication of his young adult book *Taking Sides.* In an article he wrote for *The Reading Teacher,* Soto spoke of his experiences visiting schools in the San Joaquin Valley as "Author for a Day": "I was in love with my readers, brown faces shadowing my own characters with names like their own. I could see them turning the page, a fistful of sunflower seeds in their laps. And now I could see them upfront. I had done so many book signings but was never so happy as when a little girl came up and, hands pressed together sweetly, said, 'I want to be a writer, too.' I gave her a free book and bit my tongue when I started to say, 'Sweetie, don't do that to yourself. Go into engineering.'"

In 1992, Soto published several books for young readers, including *Pacific Crossing,* about a Mexican-American boy, Lincoln Mendoza, a character from *Taking Sides,* who spends a summer with a host family in Japan and discovers more than martial arts. In 1993, Soto published the children's books *Local News,* comprised of thirteen short stories set in a Mexican-American neighborhood, and *Too Many Tamales,* about a girl who loses her mother's ring in the masa for the tamales they are preparing for a Christmas Eve party. The girl's party guests must find the ring by eating the whole batch of tamales. Gary Soto has also produced two films for Spanish-speaking children, *The Bike* and *The Pool Party.*

In 1990, Soto published a collection of poetry entitled *Who Will Know Us?: New Poems.* His poems have appeared in distinguished journals and magazines. He also edited a superb collection of short stories by various Chicano writers which was published in 1993 as *Pieces of the Heart: New Chicano Fiction.*

69

Juan "Chi Chi" Rodriguez

1935–

The fifth of six children, Juan "Chi Chi" Rodriguez was born Juan A. Rodriguez Vila to Juan Rodriguez and Modesta Vila Rodriguez on October 23, 1935, in Rio Piedras, Puerto Rico. Juan contracted sprue and rickets when he was four years old and nearly died. The illness made his bones thin and extremely sensitive to pressure, and he still takes vitamin B_{12} shots and eats steak nearly every day to increase his stamina. When he was seven, Juan's parents separated and he and his siblings went to live with their father, who labored on plantations cutting sugar-cane and worked as a dishwasher, never earning more than eighteen dollars per week.

Juan Rodriguez Sr. knew his son was a gifted athlete, and he instilled confidence in the boy to fulfill his potential. Juan boxed on street corners for sodas until he was fifteen years old and played baseball with such future stars as Roberto Clemente and Juan Pizarro, earning a reputation as a fine sandlot pitcher. Juan took the name "Chi Chi" from the baseball player Chi Chi Flores, a popular idol in the San Juan leagues. As a child, Chi Chi helped support his family by working at odd jobs, such as shining shoes, selling peanuts in the street, and bringing water to cane cutters in the fields. Chi Chi was introduced to golf at age eight when he got a job as a forecaddie at the now-defunct Berwyn Country Club. Soon he played his own version of the game with a guava branch as a golf club and a ball fashioned from a tin can.

As a regular caddie, Chi Chi joined the other caddies on the one day each week that they were permitted to play on the green at Berwyn. On these days Chi Chi made do with what equipment he had and wore on his size-five feet the size-thirteen golf shoes a club member had given him. The future pro informed his fellow caddies that he would one day be a great golfer, teeing off with the likes of Ben Hogan and Sam Snead. When he was seventeen years old, a Berwyn Club member recognized his talent and sponsored him in his first tournament, the Puerto Rican Open. Chi Chi placed second and became even more resolute about pursuing a career in golf. At age nineteen, he joined the army and was stationed at Fort Sill, Oklahoma, for a two-year stint. He improved his golf game while in the service, winning the golf championship at Fort Sill one year. Every month Chi Chi sent fifty dollars from his paycheck to his family and held on to twenty dollars to cover his own expenses.

After his discharge, Rodriguez returned to Puerto Rico in 1957, where he worked as an orderly in a psychiatric clinic at night so he could practice golf during the day. He was then hired as a caddie at the Dorado Beach Resort. His game improved under the tutelage of pro Pete Cooper, a winner of ten PGA events who still played on the tour. Cooper made changes in Rodriguez's grip and ordered him to practice fifty-yard wedge shots until he had perfected his stroke. Cooper would remain Rodriguez's teacher throughout his career.

Rodriguez played little tournament golf in Puerto Rico, preferring instead to practice with Pete Cooper. When he began to defeat his teacher and mentor, he decided it was time to head to the mainland and join the U.S. Tour. One of the owners of the Dorado Beach Resort gave him a $12,000 stake, and he and Cooper headed north to play the Tour in 1960. His first event was the 1960 Buick Open in Grand Blanc, Michigan, where, after the first nine holes, Rodriguez was tied for the lead. On the back nine he shot a 42, but still came away with $450 for his efforts in the Buick Open. In that first year on the PGA Tour, Chi Chi Rodriguez played in twelve tournaments and won about $2,000 in prize money. As Pete Cooper's protégé, Rodriguez enjoyed the privilege of playing practice rounds with golf legends like Sam Snead and Tommy Bolt. He surprised everyone by soon becoming one of the longest hitters on the Tour, although he weighed only 117 pounds.

In his early years on the PGA Tour, Rodriguez became somewhat of a jester, performing hilarious antics on the green, which some of the more straitlaced pros found distracting but the fans appreciated. In 1963, Rodriguez captured his first PGA victory at the Denver Open and closed the year with over $17,000 in winnings. In 1964 he emerged victorious in the Lucky Strike International Open, beating veteran Don January in an eighteen-hole playoff, and in the Western Open, where he defeated Arnold Palmer by one stroke. Rodriguez finished the year ninth on the list of money winners, his finest showing on the regular Tour. Then one day in 1965, Rodriguez's golfing talent mysteriously disappeared for a time.

In the aftermath of that trying experience, Rodriguez linked his father's death to his troubles on the course. His play was also marred by the stress he endured in having to support relatives in Puerto Rico and his wife, the former Iwalani Lynette Lum King, a Hawaiian of Polynesian descent, and their daughter, Donnette. Even when he was playing his worst, he never lost his sense of humor, which kept him from throwing in the towel.

Rodriguez was victorious in five more tournaments on the regular PGA Tour after 1964, including the 1967 Texas Open, the 1968 Sahara Invitational, the 1972 Byron Nelson Classic, the 1973 Greater Greensboro Open, and his last victory, the 1979 Tallahassee Open. His best finish in a major championship after 1979 was a tie for sixth in the U.S. Open in 1981. By the mid-1970s most of his earnings came from his play in exhibitions and on corporate outings. His twenty-five-year career on the regular PGA Tour brought him fame but only eight victories and a little over $1 million. Rodriguez would not fulfill the promise of his early years until he joined the Senior PGA Tour in 1985.

In 1979 the golfer founded the Chi Chi Rodriguez Youth Foundation, an educational and counseling center at Glen Oaks Golf Course in Clearwater, Florida. The foundation addresses the needs of troubled, disadvantaged, and abused children aged five to fifteen who are bused to Glen Oaks after school for tutoring, vocational training, and a few swings of the golf club. Rodriguez is actively involved in the foundation and visits the children several times each year. He is also immersed in other philanthropic projects. Each year he holds a tournament in Puerto Rico, and the proceeds from the event go to a children's hospital on the island. He also underwrites the tuition for dozens of high school graduates who go on to the University of Puerto Rico every year.

As he approached his fiftieth birthday, Chi Chi Rodriguez began to think about retiring from golf. At around that time, Jack Nicklaus bought the MacGregor Golf Company and asked Rodriguez to endorse a line of clubs. This deal provided an enormous lift to his confidence as a competitive player. Shortly thereafter, he negotiated a lifetime deal with Toyota, and together with the Nicklaus contract, Rodriguez was financially secure for life. He decided to join the Senior PGA Tour, a rigorous pursuit, since players must master a new course each week and play every day regardless of how they feel. Chi Chi joined the Senior Tour in late 1985, and as part of his preparation, he revamped his mental golf game and imagined himself a winner, visualizing nothing but the fairway instead of the traps he might hit. With his new approach to the game, Rodriguez has met with great results.

In 1986 he won three tournaments and was ranked second in earnings with $399,172. For Rodriguez 1987 was a stellar year; he captured seven tournaments, including the PGA Senior Championship, walked away with over half a million dollars, and was ranked number one. In 1988 and 1989, Rodriguez suffered a setback due to a pinched nerve. Nevertheless, he won a total of three titles in those years, earning $300,000 at the 1988 Skins Tournament in Turtle Bay in Hawaii. On April 14, 1992, Rodriguez was inducted into the PGA World Golf Hall of Fame for his humanitarian work. By 1993, he belonged to the $5 million club for overall earnings, whose members include golf greats like Jack Nicklaus, Lee Trevino, George Archer, and Bob Charles. According to the 1994 Senior PGA Tour Guide, Rodriguez was tied for second place as the golfer with the most Senior PGA tournament wins, with twenty-two titles, just two behind the leader, Miller Barber. With his spectacular performances on the green in the 1990s the golf world may see a lot more of Chi Chi Rodriguez.

70

Edward James Olmos

1947–

The second of three children, Edward James Olmos was born on February 24, 1947, in Los Angeles, California. His father, Pedro Olmos, was an immigrant from Mexico; his mother, the former Eleanor Huizar, a Mexican American. His maternal great grandparents had been radical journalists in Mexico City before they fled to Los Angeles around the time of the Mexican Revolution. Edward and his siblings grew up in a small house on Cheesebrough Lane in the Boyle Heights section of East Los Angeles, an ethnically diverse community of Latinos, Native Americans, Russians, Koreans, and Chinese, struggling to make ends meet and dodge the gangs. When Edward was ten years old, the family left the barrio and moved to the suburban area of Montebello.

His parents soon split up, which caused Edward great unhappiness. As a way of coping with his pain and taking refuge from the gangs and drugs on the street, Edward single-mindedly devoted himself to baseball, often spending seven days a week playing the game. He had so much ability that before he reached high school, he won the Golden State Batting Champ title, and when he was fourteen, he played as a catcher for major league pitchers in the California winter league. By age fifteen, Edward lost interest in baseball and took up music, although he had no talent as a singer. He taught himself to play the piano, and with several other young musicians, he formed a raucous rock-and-roll group called Eddie and the Pacific Ocean, of which he was lead vocalist and keyboardist.

Although he liked school, Edward's performance was only fair due largely to a reading disability that made it difficult for him to read and comprehend. In 1965 he graduated from the high school in Montebello. Olmos enrolled at East Los Angeles College and later Cal State, Los Angeles to study sociology and criminology, and eventually received an associate's degree in sociology. In the mid-1960s Eddie and the Pacific Ocean played gigs on a regular basis at nightclubs on Hollywood's Sunset Strip. Olmos wanted to cure his fear of public speaking, which was exacerbated in his childhood by his embarrassment over his reading disability, so he took a drama class at college.

Olmos soon realized that he had a greater affinity for acting than singing and shifted his focus. He dissolved Eddie and the Pacific Ocean, bought the band's van, and started an antique-furniture delivery business while he waited for his break as an actor. In 1971, Olmos married Kaija Keel, the daughter of M-G-M film star Howard Keel. The couple had two sons but were divorced in 1991. Olmos honed his acting skills on small experimental stages and at workshops in Los Angeles, such as the Lee Strasberg Institute. During this time he was cast in bit parts in such television series such as *Kojak* and *Hawaii Five-O,* and in 1975 he made his film debut in Floyd Mutrux's *aloha, bobby and rose,* which gained him entry into the Screen Actors Guild. Olmos went on to play a small role in Robert M. Young's motion picture *Alambrista!,* a realistic story of the plight of a Mexican immigrant living illegally in the United States.

In 1978, Olmos auditioned for the part of the streetwise El Pachuco in *Zoot Suit,* Luis Valdez's musical drama based on the

Sleepy Lagoon case in which a group of young Mexican Americans were sentenced to life in Alcatraz on trumped-up murder charges in Los Angeles in 1942. In tryouts for *Zoot Suit*, Olmos showed off his dancing expertise and spoke caló, a mixture of English, Spanish, and Gypsy used on the streets of L.A. He won the part, his first big break. As El Pachuco, Olmos played both the narrator and the conscience of the protagonists in *Zoot Suit*. The original version of *Zoot Suit* opened at the Mark Taper Forum's New Theater in Los Angeles in the spring of 1978 for a limited run of ten weeks. The critics and the public embraced the show, and it later returned to the Mark Taper Forum for eight more weeks, before moving to the Aquarius Theater for a nine-month run.

Olmos's mystical portrayal of El Pachuco garnered rave reviews, earning the actor a Los Angeles Drama Critics Circle Award for Best Performance, a Theater World Award, a Drama Loque Award, and a Nosotros Golden Eagle Award. *Zoot Suit* became the first Latino play to appear on the Broadway stage when it moved to the Winter Garden in March 1979, where it ran for two months. For his New York performance, Olmos was nominated for a Tony Award for Best Performance by a Featured Actor in a Play. The actor then went on to portray El Pachuco in the 1982 screen version of *Zoot Suit*, which did poorly at the box office and among the critics. The American Theatre Wing subsequently designated El Pachuco one of the three definitive American characters, thanks in large part to Olmos's portrayal of the character.

Olmos landed a supporting role as a Native American steelworker in the 1981 detective story *Wolfen*, an exploration of humanity's lack of respect for the environment. Olmos accepted the role based on a promise from the producers that they would first consider Native American actors before casting him as a steelworker with a mystical link to the natural world. He then appeared in the 1982 futuristic detective thriller *Blade Runner*, set in the year 2019. Olmos then starred as Cortez in *The Ballad of Gregorio Cortez* (1983), the true story of a Mexican cowhand who in 1901 eluded a posse of six hundred men for two weeks in the most famous manhunt in the history of the Texas Rangers. Olmos portrays Cortez as a man of dignity and compassion who ultimately falls victim to linguistic and cultural barriers and ethnic prejudice. *The Ballad of Gregorio Cortez* aired on PBS as an

American Playhouse presentation in 1983; Olmos later orchestrated the film's distribution to libraries, schools, and boys and girls clubs. He also turned down five straight movie roles, nearly going bankrupt, so that he could travel throughout the Southwest and show *The Ballad of Gregorio Cortez* in movie theaters he rented at his own expense. In 1983, Olmos received a National Council of La Raza Rubén Salazar Award for Communication.

After appearing in several early episodes of the popular police series *Hill Street Blues*, Olmos turned down an offer for a regular role on the series because it meant signing a standard exclusive contract that would forbid him from pursuing other projects for five years. Olmos was working in a furniture store to get by when NBC offered him a nonexclusive contract for a supporting role in another television series, *Miami Vice*. *Miami Vice* went on the air in 1984, with Olmos playing the laconic Lt. Martin Castillo, the boss of two undercover vice-squad cops played by Don Johnson and Philip Michael Thomas. Olmos's portrayal of Lieutenant Castillo won him a 1985 Emmy for Best Supporting Actor in a Dramatic Series and a 1986 Golden Globe Award. Nevertheless, Edward James Olmos, like the critics, did not think highly of the show, with its inconsistent story lines and its strong production values.

In 1988, Olmos starred in the hit motion picture *Stand and Deliver* about math teacher Jaime Escalante. After *Stand and Deliver* was completed, Olmos negotiated with corporations such as IBM and Pepsico to have the film distributed to American high schools. Olmos's portrayal of Escalante won him an Academy Award nomination for Best Actor.

Edward James Olmos was next cast in a supporting role in the 1989 motion picture *Triumph of the Spirit,* the story of Salamo Arouch, a Jewish middleweight boxing champion of the Balkans in the 1930s. After the Nazis took over Greece, Arouch was taken to Auschwitz, where he literally fought for his life in two hundred boxing matches the Nazis staged. Olmos played another prisoner, Gypsy, who is forced to entertain the Nazis with vaudevillian song, dance, and stage magic. Olmos next starred in Robert M. Young's 1991 baseball comedy *Talent for the Game*. He plays Virgil Sweet, a major league baseball catcher and a scout in search of talented pitchers for the California Angels. On the set of *Talent for the Game,* Olmos met the actress Lorraine Bracco. They were married on January 28, 1994.

Olmos coproduced, directed, and played the lead in the 1992 antigang film *American Me,* which chronicles the lives of Latino gang members who build an empire of violence, drugs, and death and end up behind bars at Folsom State Prison in Sacramento. Rather than romanticizing criminals, as many films do, *American Me*, filmed partly on location at California's infamous Folsom prison, conveys the hopelessness of crime and violence. After convincing prison officials that the film would send the message to adolescents to say no to gangs, Olmos secured permission to film three deaths and a major riot at the penal institution, using all thirty-four hundred inmates as extras. After *American Me* was released, Olmos spent months attending special screenings of the film for teenagers and community leaders around the world.

In June 1993, Olmos, together with David Hayes-Bautista, a doctor, and Gregory Rodriguez, a writer, published an Op-Ed piece in a June 1993 issue of the *Los Angeles Times,* informing readers that Anglo culture was declining in L.A. at the same time that Latino culture was beginning to flourish. The Op-Ed piece stirred heated discussions among Latinos, most of whom want access to the mainstream and do not advocate the demise of Anglo culture. While he was working on *American Me,* Olmos directed and narrated a documentary entitled *Lives in Hazard,* which shows the filming of *American Me* in East Los Angeles and in Folsom Prison. *Lives in Hazard* was aired on television in 1994. In his next television project, Olmos portrayed José Menendez in the 1994 CBS two-night miniseries *Menendez: A Killing in Beverly Hills,* about the murder of José and Kitty Menendez, allegedly by their two sons, a gruesome case which captivated American audiences tuning into Court TV.

In 1992, Eastman Kodak honored Olmos with the Eastman Second Century Award for his active encouragement of young filmmakers. Olmos has dedicated much of his free time to social and charity work. He gives around 150 lectures a year at schools, juvenile detention centers, prisons, migrant-worker camps, and Native American reservations, delivering a message of self-discipline and determination. Olmos was one of the first to organize a relief fund for victims of the earthquake in Mexico City in 1985. With other celebrities, he was instrumental in the cleanup of Los Angeles after the city was plagued by riots in the wake of the acquittal of four white police officers charged with beating of the African-American motorist Rodney King.

71

Trini López

1937–

One of twelve children, only six of whom survived childhood, Trinidad López III was born on May 15, 1937, in Dallas, Texas. His parents, Trinidad López and Petra López, were orphans from Moroleón in the state of Guanajuato, Mexico. In 1927, a few months after the birth of their first child, Trinidad and Petra López crossed the Rio Grande into Texas, without documentation, in search of a better way of life. In the late 1930s, they were made legal residents of the United States when President Roosevelt issued a blanket pardon covering thousands of "wetback" Mexican families. Trinidad and Petra López settled near Dallas and struggled to survive and keep their young family afloat. The family later moved to a one-room house in the Dallas barrio known as "Little Mexico," and Petra López washed the family's clothes on rocks in a river. Trinidad López did manual labor, such as gardening, and never ceased searching for more remunerative employment. The family's economic situation later improved when he became superintendent of maintenance at Southern Methodist University.

Despite perpetual fatigue from working two or three jobs, Trinidad López always found time at home to entertain the family singing popular Mexican songs and playing the guitar. When Trini was eleven years old, his father encouraged his musical ability by buying the boy a twelve-dollar guitar and teaching him the basics. The guitar did not come easily to Trini, but by observing his father play and listening to Frank Sinatra and Ray Charles records, he mastered the instrument. Later, when he had exhausted his father's repertoire, Trinidad López handed him over to music teachers, including the late Concho Grant, of local fame. As a youth, Trini organized a combo, which at first performed for very little pay in a Mexican restaurant in the barrio. The group gained experience, and eventually Trini secured engagements at the Ci Pango in Dallas and at other leading nightspots in the Southwest, where they performed a mix of Mexican and American folk and pop material.

Trini primarily spoke Spanish until he entered Crozier Technical High School, where he finished eleventh grade and then dropped out to pursue a music career and help out his parents financially. He bought a station wagon, and with $300 in his pockets took his combo to Los Angeles in 1960. The only engagement he could arrange was a solo fill-in booking for himself at Ye Little Club. While he had no experience performing alone, he desperately needed the money and signed up for a two-week engagement that stretched to a year. From there, he went on to perform at Ciro's, P.J.'s, and other nightclubs in Los Angeles that were clamoring for the young performer.

The big names of the entertainment world frequented these clubs, but López felt that his career was going nowhere, since no one in the crowd singled him out. He was about ready to pack his bags when Don Costa, the musical director at Reprise Records, a subsidiary of Warner Brothers–Seven Arts Records, approached him with an exclusive contract. Costa had heard Trini at P.J.'s, taped his act, and later played the tape for Frank Sinatra, the principal owner of Reprise, who was taken by his style. Early in

1963, López signed the contract with Reprise Records, as well as a long-term contract with George "Bullets" Durgom, one of the most successful show-business managers.

The tape that Costa had recorded at P.J.'s metamorphosed into Trini López's first album for Reprise. *Trini López at P.J.'s* sold over a million copies, and a single cut from the album, "If I Had a Hammer," was an overnight sensation, selling over 4 million copies around the globe and becoming the number-one song in twenty-three countries. Trini achieved international fame, and in late 1963 he set out on his first foreign tour, performing before European audiences in packed theaters. After a superb performance by López at the Olympia Music Hall in Paris, Maurice Chevalier ventured backstage to offer him his congratulations, and Brigitte Bardot requested an autographed picture. Princess Grace invited López to perform at a benefit in Monte Carlo, and he obliged.

In June 1964, López appeared in his New York debut at Basin Street East, backed by his eleven-member band, which included his brother Jesse, a singer and tenor saxophone player. López received rave reviews from the tough-minded Manhattan music critics, who found his phrasing impeccable and his approach completely original. López was one of the first musicians to fuse rock rhythms with Spanish folk music. He also relied heavily on oldies, blues, and his dynamic stage personality to win over an audience. By 1964, López had amassed more than half a million dollars and was earning $5,000 a week. He diversified his income by investing in real estate, two shopping centers, "Trini" López guitars, and a music company. Over time López succeeded in increasing his assets substantially, making it possible for him to become a generous philanthropist in the coming decade. He also created a comfortable retirement for his parents, buying them a spacious house and a new car with his earnings.

In the mid-to-late 1960s, López performed at such venues as the Off Broadway Club in San Francisco, Harrah's in Reno, the Flamingo and the Riviera in Las Vegas, the Palmer House in Chicago, and the Latin Casino in Camden, New Jersey. In 1965 he portrayed himself and sang "Sinner Man" in the comedy *Marriage on the Rocks*, starring Frank Sinatra and Dean Martin. He was later cast as Pedro Jimenez, one of twelve convicts released from prison to undertake a dangerous commando mission during World War II, in the 1967 film *The Dirty Dozen*. He enjoyed acting and hoped that an Anthony Quinn–style role in a rugged western would come his way.

In 1967 the performer went on his second foreign tour to South Africa and England, where he cut an album entitled *Trini López in London*. Later that year he performed to great reviews in Australia, the Philippines, and Japan. In the mid-1960s, López was a guest performer on the television shows of Jack Benny, Ed Sullivan, Carol Burnett, Andy Wiliams, and Dean Martin, and on August 8, 1967, he hosted the CBS television network show *Spotlight*.

In the 1970s and early 1980s, López continued to sing on the international circuit and to record his songs, many of them old favorites with his fans. In 1980 he recorded "If I Had a Hammer" with a disco beat. The star also devoted himself to various philanthropies and in the 1970s and 1980s gave numerous benefit performances for charitable and educational institutions. Among his many philanthropic enterprises, he established the International Trini López Scholarship Fund at Southern Methodist University and built an auditorium for the Corsillo de Christiandadón on the grounds of Our Lady of Lourdes Church in West Dallas. Trini López is the recipient of gold records for "If I Had a Hammer" and other songs, and in 1967 he was honored for his contributions onstage and off with the Dallas Man of the Year Award.

72

Vikki Carr

1940–

Vikki Carr was born Florencia Bicenta de Casillas Martinez Cardona on July 19, 1940, in El Paso, Texas. She was the oldest of seven children of Carlos Cardona and Florence Cardona, both first-generation Mexican Americans. Her Mexican grandparents hailed from Guadalajara, Chihuahua, and Sonora. When Florencia was an infant, the family moved to Rosemead, California, an eastern suburb of Los Angeles. Florencia was introduced to music early on, for her father, a construction engineer, played the guitar at home. Even as a small child she loved singing and at the of age four made her debut with a rendition of "Silent Night" in Latin in a Christmas play. In Rosemead, Florencia attended parochial school and Rosemead High, where she took as many music classes as possible, took part in all of the school's musical productions, and on weekends sang with local bands.

Upon graduating from high school in 1958, Florencia, who took the stage name "Carlita," landed a spot as soloist with Pepe Callahan's Mexican-Irish Band during its engagement at the Chi Chi Club in Palm Springs. She traveled with the band to Las Vegas, Hawaii, and Reno, where she teamed up with the Chuck Leonard Quartette. Florencia then went on the road as a solo performer and, following a tour of Australia, signed a long-term contract with Liberty Records in 1961. A year later she was offered the spot of feature vocalist on the Ray Anthony television series. In the 1960s the singer toured the nightclub circuit, performing coast to coast and landing her first headlining engagement at the Coconut Grove in Los Angeles in 1964. Florencia enjoyed her first smash hits in Australia with the song "He's a Rebel" and in England with "It Must Be Him," the 1966 song which sold over a million copies and catapulted the entertainer to fame. In 1967 "It Must Be Him" was released in the United States on the album of the same name. The song was a success on this side of the Atlantic, and the album captured a Grammy nomination that year.

Riding the wave of fanfare with "It Must Be Him," Florencia signed a recording contract with Columbia Records and launched a string of successful tours, traveling worldwide and winning the hearts of millions of fans. Along the way she changed her name to "Vikki Carr" despite her father's displeasure. In recognition of her international fame, she was invited to sing for Queen Elizabeth II at a Royal Command Performance in London in 1967. That year, she also toured military bases in Vietnam with Danny Kaye, one of her most fulfilling moments.

By the late 1960s, Carr had established herself as one of the foremost female vocalists in the United States. She made guest appearances on most of the major television variety shows in America, including those hosted by Dean Martin, the Smothers Brothers, Carol Burnett, and Bob Hope. She also made a name for herself in musical comedies on stage. She won critical acclaim for her performance in a 1968 production of *The Unsinkable Molly*

Brown with the John Kenley Players in Ohio and in a 1969 production of *South Pacific* at the Starlight Theater in Kansas City. In 1969, Carr also won a Grammy nomination for her album *With Pen in Hand*. In 1970, she was invited to perform at a White House dinner in honor of Venezuelan president Rafael Caldera and at the inaugural of the Kennedy Music Center in Washington, D.C. In 1970, the *Los Angeles Times* voted the singer Woman of the Year; two years later, the American Guild of Variety Artists named her Entertainer of the Year. A darling of the White House, Carr sang on occasion at state dinners and at Richard Nixon's inaugural celebration in 1973. She also entertained for Presidents Ford, Reagan, and Bush during their White House years.

Although she has risen to fame in mainstream America, Carr is proud of her Mexican roots and calls herself Mexican American. Carr began to incorporate her Mexican heritage into her work when, in 1972, she performed in Mexico for the first time and recorded her first album in Spanish, *Vikki Carr, en Español*. Carr would soon achieve enormous popularity with Latino audiences. In 1972, she was voted Mexico's Visiting Entertainer of the Year, and in the course of her illustrious career, she has hosted numerous specials on Mexican television. In 1974 Vikki Carr divorced her first husband and manager Dan Moss and said that the three years after the divorce were quite productive because with no romantic distractions she could concentrate on her career. In 1978 she met her second husband, but her celebrity status and constant touring strained their relationship, and the two separated in 1991.

In 1983, Carr made such a splash at the Westport Playhouse in St. Louis for her starring performance in *I'm Getting My Act Together and Taking It on the Road* that she broke house records. In 1985 the singer was honored with a Grammy for Best Mexican American Performance and for her Spanish-language album *Simplemente mujer* (1985). In 1988 the Nosotros group bestowed upon Carr their Golden Eagle Award for outstanding performer. She also received the Career Achievement Award of the Association of Hispanic Critics, Chicago's Ovation Award, and the YWCA Silver Achievement Award.

In 1990, Carr returned to England to perform at London's Royal Festival Hall. Two years later, Carr sold out two headlining engagements at Caesars in Atlantic City and the prestigious

McCallum Hall in Palm Springs, California. In 1992 she also put together an English-language television pilot entitled *Who Will Sing the Songs?* Vikki Carr's 1992 album, *Cosas del amor,* for Sony Music, won the performer a Grammy for Best Latin Pop that year. The title song hovered at the number-one spot for ten weeks on the *Billboard* charts and was named Single of the Year by the trade journal *Radio y musica. Cosas del amor* hit number one on the *Billboard* charts and remained in the Top 20 for over six months. It also peaked at number one in Puerto Rico, Costa Rica, Colombia, Venezuela, and Ecuador, going gold in most of these countries and in the United States. In 1992, *Cosas del amor* was voted Album of the Year in Venezuela, that country's equivalent of a Grammy. In 1993, Carr released *Brindo a la vida, al bolero, a ti,* her tribute to the bolero genre. The album is filled with romantic ballads, several of which were written by illustrious composers like María Grever and Augustín Lara. By 1994 Carr had recorded fifty bestselling records; seventeen of them went gold.

Highly respected as a humanitarian as well as an artist, Carr has contributed her time and effort to many philanthropies. She has also worked ardently on behalf of Mexican Americans. In 1968, Carr initiated the first in a series of annual benefits on behalf of Holy Cross High School in the San Antonio barrio that have enabled the once poverty-stricken school to prosper. In 1971 she launched the Vikki Carr Scholarship Foundation to encourage Mexican-American youths to go on to college. By 1992 the foundation had granted over 175 scholarships to students who pursued higher education at various universities.

For her contributions to Chicano education and the welfare of all Mexican Americans, Carr received an honorary doctorate in law from the University of San Diego in 1975. In the late 1970s she was named Woman of the World by the International Orphans Fund and in 1981 Carr was honored with the Humanitarian Award from the Hispanic magazine *Nosotros.* In 1983 the League of United Latin American Citizens named the singer Woman of the Year, and the following year, Vikki Carr received the Hispanic Woman of the Year Award from the Hispanic Women's Council. In 1990, the City of Hope bestowed upon Carr its Founder of Hope Award.

73

Fernando Valenzuela

1960–

Fernando Valenzuela was born Fernando Anguamea Valenzuela on November 1, 1960, in Etchohuaquila, Mexico, the youngest of twelve children of Avelino Valenzuela and María (Hermengilda) Valenzuela. His ancestry is Taracahitian Indian, or Mayo, as inhabitants of the state of Sonora call themselves. Avelino Valenzuela grew produce in Etchohuaquila as part of a government farm program, and some of Fernando's older brothers worked on farms and ranches in the region. In his childhood, Fernando showed talent as a baseball player, and one of his older brothers assured him that he could play professionally.

After nineth grade, Fernando dropped out of school to devote himself to baseball. In 1976, he played on the Navojoa area all-star team, which competed in a state tournament in Sonora. Later, as a member of the Sonora state all-star team, he went to the national competition in La Paz in Baja California. After returning home from La Paz, Fernando accepted an offer by the Navojoa Mayos of the equivalent of $250 to play winter ball. He spent three months with the Navojoa farm club, playing little baseball but learning from the older players. The Puebla Angels then signed him and loaned him out to the Mexican Triple A Guanajuato club. As a relief pitcher with Guanajuato in 1978, Fernando had a lukewarm 6–9 record, but led the Mexican Center League in strikeouts in averaging almost one per inning. In 1979 he moved up to the Yucatán Lions, the weakest team in the country's major league. As Yucatán's pitcher, Fernando struck out 152 batters in 181 innings, 15 in a single game, and was named the league's Rookie of the Year.

Meanwhile, major league teams in the United States were taking an interest in him. Mike Brito, a scout for the Los Angeles Dodgers, spotted him, and the Dodgers then bought his contract for $120,000, of which Valenzuela saw only $20,000. The Dodgers had been seeking a Mexican player to draw the large Los Angeles Mexican-American community to the ballpark. The club assigned Valenzuela to their Lodi team in the Class A California League, where in three starts at the end of the 1979 season he had only a 1–2 record, but his earned-run average was a remarkable 1.13. The Dodgers management was so impressed with that the following winter he was sent to the Arizona Instructional League to learn the screwball under the tutelage of the Mexican-American relief pitcher Bob Castillo. The screwball is a difficult pitch to master, since it must be delivered at two speeds to fool the batter and save the arm of the pitcher. While some pitchers take years to develop the screwball, Valenzuela perfected it within a year. His pitch became known as "Fernando's fadeaway" and was considered the best since Carl Hubbell's.

In 1980, Valenzuela advanced to San Antonio in the Class AA Texas League, where at one stretch he pitched thirty-five scoreless innings, bringing his record to 13–9 and his earned-run average to 3.10. Late in the season the Dodgers brought him up in the middle of a close race against Houston for the National League West title. Valenzuela won two critical games in relief and captured a third, surrendering no runs in ten appearances on the mound. The pitcher became an overnight sensation in the Mexican-American community around Dodger Stadium, and soon he would captivate the nation.

Valenzuela was slated to be a relief pitcher in the 1981 season, but on opening day none of the Dodgers starters were ready, so manager Tommy Lasorda chose him to pitch. He was the first rookie in Dodger history to start on opening day. An unknown, Valenzuela received no cheers as he took the mound, but as he pitched his way to a five-hit 2–0 shutout against the defending National League West champion Astros, the crowd was on its feet shouting "Fernando!" Five days later he defeated San Francisco, 7–1, and then he accumulated five more shutouts in consecutive victories. "Fernandomania" struck the nation, and each time Valenzuela pitched, he drew nine thousand more fans than usual to ballparks. At home games, the star pitcher received standing ovations, and the scoreboard flashed *OLÉ* each time he took the mound. Valenzuela's parents were flown up from Mexico as guests of the Dodgers to see their son pitch in sold-out Dodger Stadium.

In 1981, Valenzuela became one of a select few rookie pitchers to be named a starter on the All-Star team. With his stunning screwball, excellent curveball, and good slider and fastball, the pitcher ended the 1981 season with a 13–7 record and a 2.48 earned-run average and led the National League with 192 strikeouts. He then helped the Dodgers capture the National League West title. In the National League championship series against Montreal, he lost the second game but came back in the fifth to beat the Expos, 2–1, and clinch the pennant. In the 1981 World Series between the Dodgers and the New York Yankees, the Yankees led the series, 2–0. In Game Three, Valenzuela took the pitcher's mound and threw 145 pitches, the most he had ever thrown, leading the Dodgers to a stunning victory. Los Angeles then won three consecutive games to capture their first world championship since 1965.

In the closest vote in the history of the Cy Young Award, the Baseball Writers Association of America selected Fernando Valenzuela the National League Pitcher of the Year on November 11, 1981. He was the first rookie to win pitching's highest honor and the first Latino ever to be named sole recipient of the award. On December 2, 1981, Valenzuela was named the National League Rookie of the Year. For his performance that year he was also awarded the Silver Slugger as the league's best hitting pitcher and the *Sporting News* National League Pitcher of the Year Award. Valenzuela became a star not only in America but also in Mexico, where his endorsement of Miguel de la Madrid for the presidency of Mexico made front-page headlines. On December 28, 1981, Valenzuela married Linda Margarita Burgos, a schoolteacher he had met when he was pitching for the Yucatán Lions in Mexico, and the wedding was broadcast over Mexican radio.

Valenzuela began the 1982 season with the Dodgers as a holdout. In his spectacular rookie year, the Dodgers had paid the pitcher only $29,000, and Valenzuela demanded a new contract with a salary increase to $850,000. The club rejected his demand, so the pitcher refused to report to spring training in February. On March 1, the Dodgers unilaterally renewed Valenzuela's contract, raising his salary to $350,000, and the pitcher became the highest-paid sophomore in baseball history. In the 1982 season Los Angeles came in second in the National League West with an 88–74 record, and Valenzuela went 19–13 with a 2.87 earned-run average, 4 shutouts, and 199 strikeouts, finishing third in the Cy Young voting. During the winter of 1982 he won a $1 million contract in arbitration, the highest arbitration award at that time.

In 1983 the Dodgers won the National League West and faced the Philadelphia Phillies in the playoffs. Valenzuela pitched the second game and won, 4–1, striking out five batters in eight innings, but the Dodgers ultimately lost the series. In the 1984 season, Valenzuela struck out 240 batters, the most by a Dodger since 1969, but ended the year 12–17 due to a lack of support from Dodgers batters, who scored one run or less in thirteen of Valenzuela's last twenty-seven starts. Valenzuela was again named to the All-Star team and struck out baseball greats Dave Winfield, Reggie Jackson, and George Brett in one inning. The Dodger batters gave him little support in the 1985 season as well, but Valenzuela set a major league record with 41$\frac{1}{3}$ scoreless innings at the start of the season and finished with a 17–10 record and five shutouts. The Dodgers won the National League West, and Valenzuela was the starter in the League Championship series against the St. Louis Cardinals. He pitched 6⅓ innings for a 4–1 victory in Game One, but St. Louis captured the series and the pennant in Game Six.

In March 1986 the Dodgers issued Valenzuela a three-year $5.5 million contract, making him the highest-paid Latino player at the time. On September 22, 1986, Valenzuela defeated Houston, 9–2, with a two-hitter to become the first Mexican pitcher in major league history to win twenty games in a season. Valenzuela finished second in the Cy Young Award balloting, but he earned a Golden Glove for his excellence in fielding. In April 1987, Valenzuela gained his 100th win, but the season was not one of his best. His screwball was flat, and his fastball had slowed down, and while he struck out 190 batters, his earned-run average rose to a career-high 3.98. In the 1988 season Valenzuela experienced difficulty warming up due to shoulder pain. He finished the season 5–8 with a 4.24 earned-run average, and the Dodgers did not send him to the mound during the National League playoffs against the New York Mets. He threw out the ceremonial first pitch before the first game and then stayed in the dugout as his team defeated first the Mets, and then Oakland, for the world championship.

After struggling early in 1989, Fernando Valenzuela ended the season with a 10–13 record. The Dodgers signed him to a one-year, $2 million contract for 1990 because the club benefited from Valenzuela's leadership and community involvement. Among his many activities off the baseball diamond, he served as a spokesperson for a program benefiting Latinos in Los Angeles–area schools. In July 1990, Valenzuela became the third Latino to pitch a no-hitter, and he finished the season with a 13–13 record. Valenzuela ended a decade of play with the Los Angeles Dodgers in 1991 with a 141–116 career record. He then pitched for a season in the Mexican League, where he regained strength in his left shoulder.

In 1993, Valenzuela stunned major-league baseball with his astonishing comeback when the Baltimore Orioles offered him a contract for $200,000 plus bonuses. On May 18, 1993, he pitched a two-hitter for the Orioles to capture his first victory since 1990. Valenzuela ended the season with an 8–10 record and a 4.94 earned-run average, but the Orioles opted to let him go, and the pitcher returned to Mexico to play for the Jalisco Charos. With three-fifths of their pitching rotation on the disabled list, the Philadelphia Phillies signed Valenzuela to a contract in June 1994 for the remainder of the season. When Valenzuela took the mound in a sold-out Dodger Stadium on July 3, 1994, this time as a friendly rival, he received a standing ovation from Dodgers fans who remembered the glorious days when "Fernandomania" shook Los Angeles.

74

Cherríe Moraga

1952–

Cherríe Moraga was born on September 25, 1952, in Whittier, California, to Elvira Moraga, a Mexican American, and Joseph Lawrence, an Anglo. When she was nine years old, her family moved near San Gabriel, California, to be close to her mother's relatives. As a child, Cherríe constantly traversed cultural boundaries, learning Mexican traditions from her family and American ways at school and speaking both Spanish and English. Women in her extended family often spent their free time weaving stories, and Cherríe was profoundly influenced by this rich oral tradition. Her eye for detail and ability to blend English and Spanish in her later writing are rooted in the storytelling of her childhood. The gender and racial differences Cherríe witnessed within her own family, which meant that members who were male or had lighter skin enjoyed certain privileges, would later inspire her discussions of class, gender, and sexual orientation.

Cherríe was educated in California public schools and later attended a small private college in Hollywood. She was awarded a B.A. in English in 1974, one of the first in her family to earn a degree. While in college she developed a love for art, although she had always envisioned a career in education. She ignored her creative instincts and pursued pedagogy, taking a teaching job as an instructor of English at a private Los Angeles high school. Moraga also signed up for a writing class through the Los Angeles Women's Building, where for the first time she became excited about her creative work. Around this time, she came out as a lesbian and wrote some of her first works, lesbian love poems. Thus, explorations of sexuality and gender questions featured heavily in Moraga's writing from the very beginning.

Moraga's commitment to her writing conflicted with her teaching schedule, and after two years she temporarily abandoned teaching. In 1977 she moved to San Francisco to escape the negative influences of her family and experience a liberal and artistic atmosphere, where she could feel less constrained by her lesbianism. She decided that if in a year's time she did not find success as a writer, she would return to the classroom. In between odd jobs Cherríe Moraga explored lesbian literature, reading such tomes as Radclyffe Hall's classic 1928 novel *The Well of Loneliness* and the works of Djuna Barnes. She developed a supportive network of aspiring artists, feminists, and lesbians who gathered to discuss their work in San Francisco cafes.

By the year's end Cherríe Moraga was reciting her poetry to an audience. With Los Angeles poet Eloise Klein Healy, she read to an enthusiastic crowd in a coffeehouse. Around this time, she began to confront the discrimination she encountered as a lesbian, which acted as a springboard to her understanding of the race and class oppression suffered by Chicanas. Through her experiences of homophobia, Moraga realized the pain of discrimination her own mother had felt because of her darker skin. In analyzing forms of oppression, Moraga was drawn to the work of

Judy Grahn, a poet who addresses issues concerning lesbians of color. She met with Grahn, and their conversation politicized Moraga and inspired her to write from the vantage point of being both a lesbian and a woman of color.

As she began her thesis for a master's degree in feminist writing at San Francisco State University, Moraga agreed to collaborate with Gloria Anzaldúa in compiling an anthology of poems, essays, letters, and conversations by women of color, dealing with issues of feminism, lesbianism, and race. Their collaboration resulted in *This Bridge Called My Back: Writings by Radical Women of Color,* which was published in 1981 and reviewed in virtually every feminist publication in the United States. The publication of *This Bridge Called My Back* coincided with increased activism on the part of women of color, both straight and lesbian, in the early 1980s. The anthology echoed and elaborated on the concerns of these women in a feminist movement catering primarily to white women. At the same time, the publication of the anthology signaled the emergence of ties between Chicanas, other Latinas, and African-American, Native American, and Asian-American women and introduced the term "woman of color" into the political lingo. Since its publication, *This Bridge Called My Back* has been on countless required reading lists in women's studies and multicultural courses in colleges and universities across the nation.

This Bridge Called My Back was republished in 1983 and in 1988 in a revised, bilingual edition. In 1986 Moraga and Anzaldúa received the Before Columbus Foundation American Book Award. *This Bridge Called My Back* also earned its author a master's degree in 1980 and a position of prominence in feminist and lesbian scholarship. In terms of the anthology's content Moraga contributed a preface, two poems, and an essay. Her essay, entitled "La güera" ("The Fair-Skinned Girl"), explores the conflicts the writer faces as a lesbian and a minority, her guilt for being unaware of the prejudice her own mother faced due to her darker skin, and her rage that such oppression exists in a democratic society. Through the act of writing Moraga endeavors to break the silence on these issues: "I think: what is my responsibility to my roots—both white and brown, Spanish-speaking and English? I am a woman with a foot in both worlds; and I refuse the split. I feel the necessity for dialogue."

In search of a publisher for *This Bridge Called My Back,*

Moraga went to Boston and New York in 1981. That year, she cofounded the Kitchen Table/Women of Color Press, devoted to publishing the works of women of color. With Alma Gomez and Mariana Romo-Carmona, Cherríe Moraga edited *Cuentos: Stories by Latinas* (1983), one of the press's first books and the first collection of writings by feminist Latinas. *Cuentos* is as groundbreaking in its content as *This Bridge Called My Back*. The collection incorporates works in Spanish and English as well as pieces that employ both languages, thereby lending validation to the Latina experience. *Cuentos* also breaks the silence about gender and sexuality among Latinas, particularly concerning lesbianism. Moraga included her own works in this anthology, just as she did in *This Bridge Called My Back,* such as the two short stories, "Sin luz" and "Pesadilla," which confront issues of sexual orientation, racism, and homophobia.

In her next project Moraga compiled poems and essays she had written since 1976 in one volume. *Loving in the War Years: Lo que nunca pasó por sus labios* was published in 1983 as the first collection by a self-proclaimed Chicana lesbian. "A Long Line of Vendidas," a major essay belonging to the collection, explores the writer's efforts to reconcile the contradictions of her identity as both a Chicana and a lesbian. In the essay she addresses the relationship between Chicana sexuality and culture, exploring the ways women are both crippled and empowered by cultural experience. One of the overriding messages of the essays and poems in *Loving in the War Years* is that women's interests must be addressed first.

After the publication of *Loving in the War Years,* Moraga set to work on her verse play, *Giving Up the Ghost: Teatro in Two Acts* (1986). The play is a dramatic representation of the ideas explored in the essay "A Long Line of Vendidas," particularly the ways in which women are harmed by gender expectations. Set in an East Los Angeles barrio, the play chronicles the short-lived relationship of the main characters, Amalia and Marisa, after Marisa has suffered rape and Amalia the death of a male lover. Through their interaction, Amalia and Marisa come to grips with the oppressive forces that have distorted their self-images.

In 1986, Moraga returned to teaching, this time as a writing instructor in the Chicano Studies Department at the University of California at Berkeley. In 1991 she published *The Shadow of a Man,* a play exploring the effects of Catholicism on the development of a young Chicana girl's identity. The year 1992 saw the publication of a third play, *Heroes and Saints*, which was produced by Brava! For Women in the Arts in San Francisco and premiered in March 1994. *Heroes and Saints*, a mixture of realism, surrealism, and agitprop, addresses the afflictions of a Latino family of farm-workers in a San Joaquin Valley town who are poisoned by pesticides sprayed by growers. In 1993, Moraga published *The Last Generation: Prose and Poetry*, in which she discusses such issues as the AIDS epidemic and Chicano gays, the struggles of Chicana lesbians, and the disintegration of the family. In the stimulating intellectual atmosphere of San Francisco, Cherríe Moraga continues to teach and write and to speak out against the oppression that women of color and lesbians face in American society.

75

Tom Flores

1937–

The youngest of two boys, Tom Flores was born Thomas Raymond Flores on March 21, 1937, in Fresno, California. His parents, Thomas Flores, a Mexican immigrant who fled to the United States as a twelve-year-old to escape the Mexican Revolution, and Nellie Flores, were farmworkers. Tom grew up in Sanger, California, where he attended school and worked in the fields of the San Joaquin Valley alongside his parents and older brother. In 1954, Tom graduated from Sanger High School, where he was a sports star. He went on to Fresno City College, where he made Honorable Mention Junior College All-American in football. After receiving his A.A. degree, Flores enrolled at the College (now University) of the Pacific in Stockton, California, and graduated in 1958 with a B.A. degree in education. He amassed a superb college football record that included playing on several all-American teams.

An old shoulder injury frustrated Flores's attempts to turn pro in 1958 and 1959. He failed to make the grade in the Canadian Football League and was released by the Calgary Stampeders in 1958. Then he joined the Washington Redskins of the National Football League (NFL) in 1959, but again met with defeat, so he accepted a temporary coaching job at Fresno High School. In 1960 he signed as a free agent with the Oakland Raiders of the newly formed American Football League (AFL) as the team's first quarterback. In his rookie year with the Raiders, Flores led the AFL in passing efficiency, with a percentage of 54, attempting 252 passes with 136 completions for 1,738 yards. Flores missed the 1962 season due to illness, and then, on December 22, 1963, the quarterback gave his greatest performance in a game when he threw six touchdown passes. Following the 1966 season, Flores was named quarterback for the AFL All-Star Game. In his six years in the pocket for the Raiders, Flores completed 810 passes for 11,635 yards and 92 touchdowns.

In 1967, Flores was traded, with offensive end Art Powell, to the Buffalo Bills (AFL) for quarterback Daryle Lamonica, end Glenn Bass, and two draft choices. After two seasons with the Bills, Flores went to the Kansas City Chiefs (AFL) in 1969 and stayed with them until the end of the 1970 season, when he retired as a player. Flores was a reserve quarterback with the Chiefs when they won Super Bowl IV, 23–7, after a superb 1969 regular season. When he finished his quarterback career, Flores ranked second in fewest interceptions thrown, a lifetime 192 in 1,715 attempts. He had almost decided to start a business career in plastics when he received an invitation in 1972 from head coach John Madden of the Oakland Raiders to become the team's receivers coach. Flores's coaching career had begun a decade earlier when he coached the University of the Pacific's freshman squad. Then, in 1971, he was an assistant coach with the Buffalo Bills.

During Flores's seven years as assistant coach with the Oakland Raiders of the AFC Western Division, the team enjoyed great success, reaching the playoffs six times and defeating the Minnesota Vikings in Super Bowl XI. In 1979, Flores replaced John Madden as head coach, and in his debut season he posted a 9–7 mark. When the Raiders started the 1980 season with three losses in five games, discontentment spread from the locker room to the offices of management. The Raiders' prospects for a winning season looked even more grim when Dan Pastorini, the team's starting quarterback, broke his leg in the team's third loss, against Kansas City. Flores handed the football to veteran quarterback Jim Plunkett, who had sat out most of the last two seasons with the Raiders. When he was an assistant coach, Flores had urged the Raiders to sign Plunkett even though all of football was sure that the quarterback had lost his nerve, if not his arm.

With Jim Plunkett taking charge in the pocket, the Raiders rallied for an 11–5 record that season and a slot in the playoffs as a wild-card team. In the playoffs Flores piloted the Raiders to a 27–7 win against the Houston Oilers, a 14–12 defeat of the Cleveland Browns, and a 34–27 victory over the San Diego Chargers in the AFC championship game. Flores's Raiders went into Super Bowl XV as the underdogs against the Philadelphia Eagles. The Raiders played a flawless game and prevailed 27–10 to give Tom Flores a championship title in only his second year as head coach. With that spectacular victory the Los Angeles Raiders became the only wild-card team to win a Super Bowl.

The Raiders' move from Oakland to Los Angeles in 1981 represented a minor setback for Flores, who experienced his first losing season, 7–9, that year. In 1982, Flores guided the Raiders to an 8–1 mark and a division title in a season brought to a premature end by a strike. He helped the Raiders to a 27–10 victory over the Cleveland Browns before the team went down in defeat to the New York Jets in the playoffs that year. For his efforts Flores was named Coach of the Year in 1982. In 1983 the Raiders enjoyed a 12–4 regular-season record and a first-place finish in the AFC Western Division and then trounced the Pittsburgh Steelers, 38–10, and the Seattle Seahawks, 30–14, in the playoffs. In Super Bowl XVIII, Flores and the Raiders scored the biggest win ever in the history of the championship game, 38–9, over the Washington Redskins. In May 1984 the Los Angeles Board of Supervisors awarded Flores a plaque for his contributions to the city's image, especially the Super Bowl XVIII victory. In the 1984 season the Raiders finished with a respectable 11–5 regular-season record but lost their only game in the postseason. In the 1985 season, Coach Flores guided the Raiders to a 12–4 record and a first-place finish in the AFC Western Division.

Two dismal years followed for Flores and the Raiders. In 1986 the team finished with an 8–8 mark and missed the playoffs for the first time since 1981. The year 1987 saw an even worse performance from the Raiders, when they completed the strike-torn season with a 5–10 mark and again missed the playoffs. During the 1987 season rumors abounded that Flores's job was in jeopardy. When he retired from the Raiders at the end of the season, some saw it as confirmation of the rumors. The news that their head coach was leaving came as a shock to the players, with whom Flores had been very popular. Flores acknowledged at the time that it had been somewhat difficult to coach in the shadow of Raiders' owner Al Davis. He also told the *Los Angeles Times* two years later that 1987 had been the time to move on: "I knew the team needed rebuilding and I wasn't sure I had the energy to go through it. Usually, you end a season physically and emotionally exhausted, but you recharge during the off-season. I didn't recharge."

After nine full seasons with the Raiders, Flores record stood at 83–53 in the regular season and 8–3 in the playoffs and in Super Bowl competition. He retired from coaching not knowing where his next challenges would lie, although he had some business ventures in mind. Two years after his retirement, he received an offer to become president and general manager of the Seattle Seahawks, in the AFC Western Division, a franchise purchased by a longtime friend from his San Francisco days. Flores could not resist the lure of football and readily accepted the offer. The post of president and general manager provided little challenge, and Flores felt like a spectator rather than a participant. At the end of the 1991 season Seattle head coach Chuck Knox resigned, and Tom Flores began to look for a replacement. He soon realized that he himself was anxious to coach again, and so, in January 1992, Flores was named head coach of the Seattle Seahawks, with a five-year commitment to coaching. He gave up a quiet life on golf courses for the sixteen-hour days and Sunday stress of professional football.

Flores's first season with the Seattle Seahawks was fraught with the most injuries he had ever seen in his coaching career. In 1992, his first season as head coach in Seattle, the Seahawks went 2–14, the worst team in the league, with a poor offense but a very good defense. In 1993 the Seahawks completed the season with a 6–10 mark and a last-place finish in the AFC West, but they showed improvement. With Tom Flores calling the shots from the sidelines, it probably will not be long before the Seattle Seahawks are transformed into a winning football team.

76

María Grever

1885–1951

María Grever was born María de la Portilla to a Spanish father and a Mexican mother on September 14, 1885, in Mexico City. Soon after her birth, the Grever family went to Spain, where María spent much of her childhood. In those years, they often traveled about Europe. As a child she studied piano, violin, and voice, and one account of her life asserts that she learned to read music as an adult. Historians have noted that she had the gift of perfect pitch and wrote most of her songs in one key. At some point in the family's European sojourn, María studied in Paris under the French composer Claude Debussy, an exponent of musical impressionism. When María was twelve, the family returned to Mexico.

In her youth, María wrote numerous songs, and she was such a talented musician that she often created both the melodies and the lyrics of her pieces. Many of her songs evoked the folk rhythms and styles of Latin American music, and her memorable lyrics express warm and romantic sentiments. The dramatic and emotional effects of her songs appealed to American audiences of the era, and when at age eighteen Grever published her first song, "A una ola," it sold 3 million copies. She derived great enjoyment from performing before live audiences, and in 1919, after the success of "A una ola," she gave one of her earliest recitals of Spanish, French, and Italian music at the Princess Theater in New York and garnered acclaim from critics and audiences alike. In 1921, she published another hit song entitled "Besame," and 1926 saw the publication of her Spanish tango "Jurame," which garnered rave reviews from the public. "Jurame" is still sung and hummed by countless musicians and music lovers all over the world.

In the 1920s, Grever performed her music in New York City's concert halls. In addition to giving performances comprised solely of her songs, she enjoyed teaming up in concert with other musicians and combining theater, music, dance, and song. In 1927 she organized an extraordinary concert at the Little Theatre in New York, which featured opening numbers by a jazz orchestra, followed by elaborate musical dramas from Argentine cabaret. The evening ended with a short play, *The Gypsy*.

In 1934 Grever conquered the musical world with her biggest hit of all, "What a Difference a Day Makes" ("Cuando vuelva a tu lado"). It was not only the most popular of Grever's tunes during the composer's lifetime; it has lived on in perpetuity in the repertoires of numerous music stars. In the late 1930s, Grever suffered a bad eye infection which could have left her blind. Nevertheless, she managed in 1938 to write the humorous tune entitled "Ti-Pi-Tin." The song marked a departure from the style she had established for herself, and her publisher rejected it, fearing a negative response from the listening public. Bandleader Horace Heidt and his orchestra liked the song, and when they played it over the air, it became a sensation.

Grever emerged from her experience of medical complications with her eyes with a feeling of compassion for those whose eyesight was compromised, and she began to devote herself to charitable causes for the blind. In 1942 she hosted a benefit for the Spanish-American Association for the Blind, featuring musical performances by students at the New York Institute for the Education of the Blind. The funds raised at the event went toward benefiting the blind in Spanish-speaking countries.

Scholars have estimated that Grever's total musical output encompasses as many as five hundred songs. On numerous occasions the composer collaborated with American lyricists, who translated her songs from Spanish into English in order to reach mainstream audiences in the United States. Grever worked with several prominent songwriters of the era, including Stanley Adams, Irving Caesar, and Raymond Leveen. In her day, Grever's songs, such as "Lamento Gitano," "Lero, Lero from Brazil," "Magic Is the Moonlight," "My First, My Last, My Only," "Rosebud," "Thanks for the Kiss," "My Margarita," "Andalucía," "Cancionera," "Mujer Cubana," "Muchachita mia," and many more, filled the airwaves. Her melodies became so widely known because leading performers of the era included them in their repertoires, among them Enrico Caruso, Lawrence Tibbett, Tito Schipa, Nino Martini, and Jessica Dragonette. Many musicians not only performed her songs live but also included them on their albums. The 1956 album *The Bobby Hackett Horn* included an adaptation of "What a Difference a Day Makes," and Benny Goodman and his orchestra performed "Cuando vuelva a tu lado" for the 1959 Columbia Classic album *Happy Session.*

In addition to writing countless songs, Grever also composed film scores and lyrics for Broadway shows. Her song "Magic Is the Moonlight" was featured in the 1944 film *Bathing Beauty.* For the stage the composer wrote the music for such productions as the 1941 musical *Viva O'Brien.* Some of her songs in *Viva O'Brien* were "El matador terrífico," "Mood of the Moment," "Broken Hearted Romeo," and "Wrap Me in Your Serape." While Grever's legacy is her songs, she also contributed to the development of younger musicians when she worked for a time as a voice teacher.

Grever succumbed to a protracted illness on December 15, 1951. At the time she was living at the Wellington Hotel on Seventh Avenue in Manhattan. In her honor, the Union of Women of the Americas (UWA) staged a musical featuring

Grever's songs at the Biltmore Hotel. The UWA had honored her with the title "Woman of the Americas" sometime in the past.

In 1956, RCA released a retrospective of Grever's works entitled *Songs of María Grever*. The album features twelve of Grever's songs performed by Argentine singer Libertad Lamarque, accompanied by the orchestras of Chuck Zarzosa and Mario Ruíz Armengol. Along with the songs that made her famous, the album includes "Volveré," "Eso es mentira," and "Así."

77

Mary Joe Fernández

1971–

Born in 1971 in the Dominican Republic, Mary Joe is the daughter of José Fernández and Sylvia Pino Fernández. Mary Joe's parents met in Havana when José Fernández was visiting relatives living there. When Fidel Castro and his revolutionaries rolled into Havana, her parents fled first to the Dominican Republic, where José Fernández worked for an American investment company. When Mary Joe was six months old, the family moved to Miami. At age three, Mary Joe tagged along with her older sister Sylvia and her father to the tennis courts. Wishing to involve Mary Joe in the sport, José Fernández whittled down the grip of a racket to fit her small hand. As he watched Mary Joe's tennis skills rapidly develop, José suspected that his daughter had talent, so he consulted legendary U.S. champion Gardnar Mulloy. Upon seeing Mary Joe play, Mulloy advised José Fernández to enter his daughter in as many tournaments as possible, and so began a stellar career in tennis.

At age ten, Mary Joe Fernández won the U.S. Tennis Association Nationals for players twelve and under, her first victory. After winning Mary Joe was accused of being older than she claimed. Jealous parents of her opponents made the ludicrous suggestion that Mary Joe's parents had falsified her birth certificate before the family came to America.

Commencing at age eleven, Mary Joe won four consecutive singles age-group titles at the Orange Bowl, widely regarded as the world's premier junior event the first girl to perform such a feat. In 1984, Mary Joe captured the U.S. Tennis Association Championship for sixteen-and-under players and the U.S. Clay Court Championship for her age group.

Mary Joe was such a shining star on the junior circuit that by age fourteen she decided to become a pro. Agents, fellow players, and fans pressured her to drop out of high school and commit herself full-time to tennis, the course traditionally taken by young tennis talents. After much deliberation, Mary Joe announced that she would attend the Carrollton School of the Sacred Heart in Miami and play tennis part-time. Throughout her high school years, she wove tennis matches into her class schedule, managing four Grand Slam tournaments in three and one half years. Her classmates at the Carrollton School knew Mary Joe as the student who for three years in a row failed to win the President's Council on Physical Fitness Award because she could not perform the arm-hang portion of the test.

But Mary Joe excelled on the court. She played her first Wimbledon match at fourteen, losing to her idol, Chris Evert Lloyd, in straight sets. At the tender age of fourteen years and eight days, she became the youngest player to win a U.S. Open match when she defeated Sara Gomer in the first round of the 1985 U.S. Open. At the French Open in 1986, Mary Joe beat two seeds, number fourteen, Andrea Temesvari, and number four, Claudia Kohde-Kilsch, to reach the quarterfinals, where, despite a valiant effort, she was defeated by Helena Sukova, 6–2, 6–4.

In 1988, Mary Joe advanced to the semifinals of the Lipton International Players Championships, beating another young talent, Gabriela Sabatini, before losing in the finals to Chris Evert. That year, Fernández was invited to represent the Dominican Republic at the Olympics, but she declined the offer, saying she would rather represent the United States in tennis someday. Despite juggling schoolwork and tennis, Fernández became a straight-A student while earning substantial amounts in prize money and endorsements before graduating from high school. In the September 1991 issue of *Cosmopolitan,* she discussed the reasoning behind her decision to split her time between tennis and school: "I might have lost touch with reality. If you go to beautiful places all the time, as you do on the tennis tour, you think that's how it is everywhere."

Much to her disappointment, Mary Joe had to miss commencement ceremonies at Carrollton to play in the 1989 French Open. She made it to the semifinals, where she was defeated by the tournament's eventual champion, Arantxa Sanchez Vicario. Having achieved her academic goals, she concentrated fully on tennis. In 1990, her first full season as a pro, she won forty of fifty singles matches, two tournaments, and topped the $1 million mark in career earnings. In January 1990 she reached a Grand Slam singles final for the first time at the Australian Open, losing to Steffi Graf in a closely contested match. By February 1990, Fernández had made it into the top ten, without winning a pro title. In June 1990 the player reached the quarterfinals of the French Open. She captured her first professional tournament championship at the Tokyo Indoors in September 1990. She came from behind to beat Manuela Maleeva-Fragniere in a tense three-hour semifinals match and then battled cramps the next day to defeat Amy Frazier, 3–6, 6–2, 6–3, for the title.

Fernández's performance in 1990 was fraught with injuries linked to poor conditioning, including tendinitis in the right shoulder, an ankle sprain, and a minor cartilage tear in the left knee. Time spent away from the court and in the classroom had taken a physical toll. Moreover, she had never engaged in any other form of exercise besides tennis. With help from her coach, Tim Gullikson, Fernández began a conditioning regimen to build up her endurance, polished her topspin, and learned to rush the net for winning volleys and overheads. Her efforts paid off in 1991 when her ranking soared to fourth and she became the thirty-third woman in tennis to earn over $1 million in a year. Highlights of 1991 included a 6–3, 6–2 victory in a quarterfinals match against Katerina Maleeva at the Australian Open. Fernández advanced to the semifinals, where she faced Monica Seles and hung on courageously but ultimately lost the match, 6–3, 0–6, 9–7.

In 1992, Fernández worked with her coach, Harold Solomon, a French Open finalist in 1976, to introduce agressiveness into her tennis game. That year, she was a contender in women's singles at the U.S. Open, but victory eluded her. Her training paid off when she teamed up with doubles partner Gigi Fernández (no relation) to win a gold medal in the women's doubles at the Olympics Games in Barcelona. In the final, the Fernández duo defeated the Spaniards Arantxa Sanchez Vicario and Conchita Martínez, 7–5, 2–6, 6–2, before their home crowd. Mary Joe also captured the bronze medal in women's singles on the clay of Barcelona, a surface much slower than the hard courts she prefers.

Fernández again exhibited her new stamina and aggressive style in a marvelous quarterfinals singles match in the 1993 French Open on clay. She faced Gabriela Sabatini in a grueling marathon that lasted three hours and thirty-five minutes, the longest women's Grand Slam match in the Open era. Early on in the match Mary Joe was down 1–6, 1–5, but she made an extraordinary comeback to win 1–6, 7–6, 10–8. Mary Joe carried her momentum into the semifinals, where she defeated the number two seed, Arantxa Sanchez Vicario. In the finals of the French Open, Mary Joe played her best against Steffi Graf, but Graf emerged the winner that day when she took the match, 4–6, 6–2, 6–4, in a comeback effort.

Mary Joe Fernández has consistently reached the semifinals in major events, along with Steffi Graff, Gabriela Sabatini, and Arantxa Sanchez Vicario. With her textbook-perfect ground strokes, superb timing and concentration, and magnificent footwork and balance, Mary Joe Fernández has helped to bring excitement to women's tennis, making it not only the most visible women's sport around the globe, but more popular than men's tennis according to many fans.

78

Keith Hernández

1953–

The youngest of two boys, Keith Hernández was born on October 20, 1953, in San Francisco, California, to John Hernández, whose parents had emigrated from Spain, and Jackie Hernández. John Hernández played first base in the minor leagues, until he took a pitch to the head and was forced to retire from baseball. He then joined the fire department. Keith and his brother Gary grew up in the family's home in Pacifica, south of San Francisco, and then in nearby Millbrae. John Hernández was passionate about baseball; he taught his boys all the fine points of the game and organized pickup games for the kids in the neighborhood.

By the time he was eight years old, Keith had all the

fundamentals of baseball down pat. He soon mastered the art of
fielding, which his father taught him by throwing tennis balls in
the dirt, rather than hard balls, so that Keith would not injure his
arms. At the plate, Keith quickly developed into a consistent line-
drive batter, avoided bad pitches, and hit the ball to all fields.
Keith was an all-around athlete and was the first student at
Capuchino High School in Millbrae to win all-league honors in
three sports. He was a guard on the school's basketball team and
played quarterback on the football team and first base on the
baseball team. In his senior year, Keith quit baseball after a
falling out with his coach, and scouts stayed away from the
talented youth. He considered enrolling in the U.S. Naval Academy, the U. S. Air Force Academy, or the University of California
at Berkeley, the three schools that offered him a full scholarship,
when in the fortieth round of the professional baseball draft he
was picked up by the St. Louis Cardinals. His father demanded a
$50,000 salary, and the Cardinals held off signing Keith Her-
nández until the end of the summer, during which the young
player batted .500 in the semipro Joe DiMaggio League.

The St. Louis Cardinals signed Hernández as a pitcher, but
he was moved to first base soon after he joined the Class A St.
Petersburg farm club. Held back by injuries, he batted only .256
with St. Petersburg and .241 with Triple A Tulsa in 1972 and .260
with Arkansas (AA) in 1973. Before the start of the 1973 season,
Hernández ranked as the best of the Cardinal hitters, having
compiled a .300 batting average in the Florida Instructional
League. Hernández ended the 1973 season with Tulsa and hit
.333 in 31 games, helping the club capture the league championship. After leading the American Association with a .351 average
by mid-1974, St. Louis called him up to the major leagues toward
the end of the season, and Hernández hit .294 in 14 games. At the
beginning of the 1975 season he was St. Louis's starting first
baseman, but his shyness hampered his play, and by June his
batting average had fallen to a mediocre .250. Hernández was
sent back to Tulsa, where he batted .350 for the rest of the season.
In 1976, Hernández again made the Cardinals' starting lineup
and again suffered a slow start. In May the young player
demanded that St. Louis manager Red Schoendienst give him
more time to prove his ability, and he was returned to the lineup
after the All-Star game.

By 1977, Hernández had proven himself in the major

leagues, batting .291, hitting 15 home runs, driving in 91 runs, and winning the first of eleven consecutive Golden Glove Awards for fielding. In the first half of the 1978 season Hernández hit well, but he fell in a slump mid-season which lowered his batting average to .255. In the early months of the 1979 season, Hernández was still in a slump, and his father visited St. Louis to reassure his son about his swing and stance. With his family and manager Ken Moyer behind him, Hernández went on a hitting streak, batting .340 in May, .369 in June, and .333 in July. In August he was named the recipient of the Player of the Month Award, having compiled a .385 average and driven in 28 runs. In the 1979 season Hernández led the major leagues with a spectacular .344 batting average, and the National League with 116 runs and 48 doubles. He was among the league leaders in RBIs with 105 (a career high), hits with 210, and slugging percentage with .513. That season, Hernández was selected for his first All-Star game and was named 1979's Most Valuable Player. Hernández then signed a five-year $3.8 million contract with the Cardinals, making him the team's highest-paid player.

Hernández became a media hero and it hurt his game. In 1980 he lost his spark on the field, and at the end of the season he separated from his wife, Sue Broeker, whom he had married in January 1978. Hernández found solace in cocaine. Somehow, in 1980 he managed to compile a batting average of .321, score 111 runs, and drive in 99 runs. In the 1981 season, which was brought to a premature end by a strike, Hernández batted .306. Despite his top performances, Hernández felt detached from baseball, and this feeling stayed with him into the 1982 season. That year he hit .299, drove in 94 runs, hit 7 home runs, and excelled at fielding, leading the Cardinals into the World Series. After striking out in his first 15 at-bats during the series, he racked up 7 hits in his final 12 at-bats. In the deciding game of the series, Hernández played a pivotal role when he drove in a run in the eighth inning, tying the score. The Cardinals went on to win the game and clinch the World Series.

On June 13, 1983, Hernández was traded to the New York Mets, in those days one of the worst major league baseball teams. The trade shocked Cardinal fans, and Hernández as well, who likened the prospect of joining the Mets to being "shipped to the Siberia of baseball." Many questioned Manager Whitey Herzog's decision to trade a perennial Golden Glove winner and the most important player in the lineup. Some cited Hernández's drug use, which ended in early 1983, and others his lack of concentration as the reason behind the trade. Hernández packed his bags, and with the intention of declaring himself a free agent by the end of the 1984 season, sullenly played out the rest of 1983 with the Mets, hitting .293. Toward the end of the season he began to envision the Mets as viable contenders and was impressed by such young players as Darryl Strawberry.

Rather than declare himself a free agent, Hernández signed a five-year, $8.4 million contract with the Mets in early 1984. He began to instill a winning spirit in the ball club that season. With his batting average of .311 in 1984, he inspired other hitters on the team to excel. In the field he shared his knowledge of the opposing batters with his teammates, and he cheered on the Mets' pitchers. Hernández ended his first season in a Mets' uniform with another Golden Glove Award and as runner-up for the National League's Most Valuable Player Award. In 1985 the star first baseman played with incredible intensity once again, leading the Mets to 98 wins with his .309 average and 91 runs batted in.

In September 1985, Hernández testified with immunity before a grand jury investigating drug trafficking in Pittsburgh in connection with his cocaine habit of the early 1980s. In his testimony, Hernández discussed how the drug had wrought havoc in his life. Baseball commissioner Peter Ueberroth gave Hernández a one-year suspension. It was waived when the ballplayer agreed to do two hundred hours of community service, to donate 10 percent of his 1986 salary to a drug-treatment center, and to have mandatory drug testing until he retired from baseball. In the games following his testimony, Hernández's performance did not slacken under the pressure. He hit .360, enabling the Mets to hang on in a tight pennant race with the St. Louis Cardinals, to whom they lost in the end.

In the 1986 season, Hernández got off to a slow start, but his play picked up, and he helped the Mets to a victory in the pennant race against the Houston Astros. In Game Six against the Astros, he gave one of the most spectacular performances of his career. With the Mets down 3–1 in the bottom of the ninth, Hernández hit a double, driving in a run, and then went on to score the tying run. The game stretched to sixteen innings and lasted nearly five hours, during which the first baseman made stunning catches and assists. The Mets went into the 1986 World

Series as the heavy favorites against the Boston Red Sox but lost three of the first five games and were nearly eliminated in Game Six. With the series tied at three games each, the Mets fell behind 3–0 in the seventh game, before Hernández came to the plate. With one out for the Mets and one strike against him, Hernández hit a fastball to drive in two Mets' runs. In a later inning, he drove in another run, enabling the Mets to capture the game and the World Series.

In the 1987 season, Hernández was officially designated captain and led the Mets in hitting, although he compiled only a .290 average. He drove in 89 runs and hit 18 homers, a personal record. The Mets won 93 games that season but were defeated in the race for the Eastern Division title by the St. Louis Cardinals. In the 1988 season, Keith Hernández missed 67 of the 162 games due to an injured hamstring and attained a .276 average, his lowest in a decade. The Mets made it to the National League playoffs, but were defeated in the decisive seventh game by the Los Angeles Dodgers. In the 1989 season, the final year of his contract, Hernández was anxious to put his injury behind him and perform as he always had, among the top 5 percent. He outworked his teammates in spring training, but then, in mid-May, he was in a collision going into second base and broke his kneecap. The Mets declined to re-sign him, and few teams expressed any interest. When the Cleveland Indians offered him a two-year $3.5 million contract, Hernández gratefully signed on with the team. A few weeks into the 1990 season he tore a calf muscle and then tried to come back too soon and reinjured the muscle. Then his doctors recommended back surgery, which he recovered from during the 1991 season. That year, at age thirty-eight with 11 consecutive Gold Glove awards and a lifetime .296 batting average, Keith Hernández retired from baseball.

Although he has no intention of pursuing a career in Hollywood after baseball, Hernández appeared as himself in an episode of *Seinfeld,* and in 1994 he was typecast as an aging ballplayer in an episode of *Law and Order.* In 1994, Hernández published his second book, *Pure Baseball: Pitch by Pitch for the Advanced Fan,* a detailed analysis of two games from the 1993 season, and went on *Larry King Live* to promote it. His first book, *If at First: A Season With the Mets,* was published in 1986. Emotional over the game of baseball and the past, Keith Hernández refuses to go near a ballpark.

79

José Greco

1918–

With his aristocratic elegance and inimitable flair, José Greco popularized Spanish dance. While he has been touted as the greatest flamenco dancer of modern times, Greco's repertoire actually encompassed the varying complex styles of Spanish dance, such as the *farruca,* the *jota,* the *bolero,* as well as the dances of Andalusia, Malaga, Valencia, and Seville. For more than three decades he dazzled audiences at concerts, revues, nightclubs, and in films and on television. The enormous popularity of Spanish and Latin American dance in contemporary America is due largely to Greco's pioneering work.

The youngest of two children, José Greco was born Costanzo Greco in Montorio nei Frentani, a mountain village near the Adriatic Sea in northern Italy, on December 23, 1918. His father, Paolo Emilio Greco, was Italian, while his mother, Carmela, was Spanish. At seven, José was taken to Seville, Spain, where he lived with his mother's family for three years. In 1928, José's father, who had gone to the United States, sent for the family, and they settled in a neighborhood in Brooklyn where dancing, singing, and guitar and accordion playing filled the streets. José was enrolled at the St. Clair McKelway School and Franklin K. Lane Junior High School in Brooklyn. At fourteen, he left high school before graduating to attend the Leonardo da Vinci Art School in Manhattan, with the aspiration of becoming a painter. As an art student, José began visiting dance recitals to observe the body in motion.

After watching the Spanish dancer Vicente Escudero, Greco decided to make Spanish dancing his main pursuit. For two years he studied under Hélène Veola, who recognized him as a genuine dancer. Nora Kaye, then an unknown soloist with the Hippodrome Opera Company, watched Greco dance in Veola's studio. Kaye was so in awe of his talent that she proposed to the Hippodrome that Greco share her solo spot, since the management would not cover the expense of another soloist. Thus, in 1937, Greco made his professional debut in a pas de deux with Nora Kaye in the incidental dances for the opera *Carmen*. When the 1937 opera season ended, Greco took the professional name Ramón Serrano, which he later dropped, and accompanied Gloria Belmonte in an engagement at the New York nightclub La Conga. In the late 1930s, Muriel Bentley, who later joined the American Ballet Theatre, danced with Greco for a season before he became a solo dancer. In between roles, Greco studied Spanish culture and history and also taught all forms of dancing, even the Suzy-Q, at summer resorts.

The turning point in Greco's career came when the Spanish dancer Encarnación Lopez, known as La Argentinita, observed him dancing at La Conga. In 1942, her partner, Federico Rey, was drafted into military service, and La Argentinita invited Greco to join her ensemble. The two dancers performed together for the first time on January 8, 1943, with the Cincinnati Symphony Orchestra. Later that year, Greco debuted at Carnegie Hall in a dance recital with the ensemble and was soon given featured billing and several solos in La Argentinita's program. For the next two years Greco toured the country with La Argentinita and her company; they gave recitals in New York and performed as guest artists with the American Ballet Theatre at the Metropolitan Opera House.

In September 1945, La Argentinita passed away, depriving the world of a rare talent. Earlier that year, Greco had said of the celebrated Spanish dancer: "All my own dances are of my own creation and supervised by La Argentinita....I have learned unending resources of the Spanish dance since my association with the great artist." Greco and Manolo Vargas, another male partner, accompanied Pilar Lopez, La Argentinita's heartbroken sister and a member of the company, in escorting the great dancer's remains back to Spain for burial. What began as an act of humanity became a pilgrimage for Greco to the roots of Spain, to its centuries-old, mystical, proud, violent, brooding nature that would permeate the dancer's art. Upon La Argentinita's death, Pilar Lopez announced that she would never dance again, but Greco, Vargas, and cultural groups in Spain insisted vehemently, and she returned to the stage in her sister's repertoire, a valuable theatrical property, with its national dances and large-scale ballets. Lopez named the ensemble Ballet Español, and it was an immediate sensation all across Spain. Greco danced with Pilar Lopez on the Spanish stage for the first time in Madrid on June 7, 1946.

Greco soon began to choreograph and included several of his interpretations in the repertoire, such as *Cana y farruca*, *Sentimiento*, *Triana*, and a version of Manuel de Falla's *Three-Cornered Hat*. On August 16, 1946, Greco married Nila Amparo, a distinguished dancer in the Spanish idiom. The couple would later divorce, and Greco would marry two more times. For two years Ballet Español toured Spain and Portugal, with Greco practicing five hours each day. In 1948, Greco choreographed a short dance sequence for *Manolete*, a film about bullfighters. He was the principal dancer in the film, which received rave reviews from Spanish audiences. Encouraged by this positive reception, Greco decided that year to form his own company of Spanish dancers, the Ballets y Bailes de España. The company debuted in January 1949 at the Apollo Theater in Barcelona.

Greco's Ballets y Bailes de España won plaudits from French audiences when it performed that year at the Théatre des

Champs-Elysées in Paris. Greco and his dancers then toured France and northern Europe, opening the 1950 season in the Netherlands before returning to Scandinavia. At the end of the tour, Greco was invited to participate with his company at a demonstration on December 10, 1950, that Señorita Doña Dolores de Pedroso-Sturdza was conducting at London's Covent Garden Opera House. Ballet critics gave Greco's performance such an enthusiastic reception that the British Arts Council invited the Ballets y Bailes de España to return to London during the Festival of Britain. After touring South and Central America, the Ballets y Bailes de España returned to London, where, on June 18, 1951, they began a monthlong engagement at the Sadler's Wells Theater. The Broadway producer Lee Shubert saw Greco perform in London and arranged and sponsored the Ballets y Bailes de España's first tour of the United States. Greco and his troupe of thirteen dancers, a guitarist, a flamenco singer, a pianist, and a small orchestra made their North American debut at the Shubert Theatre in New York on October 1, 1951.

Greco would perform in the United States with his company (renamed the José Greco Company in 1951) for twenty-five years, a record for consecutive tours unmatched in the history of American dance companies. Throughout the 1970s and the early 1980s, Greco danced only occasionally with his company. Along with his wife and fellow dancer, Nan Lorca, he made guest appearances with major symphonies in concert, recorded albums with major labels, and gave extensive lectures and demonstrations on the art of flamenco dancing. Greco also demonstrated his expertise on television shows hosted by Ed Sullivan, Perry Como, Bob Hope, Dinah Shore, and Dean Martin. In addition, he appeared in movies, acting in such films as the 1973 western *The Proud and the Damned,* Michael Todd's *Around the World in 80 Days,* and Stanley Kramer's *Ship of Fools.* In 1976, Greco added a whole new dimension to his career when he starred as Count Dracula in a production of *The Passion of Dracula* at the State Theater in New Brunswick, New Jersey.

In 1984, Greco performed as a guest artist with the María Benitez Spanish Dance Company at the Joyce Theater in New York. After all those years his fluency was still astounding to behold, and his heel work was still perfection. After that performance he seldom took the stage. On one occasion, in September 1988, the legendary dancer was accompanied by three of his six children in a Spanish dance program entitled "The Next Generation" at the Joyce Theater. The three children, José Greco II, Carmela Greco, and Lola Greco, were from his second marriage to Lola de Ronda, a gifted Spanish dancer and for many years Greco's only dance partner. The children were raised and trained in Madrid and are considered talented dancers with their own separate careers. Greco's oldest son, José Luis Greco, from his first marriage, composed and arranged some of the music for "The Next Generation."

At the end of 1993, Greco made plans to retire from the stage, although he vowed to remain active in the management affairs of the José Greco Company. By 1993 his son José Greco II was the star of the José Greco Company, performing flamenco, classical, and folk solos and leading roles, and at the end of 1993 he inherited his father's mantle and was named the company's director.

José Greco has received many awards, including the Cross of the Knight of Civil Merit, which the Spanish government conferred upon him in 1962 "in recognition of his worldwide contribution to the culture and performing arts of Spain." In 1971 the International Platform Association honored the dancer with the prestigious Silver Bowl Award for his "brilliant contribution in establishing lasting cultural ties in the Western Hemisphere through Hispanic Dance." José Greco has also received honorary doctorate degrees from Northwood Institute and from Fairfield University in Connecticut.

80

Justino Díaz

1940–

Said to have one of the smoothest basso cantante voices, Justino Díaz is one of the world's greatest bass stars of opera. Díaz burst on the scene in 1963 when he made his debut at the Metropolitan Opera, singing the role of Count Monterone in Verdi's *Rigoletto*. At twenty-three, he was one of the youngest singers to debut at the Met. Díaz rose rapidly to stardom, performing at the world's elite opera houses in such roles as the Grand Inquisitor in Verdi's *Don Carlos*, the High Priest in Verdi's *Aida*, the leads in Mozart's *Figaro* and *Don Giovanni*, and Mephistopheles in Gounod's *Faust*. His place in the pantheon of distinguished opera singers was reconfirmed when, in 1966, the honor was bestowed upon him to open the new Lincoln Center Metropolitan Opera House in New

York City, singing the role of Antony, opposite Leontyne Price, in the world premiere of Samuel Barber's *Antony and Cleopatra*. Díaz's progress in opera in subsequent decades was both stunning and unorthodox, for he began to oscillate between baritone and bass roles and sings both with equal brilliance to this day.

The only child of Justino Díaz Morales and Gladys Villarini, Justino Díaz was born in the Condado section of San Juan on January 29, 1940. His father taught economics at the University of Puerto Rico, and in 1945 he relocated his family to Philadelphia so that he could work toward his master's degree. After the family returned to Puerto Rico, Justino took the stage for the first time at six years of age at the Robinson Grammar School in San Juan. At a music show the children gave, he sang a solo in English of "Old Black Joe" and made quite an impression on the school's music teacher. The teacher encouraged the child to sing as often as possible, and Justino joined the school chorus and the church choir. Like most young Puerto Ricans, he was an avid baseball fan, and his role models in those days were players like Mickey Mantle, Ted Williams, and Babe Ruth.

In 1954, Justino Díaz Morales took the family to Cambridge, Massachusetts, where they lived for a year and a half while he completed his doctorate at Harvard University. In Cambridge, Justino attended high school, singing in the coed glee club and working to improve his command of English. When the family returned to San Juan in 1955, Justino continued his high school education and happened upon a role in an opera. One of his friends suggested that he sign up as a super with the Puerto Rican Summer Festival, which brought eight to ten guest stars to San Juan each year. Justino had never even been to an opera, but he decided to try out for the chorus. He landed a temporary spot after his father pulled some strings on his behalf. Thus, Justino witnessed his first opera from the vantage point of the stage, as he sang in the chorus in Verdi's *La Forza del Destino*. His second performance found him in Donizetti's *Lucia di Lammermoor*.

Justino quickly progressed and in just one year was named a member of the permanent chorus. When he was barely eighteen years old, he performed his first solo, one line in the gambling scene in *La Traviata*, announcing that dinner was served. Of that performance he told *Opera News* in December 24, 1966: "Those four words put more butterflies in my stomach than anything that's happened since. It had been drummed into me to watch the conductor for my cue, but at that moment Flora walked in front of me with a big fan. I sang my line on time, though!" Upon graduating from high school in 1958, Díaz enrolled at the University of Puerto Rico, where he majored in psychology in his first year, a discipline that was helpful later in his career in interpreting roles. At the University of Puerto Rico, Diaz sang under the tutelage of María Esther Robles, a soprano of enormous talent, who found him to be a most gifted and promising student.

In 1959, Justino Diaz came to the mainland with his father, who was spending a sabbatical at Harvard. He enrolled at the New England Conservatory of Music in Boston, where he stayed for two and a half years studying Italian, French, and German, among other subjects. While at the conservatory, Díaz took voice lessons from Frederick Jagel, who had formerly been a tenor with the Metropolitan Opera Company in New York. Jagel was influential in the young opera singer's development, giving him, as Díaz once said, "the tools to work with." He took advantage of any opportunity to sing in churches or festivals so that he could pay for his living expenses. On one occasion, he sang for fifty dollars at a Richard Nixon fundraiser. While at the New England Conservatory of Music, Díaz performed with the New England Opera Company, under the direction of Boris Goldovsky, who taught the young singer to view acting as a kind of score reading. With the New England Opera Company, Díaz performed, among other roles, the singing teacher Basilio, the servant Ambrosio, and a sergeant of the guard in Rossini's *Barber of Seville*.

In 1962, Díaz went to the highly selective Metropolitan Opera Studio with a letter of recommendation from Boris Goldovsky. He was granted an audition and was promptly admitted for training. Early in 1963, while he was still at the Metropolitan Opera Studio, Díaz entered a competition sponsored by the Leiderkranz Foundation and captured first prize. In the spring of 1963 he participated in the National Council's Regional Auditions, held by the Metropolitan Opera for singers from the United States and Canada. Again he came out on top, and this time was awarded a $2,000 cash scholarship and a contract to sing at the Metropolitan Opera. That fall, Díaz made his New York debut at Carnegie Hall in the American Opera Society production of *I Puritani*. Several weeks later he debuted with the Metropolitan Opera in Verdi's *Rigoletto*.

Díaz rose swiftly to stardom and in the next three years performed at the Met and at other prestigious opera houses, singing leading roles. By 1964 he was able to sing twenty-nine roles. According to Díaz, no piece of music is easy to learn, and as he told *Opera News*: "Many times a modern piece is easier to remember, because its initial difficulty makes you master it then and there. Mozart may sound simple, but an aria like '*Aprite un po' quegli occhi*' in *Figaro* is full of words and fast repetition. Handel is hardest of all, because of the runs, ornaments, slight variations, repeated figures that could be repeated once too often."

While not onstage at the Metropolitan Opera, Díaz sang in oratorios, recitals, and music festivals, including the Casals Festival in San Juan, the Festival of the Two Worlds in Spoleto, Italy, and at Tanglewood in Massachusetts, among others. In 1965, Díaz met Anna Aragno, a ballet dancer with the Bolshoi Theatre and the Metropolitan Opera Company who performed with Rudolf Nureyev and Edward Villella, and a year later they married. Early on in the marriage they learned to balance both of their careers as well as a family life complete with children. With her ballet training, Anna Aragno coached Díaz on how to move better onstage. Díaz remained disciplined by vocalizing at home and stayed fit by swimming and working out several times a week at a gym.

Díaz went on to make important appearances in major European opera houses. He performed at La Scala in Milan in Rossini's *Siege of Corinth* and sang Manrico in *Il Trovatore* at Teatro Colón in Buenos Aires, where, in 1908, the Puerto Rican tenor Antonio Paoli, known as the "Lion of Ponce," had also made his Argentine debut singing the same role. The Argentine composer Alberto Ginastera was so delighted by Díaz's voice and delivery as Manrico and in other parts that he wrote *Beatrice Cenci* and the role of Count Cenci just for the opera singer. Díaz sang the role in 1971 at the opening week of the Kennedy Center in Washington, D.C., and then later that same year at Lincoln Center.

In April 1974, Díaz was featured as Nourabad in *Les Pecheurs des Perles* with the Opera Guild of Greater Miami and then joined the New York City Opera for Count Cenci in *Beatrice Cenci*. In May 1974 he flew to Valencia to sing the active and demanding role of Mephistopheles in *Faust*, which he had performed earlier in the season in New Orleans. That summer, Justino taped numerous recordings, doing Massenet's *Thais* with Anna Moffo for RCA and Rossini's *Assedio de Corinto* opposite Beverly Sills and Shirley Verrett for Angel.

In 1985, at the behest of the great tenor Placido Domingo, Díaz agreed to sing the archetypal baritone role of Iago in *Otello*. When the duo sang *Tosca* in Puerto Rico with Renata Scotto, Placido Domingo recommended Díaz to Franco Zeffirelli for the motion-picture version of *Otello*. Zeffirelli agreed, and the singers and the orchestra recorded the music and then went on location to shoot the film. Díaz never got to perform Iago on stage in 1985, but he got his chance in 1989 in the revival of Music Center Opera's *Otello*.

Díaz continues to perform in the world's leading opera houses and is always willing to take on the challenge of a new role with his positive approach: "The more penetration into the character the singer can accomplish as an actor, the better the voice takes care of itself. When you're concerned with pearly tones, that can't happen."

81

Fernando Bujónes

1955–

Acclaimed as one of this century's greatest dancers and the finest male classical dancer the United States has ever produced, virtuoso classicist Fernando Bujónes electrified the dance world for nearly two decades with the spectacular purity of his line, unusually high elevations, and detailed footwork. While he showed a distinct preference for classical revivals and pas de deux, the range of Bujónes's artistry encompassed roles in both established classical and contemporary masterpieces as well as bravura showpieces.

An only child, Fernando Bujónes was born on March 9, 1955, in Miami, Florida, to Cuban parents. When he was a year old, his parents divorced. His mother, María Calleiro, a dancer and theatrical stage manager, took Fernando back and forth from Miami to Havana, Cuba. She continually cultivated his appreciation of the arts and at one point wanted him to be a pianist. Concerned about her son's delicate health and poor appetite, María Calleiro sought the advice of a physician, who recommended that Fernando take classes at the Acadêmia de Ballet Alicia Alonso in Havana to build stamina. Alicia Alonso, the principal dancer with Ballet de Cuba and a regular guest artist with the American Ballet Theatre, and her husband, Fernando Alonso, the director of the Ballet Nacional de Cuba, ran the ballet school. Eight-year-old Fernando was the youngest in his class, but he was eager to learn and found great enjoyment in dance. He studied for a year and a half with the Alonsos before returning to the United States for good in 1965.

With his health vastly improved, Fernando studied ballet intensely in Miami and danced in a small troupe. His cousin, ballet coach Zeida Cecelia Mendez, gave him private lessons to develop his technique. Before long, Jacques d'Amboise, a premier danseur with the New York City Ballet, spotted Fernando and, amazed by the boy's natural facility, recommended him for the School of American Ballet. In 1967, Fernando went to New York City accompanied by his mother and cousin, where he took summer classes on a full scholarship. By the end of the summer Fernando was recognized as a prodigy and was invited to stay on. He was awarded a Ford Foundation grant covering his ballet training, piano lessons, and tuition at the Professional Children's School, where he studied for six years. Three instructors at the school were instrumental in Bujónes's development as a dancer: Alexandra Danilova, a former member of Diaghilev's Ballet Russe and then prima ballerina of the Ballet Russe de Monte Carlo; Stanley Williams, a former soloist with the Royal Danish Ballet; and André Eglevsky, a former premier danseur with the Ballet Russe de Monte Carlo and then with the New York City Ballet.

While at the School of American Ballet, Fernando awoke to the realization that he could be a great dancer, as he told *Interview* in November 1980: "...when I began to develop in the workshops the lead parts, when I saw Rudy (Nureyev) and Margot (Fonteyn) at the Royal Ballet—I began to have a vision in front of me, and I said to myself, 'You know, if Rudy's done it, I can do it.' That was always my vision, Rudy in front of me." When Fernando was fourteen years old, he was already such an exquisite dancer, with perfect feet and the manner of a true classicist, that the choreographer George Balanchine invited him to dance with the parent company, the New York City Ballet. Fernando turned down the offer, knowing instinctually that he was still too young to manage the varied and demanding repertory of that company.

At Carnegie Hall in 1970, Bujónes, age fifteen, made his professional debut as a guest student dancer with the André Eglevsky Ballet, partnering Gelsey Kirkland in the grand pas de deux from *Don Quixote*. In the spring of 1972, Bujónes graduated from the School of American Ballet, and Balanchine issued him another invitation to sign on with the New York City Ballet. Upon the recommendation of his mother and his cousin, Bujónes chose instead to join the corps de ballet of the American Ballet Theatre, citing its extensive classical repertory and the opportunities it offered for his further development as a dancer. His first corps role was in Lichine's *Helen of Troy,* and several more followed that season. In 1973, Bujónes was promoted to soloist at the American Ballet Theatre, and in April of that year he danced with Eleanor D'Antuono in the pas de deux from *Don Quixote* at the American Ballet Theatre's engagement at the Opera House of the John F. Kennedy Center for the Performing Arts in Washington, D.C. That month, he also danced magnificently in *Etudes.*

In the summer of 1973, Bujónes drew accolades again for his performance in *Don Quixote* and *Etudes* as well as in the roles of Benno in *Swan Lake,* the Third Sailor in Jerome Robbins's *Fancy Free,* and the Transgressor in Anthony Tudor's *Undertow.* In April 1974 the young dancer made his much-anticipated international debut at the London Palladium when he and partner Eleanor D'Antuono were the only Americans to dance at a highly acclaimed charity gala before members of the British royal family, showcasing renowned international dancers doing a selection of pas de deux. The pair was the biggest hit at the gala, and Bujónes received great critical acclaim. Later that year, Bujónes became the first American to win the coveted gold medal at the International Ballet competition in Varna, Bulgaria, the chief event of its kind in the dance world. At Varna the young ballet star was also awarded a special citation for "highest technical achievement."

The American Ballet Theatre honored Bujónes's astounding performance at Varna with a promotion to one of the world's youngest principal dancers. Among Bujónes's many roles in the summer of 1974 was his debut in Ballanchine's *Theme and Variations,* a taxing role, which earned him accolades for his technical precision. Despite his spectacular performances and the gold medal, Bujónes was eclipsed by the extensive publicity given that year to Mikhail Baryshnikov, the premier danseur of the Kirov Ballet, who had defected from the Soviet Union and signed on with the American Ballet Theatre. His remark that "Baryshnikov has the publicity, but I have the talent" earned Bujónes the title of "Bad Boy of American Ballet" that season.

Over the next four years Bujónes danced in many ballets with the American Ballet Theatre and also found time to perform with several regional companies. Highlights of 1975 include his debut in *Swan Lake* with Eleanor D'Antuono and in *La Sylphide* with Cynthia Gregory and his performance with partner Yoko Morishita, the 1974 Varna gold medalist in the women's category, at a gala in Tokyo in May 1975. In 1976, Bujónes debuted in *Giselle* with Eleanor D'Antuono and in Baryshnikov's *Nutcracker* with Natalia Makarova. He also made his first appearances with the National Ballet of Canada in Toronto, where he partnered both Veronica Tennant and Nadia Potts in the title role, and was featured performing in *Les Patineurs* on PBS's *Dance in America* television series. Highlights of 1977 include Bujónes's debut in Ashton's *La Fille Mal Gardée* with the National Ballet of Canada and his first appearances with the Berlin Opera Ballet, the Rome Opera Ballet, and at the Edinburgh Festival. He also landed his first role in a film that year playing a dancer in *The Turning Point,* directed by Herbert Ross. In 1978 Bujones appeared in Baryshnikov's full-length *Don Quixote,* partnering Natalia Makarova at the American Ballet Theatre, and also danced for the first time with the Vienna State Opera Ballet.

In 1980, Bujónes married the dancer Marcia Kubitschek, the daughter of Juscelino Kubitschek, the former president of Brazil and the associate director, with Dalal Achcar, of the Ballet de Rio de Janeiro. The couple had met when Bujónes was performing in Brazil in 1976. In 1980, Bujónes danced in the full-length *La Bayadère,* partnering Marianna Tcherkassky and Cynthia Harvey at the American Ballet Theatre. That year, the Library of Congress honored the dancer with the Outstanding Young Man of America Award. In 1981, Bujónes made his first appearance with the Paris Opera Ballet as its first American ballet guest star in over a century. In 1982, Bujónes became the youngest recipient of the prestigious Dance Magazine Award for the "technical excellence and joy with which he approaches and enriches dance." He also appeared that year at the American Ballet Theatre in Anastos's *Clair de Lune* in a role created specifically for him.

In January 1985, Bujónes's career took a new direction with the premiere of his first choreographed ballet for the American Ballet Theatre, *Grand Pas Romantique*. On April 17, 1985, he gave a command performance at the White House for President Ronald Reagan and the first lady. In June of the same year he made his debut with the Royal Ballet at the Royal Opera House–Convent Garden. That year he danced in Kenneth McMillan's *Romeo and Juliet* with Marianna Tcherkassky.

In 1985, Bujónes also found himself in a dispute with Mikhail Baryshnikov, who refused to talk to Maurice Béjart about creating a major new work for the dancer. At the peak of his astonishing career, Bujónes was faced with a choice: to continue performing the same classics with the American Ballet Theatre or to take a risk and face new challenges on the international circuit. He chose to abandon the American Ballet Theatre, and in the next several years he appeared with companies the world over, gaining depth and knowledge from the experiences.

In February 1986 the *New York Times* honored Bujónes with an Outstanding Artist Award. That year, he performed at the Vienna State Opera for the filming of Beverly Sills's *Gala of Stars*. He also partnered Monique Loudieres, prima ballerina with the Paris Opera, in the pas de deux in *Grand Pas Classique*. He created a leading role in the Australian Ballet's production of *The Three Musketeers* in 1987 and danced with the National Ballet of Canada as a featured guest artist in *Swan Lake*.

In 1988 he was a guest artist partnering Yoko Morishita with the Cisne Negro Grupo de Danco do Brasil at City Center in New York. In the same year, Bujónes made his debut as Lensky in *Onegin* with the National Ballet of Canada. In 1988, Bruce Marks, the artistic director of the Boston Ballet, offered him permanent guest status, which enabled the dancer a to settle down not far from New York City and continue his lucrative guest-appearance schedule. By then Bujónes's fees per event ranged from $5,000 to $15,000. The ballet star readily accepted Marks's offer and joined the Boston Ballet. In April 1988 he made his debut with Moscow's Bolshoi Ballet in *Swan Lake* as its first American male guest artist.

In 1992, Bujónes was one of nine current and former

principal dancers from the American Ballet Theatre, the New York City Ballet, the Dance Theater of Harlem, and the Joffrey Ballet to file a class-action suit against the American Guild of Musical Artists, which represents ballet and modern dancers in large companies. The dancers sought $20 million in damages for the poverty-line salaries and long working hours they had endured and a change in the union pension plan that would enable dancers to obtain benefits when they retired from dancing.

Bujónes had always dreamed of directing a ballet company one day and passing on his knowledge of ballet and life. His opportunity arose in 1993 when he was named artistic director of Ballet Mississippi. In October of that year Bujónes unveiled a strong and vigorous company in a choreographed program that saw him perform two of Béjart's *Greek Dances*.

Under the leadership of Bujónes, Ballet Mississippi and its dancers have flourished. His advice to young dancers he meets along the way, as he related to the *Washington Post*, is the same that he has adhered to throughout his career: "You should be devoted and disciplined, and never sacrifice your beliefs. You should be flexible and absorb like a sponge, but believe in yourself always."

82

Katherine D. Ortega

1934–

The youngest of nine children, Katherine D. Ortega was born on July 16, 1934, in rural south central New Mexico to Catarina (Dávalos) Ortega and Donaciano Ortega, a blacksmith and cafe owner. Donaciano Ortega instilled in the children the virtues of hard work, self-discipline, and self-reliance, while Catarina Ortega imparted religious values, encouraging the children to attend catechism and church services each Sunday. Together they made their children's education a high priority, and when Katherine was a young girl, they moved the family to Tularosa, a

396

small town at the foot of the Sacramento Mountains, so that the children could attend the local high school. The Great Depression brought financial difficulties to the Ortega family; Donaciano Ortega had to juggle several jobs, and the children lent a hand by selling perfume and vegetables door to door.

By the early 1940s, Donaciano Ortega had opened a small Mexican restaurant, which he later moved to Alamogordo, New Mexico. The family lived in the back of the restaurant in Alamogordo, and each member helped in running the business. From early childhood Katherine excelled at mathematics, and her parents were so confident of her math skills that she was allowed to operate the cash register at the family's restaurant. In her early years she took a keen interest in accounting and banking, and as a grade-school student she derived enjoyment in taking deposits from the restaurant to the bank. In her senior year of high school Katherine again put her skills in finance to use by working in the bookkeeping department of the Otero County State Bank in Alamogordo.

Upon graduating from high school, she took a position at a bank in order to save money for college. Two and a half years later, she enrolled at Eastern New Mexico State University at Portales, where she majored in economics and business and lived off the five dollars a week she made working at the university library. She graduated with honors from the university in 1957, with a plan to teach typing and shorthand in a high school. Ortega put such plans to rest when the chairman of the business school warned her that if she applied for a teaching position in eastern New Mexico, she would probably be turned down because she was Mexican American. Faced with such dim employment prospects and outright discrimination, Ortega decided to forge another career path. In an article in the *New York Times*, Ortega noted that her father was the most important influence in her life because he inspired her to overcome obstacles, including discrimination, and to succeed in a man's world: "My father taught me we were as good as anybody else, that we could accomplish anything we wanted...."

In Alamogordo, New Mexico, Ortega founded an accounting firm with one of her sisters, Ethel Olsen, a certified public accountant. In the 1960s and 1970s she held various posts in accounting in New Mexico and then in California, where she relocated in 1967. In 1969, she went to Los Angeles to take a position as a tax supervisor at the firm of Peat, Marwick, Mitchell & Co., where she was employed until 1972. From 1972 to 1975 she filled the post of vice president and cashier at the Pan American National Bank in Los Angeles. In California she also faced discrimination when she was denied service in private clubs which catered only to men.

In 1978, Catarina Ortega, who had reached her eighty-sixth birthday, beckoned her daughter back to New Mexico. There Katherine Ortega worked as a consultant until 1982 in the family accounting business, which ultimately became the Otero Savings & Loan Association of Alamogordo. In 1979 she became a California certified public accountant. Katherine Ortega had been active in the Republican party during her college days and after graduating had joined the Young Republicans and served as precinct chairperson in Alamogordo. Upon her return to New Mexico, she stepped up her activity in the Republican party, serving as a liaison at the state and local level between the party and Latino and women's organizations. She also worked on the campaigns of Pete V. Domenici, a Republican senator from New Mexico, who was later instrumental in Ortega's selection to the post of U.S. treasurer; he recommended her to President Reagan as a candidate to fill the position.

As the 1980s dawned, leaders in the Republican party took a serious look at Ortega. In April 1982 she earned national recognition when President Reagan selected her as one of ten members of a Presidential Advisory Committee on Small and Minority Business Ownership. In December, President Reagan appointed Ortega commissioner on the five-person Copyright Royalty Tribunal, a federal agency that decides on such issues as what royalty fees cable companies across the country must pay for the use of copyrighted material. In September 1983, Ortega received word that she would be nominated for U.S. treasurer, and a few weeks later the Senate confirmed her nomination.

On September 12, 1983, Ortega's nomination was officially announced at a ceremony heralding the start of Hispanic Week celebrations in Washington, D.C. She was visibly moved by the announcement and spoke on that occasion of her allegiance to the Republican party: "I have often said I was born a Republican. I am a product of a heritage that teaches strong family devotion [and] a commitment to earning a livelihood by hard work, patience, determination, and perseverance." Katherine D. Ortega was sworn in to the post by Treasury Secretary Donald T. Regan in the Rose Garden of the White House on October 3, 1983. With her swearing in, Ortega became the second Latina in history to be appointed U.S. treasurer, the first being Romana Acosta Bañuelos, selected by President Nixon in 1974. During the ceremonies, Ortega signed special forms that would be used to engrave her signature on the plates from which U.S. currency, an estimated 5.5 billion bills, would be printed during her time in office.

As U.S. treasurer, a post viewed as ceremonial for the most part, Ortega's duties were essentially to receive and pay out money for the government in handling the nation's $220 million budget and to supervise five thousand employees. Some of her particular responsibilities included overseeing the Bureau of Engraving and Printing, the U.S. Mint, and the U.S. Savings Bond Division. In addition, she tracked government spending, processed claims for lost, stolen, or counterfeit government checks, and destroyed unusable currency. In 1985, Ortega also took on the special project of promoting the sale of U.S. Liberty coins, gold and silver commemorative coins issued to raise $40 million to restore the Statue of Liberty.

In August 1984, with twelve family members in the audience, Ortega delivered the keynote address at the Republican National Convention in Dallas, which nominated Ronald Reagan for a second term in office. Her selection as keynote speaker surprised even party insiders, who had expected a better-known woman, such as Elizabeth Dole, a respected and high-profile Reagan cabinet member, to receive the honor. Ortega gave a moving speech in which she made reference to her Latino heritage and welcomed Democrats, disillusioned by their own party, into the Republican fold.

Ortega served as U.S. treasurer throughout the Reagan presidency. Since leaving her post in 1989, she has been an alternative representative to the United Nations. In 1992, Ortega was appointed to the board of directors of several major corporations, including the Ralston Purina Company and the Kroger Company, the grocery chain. She also serves on the advisory boards of Leadership America and the National Park Service and is a member of Executive Women in Government and the American Association of Women Accountants. On February 17, 1989, Katherine Ortega married Lloyd J. Derrickson.

In her long years of service Ortega has been the recipient of many awards. Her alma mater, Eastern New Mexico University, bestowed upon her its Outstanding Alumni of the Year Award in 1977, and she received honorary doctor of law degrees from Eastern New Mexico University in 1984 and from Kean College in 1985. In 1988, Villanova University awarded Ortega an honorary doctor of social science degree. Katherine Ortega has also been the recipient of the California Businesswoman's Achievement Award and the Outstanding Woman of the Year Award from the Damas de Comercio.

83

Ramón Cortines

1932–

Ramón Cortines, a Mexican American, was born in San Antonio, Texas, on July 22, 1932, to an unwed mother. When he was seventeen days old, he was given up for adoption. His adoptive mother was of English descent, and his adoptive father, once the salad chef at the Plaza Hotel on Union Square in San Francisco, was of Spanish ancestry. While they were not well educated, Ramón's adoptive parents took him on weekend excursions to museums and concerts to cultivate his appreciation of the arts. When he was seven, the family moved to San Francisco, where he attended James Lick Middle School in the Noe Valley neighborhood of the city and then enrolled at Mission High School, several blocks away from his house on Dolores Street.

In 1950, Cortines graduated from Mission High and went on

to Pasadena College, a small evangelical liberal-arts college, where he was a dedicated student with a passion for excellence. Among his many achievements at Pasadena College, Cortines was nominated to the Who's Who Among Students in American Universities and Colleges and was the recipient of numerous first-place trophies in national speech contests. Cortines's college years were interrupted by his induction into the armed forces during the Korean War. Officers in the army's Sixth Division, in which Cortines served, were so impressed by his intellect that he was chosen to teach new recruits at Fort Ord in California. After serving for two years, from 1953 to 1955, Cortines returned to Pasadena College and graduated with a B.A. degree. While teaching in California's public schools, Cortines obtained his M.A. in school administration from Pasadena College in 1964 and his M.A. in adult learning from the college in 1966.

From 1966 to 1968, he served as director of student activities at South Hills High School in Covina, California. In 1972 he was appointed superintendent of the twenty-four-thousand-student school district in Pasadena. A highlight of his twelve-year career in Pasadena was the court-ordered desegregation plan he carried out in the school district. Cortines not only had to deal with hate mail, bomb threats, and bodyguards, but in the midst of the desegregation controversy, a conservative Pasadena school board fired him, in 1978. Cortines got his job back the following year and remained at the post until 1984. During his tenure as superintendent in Pasadena, Cortines founded a camp for disabled children on land adjacent to his ranch in Porterville, California, near Santa Barbara.

From 1984 to 1986, Cortines served as superintendent of the thirty-thousand-student public school system in San Jose, where he implemented a desegregation plan for the second time in his career when the district was slapped with a desegregation lawsuit a few days after Cortines became superintendent. He forged ahead and ultimately persuaded a judge to accept a mostly voluntary desegregation plan. Meanwhile, Cortines, a proven master of school financing, restored solvency to the school district that had declared bankruptcy under the previous administration, the nation's first school system to fail since the Depression. In San Jose, Cortines not only lent financial stability to the school district, he rebuilt the curriculum, earning widespread community support.

During his tenure as superintendent of the sixty-two-thou-sand-student school district in San Francisco from 1986 to 1992, Cortines's primary task was cutting $50 million in costs due to the financial crisis gripping California. He is credited with managing to trim staff and reduce programs without firing teachers, which had happened in the rest of the state. As Cortines carefully cut costs, he aggressively sought new sources of revenue. Through various means, he raised up to $5 million a year for the city's schools from corporate donors. Cortines appealed to business executives by inviting them to be principals for a day at local schools. Many were appalled by the conditions they found and joined the superintendent's "Adopt a School" program, an extended commitment of time and money. While similar programs existed elsewhere, Cortines went a step further by publicly praising his corporate partners at every opportunity and making sure their money was used for programs, not salaries or bureaucratic expenses. In fact, he returned money to the sponsors if the school board wanted to spend it in unsuitable ways.

In creating new sources of revenue, Cortines also led a successful ballot campaign for a quarter-cent sales tax dedicated to school spending. The school district reaped $17 million in taxes in the first seventeen months. He was also the driving force behind two successful bond measures which raised $90 million for earthquake reinforcement and another $90 million for infrastructure improvements. All the while, Cortines managed to raise test scores, improve attendance, and reduce dropout rates in the school district. He was credited with bringing fiscal soundness, labor peace, and educational improvements to the system, which earned him the respect and affection of parents and teachers and the support of business and government leaders. While his school board supported his initiatives 90 percent of the time, Cortines ran into disagreements about programs and appointments for gay men and lesbians and various ethnic groups. The sharpest disputes were about plans to distribute condoms in the schools, a special counseling program for gay and lesbian students, and the exclusion of the Boy Scouts from in-school activities because of their organization's policy of discrimination based on sexual orientation. Cortines eventually went along with all three programs, although in modified form, and in the end neither alienated nor won the support of gay and lesbian activists in San Francisco.

Due to a grueling work schedule and a bad ulcer, Cortines resigned as superintendent of schools in San Francisco in July 1992 and took a part-time position as a consultant professor at Stanford University, serving as associate director of the Pew Charitable Trust Forum on School Reform. Then, in early 1993, President Clinton invited Cortines to head one of his transition teams. Later that year, he was nominated assistant secretary for intergovernmental affairs in the U.S. Department of Education. He created a minor controversy by endorsing the concept of government subsidies of private education through school vouchers, a politically charged concept that the Clinton administration opposes. He was awaiting Senate confirmation as an assistant secretary of education when he received a call from New York. In 1993 a faction of New York's Board of Education forced the ouster of Schools Chancellor Joseph A. Fernández, leaving the post open. In August 1993, Cortines became the top choice for schools chancellor of the board's four-member majority. The board voted 4–3 in favor of Cortines, who accepted the $195,000-a-year job and became the country's highest-paid Latino public official.

Cortines also became the sixth schools chancellor New York City had seen in ten years and took on what many called an impossible job that no sane person would want. When Cortines stepped in as chancellor, he inherited the nation's largest and most complex school system, with a $7.9 billion budget; an enrollment of nearly a million students, 80 percent of whom were minorities; seventy-five thousand teachers, administrators, and other staff members; and one thousand schools. He also took over a system burdened by serious problems, such as a high dropout rate, declining student achievement, ever-increasing violence, poor maintenance, and a critical shortage of funds. To make matters worse, Cortines arrived in the aftermath of fiery political battles over instruction about gays and lesbians and the distribution of condoms in the schools. Furthermore, he took the helm just as an asbestos crisis erupted, and New York City public schools were shut down, sending parents into a frenzy.

Realizing that the school community was grappling with many unsettling problems, Cortines sought, in his first days as chancellor, to restore a sense of calm and stability. As one of his first acts as schools chancellor, Cortines grappled with the maintenance crisis in the school system caused by a shortage of funds and poor management. He proposed overhauling the schools and suggested a five-year capital plan of $7.5 billion for new construction and renovation. As a preventive measure, he advocated giving local school districts the power to make minor repairs. Another issue Cortines addressed early on was preparing a core curriculum that would set citywide standards. In his first months as chancellor, Cortines also sought solutions to the problem of increased violence in the schools and proposed to appoint an administrator to supervise security and violence-prevention programs.

In 1994, Cortines and New York City mayor Rudolph Giuliani locked horns over the issue of school budget cuts. In February 1994, Mayor Giuliani, who was facing a $2.3 billion budget deficit, announced a plan to appoint a fiscal monitor to oversee board of education spending. Cortines was infuriated over this announcement, for he interpreted the plan as an attack on his handling of the school budget. In March 1994, Giuliani froze $68 million in board of education funds and demanded that the board come up with $332 million in cuts, mostly by axing administrative jobs. Cortines could not trim very much without undermining the operation of the schools and loudly protested the level of cuts the mayor demanded. After Giuliani insisted that Cortines fire two senior staff members, the chancellor threw in the towel and resigned. In the days that followed, both sides made compromises, and Cortines withdrew his resignation. However, his differences with the mayor proved irreconcilable and Cortines resigned again in June 1995, effective October 1995.

84

Jim Plunkett

1947–

The youngest of three children, Jim Plunkett was born James William Plunkett in San Jose, California, on December 5, 1947, to William Gutierrez Plunkett, of Mexican, Irish, and German ancestry, and Carmen (Blea) Plunkett, of Mexican descent. Both of Jim's parents were visually impaired, though William Plunkett could see with the aid of thick glasses. They met at a school for the blind in Albuquerque, New Mexico, and moved to California during World War II. While William and Carmen Plunkett were bilingual, they spoke only English with the children, and Jim grew up without any proficiency in Spanish. William Plunkett operated a newsstand, and the family's income was quite low, so Jim earned spending money selling newspapers, mowing lawns, tending gardens, and later working at a gas station.

Jim attended Mayfair Elementary School, where he excelled on the athletic field despite having suffered a bone disease in childhood. He competed in wrestling, track, baseball, and basketball at Lee Matheson Junior High School and, by the time he reached the eighth grade, he discovered that he had an excellent throwing arm for football. At Overfeldt High School he played quarterback on the junior varsity football team. In 1964 he transferred to James Lick High School, where he was an honor student, a superb pitcher and a .300 hitter in baseball, and the first wrestler ever to capture four consecutive Mount Hamilton Athletic League individual titles. He also excelled on the football field, and made the varsity team as a quarterback. In 1964 he led the team to the Mt. Hamilton League title, and in 1965, with Jim at the helm, Overfeldt High went undefeated. In 1964 the young quarterback was elected to the All-League team, and in 1965 he enjoyed this honor again and was also named to the North Shrine All-Star team.

When Jim Plunkett graduated from high school in 1966, many colleges and universities came knocking at his door, offering football scholarships. He chose Stanford University for its proximity to home and its fine academic reputation. Just before going off to Stanford, Plunkett discovered a lump at the base of his neck and underwent surgery for a thyroid tumor, which fortunately proved benign. Due to his recuperation from the surgery, the young quarterback entered Stanford's starting lineup late that year and played less than his best. He also fell behind in his classes and dropped back a year, but he later got a firm academic footing and maintained a B average. Jim Plunkett made the varsity football team at Stanford in 1967, but he was benched during the games because the team had three other quarterbacks. Coach John Ralston wanted to move him from the quarterback position to defensive end, but Plunkett refused to make a switch.

Plunkett made the varsity lineup again in 1968, completing 142 out of 268 passes for 2,156 yards and 14 touchdowns. He set a record in the Pacific Eight Conference for yards gained in the air and ranked tenth in the national standings for total offensive yardage. Plunkett broke some ribs and injured his right knee that year, and after the season ended, he underwent surgery on the knee to remove damaged cartilage. In 1969 the young quarterback completed 197 out of 336 passes for 2,673 yards, a new Pacific Eight record, and 20 touchdowns, also a record. His total offensive yardage and total offense in a single game also set new Pacific Eight records. That season, Plunkett was named to the all-American second team, received the Voit Memorial Trophy as the Pacific Eight's outstanding player, and finished eighth in the running for the Heisman Memorial Trophy.

Stanford's class of 1970 graduated without Jim Plunkett, who was tempted to drop out and announce his availability for the draft that year. His father had passed away in 1969, and his mother needed help financially, and he barely made enough in the summers at construction jobs to get by. Out of his allegiance to Stanford and to the Chicano kids he tutored who looked upon him as a role model, Plunkett decided to stay at Stanford and graduate the following year. In the 1970 season, Plunkett completed 191 passes in 358 attempts for 2,715 yards and 18 touchdowns and 183 yards on the ground with 3 more touchdowns, leading the Stanford Indians to an 8–3 season, the Pacific Eight championship and the Rose Bowl.

For his performance on the field that season, Jim Plunkett was named the recipient of many prestigious awards, including the Heisman Memorial Trophy, the Maxwell Award, and Walter Camp Player of the Year. With 7,887 total offense yards in his career at Stanford, he became the first football player in NCAA history to surpass the 7,000-yard mark. In his three seasons with the Stanford Indians, Plunkett completed 530 passes in 962 attempts for 7,544 yards and 52 touchdowns. At the Rose Bowl, Jim Plunkett led his team to a 27–17 victory over Woody Hayes's undefeated Ohio State, the 10-point favorite. He completed 20 passes in 30 attempts for 265 yards and ran the ball 49 yards. In his crowning moment at Stanford, Jim Plunkett was named Player of the Game in both the Rose Bowl and in the All-Star game in the Hula Bowl, where he was the starting quarterback for the victorious North team.

In the pro draft held in January 1971, the Boston Patriots, who were then the lowest-ranking team in professional football, made Jim Plunkett their first pick. Even before he took the field, Plunkett's contribution helped the Patriots. The club's stock soared by $1,500,000 in anticipation of the pick, and ticket sales skyrocketed after the team's first draft choice was announced. In the 1972 season Plunkett played every single down as quarterback and passed for 2,158 yards and 19 touchdowns. His accomplishments in the pocket earned him the title of National Football League (NFL) Rookie of the Year.

After his rookie year, Jim Plunkett was plagued by injuries during the next four seasons and finally asked New England to trade him to the San Francisco 49ers so that he could be close to his home in San Jose. The Patriots obliged and sent Plunkett to San Francisco for four draft choices and a player. However, after two mediocre seasons in which he was benched for the first time in his life, the 49ers released him. It appeared that Plunkett's football career had reached a dead end until the Oakland Raiders signed the quarterback during the 1978 season. He rode the bench that entire season, and in 1979 he made just 15 passes, but he was poised for a comeback.

In 1980, Plunkett replaced the Raiders' starting quarterback, Dan Pastorini, with whom he maintained a fierce rivalry, after Pastorini broke his leg in a game against Kansas City. In that game Plunkett threw five interceptions for a loss, but then, a week later, in his first start in nearly three years, he led the Raiders to a victory over San Diego. Oakland then won five successive games, rallying for an 11–5 record and qualifying for the playoffs. Jim Plunkett led the team past the San Diego Chargers, 34–27, in the AFC championship game to Super Bowl XV, where he passed for 261 yards and three scores, defeating the Philadelphia Eagles, 27–10. Plunkett's touchdown pass to Kenny King sailed 80 yards, a Super Bowl record. The Oakland Raiders broke another record by becoming the first wild-card team in the history of football to win the Super Bowl. With his spectacular performance, Plunkett was named Most Valuable Player of the Super Bowl, and the NFL also designated him the 1980 Comeback Player of the Year.

In 1981, Plunkett suffered a thumb injury and warmed the Raiders' bench for most of the season. In the spring of 1982 the quarterback married Gerry Lavelle. After the Oakland Raiders relocated to Los Angeles for the 1982 season, Plunkett led the team to an 8–1 record, and then threw for a career high of 386 yards in a playoff game against the Cleveland Browns. In 1983, Jim Plunkett started well, but he was sidelined in favor of Raiders' quarterback Marc Wilson. When Wilson was injured that season, Plunkett took over and steered the Raiders to an AFC title and a

38–10 victory over the Washington Redskins at the Super Bowl. That season, he enjoyed his best single-season statistics, including 230 completions for 2,935 yards and 20 touchdowns.

In 1985 Jim Plunkett was plagued by a dislocated shoulder, but he was back in action in the 1986 season. He replaced Marc Wilson as the starting quarterback after the Raiders floundered in the first few games. By the end of the 1986 season Plunkett had completed a career total 1,943 passes in 3,601 attempts for 25,882 yards and 164 touchdowns. In 1987 his shoulder condition worsened, he sat out all season, and again underwent surgery. In August 1988 the Los Angeles Raiders released him, though he would rather not have called it quits. He told the *Los Angeles Times* after hearing the news: "I love this. I've been doing it for twenty-six years. I've been putting on pads for that long and I enjoy it. I mean, I really get a thrill out of it."

In 1990 the National Football Association inducted Jim Plunkett into the College Football Hall of Fame. That year, the star quarterback served as a spokesman for a company producing the first set of Braille sportscards, a 280-card set of pro football players with raised pictures on the front and Braille descriptions on the back. Plunkett donated all his proceeds from the sale of the cards to charities dedicated to helping the visually impaired. On the back of the Plunkett card it reads in Braille: "Raiders win Super Bowl XV—Jim Plunkett named MVP." In 1991, Jim Plunkett served as a football analyst for a Los Angeles radio station, and in 1992 he became an Oakland Raiders radio announcer.

85

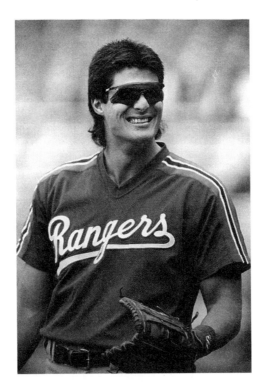

José Canseco

1964–

José Canseco is the stuff baseball legends are made of. In Detroit, Canseco once drove a ball so hard that when a Tiger third baseman got his glove on it, he was knocked over by its sheer velocity. In Seattle, he hit a home run off a broken bat. At Minnesota's Humpdome, Canseco slammed a ball 457 feet, nearly reaching the unreachable second deck, and at Toronto's Skydome he hammered a ball 540 feet to become the first player in history to hit the stadium's fifth deck. As an outfielder for the Oakland A's, José Canseco was called "baseball's Bruce Springsteen." He is one of the most exciting players in the sport and may go down in history as one of the all-time greats.

An identical twin, José Canseco was born in Havana, Cuba, on July 2, 1964, to José Canseco and Barbara (Capaz) Canseco. The Cansecos were one of the most respected and affluent families in Havana, where José Canseco Sr. enjoyed considerable clout as an oil executive for the American company Esso. Life changed dramatically for them when Fidel Castro rose to power in 1959. José Canseco Sr. lost his job, his house, and the car and struggled to make a living giving English lessons. The family was denied permission to leave Cuba until December 5, 1965. With fifty dollars and no job offers, they headed for the United States and settled in Opa Locka, just outside of Miami, Florida. There they were accepted into the large Cuban exile community. José Canseco Sr. worked as a gas-station attendant by day and a security guard at night before Amoco hired him as an executive.

José and his twin brother, Osvaldo (nicknamed Ozzie), and Teresa, their older sister, grew up in a hardworking white-collar family and were expected to excel in school. In 1975 the family moved from Opa Locka to Miami, where José attended Coral Park High School and became an honor student. While José and Ozzie played soccer and basketball in childhood, the boys ignored baseball until they were twelve years old and never competed in Little League. José tried out each year for the varsity baseball team at Coral Park High but did not survive the cuts until his senior year, when he was chosen to play third base. High school scouts considered José a good player with enormous potential as a hitter, but they feared that he had reached his peak in growth at five-eleven, making him too small for major league baseball.

Nevertheless, Canseco was picked up by the Oakland Athletics (A's) as their fifteenth-round selection in the June 1982 free-agent draft; his brother, Ozzie, went to the New York Yankees. Thanks to intensive weight training, Canseco added four inches and sixty-seven pounds to his frame within three years. Some have attributed his phenomenal growth to steroids, but he emphatically denied any drug use, and his records show he has never gained more than fifteen pounds in an off-season. Canseco made an astonishing climb through the minor leagues and began to show signs of a great offensive player in 1985 when he played fifty-eight games for the A's Class AA team in Huntsville, Alabama. Ozzie attributes José's success to the strengthening of his resolve after the boys' mother passed away in April 1984. With Huntsville, José hit a solid .318 with 25 home runs and 80 runs batted in before he advanced to Oakland's Class AAA farm team in Tacoma, Washington. In sixty games with Tacoma, Canseco raised his batting average to .348, compiling 11 more home runs and 47 runs batted in and knocked a ball out of Tacoma's Cheney Stadium, the first slugger to do so in twenty-six years. For his stellar season, Canseco received the *Sporting News* Minor League Player of the Year Award for 1985, and he was named the Southern Association's Most Valuable Player.

On September 2, 1985, Canseco was called up to the majors and played with the parent club that very day, striking out as a pinch hitter. Seven days later, he hit his first major league home run against the Texas Rangers. In the 29 games he played that season, Canseco earned a .302 batting average, with 5 home runs and 13 runs batted in. The young baseball player got off to a spectacular start in 1986. On April 12, 1986, against the California Angels, Canseco hit a ball 430 feet against a strong wind to the opposite field. At mid-season he was aiming to break Ted Williams's 1939 rookie record of 38 home runs and was recognized for his superb effort by being selected to his first All-Star team. A slump took Canseco out of contention for the Williams record. Despite a club record of 175 strikeouts in 1986, Canseco compiled 33 home runs and 117 runs batted in and was voted American League Rookie of the Year by both the *Sporting News* and the Baseball Writers Association of America.

In 1987, Canseco got off to a slow start, but ended the year with 31 home runs and 113 runs batted in, becoming the first Oakland player to drive in over 100 runs in two consecutive seasons. The 1988 season was a brilliant one for Canseco. As he had predicted early in the season, Canseco stole 40 bases and led the league with 42 home runs, making him the sole member of the "40-40" club in the major leagues. Twenty-seven of Canseco's 42 homers either tied the game or put the A's in the lead. With his 42 home runs, he became the first player in major league history to hit at least 30 homers in each of his first three seasons.

In 1988, Canseco also led the league with 124 runs batted in, a new Oakland A's record, and was named the American League's Most Valuable Player in a unanimous decision. The *Sporting News* and the Associated Press also selected him Player of the Year. Canseco helped lead the A's to the World Series in 1988, where they went down in defeat to the Los Angeles Dodgers in five games. In the opening game of the World Series, Canseco hit his first-ever grand-slam home run, the sixteenth grand slam in World Series history and just the second by a player in his first World Series game. His home run in Game Four hit the NBC centerfield camera, over 400 feet from the plate, and the next day, Canseco signed the dent. In 1988 he made his first appearance in the All-Star Game in the starting lineup, having been named on more voters' ballots than any other American League player.

On October 25, 1988, Canseco married a former Miss Miami, Esther Haddad.

In the weeks before the start of the 1989 season, Canseco became embroiled in controversy. First, the press criticized him for breaching his contract with promoters of a card show and failing to appear at a charity fund-raiser. In February 1989, Canseco was arrested in Miami for driving over 125 miles per hour. To make matters worse, the baseball player reported late to spring training in Phoenix for the third year in a row and then suffered a wrist injury that necessitated surgery and a long rest period. In April 1989 Canseco was arrested at the University of California at San Francisco for possession of a semiautomatic pistol in his car. He told the media he began carrying the weapon after receiving a series of threatening phone calls.

Due to such incidents, Canseco is both one of the most adored and vilified players in baseball. Critics cite not only his brushes with the law but his outspokenness, his supposed use of steroids, his rumored affair with Madonna, his disputes with umpires and the A's management, and his sometimes rude behavior in public. His supporters attribute his shortcomings to the pressure and intense scrutiny he undergoes as a superstar athlete and point to the player's enormous contributions to baseball, his popularity among fans, and his humanitarianism. When he is off the baseball field, Canseco works untiringly on behalf of children. He contributes time and energy to the Miami Youth Club, playing basketball with the kids, attending their spaghetti dinners, and regularly donating hundreds of pairs of sneakers. He is heavily involved in the Make-A-Wish Foundation, whose mission is to fulfill the dreams of dying children. On one occasion, the baseball player flew a leukemia-stricken child to Scottsdale, Arizona, for the A's spring training, and he once signed autographs for four and a half hours to raise money for a paralyzed child.

Canseco missed half the 1989 season, but upon his return he hit 17 home runs and 57 runs batted in, helping the A's advance to their second World Series in a row. This time Oakland emerged victorious, sweeping the San Francisco Giants in four straight games in a series that came to a standstill for ten days due to an earthquake. Canseco spent two weeks on the disabled list early in the 1990 season because of back problems. That June, he signed a five-year contract extension for $23.5 million with the Oakland A's, making him the highest-paid player in baseball at the time. Canseco missed thirty-one games in the 1990 season but still finished third in the American League in home runs with 37 and fourth in runs batted in with 101. In 1990, Oakland won the American League Western Division title for the third straight year but lost the World Series to the Cincinnati Reds. While the A's lost the Western Division title in 1991, Canseco was back in good form for the regular season. He enjoyed a career high of 44 home runs and tied for second in the league in runs scored with 115. At the end of the season, Canseco had accumulated 209 homers in the major leagues, placing him twelfth in history for sluggers at the end of the season in which they turned twenty-seven.

In 1992, Canseco was plagued by both a bad back and a sore shoulder and hit .246 with 22 home runs and 72 runs batted in. Surprisingly, the A's traded their star baseball player to the Texas Rangers, with a month left in the pennant race, in exchange for Texas slugger Ruben Sierra and pitchers Bobby Witt and Jeff Russell. The A's trade defied all logic, since the twenty-eight-year-old Canseco not only made an enormous contribution to the team but was also a pop icon who attracted fans to the ballpark. Perhaps the Oakland A's sensed a downward slide in Canseco's career, which was further evidenced by his bad start with the Rangers in 1993. Canseco had convinced the team to let him pitch an inning during a game that May, only to injure his elbow and sit out for most of the 1993 season. In the off-season Canseco renewed his commitment to baseball by working intensively with two coaches and a physical therapist to improve his hitting, throwing, and running. He also improved his mental game by overcoming the depression that had plagued him since his divorce from Esther Haddad in 1993. Canseco, one of the most exciting players in all of baseball, is poised for a dramatic comeback.

86

Miriam Colón

1930(?)–

Miriam Colón was born in Ponce, Puerto Rico, and grew up in San Juan with her brother and sister. She was born on August 20, presumably in the mid-1930s, although she has never publicly revealed the year of her birth. She became enamored of the theater when she was a child. At age eleven, while in her first year of junior high school, Miriam was cast in a school play that Marcos Colón, a drama student at the University of Puerto Rico, was directing for his thesis. From the moment Miriam stepped onstage, she aspired to be an actress. She asked Marcos Colón if she could go to the university to learn more about acting. He promised that he would inquire about the matter, and as it turned out, the dean of drama at the University of Puerto Rico, Leopoldo

Santiago Lavandero of Yale, saw the play in order to grade the thesis and was impressed by Miriam's dramatic flair. Marcos Colón told her to write Lavandero for permission to audit his classes.

Before long, Lavandero cast Miriam in a small part in a college play. After six months, she landed a three-line role, and within two years she was playing the lead in the university's productions and was made a member of its company. At the university Miriam also studied under Ludwig Schajowicz, a disciple of Max Reinhardt's. High school graduation was cause for great concern, since Miriam could not repeat the college drama courses she had taken through the years. The Drama Department at the University of Puerto Rico tailor-made a two-year scholarship to send its prodigy to study at Erwin Piscator's Dramatic Workshop and Technical Institute in New York City. Her mother accompanied her to Manhattan and worked in a garment factory as a seamstress. Miriam studied drama, voice, and dancing and knocked on producers' doors. She interrupted her training for a brief marriage to her childhood sweetheart after his discharge from the army. They were much too young, and the union dissolved after eighteen months.

Colón's acting career got off the ground when Elia Kazan and Lee Strasberg accepted her into the Actors Studio after her first audition as the first Puerto Rican ever admitted. Colón earned recognition for her talent on the New York theater scene through her performances on and off Broadway. In 1953 she was cast in the Broadway production of *In the Summer House* with Dame Judith Anderson and Darren McGavin and then performed opposite Geraldine Page and Mildred Dunnock in *The Innkeepers*. Colón then costarred with James Patterson in the Broadway production of *The Wrong Way Lightbulb*, directed by Stephen Porter. The actress soon found that Latina roles were scarce on Broadway and that the few that existed were usually as a villain or a maid. As a result, she began to act in New York's Off-Broadway productions. In 1956, Colón starred in the Off-Broadway production of *Me, Candido*.

After *Me, Candido* closed in New York, Colón went to Hollywood to play the same role at the Players Ring Gallery for twenty-five-dollars a week. She stayed in Los Angeles for several years and worked in numerous films, including the 1961 western *One-Eyed Jacks* and the 1966 western *The Appaloosa*, both opposite

Marlon Brando. She was also featured with Shirley MacLaine in the 1972 horror film *The Possession of Joel Delaney,* about a wealthy New York divorcée who tries to save her brother from death at the hands of a Puerto Rican occult group. In Hollywood, Colón appeared in many television shows, including an episode of *Dr. Kildare* in which she was cast as an East Indian princess. During a short stay in New York, she was introduced to George P. Edgar, a Wall Street securities analyst, who lured her back to Manhattan. The two married a few months later, in 1966. George Edgar had invested in Genet's *Blacks* in 1962, and in 1966 he backed the Off-Broadway production of *The Ox Cart* by Puerto Rico's foremost dramatist, René Marques, which ran for three months at the Greenwich Mews Theater. Colón was the star of *The Ox Cart* and attracted unanimous raves for her portrayal of the ill-fated Juanita. When *The Ox Cart's* three-month run ended, Colón began a project that has demanded as much of her creative energy as acting.

By the mid-1960s, Colón had decided she could not wait for roles to knock on her door and that she had to channel her energy and curiosity into her own theater. In 1967, Colón was selected to head the cultural panel of New York mayor John V. Lindsay's Puerto Rican Community Conference. Colón decided that all the leftover sets and costumes from *The Ox Cart* could travel to the parks, playgrounds, and streets of New York's most culturally deprived neighborhoods free of charge, the kind of mobile theater she had seen in Puerto Rico in the 1940s. Mayor Lindsay was keen about the idea, and in 1967 a mobile troupe of professional actors and twenty-five staff members was formed with initial funding by Lindsay's Urban Action Task Force. The Parks Department and the New York State Council on the Arts gave additional support. The mobile troupe debuted in *The Ox Cart* at the Carver Amphitheater in the barrio, and Colón played one of the leads. At the start the troupe performed only in English, then, due to popular demand, in Spanish. In the early years the troupe performed outdoors, using a flatbed truck for a stage, in parks and playgrounds and at street festivals in the summer, and during the winter months they held performances at their laboratory on West Eighteenth Street.

Before long the Puerto Rican Traveling Theater, as the troupe was called, began to bring Puerto Rican writers to the mainland and then developed young Latino writers living in the

United States. In 1977 the theater acquired a city-owned former firehouse on West Forty-seventh Street, rented to the company for $250 a month, with a lease of twenty-five years. The space needed remodeling to include a theater, drama school, rehearsal space, and an art gallery, and renovations were costly. Colón lobbied hard for financial support from corporations and foundations. In the next few years she raised the $1.6 million necessary to renovate the firehouse, and in 1981 the building was inaugurated. The simple street theater that Colón created had swiftly expanded into a theatrical organization, with a playwrights unit, a training program for youth, street theater in August, and three plays a season indoors during the other months.

In 1982, Mayor Ed Koch honored Colón with the Mayor's Award of Honor for Arts and Culture and a certificate of appreciation in recognition of her contributions to New York's cultural life. By 1988 the Puerto Rican Traveling Theater had staged over 100 productions, although Colón had acted in only five or six, including a play by Bertolt Brecht entitled *Señora Carrar's Rifles,* in which she played one of the most exhausting roles of her life. She also took time out to appear in the Al Pacino movie *Scarface* (1983). Colón devoted most of her time in the 1980s to the constant pursuit of corporate, private, and government funds to keep the company afloat, with its $650,000 annual operating budget. In addition, Colón concentrated on selecting directors, scouting for acting talent, and working on the artistic aspects of each production. With her unflagging enthusiasm and unflappable demeanor, Colón sustained the theater even in hard times.

A testament to her courage and commitment came when the country fell into an economic recession in the late 1980s, which had a profound effect on government, corporate, and private supporters of the arts in general and of the Puerto Rican Traveling Theater in particular. In 1991 the theater's annual budget came up short by almost $100,000, and Colón was forced to lay off valued staff members. She brainstormed for ways to make up the lost revenue and came up with the idea of exchanging the theater's credibility with Latino audiences for support from corporations looking to expand into the Latino market, the fastest-growing segment of the American population, with tremendous purchasing power. Her efforts proved successful enough to open the Puerto Rican Traveling Theater's twenty-fifth anniversary season in 1992 on schedule with a production of *The Ox Cart,* which won plaudits from theater critics and the public.

With the financial crisis behind her, Colón balanced the business end of running the theater with acting. In 1993 she starred in a production of *The Boiler Room* by Reuben Gonzalez, a compassionate portrait of the travails of a family of Puerto Rican immigrants in New York who must cope with a boiler in their living room. In 1994, Colón starred in *Innocent Erendira and Her Heartless Grandmother,* a drama based on a novella by Gabriel García Marquez about a young girl forced into prostitution by her grandmother. In 1994, Colón also produced *Written and Sealed* by Venezuelan playwright Isaac Chocrón.

87

Charlie Sheen

1965–

One of four children, Charlie Sheen was born Carlos Irwin Estevez in Los Angeles, on September 3, 1965, to Martin Sheen, the actor, of Cuban and Irish descent, and Janet (Templeton) Sheen. In 1968, Martin and Janet Sheen moved the family from New York to California, where Charlie was soon making Super-8 movies with older brother Emilio and his friends Sean and Chris Penn and Rob and Chad Lowe. Martin Sheen traveled the globe making films when Carlos was a boy, and he always made provisions for family members to accompany him on shoots. If the film schedules did not coincide with school vacations, the young Carlos was tutored on the set. Carlos made his professional acting debut at age nine as an extra in the wedding scene in the

CBS-TV movie *The Execution of Private Slovik,* starring his father. During the shooting of the 1979 film *Apocalypse Now* Carlos spent ten months on the set in the Philippines surrounded by Hollywood legends like Marlon Brando and Francis Ford Coppola and became inspired to pursue acting.

At Santa Monica High School, Carlos excelled on the athletic field rather than in academics or drama. He played many sports, but his real passion was baseball. In his first year and a half of high school he made top grades, but by mid-1983 he was failing subjects. By his own admission, Carlos was a truant 30 percent of the time, skipping school to cruise around Westwood, the UCLA college town in western Los Angeles, in the BMW his parents gave him for his sixteenth birthday. Shortly after getting the car, Carlos was arrested when police found him passed out over the steering wheel with a small knife strapped to his ankle.

At age seventeen and in his junior year of high school, Carlos auditioned for a part in *Grizzly II: The Predator,* but he had to wait a year to find out he was selected to costar in the feature film. In his senior year, with a cumulative average of 1.35 and ranked 778 in a class of 793, Carlos Estévez ended his high school career without earning a diploma. On the last day of class he threatened his English teacher when she refused to allow him to take the final exam without a pass to the classroom. He knew that if he did not take the exam he would not get the C he needed to graduate and would be unable to go to the University of Kansas on the baseball scholarship he had won. He reacted violently to the teacher's demand, threw a desk and a trash can, and stomped out of school. He became ineligible for the baseball scholarship and had no alternate plans for his life.

Less than three months after withdrawing from Santa Monica High School, Carlos went off to Eastern Europe on the three-week shoot of *Grizzly II: The Predator,* in which he plays a camper who gets mauled by a bear. At this point he officially took the name Charlie Sheen. He then portrayed a young fighter killed by the Russians in the 1984 war film *Red Dawn.* The film was panned by critics but was a hit at the box office. By the time *Red Dawn* was released in the summer of 1984, Charlie had appeared in his television feature debut, the CBS drama *Silence of the Heart,* which costarred Chad Lowe.

In 1985, Sheen played in the television movie *Out of Darkness,* alongside his father in a walk-on role. Sheen then embarked on another feature film *Lucas,* released in 1986, in which he portrays Cappie Roew, a high school football hero who befriends the nerdy Lucas and then steals his girlfriend. This teen film gave Sheen his first opportunity to combine sports and acting. He then performed a one-scene cameo in a major hit of the summer of 1986, *Ferris Bueller's Day Off.* In 1986 Charlie made a cameo appearance in *Wisdom,* the film written and directed by his brother Emilio Estévez.

That year Sheen went on to bigger and better films just two weeks after wrapping up filming on *The Wraith.* He left for the Philippines to play in Oliver Stone's 1986 Vietnam War epic *Platoon.* Sheen was cast as Chris Taylor, a nineteen-year-old college dropout who volunteers for service and joins the Twenty-fifth Infantry Regiment near the Cambodian border. As the narrator, Sheen delivers the anguished inner dialogue of *Platoon* just as his father did for the Vietnam saga *Apocalypse Now* seven years earlier. *Platoon* made Charlie a star, but the road to fame was fraught with danger. All the actors who starred in *Platoon* were put through a two-week intensive boot camp under the command of a marine captain, hired to transform the actors into the soldiers they would portray in the film. The military training was so rigorous that many of the actors came close to losing their lives. In the year that it was released, *Platoon* grossed over $130 million at the box office. It won four Academy Awards, making Sheen one of the leading actors of his generation.

Sheen's next feature film was the 1987 film *Three for the Road,* a youth-oriented romantic comedy based on Eliot Asinof's 1963 bestseller. In the film Sheen portrays an ambitious senatorial aide who is assigned the task of driving the senator's unruly daughter to a reform school and encounters mishaps en route. *Three for the Road* received terrible reviews, but this did not bother Sheen, who told *US* magazine in a June 1993 article: "Where film actors have the advantage is they can bomb three or four movies and then come back with a hit and they're good for a couple more bombs and then a hit, which has been my track record. Thank God, right? I'm very lucky that way."

In his next film project, the 1987 low-key thriller *No Man's Land,* Sheen played Ted Varrick, the leader of a multi-million-dollar auto-theft ring. During filming, Charlie was injured when explosives were ignited, sending debris into the air. Martin Sheen, who happened to be on the set, refused to wait for an ambulance and rushed Charlie to the hospital, where a wound on his chin was stitched up. Upon finishing *No Man's Land*, Charlie came back with a hit in the 1987 motion picture *Wall Street*, another Oliver Stone film.

After wrapping up *Wall Street*, Charlie Sheen debuted as a director with an independent short film, *RPG II*, a sequel to his first 16 mm film *RPG*. He then had the opportunity to combine his two passions, baseball and acting, in the 1988 film *Eight Men Out*. The film recounts the saddest chapter in the annals of professional American sports, the Black Sox Scandal of 1919, in which the Chicago White Sox conspired with professional gamblers to throw the 1919 World Series. After filming *Eight Men Out*, Sheen did not follow his fathers' advice to perform in Shakespeare's *King Henry IV, Part I* in New York with producer Joseph Papp, opting instead to star in the adventure movie *Johnny Utah*, released in 1988. In 1989 he was cast in another baseball movie, the low-brow comedy *Major League*. The film was a box-office hit, earning $50 million in the United States.

Sheen appeared in four films released in 1990: *Men at Work, Cadence, Navy Seals,* and *The Rookie*. In *Men at Work,* he and his brother Emilio Estévez, who also directed, play garbage collectors. Sheen portrays Lt. Dale Hawkins in *Navy Seals*, an action-packed film about a clandestine special force that performs daring rescue missions. *The Rookie* pairs Charlie Sheen as a rookie cop and Clint Eastwood as a savvy veteran. In August 1990, in the aftermath of this marathon filming, Sheen was admitted to a drug- and alcohol-rehabilitation center where he underwent thirty-two days of intensive drug and alcohol treatment. Martin Sheen, who also suffered from alcoholism, was the driving force behind Charlie's decision to enter rehab. The crisis brought the family closer together, and upon Charlie's release, he and brother Ramón played side by side in *Cadence*, Martin Sheen's directorial debut.

In 1991, Sheen starred in *Hot Shots!*, a spoof on the movie *Top Gun* about a misfit band of navy pilots being trained for a special mission. In this zany comedy, Sheen plays Topper Harley, a maverick jet pilot who is haunted by the disgraceful actions of his father. *Hot Shots!* was an enormous hit, grossing over $68 million at the box office. The year 1992 saw Sheen portray a Justice Department official who goes undercover in an outlaw motor-cycle gang in *Fixing the Shadow*. *Hot Shots!* spawned a sequel in

1993 entitled *Hot Shots! Part Deux,* in which Charlie Sheen plays an ace navy pilot on a mission to rescue hostages in the Middle East. In 1994, Sheen was one of four principals in Hollywood's latest version of *The Three Musketeers.* Charlie Sheen then starred in the 1994 sequel to *Major League,* entitled *Major League II,* which chronicles the further adventures of the fumbling baseball team. In the 1994 film *The Chase,* Sheen portrays a fugitive who heads for the Mexican border with an heiress, played by Kristy Swanson, in tow.

In addition to acting, Charlie Sheen chases baseballs, but not in the outfield. He is the proud owner of a huge collection of baseball memorabilia, which includes Babe Ruth's hat and the ball Mookie Wilson of the Mets hit through the legs of Boston Red Sox player Bill Buckner in Game Six of the 1986 World Series. Sheen paid $93,500 for the coveted baseball, the most ever invested in the round horsehide. Charlie Sheen is such a fan of the game that he modeled fashions with a baseball theme for the August 1988 issue of *Playboy.*

88

Julia Alvarez

1950–

Julia Alvarez was born on March 27, 1950, in New York City where she lived for the first three weeks of her life. She spent her early years in the Dominican Republic in an American-oriented family. For many generations, the Alvarez family had pursued its ambitions in the United States. Julia's maternal grandfather had been a cultural attaché to the United Nations, and her grandmother accompanied him on his frequent trips to New York. Julia's maternal uncles and aunts were sent to American boarding schools, and her uncles then went on to Ivy League universities.

In his university days Julia's father had been a member of the student underground. When news of his involvement with anti-government forces was leaked, he had no other choice but to flee to Canada, where he lived for nine years and worked as a doctor. In the United States he met Julia's mother, a student from the Dominican Republic, who was enrolled at an American university. The couple married and settled in New York.

Julia's mother soon became homesick for the Dominican Republic and persuaded her husband to return to the island. Her mother's influential family obtained a pardon for her father, and three weeks after Julia's birth, the family's first immigration to the United States ended, and they returned home. When she was a small child, Julia lived with her parents in an extended family of aunts, uncles, and cousins on her maternal grandparents' property. Her mother's side of the family had managed to preserve its wealth by supporting the people in power. However, her father's once affluent family became destitute after embracing the wrong side in the scramble for power in the Dominican Republic in 1930, which created tension and lopsided relationships within the communal household. Julia's maternal grandmother made matters worse by constantly reminding her daughter that she married a poor man.

Julia and her sisters lived together with cousins under the supervision of their mother, various aunts, and the family's maids. Julia enjoyed a privileged position in the family for having been born in America. In an article in the winter 1987 issue of *American Scholar* she writes of the advantages of her American birth certificate: "That technicality of birth, however, would not have amounted to anything but paper citizenship if it hadn't been backed up by a sense of honor and privilege the certificate conferred upon me." Julia's cousins were not allowed to forget for a minute that she had American citizenship. In the article Alvarez describes the attention her cousin gave to her birth: "My cousins would often ask me what I remembered about living in that magic land. I'd claim to recall a great many things from these first three weeks. Only once did my memory fail me, when I said that snow came in several colors."

In the Dominican Republic family members tried to re-create their U.S. experiences by subscribing to American magazines and mail-order catalogs, purchasing American cars and appliances, preparing typical American fare for the children, and providing them with an American education. Julia was sent to the Carol Morgan School, where each day commenced with the recitation of the Pledge of Allegiance to the American flag. At the school Julia befriended an American girl and learned English, which the adults in the household spoke when they did not want the children or servants to understand. Julia's aunts and uncles kept in touch regularly with classmates, alumni associations, and honorary societies in the United States, and during spring, summer, and Christmas vacations, the house was crowded with visiting American friends and their families.

The family's ties to the United States and the respect this engendered in Dominican society may have provided protection during the violent regime of dictator Rafael Leonidas Trujillo, which began in 1930. Trujillo was hesitant for political reasons to engage in a struggle with the well-connected family and jeopardize American support for his regime. He knew that the Americans would be immediately alerted if he tampered with the family, since Julia's grandfather rented several buildings next door to the family property to the American embassy. If Trujillo caused trouble, the family could cross over to safety in minutes. Furthermore, the American consul, an undercover CIA agent, was a Yale classmate of Julia's uncle and was treated like a member of the family during the frequent visits he paid to the Alvarez home. Thus, during the purges that Trujillo ordered, Julia's father was not rounded up.

For ten years after leaving America, Julia's father quietly practiced medicine in the Dominican Republic. As Trujillo's policies grew more threatening to the stability of the Caribbean and Latin America at the end of the 1950s, the United States decided to bring pressure against the regime. The American consul invited Julia's father to join forces with professionals and members of prominent families secretly planning to overthrow the government. Julia's father agreed to joined the American-backed forces struggling to oust Trujillo. Ultimately, it became too dangerous for the family to remain in the Dominican Republic, so the consul came up with a scheme that would enable Julia's father to travel to the United States as a member of an international heart-surgery team. Conditions rapidly worsened in the Dominican Republic as Trujillo's actions became increasingly irrational and brutal. The police planned to capture Julia's father in 1960, but an American agent known as Tio Vic warned him of impending danger and flew the family out of the country when Julia was ten years old.

Julia settled with her parents and siblings in a tiny apartment in Queens, New York. She had longed for the moment of arrival in the United States for most of her childhood, so she took delight in setting foot on American soil. However, she suffered bouts of homesickness and pined for her family's spacious home in the Dominican Republic, her cousins, and the respect the family name engendered. In trying to adjust to a new culture she became introverted, immersing herself in books and writing. She also held fast to the advice her father gave her when the family arrived in America, which she quoted in "Hold the Mayonnaise," an essay in the Hers column of the January 12, 1992, issue of the *New York Times*: "Just do your work and put in your heart and they will accept you!" This assimilationist approach to immigration, Julia Alvarez notes, is a far cry from the dictates of multiculturalism that Americans now embrace by which cultural differences are accentuated and celebrated rather than being blurred and forgotten.

Alvarez pursued higher education, earning an undergraduate and a graduate degree in literature and writing. Later, she took an academic post as an English professor at Middlebury College in Vermont. In the 1980s she won grants for her writing from the National Endowment for the Arts and the Ingram Merrill Foundation as well as a P.E.N. Oakland/Josephine Miles Award for excellence in multicultural literature. She has published several poetry collections, among them *Homecoming*, which was released in 1984, and in 1986 she won the Coordinating Council of Literary Magazines/General Electric Foundation Prize for her short story "An American Surprise."

In 1991, Alvarez published *How the García Girls Lost Their Accents*, comprised of fifteen interwoven stories chronicling in reverse the lives of the García sisters and their parents who are forced to flee the Dominican Republic for America. The narrative echoes Alvarez's own childhood experiences of immigration and the complexities of acculturation. The García family of the novel is endowed with a noble Spanish ancestry dating back to the conquistadors, and in their homeland the family enjoys wealth and influence. The Garcías flee the police state of the Dominican Republic when Dr. García gets involved in a failed plot to overthrow Trujillo. Once in New York, the García girls are fiercely determined to assimilate into the mainstream despite a lack of advice from their parents on how to navigate in the New World.

How the García Girls Lost Their Accents spans three decades, with the first chapter beginning in 1988 and the last stretching back as early as 1956 as the characters gradually disassemble their lives and personalities. Thus, the novel is in many ways a modern-day version in reverse of those ancient, and not so ancient, tales of the struggle from naïveté to knowledge, from persecution to tolerance, from darkness to light. *How the García Girls Lost Their Accents* affirms our human capacity for movement, advancement, and renewal rather than their antitheses, stagnation, decline, and disintegration.

As a work of literary merit and one of relatively few novels to address the experiences of Latino immigrants in the United States, *How the García Girls Lost Their Accents* received considerable attention from critics and the reading public. In her review of the novel in the October 6, 1991, issue of the *New York Times Book Review,* the critic Donna Rifkind applauds Julia Alvarez: "She has, to her great credit, beautifully captured the threshold experience of the new immigrant, where the past is not yet a memory and the future remains an anxious dream."

89

Celia Cruz
1929(?)–

Celia Cruz will not divulge the year of her birth, and biographers have merely estimated that she was born in 1929. It is known, however, that she was born on October 21 in Havana, Cuba, the second oldest of four children of Catalina (Alfonso) Cruz and Simón Cruz, a railroad stoker. Celia grew up in an extended family of fourteen children, including nieces, nephews, and cousins, in the Santo Suarez barrio of Havana. Her gift for song became apparent in childhood when she enjoyed the task of singing lullabies to the younger children at bedtime. Music always captured her imagination, and she often listened to the radio and

431

went to ballrooms with her aunt. She was a good student; she graduated from the República de Mexico public school in Havana and then from the Escuela Normal para Maestros. Instead of pursuing a career as a musician, however, Celia intended to enter the teaching profession. Her father encouraged her aspirations because he wanted his daughter to belong to a respected profession.

With her superb rendition in bolero tempo of the tango "Nostalgia," Celia won a talent show in 1947 called "La Hora de Te," which aired on the García Serra radio network. In addition to winning a cake, Celia received a lot of fanfare. Shortly after, she appeared in amateur shows and was soon a paid entertainer. Her first jobs included singing on Radio Progreso Cubana for one week and on Radio Unión for some months. Her specialty in those days was *pregón*, a native Cuban genre derived from the chants of street hawkers. Initially, she took singing jobs so she could purchase groceries and school books, but then a teacher encouraged her to forget pedagogy and pursue a singing career. Cruz took the teacher's advice to heart and studied voice and theory for the next three years at the Conservatory of Music in Havana. She managed to persuade her father that music was a respectable calling and that she would not bring shame to the family.

Cruz went on to sing with the female dancing troupe Las Mulatas de Fuego, entertaining audiences while the dancers changed costumes. She also performed with the orchestra Gloria Matancera, and in 1949 a radio station hired her to sing Yoruba songs. Cruz's major opportunity came in 1950 when she was selected to replace Myrta Silva, the lead singer of La Sonora Matancera, the most popular orchestra in Cuba. Cruz joined La Sonora Matancera in its weekly program on Radio Progreso. At first, Silva fans were discontented at the replacement; then they were in awe of Cruz. Riding a wave of popularity in early 1951, Cruz began to release La Sonora Matancera recordings. Cruz and La Sonora Matancera became headliners at Havana's elegant Tropicana nightclub.

In the 1950s they toured Central and South America and the United States and performed for television and film and on radio. The orchestra made appearances in five motion pictures filmed in Mexico: *Una gallega en Habana, Olé Cuba, Rincón criolo, Piel canela,* and *Amorcito corazón.* For fifteen years, known as her "golden era," Cruz sang with La Sonora Matancera. The musicians' frequent tours and the fame they enjoyed would provide them with a trump card when Fidel Castro came to power after the 1959 revolution. They escaped Cuba in July 1960 by pretending to go on another tour abroad; instead, they performed in Mexico for a year and a half and then came to the Unites States. Fidel Castro was irate over Cruz's defection and forbade the singer from returning to Cuba, even when her mother fell ill and her father passed away. She was forced to reminisce about her beloved homeland in song.

On July 14, 1962, Cruz wed Pedro Knight, the first trumpeter of La Sonora Matancera, whom she had known for over fourteen years. Knight has been her manager and musical director ever since and has influenced her career decisions and given her enormous support. In 1965, Cruz signed with Seeco Records and in just one year cut twenty albums—comprising a retrospective of her fifteen years with La Sonora Matancera. Among these many albums are *Con amor, La reina del ritmo Cubano, Gran exitos de Celia Cruz, La incomparable Celia, México que grande eres, Sabor y ritmo de pueblos, La tierra,* and her bestselling Seeco album, *Canciónes premiadas.* In 1966, she signed with Tico Records and over the next seven years cut thirteen albums. Cruz recorded eight of the Tico albums with Tito Puente, the "King of Latin Swing."

Despite her prolific production, Cruz did not sell many records in this period. She was new on the American music scene, young Latinos were captivated by rock and roll stars, and the U.S. recording industry was not geared toward promoting Afro-Caribbean musicians and their new sound. To survive in such difficult times, Cruz took the stage across the United States and South America, sometimes giving as many as six performances a day. Her popularity began to rise in 1973 when she was selected to sing the part of Gracia Divina in Larry Harlow's Latin opera *Hommy* at Carnegie Hall. Her exquisite voice and electrifying stage presence enchanted the audience, which was just warming up to salsa, those Afro-Cuban rhythms with plenty of brass and percussion. Young Latinos, enthralled by her fast-paced scatting, began to notice her, and older fans were delighted to hear the rhythms of their Cuban youth. All were amazed by her flamboyant costumes of bright fabrics adorned with lace, feathers, or sequins.

Cruz achieved stardom a year later when her contract with Tico ran out and she teamed up with Johnny Pacheco, the rumba bandleader and flutist of the charanga style. Together they revised Cruz's La Sonora Matancera songs for *Celia and Johnny,* which was released in 1974 for Vaya Records. Latinos across America raved about the album, and it went gold. Cruz collaborated on her next successful albums, *Tremendo caché* and *Recordando el ayer,* with Johnny Pacheco, Justo Betancourt, and Papo Lucca. Celia Cruz received a Grammy Award in 1974 for an album she recorded that year with conga player Ray Barretto. During the 1970s, Cruz performed in concert with Johnny Pacheco in the United States and with Tito Puente and other members of the Fania All-Stars throughout Africa and France. Her popularity soared as she brought audiences to their feet with her vibrant sound. In 1977 and 1979, New York's *Daily News* voted Celia Cruz the country's best female vocalist, as did *Billboard* in 1978.

In 1982, Cruz teamed up once again with La Sonora Matancera. They released new songs combining percussion solos and Matancero rhythms with contemporary salsa on their album *Feliz encuentro.* Later that year, Cruz took the stage in a tribute concert before twenty thousand people in Madison Square Garden and television viewers throughout the world to perform with musicians who had contributed to her career, such as La Sonora Matancera, Tito Puente, Cheo Feliciano, Johnny Pacheco, Pete Rodriguez, and Willi Colón.

In 1985, Cruz performed live with various groups and sang songs derived from ancient Yoruba religious chants in homage to West African deities. In 1986 the National Ethnic Coalition of organizations bestowed on Cruz the Ellis Island Medal of Honor, also known as the Mayor's Liberty Award. The year 1987 saw the release of her fifty-seventh album, *The Winners,* a collaborative effort with Willie Colón. That year, she also captured a fourth Grammy nomination, a New York Music Award for Best Latin Artist, and an Obie Award. A 1988 tribute to Frank Grillo, a musician who had played with Cruz for years and was instrumental in the development of Afro-Cuban jazz, was one of the singer's most memorable performances. On October 21, 1989, she performed in another memorable concert with the Cuban jazz star Mario Bauzo, along with Tito Puente, Chico O'Farill, Marco Rizo, Max Roach, and Henry Threadgill.

In 1990, Cruz won a Grammy for Best Tropical Performance in the Latin category for *Ritmo en el corazón,* an album she recorded with Ray Barretto. She portrayed Harlem nightclub owner Evalina Montoya in the 1992 film *The Mambo Kings,* which helped her win a following with non-Latin audiences. In late 1993 she performed with Puente and others in the concert "Marlboro Music's Combinación Perfecta," a salsa show at Madison Square Garden. By 1994, Celia Cruz, with her inexhaustible energy, had recorded over seventy albums. More than twenty of them have achieved gold.

90

Gigi Fernández

1964–

Gigi Fernández was born Beatriz Fernández in San Juan, Puerto Rico, on February 22, 1964. Her father is one of Puerto Rico's most prominent physicians, which afforded Gigi a privileged childhood. On her eighth birthday, Gigi's parents provided her with tennis lessons. She found that tennis came quite naturally to her and that she didn't have to practice long hours to develop her skills. She soon began to compete on the junior circuit in Puerto Rico and walked away with many victories. However, she never dreamed she would make a career of tennis, since no woman in Puerto Rico had ever made a living playing a sport. She imagined that she would eventually marry and have children, the fate of most women on the island. However, she kept winning tennis matches.

In 1981, at seventeen, Fernández won the Puerto Rico International Junior Tennis Championships girls' singles and doubles and the Jean Naté Championships. That same year, the Puerto Rico Tennis Association selected her "Amateur Athlete of the Year." Soon after, she was awarded a tennis scholarship by Clemson University in South Carolina, where she began to work hard on her game, playing every day. Her skills improved rapidly at Clemson as she faced tougher competition on the court. During her freshman year Fernández made it to the finals of the NCAA singles championship—the Wimbledon of college tennis—but lost a close match to Beth Herr, a more experienced player. At the 1984 Olympics, Fernández represented Puerto Rico when tennis was still an exhibition sport. In 1985 she turned professional and that year was recognized by *Tennis* magazine as a "player to watch" for attaining the ranking of twenty-third in the world in singles.

As it turned out, Fernández would soon emerge as a formidable doubles, rather than singles, player. In fact, the highest ranking she has achieved in singles is seventeenth, in 1991, after a victory in Albuquerque, a semifinal finish in Eastbourne, and a quarterfinal finish at the U.S. Open. But in doubles Fernández has either ranked number one or hovered near that figure. Since joining the professional tour, she has captured six Grand Slam women's doubles titles. Many tennis experts observe that her serve and volley game make her better suited for doubles. Her record attests to the validity of that claim.

Fernández credits Martina Navratilova for giving her focus as a professional tennis player early on in her career. When Fernández was still an unknown on the tennis circuit, Martina sent her a note praising her play and insisting that she had the potential to be one of the best players in tennis. Fernández took Navratilova's encouragement seriously; she improved her diet to reduce her weight from 170 pounds to 150 pounds and renewed her commitment to tennis. She would play many doubles matches with Navratilova as her partner and learn important lessons in doubles strategy from the legendary player.

The year 1990 was a spectacular one on the court for Fernández. Among her many victories, she and doubles partner Zina Garrison emerged victorious in an exciting match against a Soviet team to win the Federation Cup for the United States. That year, Fernández and Martina Navratilova also captured the doubles title at the U.S. Open when they defeated Jana Novotna and Helena Sukova, 6–2, 6–4, before the New York tennis establishment. The duo never let up as they drove the Czech team to the baseline with rapid-fire volleys and low-flying passing shots. In that match neither Fernández nor Navratilova had their serve broken, and their only error came when Fernández swung her racket wildly on the first match point, leading Navratilova to joke: "Her strings disappeared." With that crucial victory at the U.S. Open, Fernández and Navratilova became the second women's team in tennis history to win all the major championships in doubles in a calendar year. Navratilova and Pam Shriver earned this distinction first in 1984.

The following year, Fernández and her doubles partner, Jana Novotna, made it to the finals at the Australian Open, but their hopes for a title faded when they lost, 7–6, 6–1, to Mary Joe Fernández and Patty Fenwick. In August 1991, Fernández found a doubles partner in Natalia Zvereva, a player from Minsk, Belarus, known for her versatile serve. The pair met with little success and after two tournaments split up. Both were dissatisfied with other doubles partners, so they teamed up again in March 1992. This time, they astonished the tennis world with their three consecutive doubles victories at the French Open, Wimbledon, and the U.S. Open in 1992. Before playing in the U.S. Open that year, Fernández went to Spain to represent the United States at the Olympics. Both the U.S. Olympic tennis team and the Puerto Rican team had vied for her, but the United States won its bid.

Gigi teamed up with Mary Joe Fernández, the player who took home the bronze in women's singles from Barcelona. The team easily advanced to the final at the Olympics where they faced Arantxa Sanchez Vicario and Conchita Martinez on center court. They defeated the Spaniards, 7–5, 2–6, 6–2, to capture the doubles title. With that victory Fernández became the first Puerto Rican to win a gold medal at the Olympics. After clinching the gold, she declared: "I'm very proud for Puerto Rico. I'm very proud for the U.S. I'm very proud for everybody." For Fernández, her victory at the Olympics was a career highlight. She told the *Los Angeles Times* on August 9, 1992: "I said the other day to ask me if this is bigger than Wimbledon. Well, I know now it is. You represent your country, you are playing before a king and queen. It is definitely more exciting than Wimbledon, and Wimbledon is pretty darn exciting."

After returning from Barcelona with the gold, Fernández resumed doubles play with Natalia Zvereva. They captured the doubles title at the U.S. Open in 1992, their third consecutive Grand Slam tournament, and went on to clinch the Australian

Open, the French Open, and Wimbledon in 1993, their fourth, fifth, and sixth straight Grand Slams and three of 1993's four Grand Slam events. They were in hot pursuit of the doubles Grand Slam of the year, but at the U.S. Open the top-seeded team went down in defeat in a semifinals match against Helena Sukova and Arantxa Sanchez Vicario. After the match Fernández declared: "I mean, we won six Grand Slams in a row. How lucky do you want to be?" Despite the loss at the U.S. Open, Fernández and Zvereva achieved the second-longest Grand Slam doubles streak in history.

In 1994, Fernández astonished the tennis world when she advanced to the semifinals in women's singles at Wimbledon, where she met Martina Navratilova, the nine-time Wimbledon singles champion who had her eye on a record tenth and final Wimbledon crown. Before traveling to England, Fernández endured nine first-round singles losses, which led her to consider going into retirement. She went into the Wimbledon semifinals match ranked ninety-ninth, the lowest ranking for a women's singles semifinalist in Grand Slam history. Fernández lost the match, 6–4, 7–6, 8–6, to Martina Navratilova. Despite the defeat, she and Navratilova gave spectators a fabulous grass-court tennis demonstration. After the match Fernández told the press: "Today was a great example of how to play grass-court tennis, everybody coming in at the first opportunity and at times both players at the net."

Fernández attributes her achievements as a doubles player to her strong serve, solid volleys, and "some of the quickest hands in the game." There are other ingredients to her success, as she told the *Los Angeles Times* on July 11, 1993: "It's a lot of technical things, but I think more important than anything is my personality. I communicate well and I'm easy to get along with on the court and I'm very supportive of my partners." For her accomplishments in women's professional tennis, Fernández is the recipient of dozens of awards and has the distinction of being registered in the Congressional Record as an American "Model of Excellence." She spends time off the tennis court, promoting Avia products, Yonex racquets, and Whitehall Laboratories. She also does fund-raising for the National Hispanic Scholarship Fund, Yo Si Puedo (Say No to Drugs), and the Puerto Rico Tennis Association. In addition, she founded the Gigi Fernández Invitational Cup, which has raised large sums for charities.

91

Ileana Ros-Lehtinen

1952–

Ileana Ros-Lehtinen was born on July 15, 1952, in Havana to Amanda Adato Ros and Enrique Emilio Ros. In 1960, a year after Castro assumed power, the family fled to the United States and settled in Miami. Almost immediately, her parents joined other recent refugees from Cuba who were secretly plotting to overthrow Castro's Communist regime. After anti-Castro forces with backing from the American government failed in their attempt to invade Cuba at the Bay of Pigs in 1961, the Ros family abandoned their hopes of returning to their homeland and embraced the American way of life.

In 1972, Ros-Lehtinen was awarded an A.A. degree from Miami–Dade County Community College, and in 1975 she earned a B.A. degree in English from Florida International University in Miami. Eleven years later she received an M.S. degree in educational leadership from Florida International University. Since then she has continued to work toward a doctorate in educational administration at the University of Miami. For ten years she was employed as a teacher and a principal at Eastern Academy, a school she founded, before entering the political arena. She inherited her love of politics from her father, who had devoted much of his energy toward the restoration of democracy in Cuba.

In her first elected office Ros-Lehtinen served as a representative in the Florida state legislature from 1982 to 1986. She was then elected state senator and served in that post from 1986 to 1989. During her tenure in the state legislature, Ileana met her future husband, Dexter Lehtinen, who at the time also served in that legislative body and later became the U. S. Attorney in Miami. They have two daughters. In her early years in the state legislature, Ros-Lehtinen focused on broad changes in public policy, but as time passed she began to concentrate on the concerns of individuals and businesses in her district.

With the death of Claude Pepper, the seat in Florida's Eighteenth Congressional District was left vacant. In July 1989, Ros-Lehtinen resigned her state senate seat to campaign in the special election to fill the vacancy in the House. From the moment she announced her candidacy she was a early favorite on the Republican side, and it looked as if she would have to battle Miami city commissioner Rosario Kennedy, a Democrat. However, Gerald F. Richman, an attorney and a former president of the Florida Bar Association, emerged from the primary as her number one opponent. The campaign soon turned into a fierce contest fought almost entirely over ethnicity, pitting the district's Anglo, Jewish, and black voters against the Cuban Americans. By the end of the campaign it had become one of the most ethnically divided congressional races in Florida's history.

Tensions in the bitter campaign mounted when Republican party chairman Lee Atwater announced that a Cuban American was the best choice to fill the vacant seat, since the Eighteenth Congressional District was 50 percent Latino. *Time* magazine quoted Gerald F. Richman as having dismissed Atwater's claim with the declaration "This is an American seat." Before the controversy was over, Richman had accused Ros-Lehtinen of bigotry because the Republicans had said the seat should go to a Cuban American and Ros-Lehtinen had attacked Richman for being a racist with anti-Hispanic sentiments. Broadcasters on Spanish-language radio stations in the Miami area rushed to support Ros-Lehtinen, warning listeners that voting for Gerald Richman was the same as voting for Fidel Castro. President George Bush's son, Jeb Bush, who speaks fluent Spanish and whose wife is of Mexican descent, helped bolster Ros-Lehtinen's campaign. President Bush gave the candidate his personal endorsement and made a special trip to Miami to deliver a speech on her behalf.

On August 29, 1989, Ros-Lehtinen emerged victorious, capturing 95 percent of the vote of Cuban Americans, who turned out in large numbers in Little Havana. She won 53 percent of the total vote. Many viewed her victory as not so much one of Republican ideology as of Republican strategy. By winning the special election, Ros-Lehtinen became the first Cuban American and the first Latina elected to the House and the first Republican and the first woman to be elected from Florida's Eighteenth Congressional District. Claude Pepper had held the office for twenty-six years, since the seat was first established in 1962. Cuban Americans across America, Republican or not, were euphoric over Ros-Lehtinen's victory. Even members of the opposition such as José Cruz, president of the Cuban-American Coalition, an organization seeking to improve communications with Cuba, rejoiced in her historic victory.

At Ros-Lehtinen's victory celebration, the queen of salsa, Celia Cruz, shouted: "The Cubans won!" Cuba was definitely on Ros-Lehtinen's mind, for during her victory speech she suddenly switched from English into Spanish, doing so "for our brothers listening in Cuba so they can see what a democracy is like." Despite the euphoria of the moment, Ros-Lehtinen's success left deep scars in Florida's Eighteenth District. In her victory speech, the new congresswoman maintained that she would work to heal the wounds caused by the campaign: "But now it's time for healing. I know that there are a lot of people out there who feel alienated." With her family at her side, Ros-Lehtinen was sworn in to the U.S. Congress on September 6, 1989. In 1990, a year after coming to power, her seat came up for election, and she captured 60 percent of the vote and a clear mandate to stay in the political arena. This was reinforced in 1992 when she achieved victory over Magda Montiel Davis, a Cuban-born Democratic contender for the House seat.

In the House, Ros-Lehtinen has served on the Foreign Affairs Committee and its Subcommittee on Human Rights and International Organizations as well as its Subcommittee on Employment and Housing. Among her many views on the issues, Ros-Lehtinen is a staunch opponent of abortion, except in the event that a woman's life is in danger, is against the English Only movement, and favors a seven-day waiting period for the purchase of guns. One of her goals as congresswoman in Washington has been to be a voice for all of her constituents, and she has attempted to listen closely to citizens from her district by holding town meetings and opening the doors to her district office. She is particularly responsive to the concerns of young people, women, and minorities, to whom she believes the Republican party should reach out if it is to be a strong source of change in America.

In her tenure in the House, Ros-Lehtinen has spoken out about injustices committed beyond America's borders, particularly in Latin America and the Caribbean. In September 1993, in an editorial in the *Christian Science Monitor,* she cited the flagrant abuses by some officials in Nicaragua, which she deemed as cause for the United States to stop sending financial aid to that country. Faithful to her Cuban-American roots, Ros-Lehtinen condemns Fidel Castro's regime. Over the years, the congresswoman has argued against lifting the U.S. embargo against Cuba, contending that such an action would only strengthen Castro's hold on the island. In 1991 she urged international leaders to stop assisting Cuba in an effort to rid the country of Communist rule. That year, she also urged that countries boycott the Pan American Games held in Cuba each August, arguing that Castro holds the event in order to obtain hard currency to alleviate the island's economic difficulties.

In further support of the Cuban people, Ileana Ros-Lehtinen asserted in an editorial in the October 14, 1993, issue of *USA Today* that the United States should show its solidarity with Cubans by allowing TV Martí to continue beaming its message of freedom to the island. She also published an editorial in the February 11, 1994, issue of *USA Today* in which she states that the circumstances leading to the Cuban Adjustment Act of 1966 still exist today and therefore the United States must continue to grant Cuban refugees political asylum. She writes: "After thirty-four years in power, the Castro regime continues to deny the Cuban people their rights, while running the world's most ruthless police state as documented by the U.N. Human Rights Commission."

Ileana Ros-Lehtinen values the contributions Latinos have made to American society. She told *Hispanic* magazine in September 1990: "Hispanic culture has had a dramatic positive impact upon America. The Hispanic spirit and flavor add to the variety in American society. With the number of Hispanics growing in the U.S., it is important to draw on the strengths of our heritage so that we may progress into a brighter future." She appreciates in particular the achievements of Latinas, and in *Vista* she offers women a strategy for the future: "We Hispanic women must re-energize and refocus our efforts to realize the vast potential that lies within our grasp."

92

Rosie Pérez

1970(?)–

One of eleven children, Rosie Pérez was born Rosa Mary Pérez in Brooklyn, New York, to Lydia Pérez, who had been a singer in Puerto Rico, and Ismael Serrano, who was in the merchant marine. She will not divulge her age except to say (in 1993) that she is "under twenty-five." Lydia Pérez loved the rhythms of Puerto Rico, and the family's house in Brooklyn was always filled with music. In her childhood, Rosie watched her parents dance salsa on weekends and holidays, and by age thirteen she was hitting the dance floors in Manhattan clubs. The family lived a humble but happy existence, as Rosie told *Vogue* magazine in March 1993: "I didn't know I had secondhand clothes, I just thought my mother had bad taste." Until the sixth grade she called herself "Wosie" and had to take remedial classes to correct her speech impediment. While Pérez prefers to avoid talk of the past, she once confessed at a panel discussion of Forest Whitaker's HBO feature *Strapped* that she had lived in group homes because of her involvement with drugs and that an aunt had visited her every day with words of support and love, enabling her to start anew. Pérez was then raised by her aunt in the Bushwick section of Brooklyn, also known as "Little Puerto Rico."

Rosie was a good student, excelling in science. She never dreamed of building a career as a performer. In fact, as a child she went to the theater on only one occasion when her class was taken to see *The Wiz*. After graduating from high school, she moved to Los Angeles to attend UCLA, where she majored in biochemistry and danced at her favorite nightspots. She told the *Boston Globe* in an interview: "I left Brooklyn to go to college. I just wanted something different. I knew if I was to stay on my block—well, you become part of your environment. So I went as far as I possibly could, to L.A. I never learned dancing formally, I just danced a lot at clubs. Then I got a dance partner, Arthur Rainer, and we began choreographing." While doing assorted steps at the Funky Reggae cabaret, Rosie got her first show business opportunity. She was invited to dance on the syndicated television show *Soul Train*.

Pérez did a few shows before calling it quits, but while she was at *Soul Train*, she made the acquaintance of Louis Silas Jr., senior vice president of black music at MCA Records, who invited her to be part of a recording group. Pérez turned down the offer but kept in touch with Silas, who later asked her if she would choreograph one of his artists. At first, she refused the offer, but when she heard the music of the artist, who turned out to be Bobby Brown, she went ahead with the project. After seeing Brown on *Soul Train*, a new Motown recording group, the Boys, approached Pérez about choreographing their show. After those successes, work never stopped and Pérez and her partners, Heart & Soul, were busy creating stage and video choreographs for such artists as Diana Ross, Al B. Sure, LL Cool J, Heavy & the Boyz, as well as for record labels such as Capitol, Motown, and Polygram.

While she was dancing one night at the Funky Reggae, director Spike Lee, who was celebrating his birthday at the club, spotted Rosie Pérez and introduced himself. When Lee's partner gave her a business card, Pérez interpreted the situation as yet another pickup attempt and didn't call the director for a month. Lee proved sincere and offered her a small role as his hyperactive girlfriend Tina in his 1989 film *Do the Right Thing*. Pérez accepted the offer, though she had never before considered acting. In her screen debut she dances across the opening credits to the beat of Public Enemy's "Fight the Power" and gives a powerful performance as Tina, a hot-tempered, unwed Puerto Rican mother. Much to her surprise, she was criticized by Latino groups for playing the part of a Puerto Rican stereotype, but she argued that she was "not portraying something that's not really out there."

While Pérez acknowledges that *Do the Right Thing* launched her Hollywood career, she also maintains that shooting the film had its bad moments, particularly when she had to do a nude scene and when degrading gossip circulated that she got the part by sleeping with Lee. After filming, she told her agent that she did not want to portray any more "Tinas." After shooting the Lee film, Pérez made television appearances in an episode of *21 Jump Street* and on the CBS series *WIOU* as well as in *Criminal Justice*, a 1990 HBO movie in which she was cast as a young Latina prostitute addicted to crack. In her next project, Pérez made a brief appearance as a boisterous Puerto Rican woman in Jim Jarmusch's widely praised 1992 film *Night on Earth*, composed of five vignettes chronicling brief encounters on a single night between cabdrivers and passengers in various large cities. She was ready to move on to more diverse roles in which, as she once said, "I'm not screaming at the top of my lungs."

In the aftermath of *Do the Right Thing*, directors advised Pérez to take classes to lose her Brooklyn accent and slow down her speech. She told the *Boston Globe* in February 7, 1993: "Managers, agents, everybody was telling me to go to speech classes. They were telling me I'd get more work if I stopped speaking *like that*." Everybody changed their tune about Pérez's speech patterns when the actress nearly stole the show from Woody Harrelson and Wesley Snipes in the 1992 basketball comedy *White Men Can't Jump*, which was originally intended to be strictly a male-bonding movie.

In *White Men Can't Jump*, Pérez landed the more diverse role she was waiting for and was cast in the part of Gloria Clemente, who, in the film's comic subplot, spends her days cramming her head with information to fulfill her ambition of competing on the quiz show *Jeopardy!* The part was originally written for a Caucasian woman with an Ivy League education. However, when Pérez auditioned for the part, she so impressed writer-director Ron

Shelton that he transformed the character into a former Brooklyn disco queen. Pérez gives a hilarious performance throughout the film, hitting a high note in the film's *Jeopardy!* scene when she trounces her bookworm opponents with her scholarly expertise in the category "Foods Beginning with Q."

In 1992, *People* magazine named Rosie Pérez one of the year's Ten Best Dressed for her flashy style. That year, she was hired to do the choreography for the Fly Girls, a dance ensemble that combines technical dancing, acrobatics, and hip-hop moves, on the Fox television network show *In Living Color*. Rosie Pérez earned an Emmy nomination for the dances she choreographed. In February 1993 she began production on a short-lived HBO series of specials she created, "Rosie Pérez Presents Society's Ride," showcasing rhythm and blues, rap, reggae, and classic soul. Pérez was cast in a semidramatic part as a waitress alongside Marisa Tomei and Christian Slater in the 1993 romantic tale *Untamed Heart*. Although the film received lukewarm reviews, the critics applauded her performance.

In her next project, the 1993 film *Fearless*, directed by Peter Weir, Pérez costarred with Jeff Bridges and Isabella Rossellini. She played a deeply religious young mother whose faith is shaken when her child dies in a plane crash. Many actresses vied for the part, but Pérez was selected over such "name" stars as Jodie Foster and Winona Ryder. The character was originally Italian American as in the novel, but Peter Weir rewrote the part for a Latina after casting Pérez. The role demanded enormous emotional depth, and a week before shooting, Pérez panicked. Weir got her to channel her emotions into the role, and she gave a stunning performance, winning some of the best reviews of her career. Pérez's success in *Fearless* was confirmed by an Oscar nomination for Best Supporting Actress in 1994. In 1993 she was cast in Andrew Bergman's romantic comedy *It Could Happen to You*, based loosely on the true story of a New Jersey policeman who won the lottery and shared his $142 million with a waitress in a diner. As in *White Men Can't Jump* and *Fearless*, her role was originally written for a white actress and subsequently revised.

Pérez is a nonstop workaholic personality who often disappears to make business calls on the set. She told *Newsweek* in 1992: "Show business is mostly about marketing. I learned that when I was a college student in L.A., dancing at the clubs. Four different record companies offered me contracts—*and I sing like shit*. All they knew was, she's got the packaging, she's got the look, and that was enough for them. I saw that, and I said to myself, 'Approach this like a business.'" In addition to setting up meetings with directors and auditioning for films, Pérez manages a female rhythm and blues group called 5 A.M., continues her work as a choreographer, and looks toward directing in the future. And whenever she is in New York City, she goes with friends and family to the hippest Manhattan clubs to dream up new moves.

93

Carlos Montoya

1903–1993

Carlos García Montoya was born in Madrid on December 13, 1903, to Juan García and Emilia Montoya, Spanish Gypsies. His four grandparents were Gypsies from the Lavapies neighborhood of Madrid, and all had extensive experience in flamenco. Juan García, who earned a living selling mules to the Spanish army, died when Carlos was just two years old. Emilia Montoya, an amateur flamenco guitarist known as La Tula, began to give her son his first flamenco lessons when he was eight. The boy then took flamenco guitar lessons from Pepe el Barbero, a local barber, who in a short time taught Carlos all that he knew.

Carlos's uncle, Ramón Montoya Salazar, an accomplished flamenco guitarist, is generally given credit in guitar histories as being the first to give full recitals of solo flamenco guitar music.

Ramón Montoya Salazar had little spare time to teach Carlos flamenco, so the boy was left to his own devices. Through his uncle and his mother, Carlos rubbed elbows with Spain's preeminent flamenco guitarists and dancers, and he learned by following their example rather than by formal training. By the time he was fourteen Carlos had become well versed in the conventions of flamenco and the repertory of themes on which the singers and dancers improvised, and he was able to lead *café cantantes,* to take part in *cuadros flamencos,* and to perform with the dancers and singers in cafes in the region. He spent most of his modest earnings on wine, which he presented to his fellow artists in hopes that they would teach him a new technique. For a short time he worked by day as a postal clerk and later in a courthouse, but he always spent his evenings playing the flamenco guitar. By the early 1920s, he had performed with Antonio de Bilbao, Juan el Estampio, La Macarrona, and La Camísona.

Montoya served in the Spanish army from 1924 to 1927. He was stationed in Morocco, which in those years was in a state of turmoil, and between maneuvers played his guitar for any audience that gathered. Having completed his military service, he returned in 1928 to the cafes of Madrid, where he again immersed himself in the study of flamenco. That year, Antonia Mercé, the renowned flamenco dancer, who was known professionally as La Argentina, heard one of Montoya's performances and invited him to tour with her troupe. He graciously accepted the invitation and accompanied the troupe for three years on their tour of engagements across Europe. He then worked with the dancer Vicente Escudero. In 1933 he joined the troupe of La Teresina and went on a highly acclaimed tour of the United States and the Far East. Montoya's artistry was particularly appreciated by the Japanese, and affiliates from the University of Tokyo even offered him a two-year teaching position. When he turned down the offer, they compromised and made a film of the great flamenco guitarist.

In 1938, Montoya was invited to join the troupe of the legendary dancer La Argentinita. He took the stage with her in performances across Latin America and the United States until her death in 1945.

In 1940, Montoya married Sallie MacLean, an American dancer with the professional name La Trianita. After their marriage, she served as her husband's manager and interpreter for the remainder of his career. They had two sons, Carlos Montoya Jr. and Allan MacLean Montoya. In 1940, Montoya also became an American citizen and had the honor of playing for President Harry S Truman on the very day that he was granted citizenship.

After La Argentinita's death, Montoya launched his solo career, a radical move, since flamenco was rooted in folk tradition and audiences expected the standard ensemble of Spanish dancers, singers, and the guitarist. At first Montoya met with audience resistance over the fact that the dancers, the main attraction, were missing. Nevertheless, Montoya was reassured when two hundred people showed up at one of his first solo flamenco guitar concerts in New York. In the 1950s and 1960s, Montoya built an enormous following through countless solo recitals and many recordings for RCA-Victor and ABC-Paramount Records. In those decades he spent a great deal of his time on the road performing before standing-room-only audiences in the United States as well as occasionally touring on the international circuit. Montoya established flamenco guitar music as a highlight of the concert season.

Montoya's extraordinary success can be attributed in large measure to his rapport with audiences. He was always precise about creating the right ambience in the theater. In preparation for each performance he requested a chair with a seat sixteen inches high and muted pink lighting. His musical technique was no less elaborate and precise. Montoya brought not only intensity and virtuosity to his art but also the uncanny ability to suggest with his guitar the sounds of tambourines, castanets, and drums, the snapping of fingers, and the clicking of dancers' heels, so that it seemed as if an entire ensemble were present. Montoya performed many of his own compositions, which included an interpretation of a Holy Week procession in Seville. He always delighted in noting that in keeping with the improvisatory nature of flamenco, he never played a selection the same way twice.

In 1966, Montoya realized one of his early ambitions, which was to compose a flamenco suite. While he had given thought to the project over the course of two decades, it was only in the early 1960s that he was able to devote his attention to the task. With

Julio Esteban, Montoya overcame the dilemma of writing a suite for both guitar and orchestra that did not in any way place restraints on the guitar. The final product, entitled *Suite Flamenca,* the first flamenco suite for full orchestra, consisted of four sections, with solo parts for the guitar taken from Montoya's own repertoire. With the premiere of *Suite Flamenca* in January 1966 by the St. Louis Orchestra, Montoya's dream of two decades was fulfilled. He considered the concerto his most enduring work and the performance the high point in his career.

Montoya was a prolific composer, but since he never learned to write music, he always enlisted others to notate and publish his compositions. On occasion, Montoya insisted that the published scores were merely guidelines for guitarists to follow and that improvisation is the distinctive feature of flamenco. He emerged as one of the early crossover artists, and recorded arrangements of "St. Louis Blues" and other jazz and popular songs.

The world lost one of the foremost flamenco artists when, on March 3, 1993, Carlos Montoya died of heart failure in Wainscott, Long Island, his home for many years.

Nydia Margarita Velázquez

1953–

One of nine children and a twin, Nydia Margarita Velázquez was born in Yabucoa, Puerto Rico, on March 23, 1953, to Benito Velázquez and Carmen Luisa (Serrano) Velázquez. Nydia grew up in the family's small house situated amidst the sugarcane fields on the banks of Río Limón. Benito Velázquez, who had only a third-grade education, cut sugarcane for a living and later worked as a butcher and owned a legal cockfighting business. Carmen Velázquez made *pasteles*, patties made of mashed root

454

vegetables stuffed with meat and wrapped in plantain leaves, and sold them to sugarcane cutters in the fields to supplement the family's modest income. Benito Velázquez was also a local leader, who was so passionate about politics that he founded a political party in Yabucoa. Conversations in the Velázquez household often concerned workers' rights and other topical issues. During her childhood, Nydia inherited her father's social activism, and vowed to emulate him. Nydia was a gifted child, and at five she begged her parents to allow her to start school. They gave into her demands, and Nydia then skipped second, fourth, and sixth grades and became the first family member to receive a high school education.

At sixteen, she entered the University of Puerto Rico in Rio Piedras and later graduated magna cum laude, with a B.A. degree in political science. Velázquez taught for a brief period of time in Puerto Rico and then, in 1974, was awarded a scholarship to pursue graduate studies at New York University. Her father did not want her to study so far away, but two of her professors intervened and convinced him otherwise. In 1976, Velázquez received her master's degree in political science and then took a position teaching the subject at the University of Puerto Rico. In 1981 she left her teaching post there after the conservative New Progressive party came to power on the island, and she was labeled a Communist. Velázquez sought refuge from harassment in New York City, where she taught for two years at Hunter College as an adjunct professor of Puerto Rican studies.

In 1983, Velázquez entered the political arena in New York City as a special assistant to former U.S. representative Edolphus Towns, a Democrat from Brooklyn. In that capacity, Velázquez dealt primarily with immigration issues and on one occasion testified before Congress on immigration legislation. In 1984 she became the first Latina to serve on the New York City Council. Her appointment to the council came after a seat was left vacant with the conviction of former councilman Luis Olmedo on charges of federal conspiracy and attempted extortion. In the next election, in 1986, Velázquez lost her council seat to a challenger and returned to her native island, where she was appointed by the Puerto Rican governor to head the Migration Division Office of the Department of Labor and Human Resources of Puerto Rico, later renamed the Department of Puerto Rican Community Affairs in the United States.

Velázquez remained at that post until 1989, when the governor of Puerto Rico named her to a cabinet-level position as secretary of the Department of Puerto Rican Community Affairs in the United States, which serves as a bridge between the U.S. government and the commonwealth. In that capacity, Velázquez ran the New York City headquarters and four regional offices and advised the Puerto Rican government on the island's public policy and its commitment to Puerto Ricans on the U.S. mainland. In 1989, Velázquez took decisive action when Hurricane Hugo ravaged Puerto Rico. She personally contacted the head of the Joint Chiefs of Staff, Gen. Colin Powell, and soon after, the island was promised federal assistance. As secretary, Velázquez also held successful voter-registration drives in the Northeast and Midwest that signed up 200,000 voters in Puerto Rican communities. In 1991 she launched the project *Unidos Contra El SIDA* (United Against AIDS) to help fight the spread of AIDS among Puerto Ricans.

In 1992 the Twelfth Congressional District in New York City, a heavily Democratic and Latino district comprised of poor and working-class neighborhoods in Queens, Manhattan, and Brooklyn, was created so that a Latino would be elected representative. It was one of nine districts formed to enhance the voting power of minorities under the Voting Rights Act. As a result of the formation of the district, former representative Stephen J. Solarz's Brooklyn district was dissolved. Solarz, a popular nine-term congressman and non-Latino, sought to represent the newly formed district. When Velázquez declared her candidacy, she found herself in a grueling battle with Solarz and four Latino candidates in the Democratic primary. Velázquez could not afford extensive campaign literature or television advertisements, so she launched a grassroots campaign and spoke directly with people by telephone and on the sidewalks of New York.

Velázquez garnered the support of New York City mayor David Dinkins, the Reverend Jesse Jackson, and the Latino union leader Dennis Rivera, among others. Despite these endorsements, she had to prove to the diverse groups of her district that she would represent all of them, not just the Puerto Ricans from the island. Velázquez emerged the victor of the September 15 primary, which virtually assured her of election. She returned to her hometown in Puerto Rico, accompanied by Mayor David

Dinkins and Dennis Rivera, where the people rolled out the red carpet and embraced their hero. Velázquez thanked the crowd for its support and dedicated her victory to her mother and all the women of Puerto Rico. Upon her return to the United States, Velázquez traveled to Washington to discuss committee appointments with House Speaker Thomas S. Foley and to strategize with Rep. Bill Richardson of New Mexico, a leader of the Hispanic Caucus.

In early October, Velázquez's candidacy came under scrutiny from two fronts when controversies erupted over her past. An anonymous source leaked a story to several press organizations about her attempted suicide and hospitalization in 1991. Rather than deny the charge, Velázquez called a news conference, and with friends and family at her side, she confessed that she had suffered in the past from serious depression stemming from her mother's illness and a brother's drug addiction and had indeed attempted suicide. She made the point that she had put the unhappy experience behind her and had gained new strength and stamina. She also expressed her dismay that confidential hospital records, which constitute privileged medical information, had been released by the press, in violation of state law, and requested that the Manhattan district attorney and the state attorney general investigate.

Velázquez faced another political challenge before the November election. Cong. Don Young of Alaska asked the General Accounting Office to investigate a political memo Velázquez had written in 1991 on stationery from the Department of Puerto Rican Community Affairs to Governor Rafael Hernández Colón. In the memo Velázquez proposed launching a pro-commonwealth campaign to dissuade mainland Puerto Ricans and the U.S. Congress from seeking independence or statehood for the island. The memo suggested that the resources of the nonpartisan office Velázquez headed would fuel the campaign. In her defense, Velázquez stated that the campaign never took place and that her only transgression was writing the memo on office stationery.

Despite these controversies, Velázquez's supporters in the Twelfth Congressional District did not abandon their candidate. In fact, they had more respect for her ability to surmount obstacles. In the November 1992 election, Velázquez, age thirty-nine, defeated all challengers, garnering over 75 percent of the vote to become the first Puerto Rican woman elected to the U.S.

House of Representatives. At her victory party, held on election night in Williamsburg, Brooklyn, she declared in Spanish to the people of her district: "For you, I'm going to fight to gain better jobs, better lives, and better opportunities."

As a member of Congress, Velázquez has concentrated her efforts on the economy, employment opportunities, child care, housing, and eliminating crime and drugs in her district. She has worked closely with other minority and progressive members of Congress to devise strategies to overcome poverty and despair in inner cities across America and in other parts of the world.

95

Gilbert Roland

1905–1994

Gilbert Roland was born Luis Antonio Dámaso de Alonso on December 11, 1905, in Ciudad Juárez, Mexico, one of six sons of Francisco Alonso and Consuelo Alonso, both of whom were from Spain. Luis's father, paternal grandfather, and a great grandfather were well-known matadors, and the boy's early life centered on bullfighting. In Ciudad Juárez, Francisco Alonso owned a bull ring, and when Luis had time off from school, he worked there selling cushions and helping the matadors. This way of life came to an end when Pancho Villa began chasing Spanish-born people out of Ciudad Juárez during the Mexican Revolution and the family was forced to flee across the Rio Grande to safety in El Paso, Texas. Luis was sent to the Sunset School in El Paso, where a

Mrs. Alona Bartlett taught him to read, write, and speak English. All his life he felt such fondness for Mrs. Bartlett that he carried her picture in his wallet.

In El Paso, Luis developed a passion for movies, and when his father returned to Spain for a tour of the bull rings there, Luis, age thirteen, left home and jumped a freight train to California with $2.60 in his pocket and a dream of becoming a movie star. For the next three years he worked as a stevedore unloading boats in Catalina, a lithographer, a laborer in a battery plant, and finally as an extra and bit player in films with such unknowns as Clark Gable and Gary Cooper. Film producer B. F. Schulberg thought young Luis had talent and gave him a part in the 1925 film *The Plastic Age* with Clara Bow, but the budding actor earned no special recognition. Schulberg told Luis to change his name to John Adams to set himself apart from all the Latinos in Hollywood at the time. Instead, Luis came up with Gilbert Roland, in honor of his two favorite movie stars, John Gilbert, the leading silent screen idol, and Ruth Roland, a serial heroine.

Roland was picked out of a mob scene to double for Ramón Novarro in the 1925 silent film *The Midshipman* at seventy-five dollars per week. His first major role as Armand in Norma Talmadge's *Camille* came as a result of the star's insistence. With *Camille's* release Gilbert Roland catapulted from obscurity to stardom as one of the screen's most popular leading men. His fame was reinforced in such films as *Rose of the Golden West* (1927) opposite Mary Astor; *The Dove* (1927), again with Norma Talmadge; and *The Love Mart* (1928), with Billie Dove. By 1928 the talkies had arrived in Hollywood, and Gilbert Roland made a bumpy transition from silence to sound due to his accent. Nevertheless, he took the roles that came his way and made his talkie debut with Norma Talmadge in the 1929 drama *New York Nights*. After Roland made the 1930 adventure film *Men of the North* for M-G-M, he was conspicuously absent from the big screen for nearly two years. Norma Talmadge's husband, the producer Joe Schenck, was intensely jealous of Roland and made sure he didn't get any roles.

In 1932, Roland landed a supporting role in the romantic comedy *The Passionate Plumber*, starring Jimmy Durante and Buster Keaton. He was cast as the lead opposite Clara Bow in one of her last films, the 1932 melodrama *Call Her Savage*. That year, he also did two "Poverty row" quickies, *No Living Witness* and *A Parisian Romance*. Roland began 1933 as Serge Stanieff, a South American gigolo, in *She Done Him Wrong,* starring Mae West and Cary Grant. He then landed a small role opposite Constance Bennett in the 1933 motion picture *Our Betters*. During this time, Roland and Bennett became romantically involved. After starring with Mona Barrie in the B mystery melodrama *Mystery Woman* and the low-budget melodrama *Ladies Love Danger* in 1935, Roland did not appear on the screen again until 1937, when Paramount hired him for the lead in a Zane Grey B western *Thunder Trail,* about a man who returns to his family after a fifteen-year absence, and for the role of Eduardo De Soto in its all-star drama *Last Train From Madrid,* about various people's attempts to escape the Spanish Civil War. In 1939, Twentieth Century-Fox featured the actor in its all-star film *Juarez.*

Gilbert Roland played in several films in 1940, including the Errol Flynn swashbuckler *The Sea Hawk,* in which he dueled with Flynn. In 1941 Roland married Constance Bennett, and the couple became a favorite topic for society writers until their divorce in 1946. In 1941, Roland played the lead in *Angels With Broken Wings* for Republic, and a supporting role in *My Life With Caroline* starring Ronald Colman. In 1942 he appeared in *Isle of Missing Men* and *Enemy Agents Meet Ellery Queen.* After becoming an American citizen in 1942, Roland joined the U.S. Army Air Corps Intelligence in 1943 and served until the end of World War II. When he returned to civilian life, the only part he could find was the lead in the fifteen-episode serial *The Desert Hawk.* His career started rolling in 1946 when Monogram signed him to play the lead in their Cisco Kid series, and in 1946 and 1947 he starred in six Cisco Kid films. In 1948 film work became scarce again and he landed only one supporting role in *The Dude Goes West.* The next year he staged a dramatic comeback in the role of Guillermo in John Huston's downbeat adventure *We Were Strangers,* about Cuban rebels who plan to assassinate a politician. He earned rave reviews for his performance in *The Bullfighter and the Lady* in 1951.

For the next three decades Roland always had a variety of roles to choose from and was cast in featured and starring roles in numerous high-grade films and in television. On December 12, 1954, Gilbert Roland married Guillermina Cantú of Mexico, and the couple remained together for four decades, until Gilbert Roland's death.

In addition to acting in over one hundred films, Gilbert Roland also pursued writing. He penned an autobiographical novel entitled *Wine of Yesterday* and many screenplays and short stories. Three of his short stories won prizes in national literary contests. Roland also gained distinction on the tennis court. The actor twice captured the Beverly Hills Tennis Club singles championship. On one occasion tennis legend Pancho Segura commented that Gilbert Roland, at the time in his eighties, was the fittest person he had ever met.

Roland once said that his mother's dying words, which he had engraved on a gold ring, explained his philosophy of life: "My son, don't rush yourself, don't worry yourself, good-bye, my soul." While he was never actively involved in any Mexican-American organization, Roland openly condemned discrimination based on ethnicity decades before the Chicano movement was born in the 1960s. He strove to enhance the image of Mexican Americans in film and refused to portray Mexican characters according to stereotypes. In 1969 both the California legislature and the city of Los Angeles awarded the actor commendations for his unbiased depictions of Mexicans and his contributions to improving U.S. relations with Mexico. In reflecting about his heritage, Roland once noted that he was fortunate to have "the blood of Spain, the heart of Mexico, and the freedom of America."

Gilbert Roland died of cancer at his home in Beverly Hills on May 15, 1994.

96

Mariah Carey

1970(?)–

The youngest of three children, Mariah Carey was born in New York City around 1970 to Alfred Roy Carey, an aeronautical engineer, and Patricia Carey, a vocal coach and a mezzo-soprano soloist with the New York City Opera. Mariah's father is African American and Venezuelan, and her mother is Irish American. The singer's biracial heritage has been a topic of conversation among critics who want to pigeonhole her. Concerning the hullabaloo over her racial makeup, Mariah Carey once said: "Why is it such an issue. Am I black, am I white? I'm ME. I'm black. I'm also white." When Mariah was three, her parents divorced, and she and her siblings went to live with their mother, who became the mainstay of Mariah's life. From that point on she saw her father only on rare occasions. When she was just four, her mother started giving her voice lessons, and Mariah knew right away that she wanted to be a professional singer.

Patricia Carey's career meant that the family had to move thirteen times to locations around New York State before they finally settled in the mid-1980s in Huntington, Long Island. Patricia Carey took Mariah with her everywhere and encouraged her to sing in practice sessions with fellow musicians. While Mariah respected the opera in her youth, she felt a greater affinity to the gospel music of the Clark Sisters, Edwin Hawkins, and Shirley Caesar and the soul music of Gladys Knight, Al Green, Stevie Wonder, and Aretha Franklin. Mariah was thirteen when she first tried songwriting, and in high school she met the composer Brian Margulies. The two began a productive partnership that lasted until 1991. Convinced that she was going to be a rock star, Mariah expressed indifference toward her schoolwork and occasionally skipped classes. She never took part in extracurricular musical activities at school, but chose to develop her talents independently.

Upon graduating from high school in 1987, Mariah moved to New York City, where she shared an apartment with other aspiring musicians while she worked as a waitress, hat checker, and restaurant hostess. All the while she made the rounds of record companies with her demo tape, which she decided was a better route to stardom than trying to make a name for herself in the clubs. Before long Mariah Carey began to get requests to do studio session work, and a few months later, she was invited to audition as a backup vocalist for Brenda K. Starr, a pop singer with Columbia Records. They became good friends, and Starr did what she could to further Carey's career.

Carey's fortune changed at a recording-industry party in November 1988 when she met Tommy Mottola, the president and chief organizing officer of Sony Music Entertainment. Mottola showed no enthusiasm when he accepted Carey's demo, but he listened to the tape on his limousine ride home from the party, and the moment he heard Mariah Carey's voice, he knew she was headed for fame. Mottola went back to the party in search of the singer and discovered she had already left. Eventually, he tracked her down and a few days later offered her a contract with Columbia. For the next two years Carey worked industriously in the recording studio on her first album. In June 1990, Columbia Records released the album, entitled *Mariah Carey*.

Columbia launched a meticulously planned publicity campaign for the singer in the months leading up to the release of *Mariah Carey*. As part of the campaign, Carey went on a nine-city promotional tour, performing for radio and record-store executives, appearing on *Arsenio Hall,* and the *Tonight Show,* and singing "America the Beautiful" before the first game of the nationally televised NBA championship series. In 1993, she spoke of the harsh experience of being suddenly thrust into the limelight: "I just wanted to do my demos and do other odd jobs and keep the music separate. So I didn't have any experience performing live at all. I had to learn about that on shows like *Arsenio Hall* and the *Tonight Show,* which is very frightening. I don't think too many people learn about performing in front of millions of people. But I had to."

Carey cowrote all eleven songs on her debut album, six of them with Ben Margulies. Most of the songs contained on *Mariah Carey* are ballads chronicling failed relationships and other personal hardships, peppered with a few light numbers. Four weeks after its release, *Mariah Carey* rose to the number-fifteen spot on *Billboard*'s pop album chart, and before long the album hit number one, where it stayed for twenty-two consecutive weeks. By the end of 1990, 6 million copies of *Mariah Carey* had been sold, and four singles had become number-one hits: "Vision of Love," "Someday," "Love Takes Time," and "I Don't Want to Cry." "Vision of Love" crossed over as a hit to *Billboard*'s black and adult-contemporary charts. Music critics raved about the new singer, particularly the incredible range of her voice, which David Gates of *Newsweek* described as "seven octaves...from purring alto to stratospheric shriek."

Carey's success reverberated throughout the music establishment. In 1991 she won Grammy Awards for Best Pop Female Vocalist and Best New Artist and received Grammy nominations for Best Album for *Mariah Carey* and Song of the Year and Record of the Year for the cut "Visions of Love." On March 12, 1991, Carey won three Soul Train Awards for her debut album: Best Single—Female, Album of the Year—Female, and Best R&B/Urban Contemporary New Artist. In its 1991 awards issue *Billboard* ranked Mariah Carey as the top pop singles artist, top female pop singles artist, top female album artist, and top adult contemporary artist. *Billboard* also named her album the year's number-one release.

In September 1991, Carey released her second album, entitled *Emotions*. Given the extraordinary reception of the first album, Columbia gave Carey the liberty to mold the second as she saw fit, and she infused *Emotions* with gospel elements. Carey wrote all ten songs for the album, among them "The Wind," a jazz instrumental from the 1950s with moving lyrics, and "If It's Over," a sorrowful ballad which Mariah Carey collaborated on with the widely known singer and songwriter Carole King. King had urged Carey to do "A Natural Woman," but Carey preferred to record her own songs, so King flew to New York and they worked at the piano and came up with "If It's Over." At around the time of the album's release, Carey told the media: "There's more me on this album. I let myself go a lot more. I tried to sing from deep inside myself." Music critics gave *Emotions* mixed reviews, and many complained that Carey had exploited her high register to such a degree that the songs were overwhelming. *Emotions* did not enjoy the commercial success of Carey's debut album, but its title track climbed swiftly to the Top 20 on *Billboard*'s pop, rhythm-and-blues, and adult-contemporary charts. By the beginning of 1993, *Emotions* had sold over 3 million copies.

In 1991, *People* magazine selected Carey as one of the year's "Twenty-Five Most Intriguing People." She had yet to make a name for herself as an entertainer; nervous and unsure of herself onstage, Carey had only given a handful of live performances by the end of 1991, but that would quickly change. In 1992, she did a short MTV concert, "Unplugged," which boosted her standing as a live performer. Her album of the concert became a big hit, capturing two American Music awards.

In 1993, Carey married Tommy Mottola in a celebrity-studded wedding. Rumors about the couple's relationship had abounded for quite a while before they tied the knot. In the summer of 1993, Carey gave a concert in Schenectady, New York, that aired on Thanksgiving as an NBC-TV special. In August 1993, Carey released her fourth album, entitled *Music Box,* a collection of pop songs with gospel undertones. On this album, Carey sang in a much lower register than she had on previous releases. She discussed her register with the *Boston Globe* in an article in 1993: "My voice is naturally more of an alto voice, though many people think of me as a soprano because that's kind of what I've made myself known for.... I always end up writing in a key that is too high for me. I can sing it, but I'm really more comfortable singing in my low register. I think in the future I'll do more of that…it's a good sound for me, a richer sound." In November 1993, Carey kicked off her first concert tour, feeling much more confident onstage. The concert tour was kept short, for Carey feared that her voice would not hold up from the strain of performing twenty or so vocally demanding songs, one after the other, onstage.

While Mariah Carey has achieved superstardom in the music world, she is still in the process of self-discovery. She told the *Los Angeles Times:* "I'm still experimenting with my voice. Every day I do different things with it, and if I feel it's appropriate I do it on the record."

97

Antonio Moreno

1886–1967

Antonio Moreno was born Antonio Garrido Monteaguado y Moreno on September 26, 1886, in Madrid. His father, a noncommissioned officer in the Spanish army, passed away shortly after Antonio's birth. Despite the little money available, Antonio was sent to school and also worked each evening in a bakery for a peseta. Mother and son later moved to Algeciras and then Gibraltar, where Antonio became friendly with British soldiers and picked up some English. He had learned quite a bit of the language by his teens, and attracted the attention of Enrique de Cruzat Zanetti, a wealthy Cuban attorney. Zanetti was traveling with Benjamin Curtis, a friend and the nephew of Seth Lowe, president of Columbia University and mayor of New York in 1901 and 1902. Curtis suffered ill health, and Antonio was hired as both an interpreter and a companion-nurse for the remainder of the friends' stay in Spain. From this job Antonio Moreno earned enough to take his mother to Campamento, a small coastal town in Spain, where she spent the rest of her days.

When Zanetti and Curtis returned to New York, they did not forget the Spanish youth who had helped them and had tried so hard to learn English. They cabled Antonio Moreno the fare to New York so that the boy could experience America. Antonio arrived in New York in 1902 and was enrolled in a Catholic school. After a year there he had mastered enough English to transfer to a New York high school. Through a well-to-do social worker, Adeline Moffet, Antonio was introduced to Charlotte Morgan, a wealthy widow who had just lost a son the same age as Antonio. He went to live with Mrs. Morgan in her home in Northampton, Massachusetts, and was enrolled in nearby Williston Seminary. Antonio insisted on working summers and found short-term employment in a silk hosiery factory in North-ampton, then in a New England telephone company, and eventually at a gas company.

It was in Northampton that Antonio first came in contact one summer with the theater, playing bit parts with the resident stock company. These stage experiences piqued his interest in acting, and at the end of the summer he set off for New York City to work in the shadow of Broadway. He found a job as an electrician, and one day he was sent to make repairs at the Empire Theatre, where Maude Adams was rehearsing *The Little Minister*. Moreno asked for a job as a super in Adams's company, and he was signed on as an actor instead. In the next five years Moreno was cast in numerous stage productions, among them *DuBarry* and *Two Women*, with Leslie Carter, and *Thais*, with Constance Collier and Tyrone Power Sr. He also acted in two productions with William Hawtrey, performed with the musical-comedy com-pany for *The Man From Cook's*, and took the stage with the Manhattan Players at the Lyceum Theatre in Rochester for one season.

In 1910, Antonio Moreno returned to Spain to visit his mother, who urged him to reconsider his career choice. On the ship coming home, Moreno met the distinguished American actress Helen Ware, who convinced him to stick with acting, for she sensed that he would go far with his Castilian gentility and Latin good looks. Encouraged by her words, Moreno took to the stage for a season of Shakespeare repertory. While he was performing in a farce in 1912 entitled *C.O.D.*, the English actor Walter Edwin suggested to Moreno that he give motion pictures a try. Moreno soon made his screen debut when Rex-Universal Studios in Manhattan cast him as a strike leader in the 1912 film *The Voice of the Million.* Moreno was so photogenic and made such a splash that he was soon swamped with screen offers and abandoned the stage. D. W. Griffith persuaded the budding film actor to switch to Biograph, which he left a year later for Mutual-Reliance. Beginning in 1914, Moreno enjoyed a long association with the studio as the "Country Lover" in fifty-two episodes of the serial *Our Mutual Girl,* starring Norma Phillips.

By 1914, Moreno was a high-profile screen personality. Albert E. Smith, president of Vitagraph, persuaded Moreno to join his studio as a contract player. Moreno went on to star with many top actresses at Vitagraph, but he was usually featured with the popular Edith Storey. In the summer of 1917 the actor went to Pathe, where he was cast opposite Irene Castle in the films *The Mark of Cain* (1917) and *The First Law* (1918). At Pathe, Moreno also landed the lead in the 1918 film *The Naulahka,* a Kipling tale of the Far East, which featured Doraldina, a then famous Hawaiian dancer. In 1918, Pathe also cast Moreno as the male lead opposite Pearl White in the twenty-episode serial *The House of Hate.* In the serial Pearl White plays the fearless damsel in distress and Moreno is the young scientist in love with her, and in each episode, they are hounded by "the Hooded Terror," who is out to destroy them. *The House of Hate* established Moreno and Pearl as a popular team.

Albert E. Smith was impressed by Moreno's celebrity, and offered him a lucrative contract to return to Vitagraph as a serial star. The actor wanted to abandon serials and concentrate on feature films, but he was unable to convince Smith that he could attract audiences in nonserial pictures. When Smith would not allow the actor to move on to features, Moreno appeared in two pictures for Goldwyn: the action-romance movie *Lost and Found,* in which he plays an adventuresome hero opposite Pauline Starke, and *Look Your Best.* Paramount then offered Antonio Moreno, by then the silver screen's foremost Latin lover, a contract and cast him opposite Mary Miles Minter in the actress's last film and one of her best, *The Trail of the Lonesome Pine* (1923).

That year, Moreno starred opposite Gloria Swanson in *My American Wife*. As soon as the film was finished, Paramount cast him in the romantic thriller *The Exciters* (1923), after which Moreno married Daisy Canfield Danziger, a wealthy, witty, and popular socialite.

Moreno continued to play leading men, opposite such actresses as Estelle Taylor, Agnes Ayres, Jacqueline Logan, and Helen Chadwicke. Overall Moreno was displeased with the roles Paramount selected for him, and he requested a release from his contract. He moved to First National, but his only noteworthy film with the studio was the 1925 comedy *Learning to Love*, starring Constance Talmadge. In 1925, Rex Ingram, a friend of Moreno's, offered the actor the lead in the 1926 film *Mare Nostrum*, based on Vicente Blasco Ibáñez's novel of the same name.

Mare Nostrum was a major success, and after its release Metro-Goldwyn-Mayer (M-G-M) offered Moreno a contract, enabling him to play opposite some of the greatest actresses on the studio's roster. The most famous of Moreno's M-G-M pictures are *The Temptress*, Greta Garbo's second American film, and the 1927 romantic comedy *Venus of Venice*, costarring Constance Talmadge. Moreno then went to Europe to star opposite Dorothy Gish in *Madame Pompadour* (1927) as a romantic innkeeper who flees with the king's mistress and in a 1927 Spanish film entitled *En la tierra del sol*.

By the time Antonio Moreno returned to the United States, the talkies had taken over Hollywood. The advent of sound posed no threat to the bilingual actor with stage experience. In fact, the studios filmed many of their movies in several languages, and Moreno was kept busy playing leads in Spanish versions of Hollywood films. In 1931 he ventured to Mexico to help the Mexican film industry upgrade to sound film. Moreno directed Mexico's first important all-talking feature film, *Santa* (1932), as well as the country's second talkie, *Aguilas frente al sol* (1932). By this time, Moreno had separated from his wife, who gave the couple's Los Angeles villa to the Roman Catholic church after the actor moved out. In a freak accident in 1933, Daisy Canfield Danziger Moreno was killed when her chauffeur-driven limousine skidded off the side of Mullholland Drive.

In 1936, Moreno returned to Spain to star opposite Carmen Amaya in the 1936 film *Maria de la O*. Moreno contemplated remaining in his native country, but the Spanish Civil War put an end to film production. Throughout the forties, Moreno appeared in a number of films, though by then he had become a character actor. In 1943 his mother suffered an illness to which she succumbed in 1944, and during this period, the veteran actor was absent from the silver screen. During World War II, Moreno served as an air-raid warden for his Hollywood neighborhood; and at war's end he bought a house in Beverly Hills, where he resided for the rest of his life. In the decade after the war, Moreno took up acting again and appeared in such films as the 1947 spectacle *Captain From Castile*. Moreno had practically retired when John Ford invited him to play the part of an early Spanish-American trader in the 1956 western *The Searchers*, Moreno's last featured role. The actor later traveled to Havana to appear in his last film, the 1958 romantic comedy *El Señor Faron y la Cleopatra*. After shooting the motion picture, he decided to stay on and direct, but his plans were aborted when Castro rose to power in Cuba in 1959.

In May 1965, Moreno suffered a stroke and never completely recovered. He was too infirm to manage his affairs and petitioned the courts to appoint Leon P. Scammon, his longtime friend and accountant, conservator of his estate. During Christmas in 1966, Moreno's condition took a turn for the worse, and in February 1967 he suffered two strokes. Antonio Moreno died from the second stroke on February 15, 1967, at the age of eighty.

98

Lourdes López

1958–

Lourdes López was born in Havana, Cuba on May 2, 1958. Her father, Felix López, had served in Fulgencio Batista's army; when the leader was deposed and Fidel Castro came to power, life became difficult for former Batista supporters. In 1959, when Lourdes was just a year old, the family fled Castro's regime and settled in Miami where her father became the regional accountant for Ecuatoriana Airlines. At age five, Lourdes began weekly ballet lessons with a local teacher as part of a regime of physical therapy to correct her pigeon-toed and flat feet and to strengthen her legs. By eight, therapy had turned to passion, and Lourdes was a serious student of ballet. She began to study under the tutelage of Alexander Nigodoff for an hour and a half each day, six days a week.

As a youngster, Lourdes worried that she would not grow up to be willowy and would therefore have to give up ballet. Her fears were unfounded. By ten, Lourdes showed so much talent and potential that her mother took her to New York City to audition for scholarships to various ballet schools. The trip entailed financial sacrifice for the family, but the investment turned out to be sound when Lourdes received offers of full summer scholarships to three New York City schools. After giving careful thought to the matter, the young dancer chose to attend the School of American Ballet, and in 1970 she and her mother headed back to Manhattan. For the first few years, Lourdes spent summers only studying at the school.

Before long, George Balanchine, founder and director of the School of American Ballet, took note of the young ballerina's ability, and at the tender age of fourteen, she was invited to study full-time. She had to live in New York City year-round, where she shared a studio apartment with her older sister, Teresa, a student at New York University. Leaving home at such a young age was a difficult experience for Lourdes, and her mother once lamented that her daughter had lost her childhood to ballet. Despite the hardships of being separated from her home and parents, the young dancer immersed herself in rigorous and constant study. Under Balanchine's genial direction, Lourdes developed artistically at a fast rate and picked up aspects of the director's distinctive style. Her hard work and determination paid off in 1974, when Lourdes was accepted into the corps de ballet of the New York City Ballet. At sixteen, she was among the youngest dancers in the company.

By winning a spot in the corps de ballet, López accomplished a great feat, since only a few students from the approximately five hundred attending the School of American Ballet are selected each year. The press compared López to the legendary dancers Anna Pavlova and Natalia Makarova. The danseur and choreographer Peter Martins, whom López first partnered shortly after joining the corps de ballet, once called her the "new Alicia Alonso," the Cuban ballerina who popularized ballet in Latin America. In spite of the comparisons, Lourdes emerged as a unique dancer who has forged a distinctive style. While her training with Balanchine is readily apparent, López has also incorporated elements of the techniques of her favorite dancers, Kay Mazzo and Patricia McBride.

When she joined the New York City Ballet in 1974, López felt somewhat uncomfortable, since she stood out from all the other ballerinas. She told *Time* magazine in 1988: "It is hard when you've got all those blond girls and you're darker than everyone and your mother speaks a different language." She eventually overcame her discomfort and showed extraordinary talent onstage and in 1980 graduated from the corps to the rank of soloist. In 1982 she reached new heights, showing incredible command of her technique and a warmth of expression when she danced for George Balanchine in such ballets as *Apollo* and the *Stravinsky Violin Concerto.* Despite the richness she lent to these ballets and the applause she garnered from dance critics, the young dancer sincerely doubted that she would ever rise to stardom.

In spite of her self-doubt, López was named a principal ballerina for the company in 1984. In one of her first performances as a principal danseuse, she danced in Peter Martins's ballet *Réjouissance.* She also garnered applause for her performance in the *Finale (Theme and Variations)* of Tchaikovsky's Suite No. 3 in 1985. In May of that year, she made her debut in the title role of the New York City Ballet's revival of *Firebird,* choreographed by Balanchine and Jerome Robbins. She won the plaudits of dance critics, including Anna Kisselgoff of the *New York Times*, who praised the way she danced the role of the firebird: "with commanding emphasis—lending a sinuous mystery to her pas de deux with Joseph Duell's Prince and offering a stunningly phrased final exit."

In 1987 *Sports Illustrated* magazine reported that the ballerina had been honored by the equestrian world when a racehorse was named after her. The owners of the thoroughbred hoped that the horse would reflect the dancer's "speed and dignity." The ballerina wagered twenty dollars on Lourdes López in a race, and the horse won, bringing its namesake sixty dollars in winnings.

On July 26, 1987, López married Lionel René Saporta, a lawyer in New York. In 1988 she suffered a career-threatening injury when a bump on her heel destroyed her bursa and began to damage a tendon. In December 1988, she was informed that she would have to undergo surgery, and that it offered no guarantee for a full recovery. While doctors had performed this surgery on athletes in the past, they had never attempted it on a dancer, and they feared that she that might not be able to jump again.

Faced with an uncertain future and a long recuperation period after surgery, López looked on the bright side and accomplished two things she had always dreamed of: having a child and going to school. She enrolled at Fordham University, and a month after undergoing surgery in January 1989, the dancer became pregnant as planned. She told *Playbill* for an article in December 1992: "I know it sounds cold and calculated, but if you're a professional and you want both a career and a baby, things have to be planned out. I actually think it's good because you know that this is what you want." She also planned to return to ballet if her surgery was successful. She healed much faster than her doctors had anticipated, and by the time she was in her fifth month of pregnancy, she was back jumping. She soon curtailed her jumping in class because the additional weight on her knees and ankles from the baby caused pain. However, she kept attending class and was up *en pointe* until the day before she went into labor.

After Adriel's birth, López immersed herself in ballet once again and began to rehearse four or five hours a day, as was her practice before the injury. In retrospect, she realized that she should have allowed her body time to heal from all the physical and emotional stress she had endured. The day before López was supposed to make her comeback performance, she tore a calf muscle. A full year passed from the time she gave birth until López danced before an audience. She performed in *Violin Concerto* and, in spite of her initial apprehension, felt completely at home onstage. With her return to her profession, López also sensed that she had evolved as a dancer after the birth of her child. She told *Playbill*: "I feel freer, as a person as well as a dancer. I think it's from being around her. She's happy all the time and very bright and loving and warm. And I think that's what's different about my dancing. I have this to come home to, and dancing is now fun. Before it was always pressure-filled, and I would get so caught up in it."

When Adriel was a year old, López took the baby to her first ballet, a dress rehearsal of *The Nutcracker*. While Adriel has watched her mother perform in numerous ballets, including *Emeralds, Apollo,* and *The Sleeping Beauty,* López refrains from taking the child to the ballet very often because she does not want

Adriel to grow up in her shadow or to turn into a theater kid. In one rare trip to the ballet in December 1992, Adriel saw her mother dance in *The Nutcracker* as either the Sugar Plum Fairy or Dew Drop. Motherhood has meant some adjustments for López, but she has managed to strike a fine balance between career and family life. López gave two of the most spectacular performances of her career when she danced in Balanchine's *Firebird* (in January 1993) and debuted in *Dances at Gathering,* Jerome Robbins's warm and witty episodes, set to Chopin, in May 1994. Devotees of ballet are witnessing the emergence of Lourdes López as one of the greatest ballerinas of the century.

Lucille Roybal-Allard

1941–

Lucille Roybal-Allard was born on June 12, 1941, in Los Angeles, California to Mexican-American parents. Her father, the prominent California congressman Edward R. Roybal, served in the U. S. House of Representatives for over thirty years, until his retirement in 1992. In his long political career, Edward Roybal crusaded to end poverty and to fight all forms of discrimination in America; his daughter would continue the fight. At seven, Lucille began contributing to her father's political campaigns by licking stamps and stuffing envelopes. When she was a little older, she accompanied the family on voter-registration drives. She later underscored the role her mother played in supporting her father's career. During Lucille's childhood, her mother ran Edward Roybal's headquarters out of the house, registered voters, and did all she could to get her husband elected. Lucille graduated from Saint Mary's Catholic School, and then went on to California State University, Los Angeles, where she was awarded a B.A. degree in 1961.

Lucille discovered early on that politics had a negative side, for her father's political life encroached upon her privacy and caused her identity problems. She told the *Civic Center News Source* in 1992: "I remember as a freshman in college in a political science class I raised my hand to answer a question and after I finished the professor said, 'Well, now we know what your father thinks,' and went on to the next student." Such experiences led to her decision to steer clear of a career in politics. She continued to contribute her time and energy to campaigns on behalf of her father and other Latino politicians, but she chose to pursue community and advocacy work as her career. Her parents' dedication to working for change and bettering people's lives had a profound impact on her decision to serve the community.

Roybal-Allard worked as the executive director of the National Association of Hispanic CPAs in Washington, D.C., and served as assistant director of the Alcoholism Council of East Los Angeles and as a planning associate for the United Way. While she found her work enjoyable at first, she gradually grew disenchanted about her power to effect change, given the obstacles placed in her way by political policy makers. In 1987, Assemblywoman Gloria Molina was elected to the Los Angeles City Council as its first Latino member, leaving a seat vacant in the California State Assembly. Roybal-Allard had worked for some of the same community causes as Gloria Molina and was familiar with her work in the assembly. Molina urged her to run for the vacant assembly seat representing the Fifty-sixth District. In coming to a decision, she took into consideration that her children were full grown and her second husband, Edward Allard III, had his own consulting firm that took him on frequent business trips to the East Coast. With fewer responsibilities at home and a desire to head in a new career direction that would offered satisfaction, Roybal-Allard decided to run for the seat.

Edward Roybal did not pressure his daughter into entering the political arena, but once she made the decision, he strongly supported her. With the backing of Edward Roybal and Gloria Molina, Roybal-Allard defeated the nine other candidates in the running for the vacant seat by a large margin. During her tenure in the assembly, she served on a number of highly influential committees, including the Assembly Rules Committee and the Ways and Means Committee. As an assemblywoman, she pushed for the passage of laws aimed to protect women. She backed landmark legislation requiring colleges and universities to provide victims of rape with information and referrals for treatment and sponsored two bills that provided sexual-assault victims more legal power by redefining the word consent. In addition, Roybal-Allard sponsored legislation in 1989 requiring the California Bar Association to adopt, by January 1991, a formal ethics rule regulating sexual relationships between lawyers and their clients. The highly publicized allegations of sexual assault by two former clients of Marvin Mitchelson, a lawyer who represented unmarried partners in alimony cases, prompted Roybal-Allard to push for the legislation.

While serving in the assembly, Roybal-Allard also fought for legislation to protect the environment and improve the quality of life in her district. In her five years as an assemblywomen she won passage of landmark legislation regarding the environment. With the support of the influential grassroots organization the Mothers of East Los Angeles, which she had helped women in the community to found, Roybal-Allard battled proposals to install a toxic-waste incinerator in the town of Vernon. After that five-year struggle that ended in victory, Roybal-Allard authored a bill that would provide every community in California with access to an environmental-impact report before the construction or expansion of toxic incinerators took place. For her sponsorship of this legislation and because of her strong voting record on environmental issues, the Sierra Club honored Roybal-Allard with its California Environmental Achievement Award.

During her three terms in the California State Assembly, each of which she won by a wide margin, Roybal-Allard continued the battle that Gloria Molina and other local politicians had waged to put a stop to plans by California governor George Deukmejian to build a new state prison in a Chicano neighborhood of East Los Angeles. With the Mothers of East L.A behind her, Roybal-Allard loudly voiced her opposition to the prison proposal. The fight to bench the prison-construction proposal continued even after Deukmejian left the governor's office in 1990. The issue was finally resolved in September 1992 when Governor Pete Wilson signed a bill, amended by Roybal-Allard, which did away with funding for the construction of the state prison.

The resolution of the prison-proposal issue came as Roybal-Allard was leaving the assembly to serve in the U.S. Congress. In a press release she discussed the community's victory: "I started my assembly career when the East Los Angeles prison bill was approved and it feels great to be leaving the assembly on this victory note.…For seven years our community has marched against the prison, we have fought in the courts and in Sacramento—this fight has empowered us. This community was once viewed as powerless. However, the Mothers of East Los Angeles and other community groups have served notice to the state's powerbrokers that ignoring the desires of the East Los Angeles community will no longer be accepted."

For her achievements in the California State Assembly, the Los Angeles Commission on Assaults Against Women, the Asian Business Association, and the Latin American Professional Women's Association bestowed on Lucille Roybal-Allard awards and commendations. In 1992 the Mexican American Women's National Association honored her with its "Las Primaras" Award for "her pioneering efforts in creating a better future for the community through the political process." *Hispanic Business* also included Roybal-Allard in its 1992 list of "100 Influentials."

In 1992 Roybal-Allard campaigned hard in the race to represent the Thirty-third Congressional District, which is heavily Latino, even though she was clearly the favorite, since the Roybal name was the best known in California politics among Latinos and she had gained recognition for decades of community involvement and for her work in the assembly. Roybal-Allard even had trouble drumming up volunteers for the campaign, because everyone felt she was such a shoo-in. They were proved right when their candidate easily won the primary with 74 percent of the vote and then went on to capture 63 percent in the general election in November 1992 to become the first woman of Mexican ancestry to serve in the U.S. congress.

With her election to Congress, Roybal-Allard vowed to

continue her fight to safeguard the environment and to secure women's rights. In keeping with the consensus in the House, she made jump-starting the economy, cutting the deficit, and addressing health-care issues her legislative priorities. She expressed her support for efforts to channel savings from defense into health care, housing, education, and jobs. In early 1993, Lucille Roybal-Allard was assigned to the House Banking Committee, the Small Business Committee, and the Finance and Urban Affairs Committee, posts that afford her the opportunity to concentrate on economic growth and community development issues in her district.

100

Elizabeth Peña

1959–

Elizabeth Peña was born on September 23, 1959, to actor, writer, and director Mario Peña and producer Estella Margarita Toirac Peña, both from Cuba. She was named after Elizabeth, New Jersey, the city where she was born and where her parents had chosen to live while Mario Peña was studying drama at Columbia University. In 1960, when Elizabeth was an infant, the optimism of the early days of the revolution in Cuba beckoned her parents back to their homeland and the families they left behind. After returning to Cuba, however, Mario Peña was arrested and imprisoned for a poem he had written that the Castro government denounced as "antisystem." Having convinced the authorities to release him, he was left with no alternative but to flee Cuba for the United States. However, the Cuban government barred Estella Margarita Toirac Peña, Elizabeth, and her younger sister, Tania, from leaving Cuba until 1968. Even as they were boarding the plane with documents in hand, officials gave the Peñas a hard time, detaining them until just before the plane took off for freedom in the United States.

When the family was reunited on American soil, Elizabeth was eight years old. Her parents' acting careers took off soon after they settled again in New York, and they earned positions of prominence in the theater in New York. Mario Peña founded New York City's Latin American Theater Ensemble, an acclaimed bilingual company, which he and Elizabeth's mother ran. Despite her own success on the stage, Estella Margarita Toirac Peña discouraged her daughter from pursuing an acting career. Nevertheless, at a young age, Elizabeth dreamed of becoming an actor, and with lessons and inspiration from her father, she fervently pursued her career. At eight she clinched her first part, and at age ten she landed her first stage lead. She attended New York City's famous School for the Performing Arts, where she excelled despite the obstacles she had to surmount. In her senior year she came face-to-face with the discriminatory practice of typecasting Latinos when she was forbidden to play Madge in *Picnic* because of her ethnic background.

In those early days, Peña also took acting lessons from Curt Dempster at the Ensemble Studio Theater and from Endre Hules at La Mama ETC. She also took instruction in clowning from Mark Stolzenberg and speech and voice from Lynn Masters. As she excelled in her chosen field and pursued acting with the same devotion she had witnessed in her parents, her mother became increasingly supportive of her efforts. In 1979, Peña's determination and perseverance paid off when she landed the role of Aurelita in the motion picture *El Super,* a touching story of Cuban exiles living in a New York basement apartment during a frigid winter. A year later, Elizabeth Peña captured a part in the 1980 film *Times Square,* about a pair of teenage runaways. She was then cast as Rita in the 1981 film *They All Laughed,* a quirky romantic comedy about the adventures of four private detectives. She also played in numerous theater productions.

Peña then captured another big screen role as Liz in the 1985 backstage drama *Crossover Dreams*. In 1985 she moved to Hollywood with no agent, $2,000 in her pocket, and a dream of becoming a star. Soon after her arrival she read in *Drama-logue*, a casting magazine for actors, that director Paul Mazursky was making *Down and Out in Beverly Hills*, a satire about rich people and their hired help. Determined to get a part in the 1986 comedy, Peña sent countless photos and messages to the film's casting director to catch his attention, since she had no agent to do the calling. The sympathetic secretary, who took all of Peña's calls, brought her to the attention of executives, who granted the persistent young actress a screen test. By the time she auditioned for *Down and Out in Beverly Hills* she was nearly penniless. Luckily the casting director found Peña perfect for the part of Carmen, the seductive Salvadoran maid who comes to view herself as an exploited person from a third-world country serving a selfish capitalist master.

Peña received favorable reviews for her first high-profile part in *Down and Out in Beverly Hills* and has worked steadily in Hollywood ever since. Her success gave her direct access to casting directors, but she had trouble convincing them that she could play any part, not just Latinas, in her age group. Peña was next cast in an ethnic role in the 1987 feature film *La Bamba*. In this hit motion picture, Peña plays Rosie Morales, the abused wife of Ritchie Valens's elder brother, played by Esai Morales, one of Peña's old classmates from the School for the Performing Arts. The year 1987 also brought Peña a great role in Matthew Robins's *Batteries Not Included*, about foot-wide flying saucers that show up in a dilapidated New York neighborhood slated for urban renewal. After appearing in these major motion pictures, Peña turned down Robert Redford's invitation to star in his 1988 film *The Milagro Beanfield War* because she did not want to play another Mexican.

Later in 1987 the actress won a part in *I Married Dora*, a television sitcom series about a man who weds his Central American maid to prevent her deportation. Peña experienced a life crisis when the series failed and her acting career screeched to a halt. She told *USA Today* in January 9, 1990: "It was an awful time. I gave my agents nervous breakdowns, my husband wanted to divorce me, my dog wouldn't talk to me. I was hell to live with." Peña had married William Stephan Kibler in July 1988. They had met at a birthday party in Los Angeles in 1987 and had fallen in love then and there, as Peña told *People* magazine on May 13, 1991: "For me it was love at first sight. I thought 'Ohhhh, noooo! I'm doomed!'" Kibler, a movie agent and junior high school teacher, shared her sentiments and proposed to Peña on their second date. Although she played few parts in 1988, Peña did receive numerous awards that year, among them the Hispanic Women's Council Woman of the Year Award, the New York Image Award, the U.S. Congress Congressional Award, and the Nosotros Golden Eagle Award. Peña landed a part in the 1988 film *Vibes*, a mediocre fantasy about a quest for gold in the mountains of Ecuador. She also played supporting roles on the television series *Cagney & Lacey* and *Hill Street Blues*.

After a slow two years, Peña totally reimmersed herself in acting in 1990. She landed the role of the mercurial Jezzie, the girlfriend of Jacob Singer, played by Tim Robbins, in the motion picture *Jacob's Ladder*. She was also featured with Jamie Lee Curtis in Kathryn Bigelow's psychological thriller *Blue Steel*, about a rookie police officer who is stalked by a slick psycho in New York City. Peña did an NBC miniseries *Drug Wars: The Camarona Story*, in which she played the wife of slain drug agent Kiki Camarena. She believes that the series inspired viewers to take drug abuse more seriously. In 1990 she was also cast as Lucy Acosta, an intelligent and sharp-tongued secretary to the unmotivated, poker-playing lawyer Jack Shannon, on NBC's acclaimed series *Shannon's Deal*.

In 1991, Peña acted in *The Waterdance*, a drama with Eric Stoltz and Wesley Snipes, released in 1992. In 1993, Peña performed in the title role in the American Conservatory Theatre's production of *Antigone*. That year, she also played in the made-for-television movie *Roommates* with Eric Stoltz and Randy Quaid. Soon after, she launched an innovative project aimed at expanding the horizons of Latino children by introducing them to literature. As creator and director, she put together the star-studded *Celebrando la diferencia, a Latino Literature Series for Children,* which played on Sundays at the MET Theatre in Hollywood. Among the many celebrity performers who were featured on a rotating basis in the production were Brooke Adams, Sonia Braga, Lou Diamond Phillips, Richard Dreyfuss, Hector Elizondo, Edward James Olmos, and Alfre Woodard. Peña drew her material from serious literature, such as the folk and religious tales of Gabriel García Marquez, and brought it to life for the children with dancers and musicians. She described her goals for the series to the *Los Angeles Times* in its May 24 1993, issue: "If I can get a couple of kids turned on to reading, to exploring their culture—to being an American, but exploring the fact that they come from a very long history—and use it to empower them....I would be a very happy person."

Not only does she believe Latino children must take pride in their heritage, Peña considers being a Latina an asset. She told *People* magazine: "I've never thought of [being Latina] as an obstacle. I think it's good. There are certainly enough five-foot-seven blonds."

PICTURE ACKNOWLEDGMENTS

All photographs not otherwise credited below are reprinted with permission of AP/Wide World Photos. The author thanks AP/Wide World Photos and the following for permission to reprint:

Jerry Ohlinger Movies Memory Shop: Desi Arnaz, p. 32; Joan Baez, p. 37; Plácido Domingo, p. 47; Rita Hayworth, p. 57; José Vicente Ferrer, p. 67; Rita Moreno, p. 91; Geraldo Rivera, p. 96; Anthony Quinn, p. 105; Chita Rivera, p. 110; Gloria Estefan, p. 130; Linda Ronstadt, p. 144; Martin Sheen, p. 172; Julio Iglesias, p. 199; Ramón Navarro, p. 215; Ricardo Montalbán, p. 240; Cesar Romero, p. 263; Raquel Welch, p. 300; Andy Garcia, p. 305; Dolores Del Rio, p. 310; Vikki Carr, p. 347; Keith Hernández, p. 375; Charlie Sheen, p. 421; Rosie Pérez, p. 445; Gilbert Roland, p. 459; Antonio Moreno, p. 468.

NYT Pictures: Linda Chávez, p. 101; Dolores Huerta, p. 159; Ellen Ochoa, p. 168; Louis Valdez, p. 235; Piri Thomas, p. 281; María Grever, p. 367.

Carolyn Soto: Gary Soto, p. 329.

Nina Little Productions: Trini López, p. 343.

Jean Weisinger: Cherríe Moraga, p. 357.

Bill Eichner: Julia Alvarez, p. 426.

INDEX

489